starting out:
the Scandinavian

JOVANKA HOUSKA

EVERYMAN CHESS

Gloucester Publishers plc   www.everymanchess.com

First published in 2009 by Gloucester Publishers plc (formerly Everyman Publishers plc), Northburgh House, 10 Northburgh Street, London EC1V 0AT

British Library Cataloguing-in-Publication Data
A catalogue record for this book is available from the British Library.

ISBN: 9781 85744 582 4

Distributed in North America by The Globe Pequot Press, P.O Box 480, 246 Goose Lane, Guilford, CT 06437-0480.

All other sales enquiries should be directed to Everyman Chess, Northburgh House, 10 Northburgh Street, London EC1V 0AT
tel: 020 7253 7887; fax: 020 7490 3708
email: info@everymanchess.com: website: www.everymanchess.com

Everyman is the registered trade mark of Random House Inc. and is used in this work under licence from Random House Inc.

EVERYMAN CHESS SERIES
Chief Advisor: Byron Jacobs
Commissioning editor: John Emms
Assistant editor: Richard Palliser

Typeset and edited by First Rank Publishing, Brighton.
Cover design by Horatio Monteverde.
Printed and bound in the US by Versa Press.

Contents

1 e4 d5 2 exd5 Nf6

Bibliography

Books

An Attacking Repertoire for White, Sam Collins (Batsford 2005)

Modernes Skandinavisch – Band 2, Karsten Müller, Matthias Wahls and Hannes Langrock (Chessgate 2006)

Modernes Skandinavisch, Matthias Wahls (Verlag Schach 1997)

Opening for White according to Anand, Volume 3, Alexander Khalifman (Chess Stars)

Secret Weapons, Andrew Martin (Tournament Chess 1991)

The Scandinavian, 1st and 2nd editions, John Emms (Everyman Chess 1997/2004)

Periodicals/Articles

New in Chess Yearbook:

74: article on ...Bg4 in the 3...Qa5 Scandinavian by Sergei Tiviakov

77, 82 and 84: articles on critical 3...Qa5 variations by Eric Prié

81 and 82: articles on critical 3...Qd6 variations by Andreas Tzermiadianos

Secrets of Opening Surprises, Volume 6 (New in Chess 2007): article on 3...Qd6 by Sergei Tiviakov

Websites/Electronic

ChessPublishing.com (Scandinavian games chiefly annotated by John Watson and Andrew Martin)

Mega Database 2008 (ChessBase)

The Scheming Scandinavian (DVD), Andrew Martin (Bad Bishop 2003)

Preface

The Scandinavian (or the Centre Counter as it is also known) is a long established opening. Indeed, the first recorded game was played in the 15th century. In the 19th century its popularity was based on its aggressive and tactical opportunities; Black players were lunging like wild men with an early ...e5 at White's central d4-pawn. Nowadays its popularity lies in the simplicity of the "big idea" fundamental to the opening, and the fact that from the first move Black players are on their own turf. A further point to add to this is that whereas players on the White side are incredibly booked up on the Sicilian, 1...e5, the French, etc, against the Scandinavian many simply rely on some scarce knowledge in the hope that simple and natural moves will give them the advantage.

On a personal note, I began using the Scandinavian through my teens and the opening took me very easily to Woman Grandmaster level. I must confess before signing on the dotted line that I was a little nervous as to whether I should embark on this project. I was hesitant as to whether I could convey the sophistications and subtleties both sides employ against each other. However, while musing over the problem, I had a sudden brainwave as to how to categorize the information and so the year-long project (or obsession!) began.

I must also confess to be a little bit inspired to disprove the negative opinion that shrouds the opening at the highest level, but I must stress there is a big difference between the elite (with their supporting seconds) and the lone individual playing club chess on a weeknight! I remember when I played 1...d5, there was always a pause followed by an "hmmm" when my opponent contemplated what to play!

My task was helped enormously by the published work of Grandmasters Sergei Tiviakov, John Emms, Eric Prié, Karsten Müller and Matthias Wahls, whose analysis I have tried to build upon. I must also hold my hands up and admit that at times the material is slightly biased towards the black pieces, primarily because I figured that those buying a book on the Scandinavian would normally be adherents. However, I have not shirked away from tough lines and I have always tried to be honest as to which variations I prefer and which are the strongest ideas for both sides.

There is no denying that there are some tough lines for Black to master; the advent of computers has brought a much closer scrutiny on openings. However, I believe with a deep understanding of the ideas and plans behind the opening one can defeat those relying on such technological beasts, and this is what this introductory *Starting Out* book aims to do. I will always highlight which lines one needs to memorize and when the viability of a position depends on a certain move or whether there is a certain plan that one must follow.

Jovanka Houska
July 2009

Chapter One

Introduction to 2...Qxd5

The First Moves

Let's look at the first moves:

1 e4 d5

A bold move: Black hits out at the e4-pawn without even bothering to support this challenge with another pawn.

2 exd5 (Diagram 1)

Diagram 1 (B)	**Diagram 2 (W)**
Position after 2 exd5	2...Qxd5

The Scandinavian seems to be a puzzling opening, to say the least, mainly because it flaunts one of the very basic tenets of opening play: "don't move the same piece twice!" Every beginner has this maxim drilled into them, yet this is exactly what you do in the Scandinavian: whether with the knight in the 2...Nf6 line, or with the queen after 2...Qxd5.

So what is the purpose of the opening? What is the thing that Black is willing to trade his *time* for?

As 2...Qxd5 and 2...Nf6 are rather distinct, it is impossible to write a general introduction on the themes covering both these systems. So this chapter deals with 2...Qxd5 ideas, and the first part of the book covers all the 2...Qxd5 lines. Chapter Eleven onwards deals with 2...Nf6.

 NOTE: Because Black must clearly recapture the d5-pawn with a piece, we are looking to understand the position in terms of *piece placement*. In this way Black retains the flexible e6/c6 pawn structure also seen in Caro-Kann and Slav positions.

Her Majesty Enters the Game: 2...Qxd5

1 e4 d5 2 exd5 Qxd5 (Diagram 2)

So what is the whole point of the 2...Qxd5 Scandinavian? Why does Black commit one of the cardinal sins of not only moving any piece more than once, but the queen? Well, as with most things in the opening, the answer lies in the middle of the board. Black's opening two moves have achieved two things. First of all Black has freed the problematic light-squared bishop, and more importantly he has *provoked* White into attacking the queen so that White cannot establish the two-pawn centre of d4/c4.

Can White try to set up a two-pawn centre immediately? Well, to put it rather bluntly the answer is a resounding "No!" 3 d4 is convincingly met by 3...e5!, and White's advantage has already dissipated. The tricky 3 Nf3 is the most convincing try to establish the d4/c4 pawn centre and this is looked at in more detail in Chapter Ten.

Let's move on to most natural move, 3 Nc3, seizing the opportunity to develop a piece while at the same time attacking the queen. This leads us to a further crossroads. Black's main two moves here are (a) 3...Qa5 and (b) 3...Qd6 (there are also the minor options 3...Qd8 and 3...Qe5+). In all lines the onus is on White to refute Black's play. If White doesn't play actively, Black will be able to equalize in a very straightforward manner. If white starts "drifting", then Black has a very specific plan of development.

We'll move on to 3...Qd6 in Chapter Seven. For the first part of the book we concentrate on the traditional main line, 3...Qa5.

Starting Out: 3...Qa5 – The Big Idea

The basic plan for Black is not based on tactical considerations, and he is not looking to strike out early with pawns breaks such as...c5 or ...e5. Instead Black is looking for a specific mode of development that is in essence simply a favourable version of the Caro-Kann. This systematic form of development is particularly effective against White's one pawn (d4) centre.

As we can see in Diagram 3, the light-squared bishop is safely developed on f5, Black has nice control of the d5-square and if Black wishes to open the position he can make use of his flexible pawn structure and the semi-open d-file with a timely ...c6-c5 break. If Black wishes to keep the position closed then he can also play ...b7-b5 to reinforce the all-important d5-square and maintain good control of the light squares.

However, the theory in the 3...Qa5 Scandinavian has exploded in the last few years, with numerous attempts by White to refute Black's set-up. As a consequence, very important discoveries have been made for the White side. However, just like the Red Queen's race in *Alice Through the Looking Glass*, Scandinavian players have adapted too (the Red Queen is constantly running but she never gets anywhere as the surroundings run with her!). Thanks to the efforts of Grandmasters Eric Prié, Matthias Wahls, Ian Rogers, Susanto Megaranto and others, the Scandinavian is still alive and kicking, although I must admit some lines have perhaps been consigned to the historical archives...

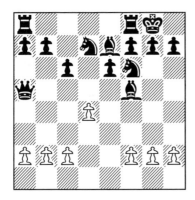

Diagram 3	**Diagram 4**
Black's set-up	Breaking with d4-d5

General Plans for White

Pawn Breaks

Here is a little jokey rule: you cannot win the game without pushing your pawns!

If we look at most lines of the 2...Qxd5 Scandinavian, we see one unusual thing: apart from 1...d5, ...e7-e6 and ...c7-c6, Black concentrates on moving his pieces. Not advancing the pawns so far forward has two effects:

1) As top Scottish Grandmaster Jonathan Rowson once mentioned to me, White has in fact a very limited number of pawn breaks (just three: d4-d5, f4-f5 and b4-b5), and this at times can be an unpleasant fact to handle. Looking at the structure in Diagram 4, it is obvious that the tactical pawn break d4-d5 is the most effective one, and the one which explodes open the board particularly if the black king is still lurking in the centre.

 NOTE: Because the d5-square is usually heavily protected, this pawn break *must* be tactically-based.

2) If White does not succeed with pawn breaks, *the focus of play will be on the wings*. White has the time and the extra space to launch a pawn storm on the flanks. Playing with pieces rather than the pawns leaves Black particularly vulnerable to rapid kingside expansions, and because his pieces having no shield to hide behind they may become vulnerable. Compare the main line of the Caro-Kann, 1 e4 c6 2 d4 d5 3 Nc3 dxe4 4 Nxe4 Bf5 5 Ng3 Bg6, and now White plays 6 h4 seizing space on the kingside.

The Big Strike: hitting the core of the c6/e6 pawn structure with d4-d5!

By sacrificing time in order to establish White's one-pawn centre, Black is playing a very risky game. This means that he must take extra care when completing the opening stage because he is behind in development. I have come to the conclusion that Black should not allow the position to open with d4-d5 at any cost. In my opinion, this is perhaps *the* most important issue in the Scandinavian – should Black be a little careless then this little pawn break can wreak untold havoc on the black position.

I cannot stress enough the danger of this pawn break. Why should Black be so vigilant to the danger? Because of the following:

 TIP: When you are ahead in development, you should open up the position!

Black has used a lot of time playing for long-term objectives, and consequently he is lagging in development. Please be extremely vigilant!

However, there are some important conditions required for a successful d4-d5:

- For the greatest effect, Black's king should be in the centre and there should be the possibility of a discovered attack on the black queen on a5.

- The light-squared bishop on c4 must be protected, otherwise Black can simply play ...Qc5! removing his queen from danger and hitting the bishop with tempo.

Such is the potency of the d4-d5 pawn break that some of the ideas behind modern move orders are based on procuring d4-d5 even at the cost of delaying the development of the minor pieces. For example, this is the idea behind playing 1 e4 d5 2 exd5 Qxd5 3 Nc3 Qa5 4 d4 Nf6 and now a very early 5 Bd2 or 5 Bc4: White intends to delay the development of the knight on g1 and follow up with Qe2 and d4-d5!

Examples of deadly d4-d5 pawn breaks

We start with a famous example: all Scandinavian players *must* drill this example into their memory.

1 e4 d5 2 exd5 Qxd5 3 Nc3 Qa5 4 d4 Nf6 5 Nf3 c6 6 Bc4 Bf5 7 Bd2 e6 8 Qe2 Nbd7 (Diagram 5)

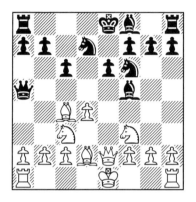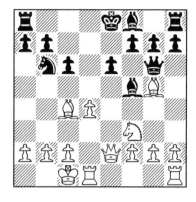

Diagram 5 (W)	Diagram 6 (W)
White plays 9 d5!	Another powerful d4-d5

Black has played the careless 8...Nbd7, oblivious to the danger. White replies **9 d5!** and is virtually winning! This has caught out many players over the years.

Here's a more recent example, arising from the main line discussed in Chapter Two:

1 e4 d5 2 exd5 Qxd5 3 Nc3 Qa5 4 d4 Nf6 5 Nf3 Bf5 6 Bc4 c6 7 Bd2 e6 8 Nd5 Qd8 9 Nxf6+ Qxf6 10 Qe2 Nd7 11 0-0-0 Nb6 12 Bg5 Qg6 (Diagram 6)

This position arose in the game G.Jones-Wang Puchen, Maastricht 2008. The talented GM Gawain Jones struck out with the deadly **13 d5!** and soon obtained a crushing position.

The f4-f5 pawn break

This is another dangerous idea White has at his disposal. This time the pawn break is aimed at the "Scandinavian bishop" (a popular term used for Black's light-squared bishop) and the e6-pawn. This plan can be enforced immediately in the opening or as part of a middlegame strategy. Diagram 7 provides an example of how White uses the f4-f5 motif in the opening.

However, the f4-f5 pawn break is particularly dangerous when associated with a kingside pawn attack, primarily because with the move f2-f4 White reinforces control of the e5-square and threatens all manner of nasties on the kingside: f4-f5, h2-h4 etc. Take this following example **(Diagram 8)**, from the notes to Game 14.

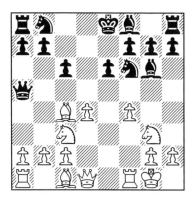

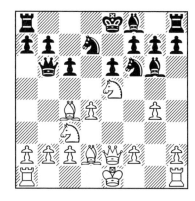

Diagram 7 (B)	Diagram 8 (W)
Aiming for f4-f5	Expanding on the kingside

Black has wasted time retreating his queen and has allowed White to jump with the knight to e5. White launches a pawn storm with **11 f4** and Black is really struggling.

The b2-b4-b5 pawn break

This queenside flank attack is usually seen as part of a middlegame strategy to provoke a weakness in the black camp or to open files. However, it is also sometimes seen as an opening strategy. Take the famous game N.Short-I.Rogers, Tilburg (rapid) 1992:

1 e4 d5 2 exd5 Qxd5 3 Nc3 Qa5 4 Nf3 Nf6 5 Be2 Bg4 6 h3 Bh5 7 b4 (Diagram 9)

White is using the weakness of the b7-pawn in order to expand on the queenside and to chase the queen away. After **7...Qb6 8 0-0 c6 9 Rb1 e6**, White employed the pawn break **10 b5!** to obtain a very dangerous initiative.

The kingside flank attack: hunting the Scandinavian bishop

Along with the tactical pawn break d4-d5, this is the most dangerous idea White has against the 3...Qa5 Scandinavian. Using the light-squared bishop as a target and often catching Black unaware, White intends to expand rapidly and dangerously on the kingside. Take this remarkable example, which John Emms gives in his book **(Diagram 10)**.

As White has castled early on the kingside (a line known not to be so challenging), Black has rather hastily followed suit with his own monarch. Normally the kingside pawn attack is at its most dangerous when White has castled queenside, but Black has been caught unaware, and **10 g4! Bg6 11 h4!** leaves the Scandinavian bishop in some trouble.

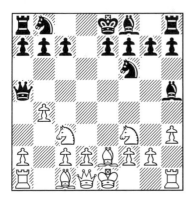

Diagram 9 (B)
b2-b4 hits the queen

Diagram 10 (W)
Black is caught unaware

Black should be especially vigilant to the possibility of a kingside pawn storm when:

- White has played a knight to e5;
- Black is considering whether to castle kingside and White has not castled;
- Black is considering developing the Scandinavian bishop to g4 instead of the more usual f5-square; and
- Black has wasted further time retreating his queen.

 NOTE: If Black unnecessarily retreats his queen to c7 or b6, jumping to e5 with the knight followed by a kingside pawn storm is the principled reaction. The general rule for Black is that he should only retreat his queen when White absolutely forces him to do so!

 TIP: As we will later learn, Black should nearly always challenge a white knight on e5 with ...Nbd7.

Black's Light-Square Strategy

This is the main strategy of the 3...Qa5 Scandinavian. Black wishes to take control of the light squares with the Scandinavian bishop, the knights and even the pawns. This theme is particularly prevalent in lines such as the old main line: 1 e4 d5 2 exd5 Qxd5 3 Nc3 Qa5 4 d4 Nf6 5 Nf3 c6 6 Bc4 Bf5 7 Bd2 e6 8 Qe2 (see Chapter Three). The whole idea is for Black to get a complete bind on the light squares using as a primary base his stronghold of d5. The critical squares for this theme are d5 and e4. Control of these squares in conjunction with overall light-square strategy helps Black in the battle against White's bishop pair. Take the following example:

1 e4 d5 2 exd5 Qxd5 3 Nc3 Qa5 4 d4 c6 5 Bc4 Nf6 6 Nf3 Bf5 7 Bd2 e6 8 Qe2 Bb4 9 0-0-0 Nbd7 10 a3 Bxc3 11 Bxc3 Qc7 12 Ne5 b5!? (Diagram 11)

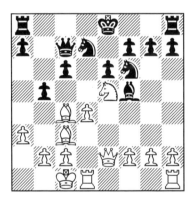

Diagram 11 (W)

Light-square strategy

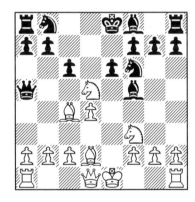

Diagram 12 (B)

The main line

13 Bb3 Be4! 14 Nxd7 Qxd7 15 Bb4 Bd5! and Black has equalized. For a more in depth look, see M.Schuster-R.Lau, Willingen 1999 (Game 8).

Move Orders and Transpositions

Move orders have now become a very important subject in the 3...Qa5 Scandinavian. Modern refinements in move orders are designed to trick Black into playing an inferior line, or in some cases to gain time to explode open the position with one of the pawn breaks.

To summarize the move orders very briefly, they are:

- ♟ White plays a very quick Nf3 and commits the bishop to c4;
- ♟ White plays a very quick Nf3 and does not develop the bishop to c4;
- ♟ White chooses to play without Nf3 but does commit the bishop to c4; and
- ♟ White eyes the queen with a quick Bd2.

In order to guide the reader through this maze of move orders I have broken down the chapters into the following:

Chapter 2: Shirov's main line: 1 e4 d5 2 exd5 Qxd5 3 Nc3 Qa5 4 d4 Nf6 5 Nf3 c6 6 Bc4 Bf5 7 Bd2 e6 8 Nd5 **(Diagram 12)**.

This is the most critical line and the most popular. The reason I deal with this first is because it has become the acid test of the 3...Qa5 Scandinavian.

Chapter 3: The old main line with 8 Qe2, either castling kingside or queenside, and lines with Ne4.

Chapter 4: White attacks immediately with Ne5, with or without Bc4.

Chapter 5: Modern move orders, delaying or omitting Nf3. White plays an early Bc4 and/or Bd2 aiming for a quick d4-d5.

Chapter 6: Lines with Bc4 and d2-d3, or where White delays moving his d-pawn.

Chapter Two

The Main Line: Shirov's 8 Nd5

▨ **The Early Moves**

▨ **Black Plays 9...Qxf6**

▨ **Black Plays 9...gxf6**

The Early Moves

1 e4 d5 2 exd5 Qxd5 3 Nc3 Qa5 4 d4 Nf6

This is by far the best move. Its advantage over 4...c6 is that in some lines Black is required to put his knight on c6 – and this is obviously not possible when a pawn is there! This may seem a little bit vague at the moment but this is a deceptively significant matter, particularly when White has not yet committed the king's knight to f3. As mentioned in Chapter One, I firmly believe that the key to Black's strategy is preventing White from achieving the d4-d5 pawn break under favourable circumstances.

5 Nf3 (Diagram 1)

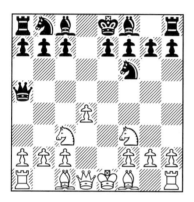

Diagram 1 (B)

White plays 5 Nf3

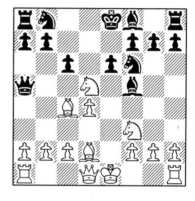

Diagram 2 (B)

A popular move

At first sight 5 Nf3 looks like an insignificant move, simply a natural precursor to what lies ahead. This is not the case. However natural 5 Nf3 looks, this move not only defines how Black should proceed with his opening play but it also determines how White will continue. By spending a tempo on committing his knight to f3 so early – a tempo that we will later see plays a great role – White keeps certain options open. Uniquely to 5 Nf3, White can play an aggressive knight hop into e5 followed by storming Black with a kingside pawn push.

5...c6 6 Bc4 Bf5

The f5-square is the ideal place for this bishop.

Here we must pause and ask why not 6...Bg4? It's true some players, including Australian Grandmaster Ian Rogers, have specialized in this move. However, after the natural 7 h3 Bh5 8 Bd2 followed by 9 g4 and Ne5, White has been given extra time to expand on the kingside.

7 Bd2 e6

 WARNING: Black should avoid 7...Nbd7 8 Qe2 e6, as 9 d5! lands him in trouble (see Chapter 3, where this position is discussed via the move order 7...e6 8 Qe2 Nbd7).

8 Nd5 (Diagram 2)

Since the world-class Grandmaster Alexei Shirov employed a novelty with devastating effect against Valery Salov, this move has become increasingly popular against the 3...Qa5 Scandinavian. In fact it has even been touted as the refutation of the Scandinavian; Grandmaster Sergei Tiviakov even went as far as to say that "simple moves sufficed" for White to secure an advantage.

8...Qd8 9 Nxf6+

The dilemma facing Black is that he must choose between accepting either a structural concession by recapturing the knight with the pawn on f6, or expending further time by recapturing with the queen. We will examine each in turn.

Black Plays 9...Qxf6

1 e4 d5 2 exd5 Qxd5 3 Nc3 Qa5 4 d4 Nf6 5 Nf3 c6 6 Bc4 Bf5 7 Bd2 e6 8 Nd5 Qd8 9 Nxf6+ Qxf6?! (Diagram 3)

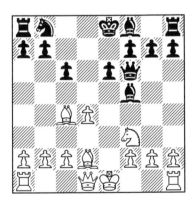
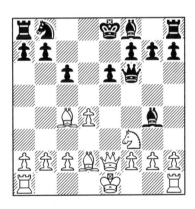

Diagram 3 (W)	Diagram 4 (W)
The 9...Qxf6 variation	Cutting out Ne5 and Bg5

Black does not wish to damage his pawn structure and places a strong trust in the closed nature of the position. He is hoping the solidity of his structure will justify his great loss of time. It is clear that White must open up the position to make full use of his lead in development and to do this he must strike with the obvious (and only) pawn break, d4-d5. However, there are some conditions for this pawn break – if White breaks too early, Black will have no problems as there are some tactical nuances that work in his favour.

In my opinion the d4-d5 pawn break is absolutely crucial to the assessment of the whole 9...Qxf6 variation. Unfortunately for Black, his lack of both development and coordination of his pieces does not put him in a position to prevent this strike. The question that must be answered is: can Black limit the consequences of this pawn thrust?

10 Qe2!

Shirov's novelty gets to the heart of the matter by preparing d4-d5.

10 Bc3 is ineffective. Black can simply play 10...Bd6, as 11 d5 doesn't promise anything because of 11...Qe7.

10 Ne5 is also not dangerous. 10...Bd6 is a reasonable answer, although John Emms prefers 10...Nd7!?, because after 11 Nxd7 Kxd7! the king is perfectly safe in the centre.

10...Bg4 (Diagram 4)

This move is designed to cut out possibilities of Ne5 and Bg5.

Usually 10...Bg4 and 10...Nd7 reach the same mainline position. The main difference is that against 10...Bg4 White has the chance to push with d4-d5 a move earlier, which gives Black additional options, as shown in Game 2.

Let's consider alternatives:

a) 10...Nd7 is covered in Game 1.

b) 10...Bxc2? is simply asking for trouble, and gets it after 11 Rc1! Bf5 12 d5! Bd6 (12...cxd5?? would be a terrible mistake because of 13 Bb5+) 13 Bg5 Qg6 14 dxe6 Bxe6 (or 14...Bb4+ 15 Kf1 fxe6 16 h4 h6 17 h5 Qf7 18 Ne5 Qc7 19 Ng6) 15 Bd3 and White has a raging initiative for the pawn.

c) 10...Bd6 (aiming to castle as soon as possible) 11 0-0-0 Bg4 (11...Qe7 is met by 12 Ne5, while 11...0-0 12 Bg5 leaves the queen in some discomfort, and here 12...Qg6 13 h4 h6 14 h5 Qh7 15 Be3 b5 16 Bd3 followed by g2-g4 was much better for White in M.Apicella-J.Chabanon, Marseille 2001) 12 d5! **(Diagram 5)** (once White has castled queenside the time is right to strike) 12...Bxf3 (12...cxd5 is met by 13 Bxd5 Nc6 14 Bc3 Qe7 15 Bxc6+ bxc6 16 Bxg7, while 12...e5? 13 Qd3 c5 14 Rde1 Bxf3 15 gxf3 Nd7 16 Rhg1 left Black in real trouble in M.Solleveld-R.Norinkeviciute, Cork 2005 – the queen is misplaced and the king won't be able to find a safe haven) 13 gxf3 cxd5 14 Bxd5 Nc6 15 Bc3 leaves Black with many problems. In K.Movsziszian-E.Prié, France 2005, Black blundered with 15...Qf4+? and White won after 16 Kb1 0-0 17 Bxc6 bxc6 18 Rd4 Qe5 19 Qd3. However, even 15...Bf4+ 16 Kb1 e5 17 Bxc6+ bxc6 18 Bb4 gives White a decisive advantage.

11 0-0-0!

11 d5?! is less accurate because it gives Black an option to play ...Qxb2 – see Game 2.

11...Nd7 12 d5 Bxf3 13 gxf3 cxd5 14 Bxd5 (Diagram 6)

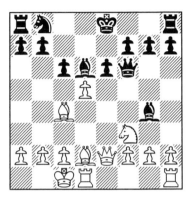 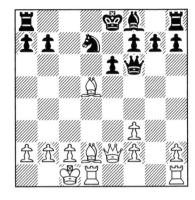

Diagram 5 (B)	Diagram 6 (B)
The typical pawn break	The tabiya position

We have reached the tabiya position for 9...Qxf6. From here Black has tried two strategies: to either play it solidly by castling queenside, or castling kingside and hoping that White's ruined pawn structure will allow Black to survive the attack. These two possibilities are covered in Games 3-4.

Game 1
☐ **G.Jones** ■ **Wang Puchen**
Maastricht 2008

---

1 e4 d5 2 exd5 Qxd5 3 Nc3 Qa5 4 d4 Nf6 5 Nf3 c6 6 Bc4 Bf5 7 Bd2 e6 8 Nd5 Qd8 9 Nxf6+ Qxf6 10 Qe2 Nd7

The idea behind this move is to limit the impact of or even to prevent d4-d5.

> **NOTE: 10...Nd7 can transpose to 10...Bg4, as 10...Bg4 11 d5 Bxf3 12 gxf3 cxd5 13 Bxd5 Nd7 14 0-0-0 and 10...Nd7 11 0-0-0 Bg4 12 d5 Bxf3 13 gxf3 cxd5 14 Bxd5 both reach the mainline tabiya (see Games 3-4).**

11 0-0-0!

The principled 11 d5?! is far too hasty here, and in fact it gives White absolutely nothing after 11...cxd5 12 Bxd5 Be7 (12...Qxb2 is also playable) 13 Bc3 (13 Bxb7? is bad because of 13...Qxb2) and now 13...Bb4!! **(Diagram 7)**.

This is the whole point of the 10...Nd7 variation – Black equalizes at once. Play continues 14 Bxb4 Qxb2 and now:

a) The optimistic sacrifice 15 Qd2 doesn't work: 15...Qxa1+ 16 Ke2 Qxh1 (this isn't forced, but taking the second rook – however nerve wracking – is perfectly safe) 17 Bxb7 a5! (the key defence) 18 Ba3 Qb1 (hitting the bishop and threatening 19...Qxc2; it's true that Black will have to give back some of the extra material, but when he has an extra rook and exchange he can afford it!) 19 Qd6 Qxc2+ 20 Ke3 Qc3+ 21 Kf4 e5+ and after a series of forced moves Black is completely winning: for example, 22 Kxf5 Qc2+ 23 Kg5 Qg6+ 24 Qxg6 hxg6 and now White cannot play 25 Bxa8 because of 25...Rh5+ 26 Kg4 f5+ 27 Kg3 f4+ 28 Kg4 Nf6 mate.

b) 15 0-0 Qxb4 16 Rab1 Qc5! (forcing the bishop to capture on b7 is the best idea; cutting down your opponent's options is always a good thing!) 17 Bxb7 Rd8 18 Be4 Bxe4 19 Qxe4 0-0 20 Rb7 Qa5 was D.Prasad-M.Kazhgaleyev, Shenyang 1999. Because of White's weak a- and c-pawns, I prefer Black here.

11...Nb6? (Diagram 8)

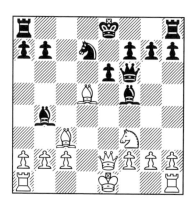

Diagram 7 (W)

Watch out for this move!

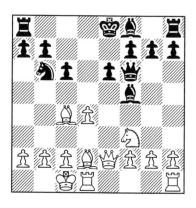

Diagram 8 (W)

Virtually refuted

This was the original idea behind 10...Nd7, but it has been virtually refuted.

A careless move like 11...Bd6? fails to 12 Bg5! Qg6 13 d5!. For example, 13...cxd5 14 Rxd5! Be7 15 Bxe7! exd5 16 Bxd5 Be6 17 Bd6 (Ye Jiangchuan-A.Hauchard, Belfort 1999) and Black has a several development problems to solve. He may well be some material ahead but his rooks are doomed to inactivity.

11...h6!? look rather passive, but the point is that if 12 d5 Ba3! Black gains a tempo, followed by another one after 13 c3 cxd5. So 12 Bc3! is stronger, forcing Black to retreat with 12...Qe7.

11...Bg4! transposes to the main line, and is Black's best choice here.

12 Bg5!

This is a very powerful zwischenzug which completely destroys Black.

12 Bb3 Bg4! was the original idea behind 10...Nd7, and here 13 d5 Bxf3 14 gxf3 cxd5 15 Bxd5 0-0-0 16 Be4 Bc5 is equal according to Wahls.

12...Qg6 13 d5! (Diagram 9)

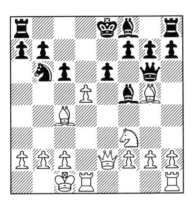

Diagram 9 (B)

Black is in trouble

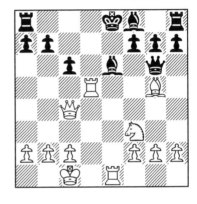

Diagram 10 (B)

Black is completely tied down

Scandinavian expert Eric Prié considers this move to be incredibly dangerous, and he is right to be concerned. 13 h4, threatening to trap the queen with h4-h5, is also good.

13...Nxc4

Black is already in some trouble. For example:

a) Attacking the bishop comes to nothing after 13...h6 14 dxe6 fxe6 15 Bh4 Nxc4 16 Qxc4 when Black is forced to play with his king stuck in the centre.

b) 13...Bc5 14 dxe6! fxe6 (14...Bxe6 15 Qe5 followed by 16 Bd3 is very unpleasant for Black) 15 h4 with the deadly threat of Ne5. Note that 15...Bxc2?? loses to 16 Bxe6, but 15...Bg4 doesn't help much either: 16 Qe5 Nd5 17 Bxd5 cxd5 18 Rxd5 Be7 19 Rd6! Bxd6? 20 Qxd6 Qf7 21 Rd1 and Black cannot stop mate on d8 without incurring a massive loss of material.

14 Qxc4 exd5 15 Rhe1+ Be6

After 15...Be4 White wins with 16 Rxd5 cxd5 17 Qxd5 f5 18 Qxb7 Rd8 19 Qb5+ Rd7 20 Qb8+ Kf7 21 Ne5+.

16 Rxd5 (Diagram 10) 16...Be7

16...h6 loses to 17 Nh4: for example, 17...Qh5 18 Rxe6+ fxe6 19 Rd8+ Kf7 20 Qf4+ Kg8 21 Qxf8+ Kh7 22 Qxh8 mate.

17 Bxe7 cxd5

After 17...Bxd5 18 Qb4 Be6 19 Bh4 Black cannot defend against the mate threat without losing material.

18 Qb4 Rc8 19 c3

This leads to a quick win, but objectively 19 Nd4! is the best move. F.Maeser-P.Kuehn, Switzerland 2002, continued 19...Rc7 20 Bd6 Rd7 21 f4! (ruthless play!) 21...Kd8 22 Qa5+ Kc8 23 Qc5+ Kd8 24 Qa5+ Kc8 25 Qc5+ (torturing Black with a repetition) 25...Kd8 and here 26 Nb5 followed by 27 Qxa7 would be devastating.

19...Qg4 20 Qd6! Qa4??

Black had to keep guard of e6 with his only active piece. 20...h5 intending ...Rh6 loses on the spot to 21 Bh4, but 20...h6! is a tougher defence, even though Black's position is still bad.

21 Rxe6 fxe6 22 Ne5 Qb5

Or 22...Qf4+ 23 Kd1.

23 Bh4 1-0

Mate is unavoidable.

Game 2
□ A.Hoogendoorn ■ L.Frost
Correspondence 2001

---

1 e4 d5 2 exd5 Qxd5 3 Nc3 Qa5 4 d4 Nf6 5 Nf3 c6 6 Bc4 Bf5 7 Bd2 e6 8 Nd5 Qd8 9 Nxf6+ Qxf6 10 Qe2 Bg4 11 d5

Although this move is the most popular, I think it is inaccurate as it allows Black an additional option.

11 0-0-0 Nd7 12 d5 Bxf3 13 gxf3 cxd5 14 Bxd5 is covered in Games 3-4.

11...Bxf3!

The best choice. Another possibility is 11...cxd5?! 12 Bxd5 Nc6, but Scandinavian experts are none too complimentary about this move, and it seems for very good reason. After 13 Bxc6+! bxc6 14 Qe4 Bxf3 15 gxf3 Rc8 16 0-0-0 Ba3 (to stand any chance Black must take away the c3-square and the long diagonal from White: after 16...Bc5 17 Bc3! Black is very vulnerable along the g-file) 17 c3 Bc5 (after 17...Be7? 18 Rhg1 g6 19 Be3 Black cannot castle because of 20 Bg5!) 18 Rhg1! **(Diagram 11)** the position is very bad for Black:

a) Just to show how things can go quickly wrong, take a look at 18...Bxf2?? 19 Bg5! Qg6 20 Qxc6+! and 1-0, D.Marciano-E.Prié, Narbonne 1997.

b) Neither does 18...0-0? save the day: 19 Bg5! Qg6 20 Qh4 (threatening Bf6) 20...Kh8 21 b4! Bb6 22 Be7 Qf5 and White has the stunning 23 Rxg7!! Kxg7 24 Rg1+, while 21...f6 22 Bh6 Qxh6+ 23 Qxh6 gxh6 24 bxc5 Rfd8 leaves White with a very pleasant endgame – Black's king is just too cut off. Perhaps Black's best bet is to sacrifice the bishop in order to open lines against the White's king. However, this also looks to be insufficient: 21...Qf5 22 bxc5 Rb8 (F.Tairi,-L.Eklund, Swedish League 2001) 23 Be7 Rb1+ 24 Kd2 Rb2+ 25 Ke3 and White runs away with his king.

c) 18...e5, providing an escape square for the queen, is probably Black's best chance for success. He hopes to distract White from the kingside by waving the e5-pawn in his face. The problem is that after 19 Rg5 0-0 20 Rxe5 Bxf2 21 Bg5 Qg6 22 Rd7, with White's rook on the seventh rank the best Black can hope for is a draw.

12 gxf3 cxd5 13 Bxd5 Qxb2!? (Diagram 12)

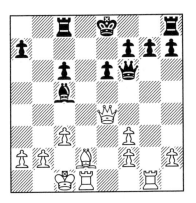

Diagram 11 (B)

Black should avoid this

Diagram 12 (W)

A computer's move

Only a computer would suggest such a move, and probably only a computer would get away with it! From now on a series of accurate moves keeps Black in the game.

13...Nd7 is met by 14 0-0-0 transposing to Games 3-4 (but not 14 Bxb7 which fails to 14...Qxb2).

13...Nc6 transposes to the previous note after 14 Bxc6+ bxc6 15 Qe4.

14 0-0 Nc6 15 Rab1 Qxc2

15...Qd4!? is also possible.

16 Rxb7 Bd6!

The best move according to Shirov. His analysis runs like this: 16...Nd4?! 17 Qe3 Qc5 and now White has the amazing 18 Qxd4!! leading to a forced win. For example, 18...Qxd5 (or 18...Qxd4 19 Bc6+ Kd8 20 Ba5+ Kc8 21 Rc7+ Kb8 22 Rb1+ Bb4 23 Rb7+ Kc8 24 R7xb4) 19 Qxd5 exd5 20 Re1+.

17 Be4

Against 17 Rc1 Black has the defensive resource 17...Nd4 18 Qb5+ (forced; 18 Qe3 Qg6+ 19 Kh1?? loses immediately to 19...Qh5 threatening mate and the bishop on d5, while 19 Kf1 0-0 20 Qxd4 exd5 is better for Black) 18...Nxb5 19 Rxc2 exd5 20 Rxb5 which leads to a drawish position, although once Black sorts out his development he will stand slightly better because of White's weakened pawn structure.

17...Nd4! (Diagram 13)

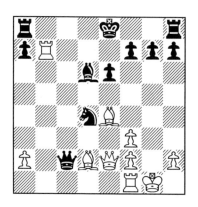

Diagram 13 (W)

The saving resource

Diagram 14 (W)

Better for Black

18 Qe3 Qc4 19 Rfb1

19 Kg2! is probably the best option. After 19...0-0? 20 Rc1 Qa4 21 Qd3 Black must deal with the attack on h7 and the threat of Rc1-c4, so 19...Rd8 supporting the minor pieces on the d-file is probably stronger.

19...Ne2+ 20 Kh1 0-0

Now that Black's king has reached safety, the situation is no longer so critical.

21 Qd3?

White cannot play 21 Bd3 because of 21...Qh4, but even trying to trick Black with 21 Bb4 is calmly met by 21...Bf4 and Black is fine.

21...Qxd3 22 Bxd3

Black is a pawn up. It looks as though White has enough compensation in the form of the bishop pair. However, this compensation is simply not enough, as Black's pieces are too well placed.

22...Nf4 23 Be4 Rfd8 24 Be3 Be5 25 Bxa7 f5! 26 Bc2 Bd4 27 Bxd4 Rxd4 (Diagram 14)

Black has survived the opening with great resourcefulness and has emerged with a better endgame. White's doubled pawns should start to tell.

28 Bb3 Rd2 29 Kg1 h6 30 h4 Kh7 31 Rb6 e5 32 a4 Nh3+ 33 Kg2 Nxf2 34 Kf1 Nd3 35 Rd1 Rxd1+ 36 Bxd1 Nf4 37 Bc2 g6 38 Rb7+ Kg8 39 Bb3+ Kh8

Black still has the advantage but his king is cornered which makes life somewhat easier for White.

40 Rb6 Ra7 41 Rb5 e4 42 fxe4 fxe4 43 Rb4 Re7 44 Bc2 Nh5 ½-½

Game 3
□ M.Zuriel ■ D.Flores
Vicente Lopez 2005

---

1 e4 d5 2 exd5 Qxd5 3 Nc3 Qa5 4 d4 Nf6 5 Nf3 c6 6 Bc4 Bf5 7 Bd2 e6 8 Nd5 Qd8 9 Nxf6+ Qxf6 10 Qe2 Bg4 11 d5 Bxf3 12 gxf3 cxd5 13 Bxd5 Nd7 14 0-0-0 Ba3

This move has all but been disregarded today. Black's plan is to provoke a queen-side weakness and castle kingside. However, White's fast development down the g- and h-files has more or less put paid to this idea.

14...0-0-0 is covered in the next game.

15 c3 0-0 16 Be4! (Diagram 15)

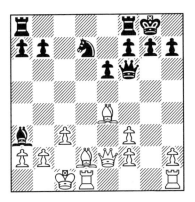

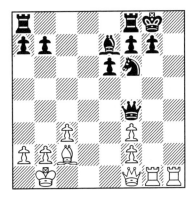

Diagram 15 (B)	**Diagram 16 (B)**
Shirov's move	Black is helpless

This move is Shirov's brainchild – the two bishops line up towards the kingside.

16...Bc5

16...Be7? has been extensively analysed to a forced loss. Here's just a summary of the main lines: 17 h4! (White threatens the deadly Bg5 and is determined to open lines whatever the cost) 17...h6 18 Bg5! hxg5 19 Bh7+!! (a beautiful idea) 19...Kh8 20 hxg5 and now:

a) 20...Qxg5+ 21 Kb1 Nf6 (or 21...Rfd8 22 f4 Qxf4 23 Rd4 Qg5 24 f4 and the queen is transferred to the h-file with deadly effect) 22 Bc2+ Kg8 23 Rdg1 Qf4 24 Qf1!! **(Diagram 16)** (a wonderful move: White simply transfers the queen to h3 or g2 and Black is just powerless to prevent this) 24...g6 25 Qg2! Rfd8 26 Bxg6 Bc5 27 Bxf7+! Kxf7 28 Qg7+ Ke8 29 Rh8+ and White wins.

b) Keeping the g-file closed doesn't help Black either: 20...Qf4+ 21 Kb1 Rfd8 (even returning the piece with 21...Bxg5 22 Rxd7 doesn't defuse the initiative, as White's pieces are simply too active) 22 Rd4 Qe5 (or 22...Qxg5 23 f4 Qf6 24 Bg6+ Kg8 and now the standard mating pattern 25 Rh8+ Kxh8 26 Qh5+ Kg8 27 Qh7+ Kf8 28 Qh8 mate) 23 Bf5+ Kg8 24 Rdh4 (a wonderful sacrifice: Black even gets to take the bishop with check!) 24...Qxf5+ 25 Ka1 and Black cannot escape the mate on h8, since 25...f6 is met by 26 g6.

17 Rhg1

Threatening to win material with 18 Bg5.

17...h6 18 Qb5 Rad8 19 Be3

This wins a pawn, but 19 Rg2 followed by Rdg1 is also strong.

19...a6 20 Qxb7 Bxe3+ 21 fxe3 Nc5 22 Qb4 Qe5 23 f4 a5 24 Qc4

24 Rxd8 Rxd8 25 Qb6 looks even stronger.

24...Qxe4 ½-½

White agreed a draw here, probably to pick up some rating points against a much higher-rated opponent. However, after 25 Qxc5 White would be a solid pawn up.

Game 4
□ M.Apicella ■ E.Prié
France 2005

---

1 e4 d5 2 exd5 Qxd5 3 Nc3 Qa5 4 d4 Nf6 5 Nf3 Bf5 6 Bc4 c6 7 Bd2 e6 8 Nd5 Qd8 9 Nxf6+ Qxf6 10 Qe2 Nd7 11 0-0-0 Bg4 12 d5 Bxf3 13 gxf3 cxd5 14 Bxd5 0-0-0 (Diagram 17)

The main line and Black's most solid choice. However, there is a big problem with this position. To put it bluntly, Black's chances are rather prospectless even if his position is actually more solid than it first appears. White must play very accurately in order to maximize his advantage, but the truth is Black is just trying to hold on for a draw.

15 Be4

The key feature of this position is that the black queen is misplaced on f6. She would in fact be better off guarding some of the light squares surrounding her king and preparing the c5-square as a base for the black pieces. This thought manifests itself in one of the best plans for Black – getting the queen to c7! However, if White is able to prevent this transfer he could very easily be winning.

In my opinion White's most dangerous plan is to simply advance the a-pawn up the board, seeking to damage the shelter of Black's monarch. In the long run, Black does stand structurally better, so should he escape the storm by exchanging a set of minor pieces – preferably a pair of bishops – then he will stand okay.

Another drawback to this line is that White has a forced draw should he choose, although with a lead in development, an open position and the bishop pair, he should really be playing for more! 15 Bxb7+ forces a draw: 15...Kxb7 16 Qe4+ Ka6 (16...Kc7 17 Bf4+ Kb6 18 Be3+ Nc5 19 Rxd8 Qxd8 20 Rd1 Qf6 21 Rd7 wins for White) 17 Qa4+ Kb7 18 Qe4+ Ka6 19 Qa4+ Kb7 and ½-½, Ye Jiangchuan-V.Malakhov, Moscow 2004.

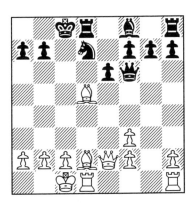

Diagram 17 (W)

A typical position

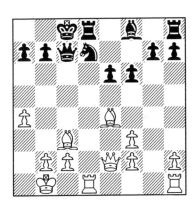

Diagram 18 (B)

Probing on the queenside

15...Qe5

Immediately transferring the queen to c7 is probably the best try for Black, and he has struggled with other moves:

a) 15...Be7? led to a swift victory for White in J.Gallagher-P. Kupper, Swiss League 1999: 16 Be3 Kb8 17 Qb5 Nb6 18 Kb1 Rxd1+ 19 Rxd1 Rc8 20 Bd4 Qh6 21 Be5+ and Black resigned – 22 Rd7 will be pretty convincing.

b) 15...Bd6 is designed to stop White's f-pawn from advancing. White has more than one promising way to continue, but 16 Kb1! is my favourite move – White nudges his king to safety and then begins to probe on the queenside. For example, 16...Nb6 17 a4! (17 Be3 was also possible, but by leaving the bishop on d2 White retains the option of Bc3) 17...Kb8 (17...Nxa4? loses a piece to 18 Qc4+ Nc5 19 Be3) 18 a5 Nd5 19 a6 b6 20 Qb5 Qe7 21 Bxd5 exd5 22 Bc3 f6 23 Rxd5 and White is a pawn up with the better position.

16 Kb1!

Just as in the previous note, White takes time out to secure the safety of his king.

16...Qc7 17 Bc3 f6 18 a4!? (Diagram 18)

The a-pawn sets out, regardless of the position of Black's queen, to do untold damage to Black's queenside. Another promising idea is 18 f4 planning f5 to rid White of one the doubled f-pawns.

18...Kb8

18...Nc5 leaves Black vulnerable on the c-file: 19 Rxd8+ Qxd8 20 Rd1 Qc7 21 Rd4 (heading for c4) 21...Bd6 22 Rc4 Kb8 23 b4 Qb6 24 Bd4 e5 (Black is hanging on to the knight, but not for long...) 25 Be3 a5 26 c3 axb4 27 cxb4 Rc8 28 Ka2 and finally White wins a piece.

19 a5

Continuing the march onwards. Black cannot allow a5-a6 opening up the light squares.

19...a6 20 f4!! (Diagram 19)

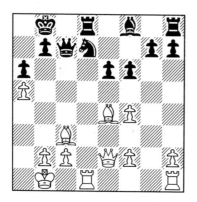

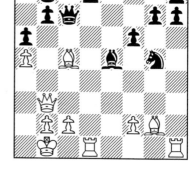

Diagram 19 (B)

A star move

Diagram 20 (B)

Planning Bb6

A deep move, worthy of two exclamation marks according to Eric Prié. The essence of the idea is that White gets ready to exchange off the problem pawn and maintains light-square control on the h1-a8 diagonal.

20...Bd6

If 20...Qxf4 21 Bg2 Qf5 (advancing with 21...e5 causes Black a whole new set of problems after 22 Bh3) 22 Rd3 Black has big problems escaping the pin without making a major concession.

21 Bg2

This move may appear mysterious to begin with, but Black must now be vigilant at all times due to the weakness of b7.

21...e5

21...Bxf4? is met convincingly by 22 Rd4 Be5 23 Rc4 Qd6 24 Bb4.

22 Qf3 Nc5 23 fxe5

Perhaps 23 Bb4 was stronger, setting the trap 23...exf4?? 24 Rd5 and Black cannot escape the loss of material.

23...Bxe5 24 Bb4 Ne6 25 Qe4 Ng5

A mistake according to Eric Prié: the knight must stay on e6 as it is the only way for Black to contest the d-file. After 25...g6! Black has no weaknesses.

26 Qe3 Bxh2 27 Qb3!

A dual-purpose move, not only eyeing b7 but also preventing the knight rejoining the action with ...Ne6.

27...Be5 28 Bc5! (Diagram 20)

Threatening Bb6. With the d-file secured for White, Black's position quickly falls apart.

28...Ne6

Too late!

29 Bb6 Rxd1+ 30 Rxd1 Qe7 31 Bh3! f5

The only move to prolong death, but it's all futile.

Against 31...Nc5 White simply plays 32 Qb4 Bd6 33 Qd4 and Black must drop a piece, as 33...Ne4 fails to 34 Bf5.

31...Nc7 allows White to penetrate the seventh rank: 32 Rd7 Qe8 33 Qc4 Nb5 and here 34 Rxb7+!! is a devastating blow. After 34...Kxb7 35 Bg2+ Kb8 36 Qe4 the threat of checkmate is decisive, and 36...Nc3+ 37 bxc3 Qb5+ 38 Ka2 leaves Black out of checks and unable to avoid his fate.

32 Re1!

Keeping up the pressure and not falling for 32 Bxf5?, which would allow Black to escape trouble with the Houdini-like 32...Nd4 33 Bxd4 Bxd4 34 Rxd4 Qe1+ 35 Ka2 Qxa5+ and 36...Qxf5.

32...Qd6 33 Bg2 Re8?

Allowing White to land the final blow, but Black's position was losing in any case.

34 Ba7+ 1-0

35 Qxb7+ is coming.

Black Plays 9...gxf6

1 e4 d5 2 exd5 Qxd5 3 Nc3 Qa5 4 d4 Nf6 5 Nf3 c6 6 Bc4 Bf5 7 Bd2 e6 8 Nd5 Qd8 9 Nxf6+ gxf6 (Diagram 21)

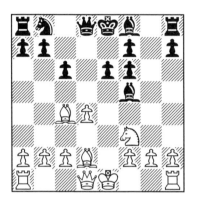

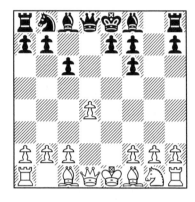

Diagram 21 (W)	Diagram 22 (W)
9...gxf6	The Bronstein-Larsen Variation

We have reached a position similar to the Bronstein-Larsen Variation of the Caro-Kann: 1 e4 c6 2 d4 d5 3 Nc3 dxe4 4 Nxe4 Nf6 5 Nxf6+ gxf6. **(Diagram 22)**

One should also be aware that this discussion of positional themes is highly relevant to lines such as 1 e4 d5 2 exd5 Qxd5 3 Nc3 Qa5 4 d4 Nf6 5 Bd2 c6 6 Ne4, or 1 e4 d5 2 exd5 Qxd5 3 Nc3 Qa5 4 d4 Nf6 5 Bd2 c6 6 Bc4 Bf5 7 Nd5.

Because the pawn structure is the exact replica of the Bronstein Larsen, one should compare and contrast the two positions to see whether the extra moves give Black an advantageous or disadvantageous version. The commonly held opinion seems to be that Black has an inferior version, but the first important thing to note is that White has already determined the placement of his pieces. This therefore rules out some of the options available to him in the Caro-Kann.

Ideas for White

There are two recurring themes for White in this pawn structure:

1) Hunting the bishop

Hunting the bishop is very much based on a light-square strategy, so control of the f5-square is an important theme. White intends to destroy the black structure with an f4-f5 pawn break or to provoke ...f6-f5 from Black, whereupon Black in effect traps his own light-squared bishop on g6. Should Black entrap his bishop,

White then proceeds to work on the queenside. The perfect example of this strategy is seen in Grischuk-Bauer (see the note to Black's 11th move in Game 5).

The fundamental issue is: can White make the light-squared bishop bad? If he manages to force ...f6-f5 and is able to re-route the knight from h4 to f4 via g2, then Black will stand very badly. Another idea for White is to try to force Black's dark-squared bishop to go to g7 (Qf3-h3 is the most dangerous plan), so that the bishops interfere with each other: to free the dark-squared bishop with ...f5, Black must imprison his light-squared bishop. Furthermore, the bishop on g7 also interferes with Black's counterplay along the g-file.

As I mentioned earlier, this pawn structure can arise when the white knight is still on g1. When this occurs White gains the added option of hunting the bishop via Ne2-g3 followed by f4-f5 or h4-h5.

2) Piece sacrifices on e6

Black should take particular care with regards to e6, which is a vulnerable point. To exploit this weakness, White may place the queen on h3 to target e6 and to place pressure on the h-file.

Another option for White is to castle kingside and "work" the queenside by playing b2-b4, although this occurs rarely and Black often gets good counterplay along the g-file.

Ideas for Black

Black must play dynamically but not recklessly to nullify White's initiative, at times utilizing every possible square that is granted to him. A perfect example of this is seen with 10 c3 Nd7! 11 Nh4 Nb6!? 12 Bb3 Bd3! (see Game 5).

Playing for a kingside attack is a natural consequence of the opening of the g-file, but Black should only proceed with this once he has solidified his position. Black must always ensure that he has control of the e4-square, because in most lines this forms the basis of his counterplay and is a source of long-term strength.

In the Botvinnik-Larsen Variation Black often plays ...e7-e5. However, given that Black has already spent a move on ...e7-e6, a further advance with ...e6-e5 is more or less ruled out, at least in the opening stages, and a break in the centre with ...c6-c5 is more likely.

Game 5
□ **J.Mullon** ■ **E.Prié**
Creon 2007

1 e4 d5 2 exd5 Qxd5 3 Nc3 Qa5 4 d4 Nf6 5 Bc4 c6 6 Nf3 Bf5 7 Bd2 e6 8 Nd5 Qd8 9

Nxf6+ gxf6 10 c3 (Diagram 23)

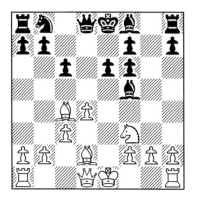
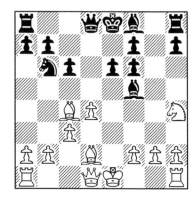

Diagram 23 (B)

Supporting d4

Diagram 24 (W)

A crucial move

Supporting the d-pawn and getting ready to play the dangerous plan of Nh4 followed by f2-f4. It is very important for Black to respond accurately. He must be ready to deal with White's two plans: aiming to trap Black's light-squared bishop by provoking ...f6-f5, or a kingside pawn advance.

10 0-0 should be met by 10...Nd7!, intending to castle queenside and then to get on with some action down the g-file. After 11 Re1 Qc7, the advance 12 d5 is not dangerous, because 12...cxd5 13 Bxd5 0-0-0 sees Black's queen ideally situated on the queenside, protecting the king. E.Sutovsky-V.Ivanchuk, Sochi 2006, continued 14 Be4 Bg6 (14...Bg4 is actually more consistent – Black plans to attack down the g-file and at an appropriate moment jump with the knight to e5) 15 Qe2 Bd6 and a few moves later it was White who had to force a draw.

Lines such as 10 Be3 Nd7 11 Bd3 Bg6 don't really offer White much, and here 12 h4 is simply too ambitious: 12...Qb6! (developing with tempo, as d4-d5 is not a threat) 13 h5 Bxd3 14 Qxd3 Qxb2 15 0-0 Qb5 16 Qxb5 (otherwise Black wins a second pawn) 16...cxb5 17 Rfb1 b4 18 Bd2 (M.Socko-J.Houska, Beijing 2008) and now instead of the game's 18...Rc8, Black should play 18...a5! 19 a3 Nb6 20 axb4 a4 followed by the clamping ...Nc4.

10...Nd7!

There are some pressing issues for Black to deal with before he can complete his development. He must get ready to utilize every square offered to him by White, and in this case I am referring to d3.

10...Qc7?! can be met by a key idea introduced by the Hungarian GM Zoltan Almasi: 11 Nh4 Bg6 12 Qf3! Nd7 13 Qh3!. This is the whole point! By threatening to capture on g6, White forces Black to play 13...Bg7 developing the dark-squared bishop on an inferior square. White is better here: 14 Qg3!? Qxg3 15 hxg3 0-0-0 16 0-0-0 Nb6 17 Be2 Bf8 18 Nxg6 fxg6 19 Rh4 Rd7 20 Rdh1, V.Chekhov-E.Atalik, Moscow 1999; or 14 0-0 0-0-0? 15 b4! and White's queenside initiative looks overwhelming, Z.Almasi-S.Kindermann, Austrian League 1995.

11 Nh4

11 Qe2 is not testing enough. Even though White can gain the bishop pair, Black's pawn structure is extremely solid. For example, 11...Qc7 12 Nh4 Bg6 13 0-0-0 0-0-0 14 g4 Nb6 15 Bb3 Nd5 with good control of the f4-square, T.Gara-L.Drabke, Budapest 2002.

11...Nb6! (Diagram 24)

This move is absolutely vital for Black.

Retreating with 11...Bg6 is simply far too passive, as the world-class grandmaster Grischuk demonstrated. His game against Christian Bauer is a perfect example of how one should play with the white pieces: 12 Qf3 Nb6 13 Bb3 Be7 14 g3! (preparing the retreat of the knight in the event of ...f5) 14...Qd7 15 0-0. Playing ...f6-f5 is tempting here, but the positional cost of locking in the light-squared bishop may simply be too great. However, 15...0-0-0 16 a4 leaves Black in a quandary: the problem is that the g6-bishop hinders plans for an attack along the g-file, so the question is how should Black continue? The only viable option I can see is to make use of the important e4-square with 16...f5. It's ugly, but Black must generate counterplay from somewhere. After 17 Ng2 Nd5 18 Nf4 Black must try to activate his bishop with 18...h5 threatening ...h4. However, after 19 h4! Black is struggling to make sense of the bishop on g6.

So in A.Grischuk-C.Bauer, Port Barcares 2005, Black did choose 15...f5, but after 16 Ng2 Nd5 17 Nf4 0-0-0 18 Rfe1 Nxf4?! (18...Bd6 is stronger, but Black still stands much worse) 19 Bxf4 Bd6 20 Bxd6 Qxd6 21 Re5 Black was positionally lost.

12 Bb3 Bd3! (Diagram 25)

This is the problem with 10 c3 when compared to 10 Bb3 – Black can use the d3-square!

13 Qf3

After 13 Bf4 Ba6! White has big problems trying to castle, and this led to a swift defeat for him in H.Atienza-B.Herbst, Tallinn 1997: 14 Bc2? Nd5 15 Bg3 Qb6 16 Bb3 Nb4! 17 Bc2 Rd8 18 Nf3 Bh6 19 a3 Nd5 20 Bb3 e5 and Black soon won.

13 Bh6 Bxh6 14 Qxd3 Qc7 15 0-0 0-0-0 16 g3 led to a complicated position in S.Gonzalez de la Torre-E.Prié, Elgoibar 2006.

13...Bc4 14 Bxc4

The alternative is to avoid the exchange: 14 Bc2 Bd5 (14...Be7?! relies on the fact that ...f5 comes with tempo, and if 15 b3 Bd5 16 Qg3 f5 17 Nf3 Bxf3 18 Qxf3 Bg5! Black will exchange of a pair of bishops, when his light-square pawn wedge will ensure that he has at least equalized) 15 Qg3 (15 Qh5 is an interesting try – White is hoping that the queen on h5 somehow disturbs Black's plans a little bit) 15...Qd7! (Prié's important improvement) 16 b3 0-0-0! **(Diagram 26)** and now:

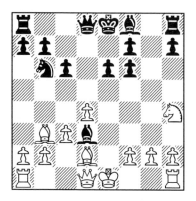

Diagram 25 (W)

Using every square!

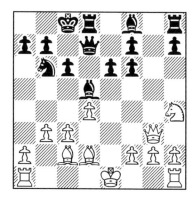

Diagram 26 (W)

Black doesn't fear c3-c4

a) White doesn't win a piece with 17 c4? because 17...Be4!, as indicated by Prié, saves the day and gives Black an advantage after 18 Bxe4 Qxd4 19 0-0 Qxd2.

b) 17 0-0 f5 18 c4 is met by 18...Be4, when again we see the use of the important e4-square!

c) 17 a4 (getting on with the queenside attack) 17...Bd6 18 Qh3 e5 19 Qxd7+ Nxd7 20 0-0 exd4 21 cxd4 and both sides have pawn weaknesses. As long as Black keeps the minor pieces on the board he should be fine – the main concern is finding a suitable square for the knight.

14 0-0-0 doesn't promise White much, and after 14...Be7 15 Rhe1 Qd5! 16 Qxd5 cxd5 17 Bf4 a5 he was only very slightly better in I.Cheparinov-C.Bauer, Kemer 2007.

14...Nxc4 15 Bc1

Unfortunately for White this move is forced. However, the situation is still not clear, as is usually the case when both sides have intentions of opposite-side castling!

15...Qd5! 16 Qe2 Rg8 17 0-0 0-0-0

Black has a pleasant initiative down the g-file.

18 g3 Nd6 19 Re1 h5 20 Ng2 Qf5 21 a4 Qh7!? (Diagram 27)

This move facilitates the pawn push ...h4. Black must begin to break down the wall protecting White's king.

22 b4

22 Kh1 Nf5 23 h4?? would be a great blunder because of 23...Rxg3!.

22 h4 is probably the safest move, although this may leave White open to piece sacrifices on g3.

22...h4 23 b5!

Eric Prié considers this position to be very double-edged. Both sides must play very actively and inflict as many weaknesses as possible.

23...hxg3 24 fxg3 c5 25 a5 Rh8 26 Nh4 Qh5! 27 Qf2

27 Qxh5 Rxh5 leaves White's queenside a little vulnerable.

27...cxd4 28 cxd4 Nxb5 29 a6 b6 30 Qc2+

30 Qg2 is ineffective due to 30...Qd5.

30...Kb8?

Ironically enough 30...Kd7 is probably safer, and after 31 Bf4 Nxd4 32 Qc7+ Ke8 33 Qxa7 Bc5 it is White who is on the defensive.

31 Bf4+ Bd6 32 Re5!! (Diagram 28)

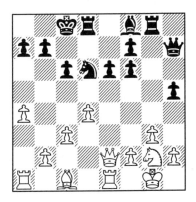

Diagram 27 (W)

Intending ...h4

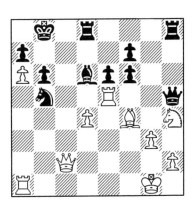

Diagram 28 (B)

This should be good

A great interference sacrifice.

32...Bxe5 33 dxe5?

The decisive mistake. After 33 Qc6! Nd6 34 dxe5 fxe5 35 Be3 (threatening 36 Bxb6) 35...Qh7 (trying to defend horizontally along the second rank; 35...f5 36 Bxb6 Rc8 37 Qxd6+ Ka8 38 Bc7 Qe8 39 Nxf5!! wins) 36 Bxb6 f6 37 Bxd8 Rxd8 38 Rc1 Black is being caned.

33...Nd4!

Now it is all over. Black can easily defend the position and White is lost.

34 Qe4 Rd5 35 exf6+ Ka8 36 Re1 Qh7 37 Qg2 Qd3 38 Kh1 Qxa6 39 Rc1 Rc8 0-1

Game 6
□ F.Libiszewski ■ E.Prié
Aix-les-Bains 2007

---

1 e4 d5 2 exd5 Qxd5 3 Nc3 Qa5 4 d4 Nf6 5 Bc4 c6 6 Nf3 Bf5 7 Bd2 e6 8 Nd5 Qd8 9 Nxf6+ gxf6 10 Bb3!? (Diagram 29)

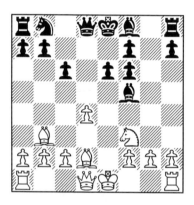

Diagram 29 (B)

Protecting c2

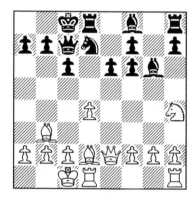

Diagram 30 (W)

White has two plans

This move is recommended by former FIDE World Champion Alexander Khalifman in his *Opening for White according to Anand* series. Unlike 10 c3, it doesn't give Black access to the d3-square. Now ideas such as ...Nb6 are not so effective, and White still has the same plan of Qf3-h3 available to him. On the downside, the bishop on b3 gets in the way of a queenside pawn march, and this makes the plan of castling queenside far more attractive to Black.

10...Nd7 11 Qe2 Qc7

The optimistic 11...a5 is rather double-edged, as Black weakens the place where his king will seek shelter. However, Eric Prié's idea is based on timing – White is effectively forced to play 12 a4 as 12 a3 loses a pawn to 12...a4 13 Ba2 Bxc2. The game V.Bologan-A.Hauchard, Belfort 1999, continued 12...Be7 13 0-0-0 Nb6?! 14 c4 Nd7 15 Bf4 Qb6 16 Bc2 Bxc2 17 Qxc2 Nf8 18 Kb1 with a very murky position. It is not clear whether Black will have a safe place for his king, which makes things a bit tricky for him. 14 Nh4!? is more interesting, especially as after 14...Bg6 15 f4 f5 16 g3! White has successfully locked out the light-squared bishop. Here 16...Bxh4

17 gxh4 Qxh4 18 d5! is incredibly dangerous – the presence of opposite-coloured bishops only strengthens White's attack.

12 0-0-0 0-0-0 13 Nh4!

White hunts down the Scandinavian bishop.

13...Bg6 (Diagram 30)

White has to make a decision, and can do one of two things:

1) Exchange the Scandinavian bishop and utilize the advantage of the bishop pair. This, however, does iron out Black's pawn structure.

2) Re-route the knight to f4 and follow up with h2-h4, which forces Black to play ...h7-h5, so that Black's h-pawn becomes incredibly weak.

14 g3

After 14 Nxg6 hxg6 15 g3 Bh6! Black has the better long-term chances. The position is not open and furthermore his pawn structure is perfect for blockading White's light-squared bishop.

14...Kb8!? (Diagram 31)

Diagram 31 (W)

Black waits

Diagram 32 (B)

The most dangerous plan

A waiting move, but one with considerable purpose. Black remains on guard for an exchange on g6, so that if this does occur he can still exchange off the dark-squared bishops (with ...Bh6). In addition, ...Kb8 also contributes to the plan of breaking with ...c6-c5 at the right time.

If Black breaks immediately with 14...c5, now is the time for White to exchange on g6: 15 Nxg6 hxg6 16 d5. This is the point – Black is not well placed to deal with this strike and now White gains a small advantage after 16...c4 17 Qxc4 Qxc4 18 Bxc4 Nb6 19 Be2 Nxd5 20 h4.

14...Bd6!? is a small concession, as the bishop is slightly misplaced here. Now:

a) 15 Rhe1 Kb8 16 Kb1 Ka8 17 a3 (both sides are waiting patiently, reorganizing their forces in preparation for the coming battle) 17...Rhg8 18 Ka1 Rc8 19 Qf3 Rgd8 20 Ka2 Be7 21 c3 c5 (Black loses patience and makes the first active break) 22 Bf4 Qa5 23 Nxg6 hxg6 24 dxc5 Nxc5. The pawn break has been successful, and thanks to the activity of his pieces Black doesn't stand worse, Zhang Zhong-S.Megaranto, Jakarta 2007.

b) Another enterprising approach is to play on the wing with 15 Nxg6 hxg6 16 h4, planning to open the h-file. For example, 16...Kb8 (16...f5 17 Bg5 prevents the desirable ...Nf6) 17 Kb1 a6 (again Black waits before committing himself to a plan) 18 c3 f5 19 Bg5! (again preventing ...Nf6-e4) 19...Rde8 20 h5 gxh5 21 Rxh5 Reg8 22 Rdh1 Rxh5 23 Rxh5 Ka8 24 a3 Nf8. The closed nature of the position and Black's light-square pawn blockade minimizes White's advantage of the bishop pair, M.Palac-S.Megaranto, Dresden Olympiad 2008.

15 Ng2! (Diagram 32)

White opts for the most dangerous plan: to re-route the knight to f4 and force Black to play ...h7-h5.

15...Bd6?!

15...Nb6!? is the move I prefer. White has to defend the d4-pawn which gives Black time to react to the plan of Nf4 followed by h2-h4. Now:

a) 16 Bf4?! plays into Black's hands by swapping the dark-squared bishops, and Black was doing well after 16...Bd6 17 h4 Bxf4+ 18 Nxf4 Nd5 in K.Arakhamia Grant-E.Repkova, Triesen 2007.

b) 16 Ba5, planning c2-c4, is the best response: 16...c5 17 d5 Bh6+ 18 Kb1 exd5 19 Bxb6! (19 Bxd5 is resoundingly met by 19...Rxd5 20 Rxd5 Qc6 and Black has the advantage – the h1-a8 diagonal is ominously overpopulated!) 19...Qxb6 20 Bxd5 Rhe8 and Black's active pieces compensate for his weakened pawn structure.

16 h4 h5 17 Nf4 Bf5 18 Nxh5

White has used up a lot of time to win a pawn, and now his knight is awkwardly placed on h5.

18...c5 19 g4 Rxh5! (Diagram 33)

Black plays energetically in order to preserve the initiative.

20 gxf5!

White correctly ignores the offered exchange and settles for having a passed h-pawn accompanied by the two bishops.

Let's take a step back and see what compensation Black would get in return for the exchange:

1) There would be uncomfortable pressure down the c-file, and in particular against the c2-pawn.

2) The white bishop on b3 would be cut off from play, and the passed pawns on the h-file would become very weak.

Let's take a look at what could happen if White accepted Black's challenge: 20 gxh5 cxd4 21 Qc4 Qb6 22 Kb1 Rc8 and now 23 Qe2 would be a blunder as 23...Nc5! picks up some material – b3 and c2 are under threat!

20...Rxf5

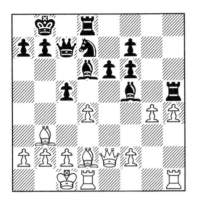

Diagram 33 (W)

A creative sacrifice

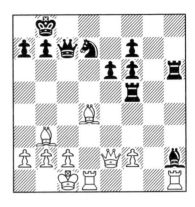

Diagram 34 (W)

White misses a chance

A critical position has been reached. White has a menacing h-pawn which Black should take great measures to prevent from advancing up the board.

21 Be3 cxd4 22 Bxd4 Rh8

Eric Prié's old suggestion of 22...Nc5 is dubious: 23 h5 Nxb3+ 24 axb3 Rh8 25 h6 Bf4+ 26 Be3 and the h-pawn is just too strong.

22...Bc5 liquidates the position in White's favour: 23 Bxc5 Nxc5 24 Rxd8+ Qxd8 25 h5 Nxb3+ 26 axb3 Qd5 27 Qd1 and White is winning, R.Ponomariov-I.Papaioannou, Plovdiv 2003.

Other moves such as 22...Be5 should be met by 23 h5.

23 h5! Bh2 24 h6 Rxh6 (Diagram 34) 25 Kb1?

This is too slow. White has the deadly knock-out blow 25 Bxe6!!, as shown by Pontus Carlsson. White seizes the opportunity now that Black's pieces are some-what clumsily placed and attacks the back rank: 25...fxe6 26 Qxe6 Rfh5 (26...Bf4+! is best for damage limitation, but the prognosis is still not good after 27 Be3 Rxh1 28 Rxh1 Bxe3+ 29 fxe3 when Black cannot escape the threat of a back rank mate without losing material) 27 Qg8+ Qc8 28 Bxa7+ (this is the winning tactical shot) 28...Kxa7 29 Qxc8 Bf4+ 30 Kb1 Nb6 31 Rxh5! Nxc8 32 Rxh6 Bxh6 and, as Carlsson indicates, this position is advantageous for White: the two minor pieces are no match for the rook and extra pawns when the position is so open.

25...Nc5!

Now Black is fine.

26 Be3 Rh8 27 f4 Rfh5 28 Qg2 a6!

Black has neutralized the initiative, won the h2-pawn and is holding tight. It doesn't matter that the bishop is trapped on h2 for the time being, as it is safe there.

29 Bxc5 Qxc5 30 Rd7 Qb6 31 a4!

White quite correctly generates counterplay on the light squares.

31...Bxf4 32 Rxh5 Rxh5 33 Qg8+ Ka7 34 Qxf7 Rh1+ 35 Ka2 Be5

Tying the bishop to the defence of b2.

36 Qxe6 Qc5 37 Qe7 Qxe7 38 Rxe7 ½-½

The position is completely drawn after a move such as 38...Rd1 preventing 39 Bd5.

Game 7
□ **Zhang Zhong** ■ **L.Nisipeanu**
Cap d'Agde (rapid) 2000

---

1 e4 d5 2 exd5 Qxd5 3 Nc3 Qa5 4 d4 Nf6 5 Nf3 c6 6 Bc4 Bf5 7 Bd2 e6 8 Nd5 Qd8 9 Nxf6+ gxf6 10 Qe2 Bxc2! (Diagram 35)

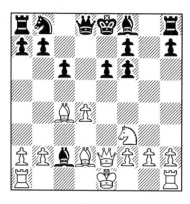

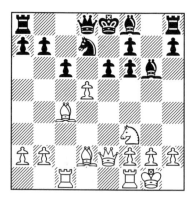

Diagram 35 (W)
Black accepts the challenge

Diagram 36 (B)
This should be avoided

Black must accept this challenge, otherwise White has not made any positional concessions to obtain his ideal piece placement and Black will simply stand worse.

However, the consequences of grabbing the pawn are not entirely clear.

11 Rc1

After 11 0-0 Be7 12 Bh6 Bg6 13 Rad1 Nd7 Black's position is rather solid, so in order to achieve anything White must play radically with 14 d5!?. However, after 14...cxd5 15 Bxd5 Qb6 (15...exd5 looks very risky) 16 Be4 Nc5 Black should have no problems, L.Nisipeanu-A.Stefanova, Krynica 1998.

11...Bg6 12 0-0 Be7

12...Nd7 allows 13 d5 **(Diagram 36)**, which is favourable for White. For example, 13...cxd5 14 Bxd5 Nc5 15 Bc4 a6 16 Rfd1 Bd3 17 Qe3 Bxc4 18 Rxc4 with very good compensation for the pawn, Xu Yuhua-Huang Qian, Beijing (blitz) 2008. Black now blundered with 18...Rc8 and White should have played 19 Rdc1, when Black cannot extricate herself from the pin.

13 Rfe1 0-0 14 Nh4 Re8

14...Qxd4? would be a big mistake: 15 Nxg6 hxg6 16 Bh6 Re8?! and now White has the obvious sacrifice 17 Bxe6 fxe6 18 Qxe6+ Kh7 19 Qf7+, winning.

14...Nd7 is also possible if Black wants to flirt with danger. After 15 Nxg6 hxg6 16 Bh6 Re8 17 Bxe6, amazingly it seems as though Black is surviving the onslaught following 17...fxe6 (17...Bb4?? 18 Bxf7+! wins) 18 Qxe6+ Kh7 19 Qf7+ Kxh6 20 Re3 Bd6 (covering g3) 21 Rh3+ Kg5 22 Rh7 (threatening h2-h4, so Black must defend the g6-pawn; a series of "only moves" keeps Black alive!) 22...Nf8 23 h4+ Kg4 24 Rh6 Bf4 and I don't see the checkmate.

15 Nxg6 hxg6 16 Bxe6!? (Diagram 37)

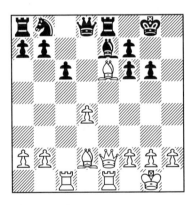

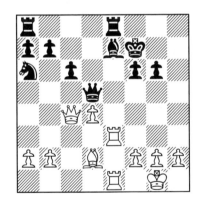

Diagram 37 (B)	Diagram 38 (W)
Extreme measures are necessary	White must head for the draw

Black is slowly consolidating his position, so White takes extreme measures to keep the momentum going.

16...fxe6

16...Bf8 provides a comfortable bail-out for players happy with a draw: 17 Qd3 fxe6 (17...Rxe6? will lose too many pawns as the eighth rank is not covered) 18 Qxg6+ Bg7 19 Bh6 Re7 20 Rxe6 (this move secures the draw) 20...Nd7 21 Rce1 Nf8 22 Rxe7! Nxg6 23 Rxg7+ Kh8 24 Rxg6 Kh7 25 Rg4 Qa5 26 Re7+ Kxh6 27 Re3 Kh5 28 Rg7 Kh6 29 Rg4 with a repetition of moves.

17 Qxe6+ Kg7 18 Rc3

18 Qe3? doesn't work: 18...g5 19 Bb4 c5! 20 Bxc5 and here the developing 20...Nc6 cements Black's advantage.

18...Qd7!

The best defence, and playing for some advantage.

After 18...Qd5 19 Qh3 Qh5 20 Qe6 Qf5 21 Qxf5 gxf5 22 Rg3+ Kf7 23 Rh3 it is difficult for Black to meet the check on h7 without repeating moves. If 23...Bd6 24 Rh7+ Kg8 25 Rxe8+ Kxh7 26 Rd8 and White can force a draw by continuously attacking the bishop.

19 Qe2

The tempting 19 Bh6+ does not work: 19...Kxh6 20 Qf7 Rf8 (the key defensive move – the point is that 21 Rh3+ Qxh3 wins) 21 Qxe7 Qxe7 22 Rh3+ Kg7 23 Rxe7+ Rf7 24 Rh7+ Kxh7 25 Rxf7+ Kh6 and Black is better.

19...Na6 20 Re3 Kf7

Black holds the position tight.

21 Qc4+ Qd5 (Diagram 38) 22 Qd3?

Too ambitious. White was forced to play 22 Qe2! even though Black could choose to repeat moves, at the very least, with 22...Qd7.

22...Bb4?!

22...Nc7 would have won, as Black can block the check on the a2-g8 diagonal with the knight.

23 Rh3?!

The final mistake. 23 Rxe8 Rxe8 24 Rxe8 Kxe8 25 Qxg6+ would have given White a little hope.

23...Rxe1+ 24 Bxe1 Bf8

With the extra material, Black is easily winning.

25 Rg3 f5 26 h4 Re8 27 Bc3 Bd6 28 Rf3 Qe4 29 Qd1 Nc7 30 h5 Nd5 31 hxg6+ Kxg6 32 Rh3 Qe2 33 Qc1 Bf4 0-1

Summary

In this chapter we have looked at the aggressive and trendy line 8 Nd5, forcing the queen back to d8. After 8...Qd8 9 Nxf6+ there are two recaptures for Black, but unfortunately 9...Qxf6 has proved one queen move too many, and Shirov's 10 Qe2 is a convincing reply for White. As we have seen in Game 1, Wahls's ...Nbd7-Nb6 manoeuvre has been refuted by 12 Bg5! followed by the magnificent 13 d5!.

Black's best chance for equality lies with 10...Bg4 (or 10...Nbd7 followed by ...Bg4 to transpose) and after 11 0-0-0! Nbd7 12 d5! Bxf3 13 gxf3 cxd5 14 Bxd5 Black should castle queenside and re-route the queen to c7. However, White has the very convincing continuation of Kb1 followed by a2-a4, prodding for weaknesses. Black's position is defensive, but playable if a draw is his main objective.

This leaves us with 9...gxf6, which leads to somewhat more fluid positions where it is important that Black adopts a strategy based around controlling the light squares. It is very easy for Black to play in the opening stage; but once the natural moves have been completed he must castle queenside and aim for ...c6-c5, although only after securing the placing of the king first! It is also beneficial for Black to exchange off the dark-squared bishops, especially if White has exchanged the knight on f3 for the bishop on g6.

On the other hand, White's sport is to hunt Black's light-squared bishop. Ideas for White include: provoking Black into playing ...f6-f5; forcing Black to develop the dark-squared bishop to g7, so that the two bishops interfere with each other's movement; and re-routing the knight to f4 via h4-g2, followed by h2-h4.

Black must be very vigilant to these ideas and should be prepared to use *every single square* conceded by White. For example, as we saw against 10 c3, Black should play 10...Nbd7 intending to meet 11 Nh4 with 11...Nb6! and then 12 Bb3 with 12...Bd3! (see Game 5). In Game 6 White employs the dangerous manoeuvre Nh4-g2-f4, and the best remedy for Black is to ensure that when the knight arrives on f4, he should be ready to challenge it with ...Nd5!. Finally, 10 Qe2 (Game 7) is a dangerous pawn sacrifice. Black *must* accept this, and then hide his king on the kingside without hesitation.

Chapter Three

Qe2 and Ne4 Lines

8 Qe2: Introduction

1 e4 d5 2 exd5 Qxd5 3 Nc3 Qa5 4 d4 Nf6 5 Nf3 c6 6 Bc4 Bf5 7 Bd2 e6 8 Qe2 (Diagram 1)

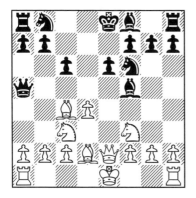

Diagram 1 (B)	Diagram 2 (W)
The old main line	The correct move

This line was historically seen as the most effective way for White to get an advantage. 8 Qe2 protects the light-squared bishop and lays down the groundwork for an effective d4-d5 break to open up the position for an attack.

8...Bb4! (Diagram 2)

Correct! This is the only move that prevents White's dangerous threat of d5-d5 while at the same time doing something constructive. Any other move either wastes time or does not deal with the fundamental problem.

I can tell the reader from past experience that 8...Nbd7? is a horrible mistake: 9 d5! (of course, what else?) 9...cxd5 10 Nxd5 **(Diagram 3)** 10...Qc5 11 b4! (11 Bb4 is also promising) 11...Qc8 12 Nxf6+ gxf6 (12...Nxf6 loses on the spot after 13 Bb5+) 13 Nd4 Bg6 14 h4 h5 15 f4! Be7 16 Rh3 Qc7 17 0-0-0 leaves Black with problems over what to do with his king, B.Spassky-B.Larsen, Montreal 1979.

 WARNING: There are very few circumstances in the Scandinavian when it pays to be greedy, and this isn't one of them! After 8...Bxc2?? 9 d5! cxd5 10 Bb5+ Nc6 11 Nxd5 Qd8 12 Nxf6+ gxf6 13 Rc1 Bg6 14 Rxc6 White wins.

Wahls thinks that 8...Qc7?! is bad, but perhaps this assessment is too harsh. Black's position is still very tough to crack, but I must stress that Black should be very careful because he has wasted too much time with his queen. White, of course, should react with principled Ne5 and get those kingside pawns rolling.

Despite appearances, 8...Qb6 is actually inferior to 8...Qc7, as Black fails to fight for control of the e5-square. After 9 0-0-0 Nbd7 10 Ne5 Qxd4?! **(Diagram 4)** (grabbing the pawn is consistent with Black's previous play but it does grant White a very strong initiative; instead 10...Nxe5 11 dxe5 Nd5 12 g4 gives White a very pleasant position – he will soon follow up with f2-f4 hunting the Scandinavian bishop) 11 Nxd7 Nxd7 (11...Qxd7? would be a catastrophic mistake, allowing 12 Bf4! Qc8 13 Nb5 and White is winning) 12 Be3 Qh4 13 Rd4 Qf6? 14 g4 Bg6 15 h4 h6 16 h5 Bh7 17 Rhd1 White has an overwhelming position for the sacrificed pawn.

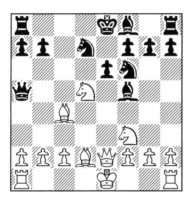

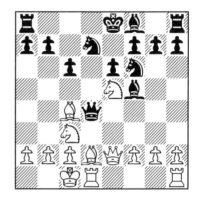

Diagram 3 (B)	Diagram 4 (W)
This must be avoided	Consistent but risky

Returning to the position after 8...Bb4, White has two main choices: 9 0-0-0 and 9 Ne5, and we will deal with each of these in turn.

9 a3 is also possible, and this is covered in Game 11. White normally castles long, but in Games 12-13 we look at lines where he castles kingside.

White Plays 9 0-0-0

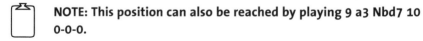

1 e4 d5 2 exd5 Qxd5 3 Nc3 Qa5 4 d4 Nf6 5 Nf3 c6 6 Bc4 Bf5 7 Bd2 e6 8 Qe2 Bb4 9 0-0-0 (Diagram 5)

White simply castles queenside and aims to gradually kick back the black pieces.

9...Nbd7 10 a3

> **NOTE: This position can also be reached by playing 9 a3 Nbd7 10 0-0-0.**

Here are some other possibilities for White:

a) 10 Nh4?! allows the trick 10...Bg4! 11 f3 Bxc3 **(Diagram 6)**.

White is forced to weaken his queenside with 12 bxc3, as after 12 Bxc3? Qg5+ the trick has revealed itself. Following 12...Bh5 13 g4 Bg6, 14 Bb3! is the best: White protects the king while preparing a central strike with c3-c4 followed by the familiar d4-d5 (after 14 Nxg6 hxg6 15 Kb1 Nd5 16 Ka1 b5 Black is the one with the slight advantage, M.Apicella-E.Relange, Nantes 1993 – he has a strong knight on d5 and his king is perfectly safe). Then 14...Nb6! (14...b5 is tempting but after 15 Kb2 Qc7 16 Ng2 a5 17 a3! Nd5 18 h4 h6 19 f4 White had a very dangerous initiative in J.Dworakowska-H.Hunt, Elista 1998) 15 Kb2! (covering the queenside entry squares) 15...0-0-0 (it is too dangerous for Black to castle kingside) 16 Rhe1 c5 reaches a double-edged position: both sides must try to take advantage of the exposed kings.

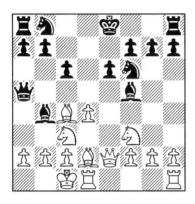

Diagram 5 (B)
The main continuation

Diagram 6 (W)
A trick

b) 10 Kb1 gets the king into safety and also prepares Nh4!? without the problem of the previous note. However, this move is a little slow. J.Hjartarson-C.Hansen, Reykjavik 1995, continued 10...Nb6! 11 Bb3 Bxc3 12 Bxc3 Qb5! **(Diagram 7)**.

In the quest to dominate the light squares Black is willing to double his pawns, which ironically improves his control of the centre and opens up the c-file for his rooks. After 13 Qxb5 cxb5 14 Ne5 (the prophylactic 14 Ba5! was the best move) 14...a5! 15 a3 Be4! Black had no problems at all.

c) Funnily enough, it is now a little premature for White to occupy the centre with 10 Ne5. After 10...Nxe5! 11 dxe5 Nd5 12 Nxd5 Bxd2+ 13 Rxd2 cxd5 14 Bb5+ Ke7, although it might appear that the king is suspiciously placed on e7, it is perfectly safe and Black has no problems. In fact, with a powerful Scandinavian bishop and the open c-file, I quite like Black's position.

WARNING: Black should exercise some caution when the white knight is on e5: 10...Nb6? (instead of 10...Nxe5!) 11 Bb3 Nbd5 12 Nxd5 Bxd2+ 13 Rxd2 cxd5 14 g4 is very bad for Black.

10...Bxc3

10...Nb6 is a messy affair which is very difficult to assess: 11 axb4!? (the most principled) 11...Qa1+ 12 Nb1 Na4 13 Bc3 Ne4 (threatening to capture on c3) 14 Rd3! and now:

a) 14...a5 15 d5!? (after 15 bxa5 Rxa5 16 Bb3 Nexc3 17 bxc3 0-0 the position is rather bizarre: Black is a piece down and has no material compensation, but White can barely move and is continuously tied down to the defence of the c-pawn) 15 ..Nexc3 16 bxc3 axb4 17 dxe6. Here the inaccurate 17...0-0 gave White the better chances after 18 exf7+ Kh8 19 Qe5! in M.Zlatic-S.Saric, Novi Sad 2005. Instead Black must keep the position closed with 17...f6!, when 18 cxb4 Bxd3 19 cxd3 Qxb1+ 20 Kxb1 Nc3+ reaches an unclear position. White has compensation for the exchange in the form of the e-pawn, and the knight gets trapped on e2.

b) 14...Nexc3 15 bxc3 Bxd3 16 Qxd3 a5 17 Bb3 is another possibility. White has two minor pieces for the rook, but the position is very tense as both sides' pieces are somewhat awkwardly placed. Even so, I think the advantage lies with White, as it is very difficult for Black to make any inroads into White's position.

11 Bxc3 Qc7 (Diagram 8)

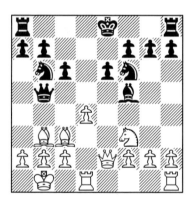

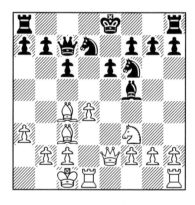

Diagram 7 (W)

Light-square strategy!

Diagram 8 (W)

A tabiya

We have now reached a tabiya for the 9 0-0-0 variation. Taking a step back, let's look at the position afresh. What are the plans for Black and why has he so willingly conceded the bishop pair? The answer lies in the semi-closed nature of the position and the misplaced dark-squared bishop sitting on c3. Black's long term plan is to swap off pieces and to reach a position where he has a strong knight on d5 completely dominating the dark-squared bishop. In fact, this is Black's strategy even with the light-squared bishops on the board. See Game 8 for further details.

Game 8
☐ **M.Schuster** ■ **R.Lau**
Willingen 1999

---

1 e4 d5 2 exd5 Qxd5 3 Nc3 Qa5 4 d4 c6 5 Bc4 Nf6 6 Nf3 Bf5 7 Bd2 e6 8 Qe2 Bb4 9 0-0-0 Nbd7 10 a3 Bxc3 11 Bxc3 Qc7 12 Ne5

This is a typical idea for White.

> **NOTE: 12 Kb1 0-0-0 13 Bd2 Ne4 14 Be1 Nd6 is an important manoeuvre for Black to remember, and 15 Bb3 h6 16 Ka2 c5 17 dxc5 Nxc5 left him with a comfortable position in I.Martic-M.Savic, Zlatibor 2007.**

12...b5!? (Diagram 9)

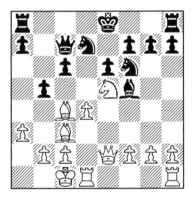
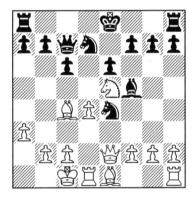

Diagram 9 (W)	Diagram 10 (B)
An equalizing plan	Planning f3 and Bg3

This plan equalizes – Black seizes space on the queenside and secures the d5-square.

12...Nxe5!? makes White's life a little easier, as his plan becomes very simple: control the d6-square and push those kingside pawns! Play continues 13 dxe5 Nd5 14 Bd2 0-0-0 15 g4! Bg6 16 f4 h5! 17 h3 Qb6! (Black must keep all his pieces as active as possible; 17...Ne7? guarding f5 is too passive, and 18 Rhf1 Kb8 19 f5 exf5 20 e6 – the point: White threatens 21 Bf4 winning the queen – 20...Ka8 21 Bf4 Rxd1+ 22

Qxd1 was better for White in M.Zufic-D.Sebastianelli, Porto San Giorgio 2002) 18 Rhf1 hxg4 19 hxg4 Qc5 20 Bb3 and now Black should play 20...Rh3!, threatening ...Rxb3, before White can play f4-f5. After 21 Rf3 Rdh8 Black's activity is holding his position together.

12...Ne4?! is dubious as White simply retreats with 13 Be1! **(Diagram 10)**.

Transferring the dark-squared bishop to a better diagonal with Be1 followed by f2-f3 and Bg3 is often in White's plans, and here Black is just helping White to achieve his goal.

13 Bb3

The game Wang Pin-N.Zhukova, Shenyang 2000, is very instructive: 13 Ba2 Be4! (perfect strategy!) 14 Rhe1 Bd5. This idea is critical: Black removes the potential danger on the a2-g8 diagonal (sacrifices on f7 or e6) and organizes favourable conditions for counterattack. The position, however, remains incredibly complex for both sides: 15 Bxd5 Nxd5 16 Bd2 0-0 17 Qg4 (Black must play very carefully and wait for the right time to counterattack) 17...Kh8 18 Qh3 Rac8 19 Nxd7 Qxd7 20 Re4 f5! (an important move, defending h7 horizontally) 21 Rh4 g6 22 Qg3 Kg8 (again Black defends calmly against the threat of 23 Qxg6) 23 Rh3 Qc7 (the knight is powerful on d5 so it would be beneficial for Black to exchange queens) 24 Qh4 Rf7! (the queen is a bad defender so Black should give this task to an "inferior" piece!) 25 Kb1 a5 26 Re1 Re8 27 c3 c5 (Black has laid the foundations for the counterattack – it is the perfect time to strike) 28 a4 c4 29 axb5 Qb8 30 Rg3? (under pressure, White doesn't handle the change of circumstances well) 30...Qxb5 31 Qh6 a4. Black has defended perfectly and now ...a4-a3 will be deadly.

13...Be4! (Diagram 11)

Excellent strategy – Black re-routes the bishop in order to secure the d5-square for the knight.

14 Nxd7

14 Rhe1 0-0 15 Nxd7 Qxd7 16 d5!? is an interesting sacrifice, and 16...Bxd5 17 Bxf6 gxf6 18 Bxd5 cxd5 19 Qf3 left Black's king exposed in P.Kruglyakov-N.Zhukova, Odessa 2007. However, Black can avoid this with 14...Bd5, as recommended by Dautov.

14...Qxd7 15 Bb4

At first sight this move looks crippling – White has prevented Black from castling to safety. However, Black can prove that his position is almost unbreakable.

15...Bd5! 16 Bxd5

After 16 c4 bxc4 17 Bxc4 Bxc4 18 Qxc4 a5 19 Bc5 Qd5! 20 Qc2 Rb8 21 f3 Nd7, Black will follow up with ...Nxc5 and castle into safety.

16...Qxd5 17 Qe5 0-0-0! (Diagram 12)

This is the point: Black's king is well placed in the ensuing endgame. After

17...Qxe5 18 dxe5 Nd5 19 Bc5 White has the better endgame – he enjoys more space and control of the d6-square, which is a significant factor but not always critical as we see in the main game.

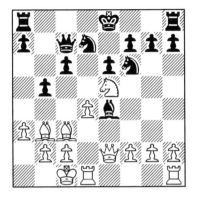

Diagram 11 (W)

Heading for d5

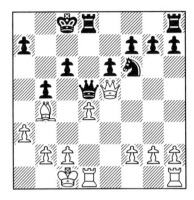

Diagram 12 (W)

Safe on the queenside

18 Be7

White was afraid of Black penetrating the queenside with ...Qa2, but it is doubtful whether this move is too scary. 18 Qg3 Rhg8 19 Rhe1 Qf5 would have kept more pressure on Black.

18...Qxe5! 19 dxe5 Rxd1+

Exchanging a set of rooks makes Black's task easier. Thanks to his control of d5, Black stands perfectly fine.

20 Rxd1 Ng4 21 Bd6 Rd8 22 a4

If 22 h3 Black can get away with capturing on f2: 22...Nxf2 23 Rf1 Ne4 24 Rxf7 Nxd6 25 exd6 Rd7 and White should force a repetition of moves.

22...a6

It is very instructive to see how Lau plays round White's apparent strength – the d6-square – and outplays his opponent completely.

23 axb5 axb5 24 c4?

Not the best – White only creates another weakness.

24...Rd7

Black safeguards the f7-pawn to give the knight on g4 extra purpose. Now White must give up a pawn.

25 cxb5 cxb5 26 Rd2 Nxh2

Black's knight is completely safe on h2.

27 Rc2+ Kb7 28 Rc5 Kb6 29 Rc3 h5

Now the knight has been completely secured, and Black is simply a pawn up.

30 Bc5+ Kb7 31 Rh3 Ng4 32 Rxh5 Rc7 33 b4 Nxf2 34 Kb1 Ne4 35 Bd6 Rc4 36 Bf8 g6 37 Rh7 Rc7 38 Rh4 Nd2+ 39 Kb2 Nc4+ 40 Kb3 Rd7 41 Bc5 Nxe5 42 Rh1 Rd3+ 0-1

White Plays 9 Ne5

1 e4 d5 2 exd5 Qxd5 3 Nc3 Qa5 4 d4 Nf6 5 Nf3 c6 6 Bc4 Bf5 7 Bd2 e6 8 Qe2 Bb4! 9 Ne5 (Diagram 13)

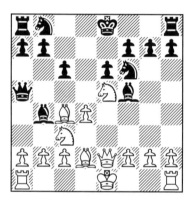

Diagram 13 (B)	**Diagram 14 (B)**
White plays 9 Ne5	Two choices for Black

Here are some points to remember:

1) Black should normally delay castling until White has done so, and then head the same way!

2) White's knight on e5 should generally be challenged by ...Nbd7.

3) Black should only exchange these knights on e5 when he can follow up effectively with ...Nd5, otherwise White's kingside pawn march can be very strong.

4) Black should hardly ever exchange the white knight on e5 if he doesn't have control of the d6-square, for example if he has exchanged his dark-squared bishop for the knight.

9...Nbd7!

Generally this is the best reaction to Ne5. Black seeks to exchange minor pieces and alleviate space problems. However, as explained above, one should be aware of the specific conditions for this.

WARNING: Whatever Black does, he must not allow White to achieve an overwhelming space advantage.

For example, 9...0-0? would be a grave mistake because of 10 0-0-0 (10 g4!? also looks very dangerous) 10...Nd5 11 g4 Bg6 12 h4 Bxc3 13 bxc3 Nxc3 14 Bxc3 Qxc3 15 Kb1 b5 16 Bb3 and now h4-h5 is impossible to meet. After 16...a5 17 h5 a4 18 hxg6 axb3 19 gxh7+ Kh8 20 cxb3 White is winning.

10 Nxd7 (Diagram 14)

10 0-0-0 transposes to 9 0-0-0 Nbd7 10 Ne5.

After 10 Nxd6, Black has two possible recaptures: 10...Kxd7 is covered in Game 9, and 10...Nxd7 is the subject of Game 10.

Game 9
□ O.Koskivirta ■ B.Martin
Correspondence 1991

---

1 e4 d5 2 exd5 Qxd5 3 Nc3 Qa5 4 d4 c6 5 Bc4 Nf6 6 Nf3 Bf5 7 Bd2 e6 8 Qe2 Bb4 9 Ne5 Nbd7! 10 Nxd7 Kxd7 (Diagram 15)

Diagram 15 (W)	**Diagram 16 (B)**
Castling by hand	d4-d5 again!

This is an idea from David Taylor: in effect Black is castling by hand. This is not just a flashy move to mock White – it contains a strategic point in that Black doesn't remove the knight from its good post on f6.

10...Nxd7 is considered in the next game.

11 0-0-0

11 a3 Nd5 prevents any tactical d4-d5 advances and simplifies the position in or-

der to minimize White's advantage. Indeed, 12 Bxd5 cxd5 13 0-0 Bxc3 14 Bxc3 Qc7 15 Rac1 Rac8 16 f3 Qc4 17 Qe3 is only marginally better for White, due to the slightly exposed black king, J.Shaw-N.Mohota, British Championship 2003.

11...Rad8

This is a mistake as it allows White to force the pace of the game.

11...Nd5! looks to be the safest. After 12 Bxd5 cxd5 13 g4 Bg6 14 f4 Rac8 15 Rhf1 Bxc3 16 Bxc3 Qa6 17 Qxa6 bxa6 18 Rd2 Be4 the presence of opposite-coloured bishops makes it rather drawish, J.Sodoma-A.Pakhomov, Pardubice 2007.

12 a3 Bxc3

12...Be7 13 d5 is very unpleasant.

13 Bxc3 Qc7

As Wahls, Müller and Langrock have pointed out, playing with the king in the centre is not without its dangers.

14 d5! (Diagram 16)

Opening the position with a bang. A slower plan is 14 f3!? Kc8 15 Be1! intending Bg3, an idea we've seen previously. 15 Kb1 is less accurate because of 15...h5! 16 Be1 h4! preventing Bg3, as played in B.Trabert-L.Nisipeanu, Naujac 2000.

14...Nxd5?

A big mistake. 14...cxd5 is better, although the resulting position is still very difficult for Black. For example, 15 Be5 Qb6 (15...Qa5? 16 Bb5+ Kc8? leaves the king only superficially safe and White can expose its vulnerability by playing 17 Rd4 threatening both Ra4 and Rc4+, P.Marxen-H.Kues, German League 1999) 16 Bxf6 gxf6 17 Bxd5 Kc8 18 Bf3 with a very pleasant position for White: the bishop on f3 is much better than its counterpart, and the black king can never feel safe with it pointing at b7.

14...exd5 is also stronger than the move in the game, but 15 Be5 Qa5 16 Bxf6 gxf6 17 Qf3 Be6 18 Qxf6 Kc8 19 Bd3 d4 20 f4 h5 was still good for White in L.Maurino-G.Soppe, Buenos Aires 1998.

15 Be5!

Black's position suddenly becomes very difficult: his king is left in the centre and White can advance on the kingside.

15...Qb6 16 g4! Bg6 17 Bxg7 Rhg8 18 Bf6 Rde8 19 h4 Kc8 20 Bd4 c5 21 Be5

It is noticeable how White terrorizes Black with the power of his bishops.

21...f6 22 Bg3 Bf7 23 g5

Suddenly the dark squares become even more vulnerable and Black's position quickly disintegrates.

23...Rg6 24 gxf6 Reg8 25 Qe5 a6 26 Bd3

With a vulnerable black king and a passed pawn on f6, the result is not in doubt.

26...Rh6 27 Bf5!

Opening up the position.

27...exf5 28 Rxd5 Bxd5 29 Qxd5 Rxg3 30 Qxf5+ Kc7 31 Qf4+ Qd6 32 Qxh6 Rf3 33 Qxh7+ Kb6 34 Qe7 Qf4+ 35 Kb1 Rxf2 36 Rh3 c4 37 Re3 Qd4 38 Re4 1-0

Game 10
□ **R.Seger ■ D.Artunian**
Pardubice 2008

1 e4 d5 2 exd5 Qxd5 3 Nc3 Qa5 4 d4 c6 5 Bc4 Nf6 6 Nf3 Bf5 7 Bd2 e6 8 Qe2 Bb4 9 Ne5 Nbd7 10 Nxd7 Nxd7! (Diagram 17)

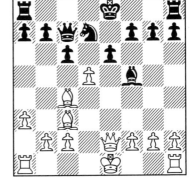

Diagram 17 (W)
Safest and best

Diagram 18 (B)
Solving the problem

In my opinion, the safest and the best move.

11 a3

With 11 0-0-0 White intends to seize as much space on the kingside as possible with g2-g4. However, Black can play 11...Nb6! 12 Bb3 followed by the natural 12...Nd5! when he shouldn't have any problems.

11...Nf6

Black aims to prevent any future d4-d5 by blunting the hidden potential of the future bishop on c3.

11...Bxc3 allows White to blow open the position with 12 Bxc3 Qc7 13 d5! **(Diagram 18)**, solving the problem of the bad bishop on c3. One of the fundamental ideas for Black is to nullify the bishop pair, and he should be very wary of allowing White to play d4-d5 like this. Now:

a) 13...0-0?! is met by 14 d6! intending 14...Qxd6 (14...Qd8! is forced but Black's position looks bad) 15 Rd1 Qc7 16 Rxd7 Qxd7 17 Qe5 and Black cannot defend the mate on g7 without losing material.

b) After 13...cxd5 14 Bxd5 0-0 15 Bf3 the bishop pair in an open position appears to offer White the easier game. Black has no squares for his knight but he does have one vital asset – pressure against the c2-pawn – which gives him some leverage. For example:

b1) After 15...Rac8 I would worry about the radical 16 h4!? threatening g2-g4. Then 16...e5 17 g4 e4 18 Bg2 e3! 19 0-0-0 Be6 leads to a double-edged position, although White has the better chances because of the bishop pair.

b2) 15...e5 16 0-0 Rfe8 17 Bd5? just wastes time, and after 17...Nf6 18 Bb3 Ne4 White had lost his advantage in K.Beckmann-R.Lau, Dresden 1998.

 WARNING: 11...Nb6? is a decisive mistake, and 12 0-0! Nxc4 13 axb4 Qxb4 14 Ra4 was winning for White in M.Chandler-I.Rogers, Bath 1983.

12 0-0

12 0-0-0 is the most promising move, as after 12...Bxc3 (12...Bxa3? doesn't look to be quite sufficient) 13 Bxc3 Qc7 White is still able to play the tactical break 14 d5. White obtained a very dangerous initiative for the pawn in V.Kalisky-E.Repkova, Slovakian League 2003, after 14...cxd5 15 Bb5+ Kf8 16 f3 a6 17 g4 Bg6 18 Bd3 Qf4+ 19 Kb1 Nd7 20 h4 Kg8 21 h5 Bxd3 22 Rxd3 h6 23 Rd4 Qd6 24 f4.

12...Bxc3 13 Bxc3 Qc7 14 Rfd1?!

A slight inaccuracy.

14...0-0-0!? (Diagram 19)

An interesting choice by Black. He can get away with castling on the opposite wing because of two factors:

1) The natural b2-b4-b5 does not work immediately because the bishops on c4 and c3 are rather awkwardly placed.

2) White must also take time out to defend against the threats of ...Ng4 and ...Bg4. In a game of opposite-side castling, time and weaknesses take on great importance.

15 Be1

After 15 b4?! h5, before White can push the b-pawn any further he must spend some time placing one of the bishops on a better square.

15...h5!

Of course Black should prevent f2-f3 and Bg3. The rest of the game is very instructive.

16 Bd3 Ng4 17 g3 Nh6

17...h4 is another possibility.

18 c3 g5 19 Be4 Bxe4 20 Qxe4 Qa5 21 Bd2 Rdg8 22 c4 Qf5! (Diagram 20)

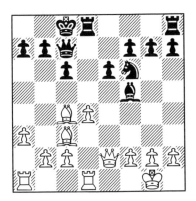 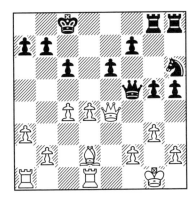

Diagram 19 (W)

Difficult to attack

Diagram 20 (W)

Seeking simplification

Now that Black has provoked the slightly weakening c3-c4, leaving the d4-pawn vulnerable, Black exchanges into a completely equal endgame.

23 Qxf5 Nxf5 24 Bc3 Rh6 25 Rac1

Or 25 d5 exd5 26 cxd5 c5 and Black will blockade the passed pawn. 27 b4 is unconvincing, as 27...c4 28 b5 Kd7 29 Rac1 Nd6 30 Bb4 Rc8 is fine for Black.

25...Rd8 26 h3 g4 27 h4 Rg6 28 Kf1 b6 29 a4 Kb7 30 b3 Rd7

Black has secured the f5-square for the knight and has ensured that the d4-pawn is a permanent liability.

31 Rd2 Rg8 32 Re1 Rgd8 33 Re5 Rd6 34 Ke1 Kc8 35 Re4 R8d7 36 Kd1 Kd8 37 Kc2 Ke8 38 Re5 f6 39 Re4 Kf7

Improving the king before undertaking any active measures. The time has come for this break and now Black is virtually winning.

40 Rde2 c5! 41 dxc5 bxc5 42 Kb2 e5 43 Rc2 Rb7 44 Ka3 Rd3 45 Ka2 Nd4 46 Bxd4 cxd4 47 Rb2 a5 48 Ree2 Rc3 0-1

Game 11
□ **L.Van Wely** ■ **M.Wahls**
Training Game (rapid), 1992

---

1 e4 d5 2 exd5 Qxd5 3 Nc3 Qa5 4 d4 c6 5 Bc4 Nf6 6 Nf3 Bf5 7 Bd2 e6 8 Qe2 Bb4 9 a3 (Diagram 21)

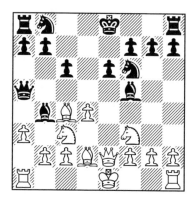

Diagram 21 (B)

A big choice for Black

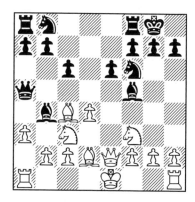

Diagram 22 (W)

Too committal?

Attacking the bishop immediately gives Black an alternative plan.

9...Bg4!?

With the idea of switching the queen to the kingside and ruining White's kingside pawns. The only question here is does Black have enough time?

 WARNING: 9...Bxc2?? loses a piece to 10 Rc1 when both bishops are attacked. In addition, retreating the bishop, say with 9...Be7, is simply not possible as White immediately hits out with 10 d5.

Here's a summary of alternatives:

a) 9...Nbd7!? 10 0-0-0 transposes to Game 8, whereas if White chooses 10 0-0 we reach Game 12.

b) 9...Bxc3 is also possible, and here 10 Bxc3 Qc7 11 Ne5 Nbd7 12 0-0-0 transposes to Game 8.

c) The thematic 9...Nd5?! doesn't work here: 10 Bxd5! cxd5 11 Qb5+ Qxb5 12 Nxb5 Bxd2+ 13 Kxd2 and now Black cannot prevent White from ruining his structure with 13...Na6 14 Nd6+ Ke7 15 Nxf5+ exf5.

d) 9...0-0!? **(Diagram 22)** perhaps commits the king too early, particularly as White can use the Scandinavian bishop as a target. However, there is an upside to Black's play in that White has an imperfect queenside pawn structure (remember, three pawns in a row is the perfect defensive formation), so Black can break more easily with ...b7-b5-b4. Now:

d1) 10 0-0 Bxc3 11 Bxc3 Qc7 transposes to Game 12.

d2) 10 0-0-0 Bxc3 11 Bxc3 Qc7 is similar to lines covered in the 9 0-0-0 section with one difference – Black has castled kingside: 12 Ne5 (White can also play 12 Qe5!? or 12 Bb4 Rc8 13 Qe5) 12...b5!? (12...Nbd7 may be the most accurate) 13 Bd3?! (it is important to use the bishop on f5 as a target to gain time with g2-g4, so White should prefer 13 Bb3!) 13...a5! 14 Bxf5 exf5 15 Qf3 b4!? 16 axb4 axb4 17 Bxb4 Ra1+ 18 Kd2 Ne4+ with good counterplay according to Wahls.

d3) 10 Ne5 with the idea of g2-g4 is the principled continuation: 10...Nd5!? 11 Bxd5 cxd5 12 g4 Bg6 (12...Bxc2 again loses a piece to 13 Rc1) and now White should play 13 h4!, because the situation becomes enormously complicated after 13 0-0-0 as Black suddenly has some tactical tricks against the white king.

10 0-0-0

10 h3 Bxc3 11 Bxc3 Qh5 is the whole point of 9...Bg4; White's pawn structure will be weakened.

10...Bxc3 11 Bxc3 Qh5 (Diagram 23)

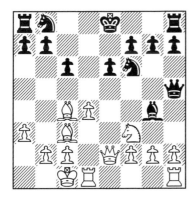

Diagram 23 (W)

Pressure against f3

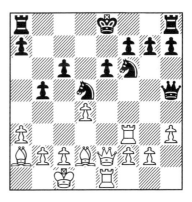

Diagram 24 (B)

Clear advantage for White

12 Rd3

After 12 h3? Bxf3 13 gxf3 Nbd7 Black's position is solid enough. While it is true that White has the open g-file, his kingside pawns are crippled and of course Black has a strong outpost on d5.

Gambiting a pawn with 12 d5!? doesn't seem to give White much: 12...cxd5 13 Bxf6 Bxf3 14 gxf3 Qh6+! (recapturing the bishop in a favourable way) 15 Kb1 Qxf6 16 Bxd5 Nc6 17 Bxc6+ bxc6 18 Qe4 0-0 19 Qxc6 is unclear, but I think the open b- and c-files provide sufficient counterplay for the material deficit.

 NOTE: The most important elements when only heavy pieces and pawns remain on the board are king safety and piece activity.

12...Nbd7

Attacking the rook with 12...Bf5?! doesn't help Black, as after 13 Re3 the rook is rather dangerous, bolstering the e-file. After 13...Nbd7 14 h3 Nb6 15 Re1 the bishop becomes a target on f5, and 15...Nxc4 16 Qxc4 Nd5 17 g4 Nxe3 18 Rxe3 Bxg4 19 hxg4 Qxg4 20 Qc5 leaves Black without a safe place for his king.

13 h3 Nb6 14 Ba2 Nbd5?

A blunder. Much better was 14...Bf5 forcing the rook backwards. After 15 Rdd1 Black reverts to the typical plan of 15...Be4! intending ...Bd5, when he stands fine.

15 Bd2 b5 16 Re1 Bxf3 17 Rxf3 (Diagram 24)

With the bishop pair and play on all areas of the board, White has the better chances.

17...0-0 18 g4 Qh4 19 Qe5

Threatening to trap the queen with 20 Bg5.

19...Nd7 20 Qd6 N7b6 21 Qxc6 a6

Now Wahls played 22 Qb7 with a clear advantage (the rest of the game is unavailable) but in fact he missed the tremendous blow 22 Bxd5! Nxd5 23 Rxf7!! picking up a huge amount of material.

Game 12

□ J.Cuartas ■ N.Mohota

Barbera del Valles 2007

---

1 e4 d5 2 exd5 Qxd5 3 Nc3 Qa5 4 d4 c6 5 Bc4 Nf6 6 Nf3 Bf5 7 Bd2 e6 8 Qe2 Bb4 9 0-0 (Diagram 25)

This line is known not to be dangerous for Black. In fact, Black has managed to achieve the main Scandinavian objective of developing his pieces while preventing White from establishing a two-pawn centre. However, that is not to say that Black can simply sit back and relax – far from it. There are still positional dangers lurking which are typical in this e6/c6 pawn structure. Black must be wary of the weakness of the d6-square and the fact that White may still establish a knight on e5 and expand dangerously on the kingside.

Typical ideas for Black include play along the half-open d-file and pawn expansion on the queenside: light-square strategy with ...b5 or breaking White's centre with ...c5 (usually as a reaction to White's expansion on the kingside). One thing Black must always do, especially when playing against White's two bishops with his knight and bishop, is to ensure that the knight always has a stronghold square – in this case d5.

9...Nbd7

TIP: Black should not exchange on c3 without being forced to do so. If Black exchanges too early, then White may gain the option of playing Bb4(-a3) preventing kingside castling.

9...0-0 is also popular. 10 a3 Bxc3! 11 Bxc3 Qc7 12 Nh4 **(Diagram 26)** is critical, testing the power of the two knights versus the might of the two bishops. If White can deprive the knights of useful bases then he will simply be better. 12...Nbd7! is the best reply – Black must get as many squares as possible. Here 13 d5 is not really a problem because of 13...Bg4 or 13...cxd5.

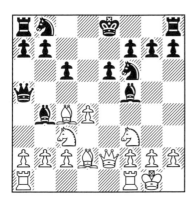

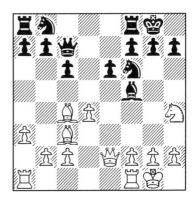

Diagram 25 (B)

The quieter 9 0-0

Diagram 26 (B)

Knights versus bishops

NOTE: If 12 Bd3? (instead of 12 Nh4) White loses his potential advantage by exchanging bishops. After 12...Bxd3 13 Qxd3 Nbd7 he is left with his inferior bishop and Black, who will secure the d5-square with ...b7-b5, experiences no problems all.

10 a3!

The most accurate move order. White's plan is simply to maximize all the advantages the bishop pair can give him.

10 Ne5 **(Diagram 27)** allows Black to simplify to an equal ending with 10...Nxe5 11 dxe5 Nd5 12 Bxd5 (if 12 Nxd5? Bxd2 White doesn't have an adequate square for the knight, and 13 b4 Bxb4 14 Nxb4 Qxb4 15 g4 Bg6 16 f4 b5 17 Bb3 Be4 was good for Black in J.Solberg-C.Hanley, Oslo 2005) 12...cxd5 13 a3 Bxc3 14 Bxc3, and now 14...Qa6! 15 Qxa6 bxa6 was very drawish in E.Solozhenkin-V.Bagirov, Jyvaskyla 1994 (rather than 14...Qc7? 15 Bb4! which is uncomfortable for Black as he cannot challenge White on the dark squares).

10...Bxc3 11 Bxc3 Qc7 12 Ne5

12 Bb3 is a multi-purpose move. Firstly White adopts some prophylaxis against ...Nb6 followed by ...Nd5 and ...b5; secondly, White clears the way for c2-c4. In addition, after Ne5 and g2-g4, the move ...Nxe5 no longer hits the bishop on c4. When both players castle kingside, despite appearances Black must still play carefully – allowing White the very dangerous Ne5 followed by g2-g4 is not usually a good idea. J.Nunn-J.Hodgson, Dutch League 1994, continued 12...0-0 13 Rad1 a5 (seizing space on the queenside to secure squares for his minor pieces; I cannot stress enough that when one is playing with two knights they should be given the freedom or the potential to move, and this usually means securing outposts or space) 14 Ne5 b5 (as John Emms stresses, 14...Nd5 15 g4! Bg6 16 f4! is something that Black really needs to avoid) 15 Bd2?! (White's position isn't strong enough to play in such a quiet manner; critical is 15 g4! Nxe5! 16 gxf5 Nc4! – Wahls – 17 fxe6 Nd5 when White's weaknesses on the kingside promise Black reasonable compensation for the pawn) 15...a4! 16 Ba2 Bxc2 17 Rc1 Be4 18 Bg5 Bd5! 19 Bxf6 Nxf6 20 Bxd5 Nxd5 21 Rxc6 Qb7 22 Rfc1 b4! 23 h3 h6 24 axb4 Qxb4 and Black had a small advantage due to his stronger pawn structure and well-placed knight on d5.

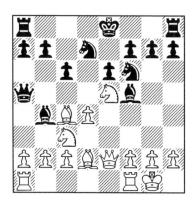

Diagram 27 (B)

Allowing simplification

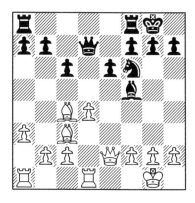

Diagram 28 (B)

The right rook

12...0-0

Or 12...Nd5!? and now:

a) The hyper-aggressive 13 g4 leads to an incredibly sharp position after 13...Nxe5 14 dxe5 Bg6 15 f4! Qb6+ 16 Kh1. Here Black has the counterattacking 16...h5! 17 f5 Bh7 intending ...0-0-0.

b) 13 Bd2!?, re-routing the bishops in order to push for c2-c4, allows 13...Bxc2 14 Rfc1 Nxe5 15 Bxd5 cxd5 16 dxe5. It looks as though White will win the bishop, but Black can reach a roughly level position with 16...0-0 17 Bc3 (after 17 Bf4 Rac8 18 b4 d4 Black saves his bishop and gets a huge pawn on d3!) 17...Rac8! 18 Qxc2 d4.

13 Nxd7

White plays very simply, avoiding the risks of 13 f4. After 13...a5 14 Rad1 Rfd8 15 h3 b5 16 Bd3 Nd5! it is difficult for White to shift the f5-bishop without taking further risks.

13...Qxd7 14 Rfd1! (Diagram 28)

The best move, as White now has another convenient retreat square for the bishop. 14 Rad1 Rfe8 (14...Nd5 is also possible, as 15 Be1 looks a little clumsy) 15 Bd3? relinquishes any claim for the advantage: 15...Bg6 16 Bxg6 hxg6 17 b3 a5 18 Bb2 b5 19 c4 Qb7 20 Rb1 Reb8 21 Bc1 bxc4 22 Qxc4 and Black has secured the d5-square for his knight, G.Mazziotti-D.Flores, Villa Ballester 2004.

14...Qc7 15 f3!? Nd5 16 Be1 Qf4 17 c3 h5?

This move looks a tad ambitious. I think it's easier to play for ...c6-c5 and take control of the d-file: 17...Rfd8 18 Bg3 Qg5 19 a4 a5 20 Qd2 Qg6 21 Rac1 h6 followed by ...Rd8-d7 and aiming for a timely ...c6-c5. Black's pieces are quite active, and both sides must play patiently and look to improve their position.

18 Bd2 Qc7 19 Qf2 b5 20 Bf1 Rad8 21 Re1 Nb6 22 Qh4 Bg6 23 Bf4 (Diagram 29)

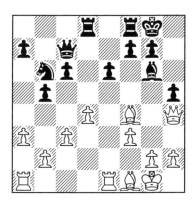
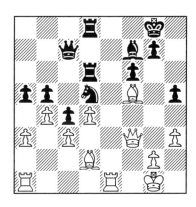

Diagram 29 (B)

White is better

Diagram 30 (B)

Black should hold tight

White's grip on the board increases and Black's kingside weakness is starting to tell – White has won the opening battle.

23...Qc8 24 Qg3 Na4 25 Qf2 Nb6 26 h3 Rd5 27 b3

As John Watson writes, "White is bluffing a bit with c4, but Black has to devote his forces to stopping it."

27...Rfd8 28 Be3 R5d7 29 Bg5 f6

29...Re8 allows 30 c4.

30 Bc1 Bf7 31 f4!

Preventing any form of counterplay with ...e6-e5.

31...Qc7 32 Qf3 Rd5

Playing for ...c6-c5, but 33 Be3 would prevent this.

33 Bd3?! c5! 34 Be4

34 Bxb5 cxd4 35 c4 R5d6 allows Black some activity.

34...R5d6 35 Be3 c4!

Securing some extra space.

36 b4 Nd5 37 Bd2 a5 38 f5 exf5 39 Bxf5 (Diagram 30)

39 Qxf5 is perhaps stronger – at the very least it forces Black to accept an additional weakness.

39...axb4?

Bad strategy – Black simply opens up another file for White to attack down. As John Watson points out, 39...Ra6 is better.

 TIP: When defending, don't allow yourself two (or more!) weaknesses. This makes it much more difficult to defend!

40 axb4 Qb7 41 Qg3 Kf8 42 Bf4 Nxf4 43 Qxf4 Ra6 44 Rxa6 Qxa6 45 Qc7

It looks as though White's position is overwhelming, but with so few pieces on the board Black's position is still a tough nut to crack.

45...Qd6 46 Qc5 g6 47 Be4 Kg7 48 Bf3 Qf4 49 Qa7 h4 50 Qa1 Re8 51 Rxe8 Bxe8 52 Qe1 Kf8 53 Bd5 Bd7 54 Kh1 Be8 55 Be6 Qg3 56 Qd2 Ke7

It is incredibly difficult for White to make progress. The problem is that if the queen moves to a more menacing position, Black can force a draw.

57 d5!?

White loses patience and pushes forward.

57...Qd3?!

57...Bd7 exchanging bishops is the most logical move – then the d5-pawn will simply become a liability. Indeed, 58 Qe2 Qe5 would have caused some problems!

58 Qf2! f5?? 59 Qxh4+ Kd6 60 Qf4+ Ke7 61 Qe5 Qd1+ 62 Kh2 Qd2 63 Bxf5+ 1-0

Game 13
□ **N.Pogonina** ■ **J.Houska**
World Mind Sports, Beijing (rapid) 2008

---

1 e4 d5 2 exd5 Qxd5 3 Nc3 Qa5 4 Nf3 Nf6 5 d4 c6 6 Bc4 Bf5 7 0-0 e6 8 Bf4!? (Diagram 31)

A very simple and natural developing move, and one I must confess I have rarely encountered before. 8 Bf4 reinforces control of the e5-square, and White's plan is quite straightforward. White intends to occupy the centre and use the extra space to build up pressure, and only then expand on the kingside. A slow build-up plan if you like.

8...Nbd7 9 a3

A dual-purpose move: White prevents ...Bb4 but also lays the foundation for gradual queenside expansion should Black play quietly.

9...Nd5!?

The most accurate try, which cuts out a lot of the options for White. 9...Be7 10 Re1 0-0 11 Qd2! prevents ...Nd5, although even here 11...Rfe8 is fine for Black.

10 Nxd5 cxd5 11 Bd3!

The only move: other retreats leave the bishop out of play.

11...Bxd3 12 Qxd3 (Diagram 32)

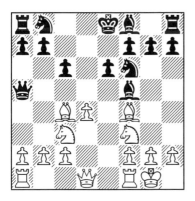

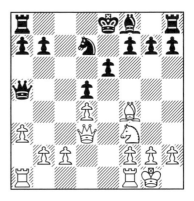

Diagram 31 (B)

Bolstering e5

Diagram 32 (B)

The plans are set

The pawn structure says it all: White will begin to work on the kingside whereas Black maintains a long-term initiative on the queenside. Should Black manage to exchange queens his position will become very pleasant, as the queenside minority attack is hard to repulse. Black, however, is not in a good position to blindly ignore White's kingside threats and must concentrate on defusing White's initiative.

12...Be7

12...Qb6!? is very interesting, tying White to the defence of his queenside. After 13 b3 Bd6 14 Bxd6 Qxd6 Black is fine.

13 Ne5?!

13 Rfe1 keeps more tension in the position and looks more worrying for Black. After 13...0-0 14 Ng5 Bxg5 15 Bxg5 Qc7 16 Re3 (swinging the rook over to the kingside) 16...f6 17 Bh4 Rac8 18 c3 Rfe8 19 Rae1 Qb6 both sides have weaknesses and the lack of minor pieces on the board indicates that the position is level.

13...Nxe5 14 Bxe5 0-0 15 Rae1 (Diagram 33)

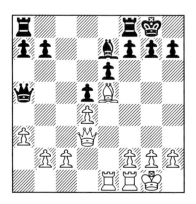

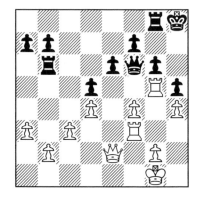

Diagram 33 (B)

Active defence is required

Diagram 34 (B)

Black must beware f4-f5

15 Rfe1 is still met by 15...Qb6!.

15...Qd8?

With limited time on the clock, I reacted a bit too cautiously.

15...Qb6! is the most active defensive resource and the best choice. Here 16 Qg3 leads to nothing after 16...f6 17 Bf4 Rac8! 18 Qh3 (or 18 c3 Qxb2 19 Rxe6 Rxc3) 18...f5, when White must hurry back to defend his queenside pawns.

16 c3 Rc8 17 Re3 Bf6 18 Rfe1 Bxe5 19 Rxe5 Rc4 20 f4 g6

Black is defending now, and my plan was to hold tight as much as I possibly could.

21 Qg3 Kh8 22 h4 h5 23 Rg5 Rg8

Not letting White in anywhere.

24 Qf3 Rc6 25 Re3 Rb6 26 Qe2 Qf6 27 Rf3 (Diagram 34) 27...Qd8?

A bad mistake. By now both my opponent and I were surviving only on the bonus time we were getting after each move, and after playing carefully on every turn I finally missed the f4-f5 shot.

27...Rc8! was better, as 28 f5 no longer works: after 28...exf5 29 Rfxf5 gxf5 30 Qxh5+

Black has 30...Qh6.

28 f5 exf5 29 Rfxf5 Re6

29...Re8! was the only move to hold on.

30 Qf3?

30 Rxh5+! would have won after 30...Kg7 31 Rh7+!.

30...f6 31 Rxd5 Qe7 32 Rg3 Re1+ 33 Kh2 Re4 34 Rh3 Re8

The rest of these moves were played very quickly.

35 Qg3 Rg4 36 Qf2 Qc7+ 37 Kg1 Qc6 38 Rc5?? Qe6??

Missing the opportunity to play 38...Re1+ 39 Kh2 Qd6+ winning.

39 Rf3 Qe1+ 40 Qxe1 Rxe1+ 41 Kf2 Rb1 42 Rc8+ Kg7 43 Rc7+ Kh6 44 Rxb7 f5 45 g3 Rc1 46 Rf4 Rxf4+ 47 gxf4 Rh1 48 d5 Rxh4 49 Kg3 Rg4+ 50 Kf3 Rg1 51 d6 Rd1 52 d7 h4 53 c4 Kh5??

The final mistake. 53...h3 was the only chance to hang on, and Black is still fighting after 54 Kg3 Rd3+ 55 Kh2 g5 56 fxg5+ Kxg5 57 c5 Kg4.

54 d8Q 1-0

Oh dear – it's checkmate with Rh7.

Ne4 Lines

In this section we look at two lines with an early Bd2 and Ne4 by White, who can play this idea with or without the light-squared bishop developed to c4.

A) 1 e4 d5 2 exd5 Qxd5 3 Nc3 Qa5 4 d4 Nf6 5 Nf3 c6

 WARNING: 5...Nc6? is simply a bad mistake, and 6 Bd2! (rather than 6 Bb5 Ne4) is the refutation of Black's idea: 6...Bg4 (or 6...a6 7 Bc4 Qh5 8 Ne5!) 7 Nb5 Qb6 8 c4 Bxf3 9 Qxf3 Nxd4 10 Nxd4 Qxd4 11 Qxb7 Qe4+ 12 Qxe4 Nxe4 13 Be3 with a very good two-bishop ending for White.

6 Bc4 Bf5 7 Bd2 e6 8 Ne4 (Diagram 35)

White has two options here: he can exchange knights and enter positions similar to those seen with 8 Nd5, or he can try to utilize ideas seen more often in the Classical Caro-Kann by transferring the knight to g3 and getting ready to establish a two-pawn centre with c2-c4. However, I must admit that 8 Ne4 has always seemed illogical to me. Why allow the black queen to reach a more favourable square than d8?

8...Qc7

This is probably the most accurate move. The positions are incredibly similar to those seen in the 8 Nd5 main line but with one exception: Black is a tempo up!

8...Qd8?! 9 Ng3 provides a perfect example of how White wishes to utilize his lead in development with piece play. The aim is simply to drive back and exchange Black's light-squared bishop while at the same time redeploying the irksome knight on c3, which prevents White from establishing a two-pawn centre. After 9...Bg6 (9...Bg4 10 c3 Nbd7 11 h3 Bxf3 12 Qxf3 leaves White with the bishop pair and a space advantage) 10 h4 **(Diagram 36)** the whole idea is revealed: White wishes to transpose to favourable version of the Caro-Kann, having obtained the "free" moves Bd2 and Bc4. Now:

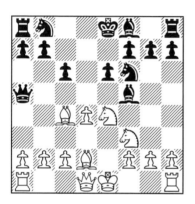

Diagram 35 (B)	**Diagram 36 (B)**
Similar to 8 Nd5	A good Caro-Kann for White

a) Black doesn't have the time to treat the position as if it were a Caro-Kann, because after 10...h6?! 11 Ne5 Bh7 12 Qe2 Nd5 (12...Qxd4?? would be a terrible mistake in view of 13 Nxf7!, and 12...Bd6?? fails for the same reason) 13 0-0-0 Nd7 14 f4 White has a very pleasant position: his knight is comfortably supported on e5, and Black cannot eliminate it without opening the f-file.

b) 10...h5 isn't usually played in these positions, as the h-pawn simply becomes a liability. Furthermore, Black cedes control of the g5-square.

c) This means that Black must deal with the problem radically by playing 10...Nh5!, but even this is good for White. For example, 11 Qe2 Nd7 12 0-0-0 Bd6 13 Ne5 Nxg3 14 fxg3 Bxe5 15 dxe5 h5 16 Bb4!? and White has complete control of the dark-squares, P.Svidler-L.Oll, Ter Apel 1996.

8...Qb6 was initially my choice, but my enthusiasm for this move has dampened just a little bit: 9 Nxf6+! (9 Ng3 is less dangerous here, and after 9...Bg4 10 Bb3 Nbd7 11 0-0 Bd6 Black has a comfortable position: he will castle kingside, place a rook on the d-file and break up White's centre with ...c6-c5) 9...gxf6 10 0-0! **(Dia-**

gram 37) (offering the b-pawn is the best option; 10 Bb3 hampers a queenside pawn storm, although White may intend to play more positionally after 10...Nd7 11 Qe2 0-0-0 12 0-0-0 Bd6 – otherwise White will establish control of the h2-b8 diagonal – 13 Nh4 Bg6 14 Nxg6 hxg6) 10...Nd7 (after 10...Qxb2 11 Rb1 Qxc2 12 Qxc2 Bxc2 13 Rxb7 White's control of the seventh rank gives him compensation for the pawn) 11 b4! Bd6 12 a4! (starting this pawn advance is in my opinion the best option; after 12 Re1?! Rg8 13 Kh1 0-0-0 14 Bf1 e5 15 c4 Bxb4 Black had the advantage in J.Dworakowska-J.Houska, German League 2000) 12...Rg8 13 a5 Qc7 14 Re1 Bg4 15 g3 a6! (to halt the queenside pawns) 16 Be2 (breaking the pin and preparing c2-c4) 16...f5! (Black must also begin to batter the protection surrounding White's king) 17 c4! Nf6 18 b5 axb5 19 cxb5 Ne4 threatens a double sacrifice on g3, but this position is extremely complicated.

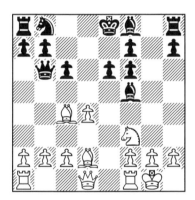

Diagram 37 (B)

Offering the b-pawn

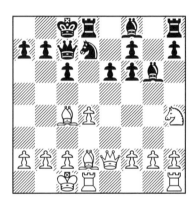

Diagram 38 (W)

Black enjoys an extra tempo

9 Nxf6+

9 Ng3?! is no longer so effective now that Black has some control of the e5-square: 9...Bg6 10 Qe2 (or 10 h4 Nh5! 11 Ne5 Nxg3 12 fxg3 Nd7 13 Bf4 Nxe5 14 Bxe5 Bd6 and Black has already equalized) 10...Nbd7 11 0-0-0 Bd6 and White has a poor version of the Classical Caro-Kann, with no kingside expansion, L.Psakhis-J.Pomes, Andorra 1996.

9...gxf6 10 Qe2!?

Just as in the 8 Nd5 main line, White intends to exploit Black's slight structural weaknesses by either exchanging the light-squared bishop for the knight or by advancing his pawns on the kingside.

10...Nd7

10...Bxc2!? isn't exactly the same as Game 7, as Black's queen on c7 grants White the option of 11 Rc1 Bg6 12 d5 which is rather menacing.

11 0-0-0 0-0-0 12 Nh4 Bg6 (Diagram 38)

Here the prophylactic 13 Bb3 (guarding against ...Nb6) is very similar to Game 6 but with an extra tempo for Black, which should certainly prove to be useful.

13 g3 can even be met by 13...Bd6!?. Of course it would be ideal if the dark-squared bishops were exchanged, so preferably Black should wait for Nxg6 hxg6 and then aim for ...Bh6. However, Black's position is still very solid even with this minor concession. For example, 14 Nxg6 hxg6 15 h4 f5 16 h5 gxh5 17 Rxh5 Nf6 18 Rhh1 Ne4 19 Be3 Qa5 20 Bb3 and Black's knight is far superior to the badly placed bishop on b3, D.Sarenac-M.Savic, Belgrade 2007.

B) 1 e4 d5 2 exd5 Qxd5 3 Nc3 Qa5 4 d4 Nf6 5 Nf3 c6 6 Bd2 Bf5 7 Ne4 (Diagram 39)

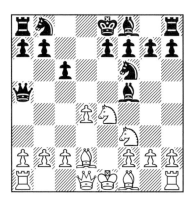

Diagram 39 (B)	Diagram 40 (B)
The subtle 7 Ne4	The best choice for the bishop

NOTE: There is a subtle point behind this move order. By keeping the bishop at home on f1, White can exchange on f6 and then develop this bishop to its optimum diagonal. Note also that White avoids the wild complications that arise after 5 Bd2 Bg4 and 5 Bc4 Bg4 (see Chapter Five).

We will now look at 7...Qc7 and 7...Qb6 in turn:

B1) 7...Qc7 8 Nxf6+ gxf6 9 g3! (Diagram 40)

This was John Emms's dangerous recommendation in *Attacking with 1 e4*. The idea is simple: the fianchettoed bishop not only protects White's king, it also doesn't impede White's pawn storm on the queenside. The only drawback to this plan is that Black can achieve the central pawn break ...e7-e5 more easily, but after some analysis I'm not too sure how much of a problem this is for White anyhow.

9...Nd7!

9...e6?! is too slow, and 10 Bg2 Nd7 11 0-0 0-0-0 12 Re1 Bd6 13 c4! e5 left White with the initiative in I.Glek-H.Nakamura, Minneapolis 2005. Here IM Andrew Martin indicates that White could have gained the upper hand with 14 c5 Be7 15 Qa4!. Black is forced to play 15...Kb8 but after 16 Ba5 b6 17 cxb6 axb6 18 Bc3 he is really struggling with his queenside weaknesses.

10 Bg2 0-0-0 11 0-0 e5! (Diagram 41)

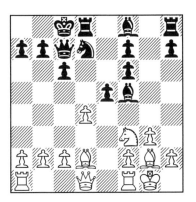

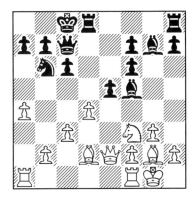

Diagram 41 (W)	**Diagram 42 (B)**
...e5 in one jump	A critical position

This is the idea – Black gets to play ...e5 in one go! However, the next question is how Black should continue, whereas it is clear that White will simply begin to push his queenside pawns.

12 c3 Nb6!?

Intending ...Nc4 to exchange off White's dark-squared bishop.

I looked at 12...h5!? but White can simply play the direct 13 a4!, which not only begins to break down Black's defences but also intends to lock the black knight on d7 out of the game! After 13...Kb8 14 a5! a6 White should simply play 15 Nh4 Be6 16 Qc2 when it's not clear how Black should continue.

12...Be4 is also dubious. The big problem is that 13 Re1 Bd5 14 Qc2 h5 15 a4 threatens a4-a5, again locking the knight out of the game and leaving Black's pieces very uncoordinated.

13 Qe2!

13 a4 allows 13...Nc4 when Black will either exchange off the dark-squared bishop or force the white pieces back.

13...Bg7 14 a4 (Diagram 42)

A critical moment: Black must try and somehow coordinate his pieces.

In H.Hunt-E.Repkova, Calvia 2004, Black played 14...Rhe8? overlooking 15 a5! (now White has a very strong position) 15...Nd7 16 Be3 Bg4 17 Qc2 a6 18 Qxh7! (White boldly takes all the material) 18...Rh8 19 Qxg7 Be6 20 dxe5 Rdg8 21 exf6 Rxg7 22 fxg7! Rg8. The g-pawn is just too much for Black to handle. Harriet eventually won with 23 Bh6, but she missed a chance to speed up the end of the game with 23 Bf4! Qd8 24 Ng5 (the check on d6 will be deadly) 24...Rxg7 25 Ne4! Qf8 26 Nd6+ and White wins further material.

14...Be6! is Black's best move. It makes sense to aggressively pursue control of the c4-square as this blockades White's attack, even if it does look scary to allow the pawn to advance to a6. Let's take a look a bit further at what might happen: 15 a5 Nc4 16 a6 b6 17 Bc1! (although this move looks a bit strange, it is probably White's best bet; after 17 Be3 Kb8 18 Ra4 Nxe3 19 Qxe3 Rhe8 it is not easy for White to co-ordinate an attack on the light squares) 17...Rhe8 18 Ra4! Nd6 and now 19 c4!? is interesting: 19...exd4 20 Nxd4 is just very good for White, as there is no effective discovered attack on the queen; 19...e4 is stronger, and after 20 Nh4 f5 21 c5 bxc5 22 dxc5 Nb5 Black is saved by his good piece coordination.

B2) 7...Qb6!? (Diagram 43)

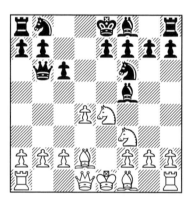

Diagram 43 (W)
Attacking b2

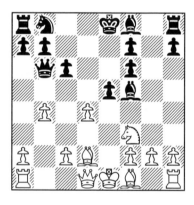

Diagram 44 (W)
The principled answer

This is probably the best move.

8 Nxf6+ gxf6 9 b4!?

White pre-empts Black's plan of castling queenside, but this does allow Black to react in the centre. Alternatively:

a) 9 Bc4 transposes to 7 Bc4 e6 8 Ne4 Qb6 9 Nxf6+ gxf6.

b) 9 Bc3 Nd7 10 g3 0-0-0! (for the time being Black should simply continue with his development and refrain from making committal moves) 11 Bg2 e6 12 Nh4 (if White prevents ...Bb4 with 12 Qd2, Black can continue calmly with 12...Qa6 preventing White from castling kingside) 12...Bg6 13 0-0 Bb4 14 Qd2 Bxc3 15 Qxc3 f5 (Black voluntarily shuts in his light-squared bishop in order to establish a grip on the important e4-square) 16 d5 exd5 17 Bxd5 Qc5 18 Bc4 b5 19 Bd3 Qxc3 20 bxc3 Nc5 21 Bxf5+ Kc7 and Black's pawn deficit doesn't count for much as he will win the c3-pawn, N.De Firmian-C.Matamoros Franco, Las Palmas 1999.

9...e5!? (Diagram 44)

This is the principled answer to White's rather adventurous play.

9...e6!? is more restrained but equally viable. For example, 10 a3 Nd7 11 c4 (this looks very tempting but in his haste to rush pawns forward White creates a weakness on d4) 11...Bg7! 12 Be3 Qc7 13 Nh4 Bg6 14 Be2 f5 15 Qc1 0-0 16 0-0 e5! 17 Bh6 (17 dxe5 is not possible because 17...Bxe5 18 h3 f4! is good for Black) 17...exd4 18 Bxg7 Kxg7 19 Qb2 Qe5 and Black had no problems in O.Korneev-J.Pomes Marcet, Navalmoral 2000.

10 Bc4!

The best continuation: White isn't swayed by the lure of material and instead chooses to complete his development. If 10 dxe5 Black should not recapture the pawn but play 10...Nd7 11 exf6 0-0-0 developing his forces rapidly. After 12 Be2 Nxf6 13 0-0 Rg8! Black threatens the unpleasant 14...Bh3 and 14...Ne4.

10...Nd7

After 10...Bxb4? 11 0-0 Bxd2 12 Qxd2 Nd7 13 dxe5 fxe5 14 Nxe5! Nxe5 15 Rae1 f6 16 Qd6 Black was in terrible trouble, as 17 Rxe5 was coming, in V.Jansa-M.Konopka, Plzen 2003.

Black should not even think about leaving his king vulnerable to attack after 10...exd4, even if it does win a pawn!

11 0-0 0-0-0! (Diagram 45)

Again the most principled continuation; Black doesn't waste any time and starts preparing his counter-attack.

11...Bg6? is too cautious and 12 dxe5! fxe5 13 Qe2 is incredibly strong: 13...Bg7 14 Rad1 0-0! (the best defensive move; 14...0-0-0 is just suicidal as none of Black's pieces will be able to attack White's king: 15 Nh4! Bxc2 16 Rc1 Ba4 – 16...Bg6 17 Nxg6 – 17 Nf5 Bf8 18 Bxf7 with an advantageous position) 15 Bg5! Nf6 16 Rd6!, forcing the knight to retreat to the back rank. White has the advantage due to his better placed pieces and queenside initiative.

After 11...0-0-0, play can become very complicated. Here are just a few possible continuations:

a) 12 a4 exd4 13 a5 Qc7 14 a6 b6 and Black will follow up with 15...Bg4 or 15...Ne5. It's useful for Black that 15 Nxd4 is met by the strong 15...Ne5! when too many white pieces are hanging.

b) After 12 Bxf7 exd4 13 Nh4 Ne5 14 Nxf5 Nxf7 15 Qh5 Ne5 it is not so clear how White will continue the attack.

c) 12 c3! exd4! 13 Nxd4 Ne5 14 Be2 (14 Bxf7 fails to 14...Rxd4) 14...Be4! **(Diagram 46)** (inducing a weakness, such as g2-g3 or f2-f3, or a piece exchange – being passive is not the name of the game!) 15 f3!? (15 Be3 c5 16 bxc5 Bxc5 17 f3 Bg6! keeps an eye on the important b1-square, while 15 a4 fails to 15...Bxb4 intending to meet 16 f3 Bg6 17 f4? with the stunning 17...Rxd4! 18 cxd4 Qxd4+ 19 Kh1 Bxd2 20 fxe5 fxe5 and Black has many pawns for the exchange) 15...Bd5 16 a4. Here Black should remove his queen from attack with 16...Qc7 17 a5 Bd6, when an exciting game has developed: Black will continue his attack on the weakened dark squares around White's king, whereas White will still prod the queenside for weaknesses but must be mindful of his own king's safety.

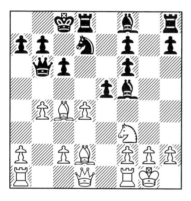

Diagram 45 (W)

A complicated position

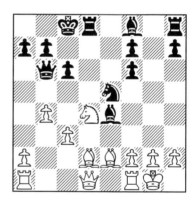

Diagram 46 (W)

Trying to create a weakness

Summary

In the old main line with 8 Qe2 we've see a series of interlinking ideas for White: gaining the bishop pair with a2-a3, and occupying the centre with Ne5 or playing to exchange the Scandinavian bishop with Nh4.

After 9 0-0-0 followed by 10 a3, Black is forced to give up the bishop pair and he then plays on the light squares. In Game 8 Black secures these by ...b7-b5 followed by a most instructive ...Be4-Bd5 manoeuvre, gaining absolute control of the d5-square.

Instead of castling queenside immediately, White may decide to occupy the centre with 9 Ne5. Because 9 Ne5 is always a prelude to a kingside pawn storm, Black must challenge this knight immediately with 9...Nbd7!. After 10 Nxd7 there are two possible recaptures: 10...Kxd7 or 10...Nxd7. If one opts for the former, be advised to look at Game 9, where Black carelessly allowed White the tactical shot d4-d5. 10...Nxd7 is more solid, and in Game 10 Black creatively demonstrates the problems White has playing with two bishops in a semi-closed position. Black should not let White's dark-squared bishop reach the h2-b8 diagonal, so make a note to take proactive measures with ...h7-h5-h4!

If White castles kingside as in Game 12, a quieter position arises, although again Black should be alert to the possibility of a kingside pawn storm if White has propelled the knight to e5. Once more the d5-square is a source of strength, and Black should seek counterplay along the d-file. White, on the other hand, aims to obtain as much space as possible on both wings and plays on the typical weakness of d6 (created by the c6/e6 pawn formation). Game 13 is a crude version of the old main line with 0-0, and here White plays on two factors: the inherent strength of the e5-square and White's space advantage. Black must deal with these issues actively otherwise he is left with a solid, if a little passive position.

Summarizing the early Ne4 lines, 8 Ne4 Qc7 isn't particularly threatening for Black, who often just ends up a tempo ahead of the 8 Nd5 main lines. However, 6 Bd2 Bf5 7 Ne4 intending a kingside fianchetto is more dangerous. Both 7...Qc7 and 7...Qb6 are playable, but Black must play energetically in these complicated positions.

Chapter Four

Ne5 Lines

Early Ne5 lines are notoriously aggressive. White intends to punish Black's loss of time in the opening immediately, and placing the knight into the centre of the board is usually the prelude to a kingside pawn storm with g2-g4, f2-f4 etc. By hunting the bishop, White is hoping to extract by sheer aggression some form of structural and positional advantage. Black in turn hopes that by playing in such a radical manner White will overextend and be left with a position full of gaping holes.

White can play with an early Ne5 in two ways: he can choose to develop the light-squared bishop to c4; or he can leave the bishop at home, and later develop it to either d3 or, better still, on the long h1-a8 diagonal.

 NOTE: Due to its totally aggressive nature, both sides are advised to study this variation carefully.

Ideas to remember include g2-g4, f2-f4-f5, piece sacrifices on e6 (especially when the bishop is developed to c4) and the d4-d5 pawn push. In this chapter Black's play is very much reactive to White's attack and concrete analysis takes precedence. There are fewer general rules, but some principles still apply. For example, when a knight arrives on e5 it should still be challenged as soon as possible, and when White has played Qe2 and Bd2 Black should intercept the potential discovered attack on the queen with ...Bb4!.

 TIP: Black should never allow his position to become constricted, and in the case of a kingside pawn launch he should be always ready to meet the lunge f4-f5.

White Plays 7 Ne5

1 e4 d5 2 exd5 Qxd5 3 Nc3 Qa5 4 d4 Nf6 5 Nf3 c6 6 Bc4 Bf5 7 Ne5 e6 8 g4 (Diagram 1)

The quieter 8 0-0 is covered in Game 16.

8...Bg6!

It is important for Black to retreat his bishop in order to provoke White into further compromising his pawn structure, as this will then become a basis for Black's counter-attack.

8...Be4 is considered to be dubious by theory because of 9 0-0 (9 f3?! weakens the king and Black should be fine after 9...Bd5 10 Bd3 Nbd7 11 Nxd7 Nxd7 12 0-0 Be7 13 Bd2 Qb6). However, the situation is not so clear cut. For example, 9...Bd5 10 Bd3 Nbd7! 11 f4 h5 12 g5 Nxe5 13 fxe5 Ng4 14 h3 Qb6! and White's king is all over the place.

9 h4 (Diagram 2)

Going directly for the bishop. This was once considered the most dangerous variation in the 3...Qa5 Scandinavian, and it is discussed in Game 14. White's main alternative is 9 Bd2, which is covered in Game 15.

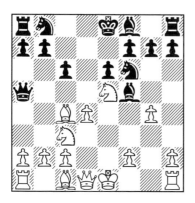

Diagram 1 (B)	Diagram 2 (B)
Ultra-aggressive play	Hunting the bishop

Game 14
□ **T.Moriuchi** ■ **E.Prié**
San Sebastian 2005

This is a very convincing game from Black's point of view.

1 e4 d5 2 exd5 Qxd5 3 Nc3 Qa5 4 d4 Nf6 5 Nf3 Bf5 6 Bc4 c6 7 Ne5 e6 8 g4 Bg6 9 h4 Nbd7!

9...Bd6!? **(Diagram 3)** is Andrew Martin's recommendation on his *Scheming Scandinavian* DVD. Now:

a) 10 f4 Ne4 11 Nxg6 hxg6 12 Qf3 Nxc3 13 Bd2 Nd7 is actually better for Black. White's kingside pawns look impressive but in actual fact they are quite weak. The reason is simple – they cannot advance.

b) 10 Bf4 Bxe5 11 Bxe5 (if 11 dxe5 Ne4 12 Rh3 h5! and Black has successfully undermined the kingside) 11...Nbd7 and Black is at least equal: once the attacked bishop on e5 retreats he will play ...h7-h5 followed by ...Nf6-e4.

c) 10 h5 is critical, but 10...Be4 11 0-0 Bd5 (11...Bxe5 12 dxe5 Qxe5 13 Re1 Nbd7 is very complicated) 12 Bd3 Nbd7 is fine for Black: he has developed his pieces and White has severely weakened his king.

10 Nxd7 Nxd7 11 h5

White must strike quickly, otherwise he is in danger of having overstretched. 11 Qe2? is a mistake, allowing Black to strike back with 11...h5.

11...Be4 (Diagram 4) 12 Rh3

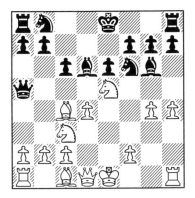

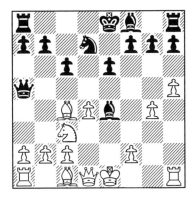

Diagram3 (W)

Another good option

Diagram 4 (W)

12 Rh3 or 12 0-0?

Against 12 0-0 Wahls recommends 12...Bd5!. For example, 13 Nxd5 cxd5 14 Bd3 Bd6 (14...g5 is also interesting: Black intends to secure the dark squares, and if White captures the g5-pawn he opens a line of attack) 15 Be3 g6 (Black's pressing issue is to arrange a breakthrough, so as to be able to exploit the white king's position) 16 h6 (this is the problem – White shuts out Black attempts) 16...0-0-0 (Black plans to play ...f7-f5-f4) 17 Rc1 Kb8 18 c4 dxc4 19 Bxc4 Nb6 and Black is doing fine.

12...Bg2!?

12...Bd5 is a very good alternative, with the idea being that if 13 Bd3 then 13...c5! is quite strong.

13 Re3

This looks more promising than 13 Rg3 Bd5 14 Bxd5 cxd5 15 Bd2 (A.Fedorov-A.Hauchard, Belfort 1999), when 15...Qb6! is better than the game's 15...Qd8. Because of his uncastled king, White really must seriously consider the defence of the b-pawn.

13...Qc7!

A great idea, discovered by Prié.

13...Nb6 was played in the legendary game V.Anand-J.Lautier, Biel 1997: 14 Bd3 Nd5 15 f3 Bb4 16 Kf2 (White traps the bishop but Black gets some pawns for his troubles, or so he thinks...) 16...Bxc3 17 bxc3 Qxc3 18 Rb1 Qxd4 19 Rxb7 Rd8 and here Anand unleashed the stunning 20 h6!! which kills off Black completely. The magnificent point is that after 20...gxh6 21 Bg6!!, Black cannot play 21...Qxd1 because 22 Rxe6+ Kf8 23 Bxh6+ Kg8 24 Bxf7 is checkmate.

14 f4?! (Diagram 5)

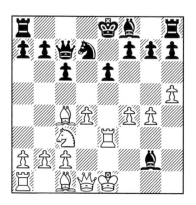
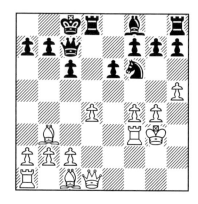

Diagram 5 (B)	Diagram 6 (B)
White has overstretched	A picturesque image!

This move is superficially aggressive but actually quite dubious. Not only does White shut out his bishop on c1, he also makes no attempt to inconvenience the bishop on g2, which can escape easily to d5. I would even go as far as to say that as a result of this move White has overstretched and now it is only Black who can reap the rewards from the position.

14 Rg3! Bd5 15 Bxd5 cxd5 16 Qe2 Be7 17 Bd2 Qb6 (simplifying with 17...Rc8 18 0-0-0 Qc4 looks like the best solution for Black) 18 0-0-0 Qxd4 is highly risky, as Black can fall into a trap: 19 h6! (in the style of Anand!) 19...g6 20 Be3 Qb4 21 a3 Qa5 22 Nxd5! (this is the idea: White gets the necessary tempo to attack) 22...exd5 23 Bd4 and White regains the piece with a winning position.

Of course not 14 f3? Qh2, and White is the one with the red face.

14...Nb6 15 Bb3 0-0-0 16 Kf2 Bd5 17 Nxd5 Nxd5 18 Rf3

Protecting the f4-pawn with 18 Re4 leaves the dark squares vulnerable, and after 18...Nf6 19 Re1 g5! White's king will be exposed even further.

18...Nf6 19 Kg3 (Diagram 6)

19 Rd3 was stronger, although after 19...g6 20 h6 Nd5 White is forced to play 21 Bxd5 and his kingside is simply too vulnerable. Following 21...exd5 22 g5 Bd6 23 Qf3 f5 Black has an outpost on e4 and is positionally winning.

19...g6

The decisive breakthrough – the opening of the h-file is fatal for White.

20 hxg6 hxg6 21 g5 Ne4+ 22 Kg2 Nxg5! 23 Rd3 Ne4 24 Qf3 Nd6 25 Be3 Nf5 26 Bf2 Bd6 27 d5 exd5 28 Bxd5 Nh4+ 29 Bxh4 Rxh4 0-1

White resigned because the f4-pawn will fall.

Game 15
☐ **J.Blit** ◼ **M.Leon Hoyos**
Buenos Aires 2005

---

1 e4 d5 2 exd5 Qxd5 3 Nc3 Qa5 4 d4 Nf6 5 Nf3 c6 6 Bc4 Bf5 7 Ne5 e6 8 g4 Bg6 9 Bd2 (Diagram 7)

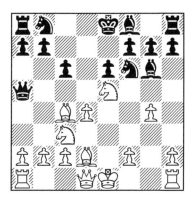

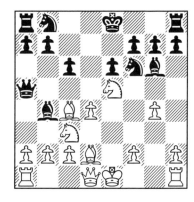

Diagram 7 (B)
A tricky move

Diagram 8 (W)
Not recommended

This move is designed to bluff Black into retreating his queen. The general plan for White is first to develop and then to continue with kingside expansion. By doing this he is hoping to catch Black unaware.

 NOTE: 9 Qe2 Bb4 10 Bd2 Nbd7 is an alternative move order to get to the position we reach in the game.

9...Nbd7!

9...Qb6? would be a mistake, as White is not obliged to defend the pawn: 10 Qe2! Nbd7 (it is best to reject the pawn offer: 10...Qxd4 runs into problems after 11 0-0-0 when the open d-file is a great source of danger to Black, and White is winning after 11...Qb6 12 f4; while if 10...Qxb2 11 Rb1 Qxc2 12 Rxb7 Black's position is in tatters) 11 f4! 0-0-0 12 0-0-0 and White's better placed pieces and extra space give him a pleasant advantage. For example, 12...Nxe5 13 dxe5 Nd5 14 Rhf1! (the threat of f4-f5 is very uncomfortable for Black) 14...h6 15 f5 Bh7 16 Rf3! (this rook manoeuvre is incredibly strong) 16...Be7 17 Nxd5 exd5 18 Rb3 Qc5 19 Ba6 is winning for White.

9...Bb4 **(Diagram 8)**, blocking the diagonal, is also possible but not something I would recommend, since ...Bb4 is something Black should really only play when the white queen is on e2. Now 10 a3! Bxc3 11 Bxc3 Qb6 12 Qe2 is good for White. For example, 12...Ne4? (12...Be4 13 Rg1 Bd5 14 Bd3 Nbd7 15 g5 gives White a tremendous position – Black is playing without space or any piece coordination) 13 Nxf7!? Kxf7 14 f3 Nxc3 15 Qxe6+ Kf8 16 Qc8+ Be8 (or 16...Ke7 17 Qxh8 Qxd4 18 bxc3 Qxc3+ 19 Kf2 and the white king will hide away on h3) 17 Qf5+ Ke7 18 Qe5+ Kd8 (18...Kf8 19 Qd6 mate) 19 Qxg7 Qxb2 20 0-0. The rook on h8 is lost and to add to Black's woes his king is too exposed in the centre.

10 Qe2 Bb4

> **TIP: Black should wait for Qe2 before playing ...Bb4 otherwise White can simply play a2-a3.**

11 0-0-0

11 h4?! **(Diagram 9)** mixes plans, and analysis by Ricardi shows this move to be premature: 11...Nxe5 12 dxe5 Nd5! (this move equalizes) 13 Bxd5 (if White tries to trap the bishop with 13 h5?, then 13...Nxc3 14 bxc3 Bxc3 15 hxg6 Bxd2+ is the point – White cannot recapture, as 16...Qxe5+ would pick up the rook) 13...exd5 14 h5 (or similarly 14 0-0-0 0-0-0 15 h5? Bxc2! 16 Kxc2 d4 and White must return the piece) 14...Bxc2 15 Rc1 d4! 16 Rxc2 0-0-0! (threatening 17...d3) 17 Qe4 Rhe8 (Black can recover the piece, but instead chooses to create some more threats first) 18 0-0 Rxe5 19 Qxh7 dxc3 20 bxc3 Bf8 and Black's king looks the safer.

11 f4 0-0-0 12 0-0-0 should be met by 12...Nb6 reinforcing the d5-square. Here White has a choice:

a) 13 a3 allows Black to complicate with 13...Bxa3 and then:

a1) 14 bxa3 Qxa3+ 15 Kb1 Rxd4 16 f5 (White must block off the b1-h7 diagonal) 16...Nxg4! (distracting the e5-knight; White must tread incredibly carefully not to lose on the spot) 17 Bc1 Qxc3 18 Rxd4 Qxd4 19 Bb2 Qf2! 20 Qxg4 (or 20 fxg6 Qxe2 21 Bxe2 Nxe5 22 Bxe5 f6) 20...Bxf5 21 Qe2 and Black has a tremendous number of pawns in exchange for the piece.

a2) 14 Na2! (the best defence) 14...Qa4! 15 Bb3 Qxd4 16 c3 and here Black has the stunning 16...Na4!. The position is completely wild, with Black paying no attention to material matters. Of course the queen cannot be taken, but White can play 17 Nxg6 Qb6 18 Kc2 hxg6 19 bxa3 Nc5 20 Rb1 Qa5 when Black's activity and White's exposed king offer Black compensation for the piece.

b) 13 f5?! was proven to be dubious in the game I.Smirin-P.Ricardi, Yerevan Olympiad 1996: 13...exf5 14 a3 Rhe8! (a marvellous sacrifice, and Black's attack is crushing) 15 axb4 Qa1+ 16 Nb1 Na4 17 Bc3 Ne4! (threatening ...Nexc3) 18 Rd3 f4! (a superb move – White can barely move a piece) 19 Qf3 Nexc3 20 bxc3 Qb2+ 21

Kd2 Nb6! 22 Ba6 (22 Bb3 fails to 22...Rxe5) 22...bxa6 23 Qxc6+ Kb8 24 Nc4 Nxc4+ 25 Qxc4 Re3 and White resigned.

11...Nxe5!

Black does not have any problems after this move.

12 dxe5 Nd5 (Diagram 10) 13 Bxd5

Diagram 9 (B)
Confusing plans

Diagram 10 (W)
No problems for Black

13 Nxd5 is answered by 13...Bxd2+ 14 Rxd2 exd5 15 Bb3 Qb4, preventing f2-f4. Here 16 e6 achieves little, as Black simply plays 16...0-0 with a very comfortable position now that the bishop on b3 is shut out.

Funnily enough, 14...cxd5 (instead of 14...exd5) leaves the black king more vulnerable than its counterpart. After 15 Bb5+ Ke7 16 Kb1 Rac8 17 f4 Rc5 18 Bd3 Wahls reckons that White's king is the safer one. The whole point is that following 18...Bxd3 19 Qxd3 Qb4 20 Rf1, the f4-f5 advance will be rather unpleasant for Black.

 TIP: After 13 Ne4!? Bxd2+ 14 Rxd2 it is important to play 14...Bxe4! to remove any potential problems the knight may cause. Remember, the d6 point is particularly vulnerable.

Black should meet 15 Qxe4 with 15...h5. Now that the rook is undefended on h1, undermining the g4-pawn looks very logical, and after 16 Bb3 hxg4 17 c4 Ne7 18 Qxg4 Qxe5 Black has a material and a structural advantage.

13...cxd5 14 Qb5+

White exchanges off into an inferior endgame. This time it is Black who has the bishop pair and a superior pawn structure!

14 f4 entails considerable risk and Black can simply carry on with 14...0-0! before aiming at the weak c2 point. If 15 Kb1 Black can reply 15...d4 16 Ne4 Bxd2 17 Nxd2 Rac8 and the pressure down the c-file looks likely to generate an advantage. 15 Nxd5 doesn't achieve much either: 15...Bxd2+ 16 Qxd2 Qxa2 17 Ne7+ Kh8 18 Qb4 Qa1+ 19 Kd2 Rfd8+ and with the white king in the open, Black is doing well.

14...Qxb5 15 Nxb5 Rc8! (Diagram 11)

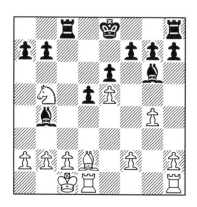

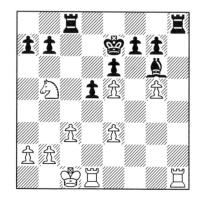

Diagram 11 (W)

Advantage to Black

Diagram 12 (B)

White has weak pawns

From now on, the advantage is firmly in Black's hands.

16 c3

16 Nd4 fails to 16...Bc5 17 Bc3 h5, undermining White's position.

16...Bc5?!

16...a6 17 Nd4 h5 would have given Black great chances to outplay White.

17 Be3 Bxe3+ 18 fxe3 Ke7 19 g5?!

White unnecessarily weakens his pawn structure.

19...h6 20 h4 hxg5 21 hxg5 (Diagram 12)

The g5-, e3- and e5-pawns are exceedingly weak, and it is only a matter of time before they drop off.

21...Be4

Seizing control of the h-file.

22 Rhf1 Bg6 23 Rf2

23 Rh1 should have been played.

23...Rh5 24 Rg1 Rch8 25 Kd2 a6 26 Nd4 Rh1

The black rooks enter White's territory. Black is practically winning now.

27 Rxh1 Rxh1 28 Rg2 Rb1 29 Rg3 Rxb2+ 30 Kc1 Rb1+ 31 Kd2 Rb2+ 32 Kc1 Rxa2

Black is two pawns up and the result is not in doubt.

33 Rh3 Rg2 34 Rh8 Rxg5 35 Rb8 Rxe5 36 Rxb7+ Kf6 37 Kd2 Rg5 38 Rb6 Rg2+ 39 Ke1 Ra2 0-1

Game 16
□ **J.Friedman** ■ **H.Nakamura**
Parsippany 2005

---

1 e4 d5 2 exd5 Qxd5 3 Nc3 Qa5 4 d4 c6 5 Bc4 Bf5 6 Nf3 Nf6 7 Ne5 e6 8 0-0

Instead of lunging like a caveman with 8 g4, White takes the positional route. However, this game shows that there are some inherent dangers in playing an early unsupported Ne5.

8...Nbd7 (Diagram 13)

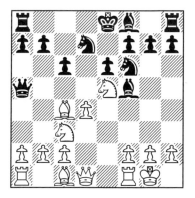
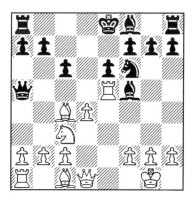

Diagram 13 (W)	Diagram 14 (B)
Black follows the rules	White's rook is vulnerable

Following the basic rule that the e5-knight should be challenged as quickly as possible.

9 Re1

Surprisingly this natural move is very bad. Some alternatives:

a) 9 f4? is too committal, and Black should eye that e4-square with glee: 9...Rd8 10 Qe2 Be7 11 Bb3 (11 g4?? loses to 11...Nxe5 12 fxe5 Nxg4 13 h3 Rxd4) 11...h5! (securing the strong bishop on f5) 12 Kh1 a6 13 Bd2 Qc7 14 Rae1 Nb6 15 Be3 Nbd5 16 Bg1 Nxc3 17 bxc3 0-0 18 c4 c5 and Black had a perfect position in I.Morovic Fernandez-Cu.Hansen, Wijk aan Zee 1994.

b) 9 Nxd7 Nxd7 10 Bf4 Bb4 11 Ne2 0-0 12 c3 Be7 13 Ng3 Bg6 14 Re1 b5 15 Bb3 Nf6 and Black has emerged from the opening with the desired favourable Caro-Kann type of position, V.Jansa-L.Van Wely, Gausdal 1992. As per usual, Black will aim to occupy the d5-square and utilize the semi-open d-file.

c) 9 Qe2 Nxe5 10 dxe5 Nd7 11 f4 (although tempting, this move is somewhat positionally suspect as it shuts out White's dark-squared bishop) 11...0-0-0 (a good decision: the black king will be safe on the queenside as White's minor pieces interfere with the desired pawn push) 12 Ne4 (12 a3 g5! undermines White's position completely, and here 13 b4 fails to 13...Bxb4) 12...Bxe4! (a masterful exchange: Black realizes that the knight will be much stronger than the light-squared bishop) 13 Qxe4 Nb6 14 Bb3 Bc5+ 15 Kh1 Qa6 16 Be3 Bxe3 17 Qxe3 g6 18 Rad1 and Black has a slight advantage due to the awkwardly placed bishop on b3, A.Olcayoz-T.Gelashvili, Ankara 2002.

d) 9 Bf4 Nxe5 10 Bxe5 (after 10 dxe5 Nd7 11 Qe2 Be7 12 Rfd1 I would be a little tempted to play the enterprising 12...g5 13 Bg3 h5 followed by castling queenside) 10...Nd7 11 Bg3 Bb4 12 Ne2 0-0 13 c3 Be7 14 Re1 Rad8 and White is only very slightly better, N.Somborski-M.Savic, Kragujevac 2000. Once Black has taken all the necessary precautions he will aim for ...c6-c5, playing ...b7-b6 if necessary. White needs to find a way to turn his attention to the kingside or try to discourage Black's plans.

9...Nxe5! 10 Rxe5 (Diagram 14)

The awkward placing of the rook causes White some problems, which Nakamura exploits ruthlessly.

The problem for White is that 10 dxe5? Ng4! attacks e5 and f2: 11 Qe2 (White must protect the bishop and the e5-pawn, as 11...Nxf2 followed by 12...Qc5+ was threatened) 11...Bc5 12 Nd1 Bxc2!? (winning a pawn, although admittedly play does become rather complicated from here; 12...Rd8! intending 13 h3 Rxd1! is stronger) 13 Bd2! Qd8 14 h3! (14 Qxg4? Qxd2; or 14 Bf4 Bxd1 15 Raxd1 Bxf2+ 16 Qxf2 Nxf2 17 Rxd8+ Rxd8 18 Kxf2 Rd4, winning one of the bishops) 14...Bxd1 15 Rexd1 Nxf2 16 Be3 Nxd1 17 Bxc5 Nxb2 18 Qxb2 Qa5 19 Qd4 Rd8 and White's two powerful bishops give him considerable compensation for the slight material deficit.

10...Qc7

With the threat of 11...Bd6.

11 h3 0-0-0!

An excellent attacking move: Black places pressure on the centre and forces White to make another concession.

12 Bg5 h6 13 Bh4 Bd6 14 Re3 Bf4 (Diagram 15) 15 Bg3 g5 16 Ne2 Rhg8 17 Ra3 Kb8 18 Nxf4 gxf4 19 Bh4 Rg6 20 Bf1 e5

Attacking in the centre; Nakamura is relentless.

21 c3 e4 22 Bxf6 Rxf6 23 c4 Rg6 24 Qh5 Bc8 25 d5 c5 26 Re1 Re8 27 Kh1 Qd8 28

Rc3 Qf6 29 a3 Re5 30 Qe2 Ka8 31 b4 Reg5 32 Qd2? (Diagram 16)

Now Black has a tactical shot.

32...e3 33 fxe3 f3!

Black crashes through.

34 g4 f2 35 Re2 Qf3+ 36 Bg2

36 Kh2 also ends in disaster: 36...Rxg4 37 hxg4 Qxg4 and mate is unstoppable.

36...f1Q+ 0-1

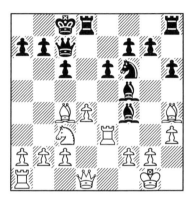

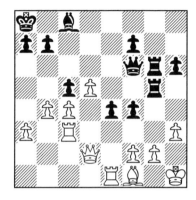

Diagram 15 (W)

Still harassing the rook

Diagram 16 (B)

A big mistake

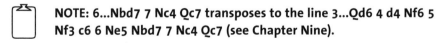

White Plays 6 Ne5

1 e4 d5 2 exd5 Qxd5 3 Nc3 Qa5 4 d4 Nf6 5 Nf3 c6 6 Ne5 (Diagram 17)

With 6 Ne5 White tries to get a favourable version of the Ne5 lines. By keeping the bishop on f1 for the moment, White maintains the important option of developing it on the desirable h1-a8 diagonal. Another possibility is to exchange off the Scandinavian bishop with Bd3, and play with the extra space. It is for these reasons why after 5 Nf3 it is advantageous for Black to play 5...c6 rather than 5...Bf5. With the bishop not committed, Black can meet 6 Ne5 by playing:

6...Be6!? (Diagram 18)

6...Bf5 is, of course, possible and this move is examined in Game 19.

> NOTE: 6...Nbd7 7 Nc4 Qc7 transposes to the line 3...Qd6 4 d4 Nf6 5 Nf3 c6 6 Ne5 Nbd7 7 Nc4 Qc7 (see Chapter Nine).

In light of White's ambitions, 6...Be6 is the most principled continuation for Black.

Although at a glance the bishop looks a little clumsy, situated in front of the e7-pawn, it cannot be harassed on e6 as the knight has already jumped to e5! Black also reasons that he has the option of developing the dark-squared bishop through a ...g6 fianchetto, and a chance to challenge the knight on e5.

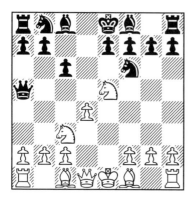

Diagram 17 (B)

An accelerated Ne5

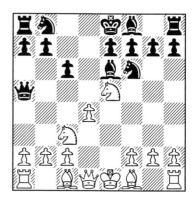

Diagram 18 (W)

The principled reply

The next decision for White is to choose whether to play the position with the light-squared bishops on the board or not: 7 Nc4 is covered in Game 17, while 7 Bc4 is the subject of Game 19.

7 Bd3 was Kasparov's choice against Anand when surprised by the Scandinavian in their 1995 world championship match, but it doesn't promise much: 7...Nbd7 (7...g6 is also good) 8 Nxd7 (8 f4?! was famously played by Kasparov, but Anand showed that this aggressive pawn move is simply too ambitious: 8...g6 9 0-0 Bg7 10 Kh1 Bf5! is a common strategic idea found normally in the Caro-Kann – Black is prepared to double his pawns in order to secure the e4-square and make White's dark-squared bishop bad) 8...Bxd7 9 0-0 Bg4 10 Ne2 e6 (with a pair of minor pieces off the board, Black's space worries have been alleviated) 11 c3 Bd6 12 Qc2 Qc7 13 h3 Bh5 14 Re1 Bg6 with equality, M.Kaminski-M.Van der Werf, Groningen 1992.

Game 17
□ M.Petrov ■ R.Ibrahimov
European Team Championship, Leon 2001

1 e4 d5 2 exd5 Qxd5 3 Nc3 Qa5 4 d4 Nf6 5 Nf3 c6 6 Ne5 Be6 7 Nc4 Qc7

7...Bxc4 8 Bxc4 e6 is a more solid way to play, but White is slightly better due to the bishop pair. The main consideration for Black is to ensure that White cannot play c2-c4 followed by d4-d5 too easily.

8 Bg5

8 Qf3 intending Bf4 is also pretty dangerous:

a) 8...Bg4 gives White the better ending after 9 Qf4 Qxf4 10 Bxf4. It is difficult for Black to develop the dark-squared bishop without conceding something, and after 10...Bf5 11 0-0-0 Ne4 12 Nxe4 Bxe4 White could have won in P.Roberts-I.Marks, Edinburgh 2007, had he chosen 13 Re1.

b) 8...Nbd7 9 Bf4 Qd8 10 0-0-0 Nb6 11 Ne3 Nbd5! is best. Black must aim to exchange pieces to alleviate his space difficulties.

8...Nbd7 9 Qf3

9 Qd2 with the idea of discouraging ...g7-g6 can be met by 9...Bxc4 10 Bxc4 e6 11 Bf4? (this seems a little bit pointless) 11...Bd6 12 Ne2 0-0 13 Bxd6 Qxd6 with a level position, K.Petschar-M.Konopka, Austrian League 2000. Black has the rather straightforward plan of playing down the d-file, possibly followed by a ...c6-c5 pawn break or securing the d5-square (...Nd5, ...b7-b5 and ...a7-a5-a4 would be perfect, although White would have to be pretty careless to allow that!).

9...g6 10 Ne3 Bg7 11 h4? (Diagram 19)

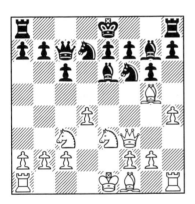
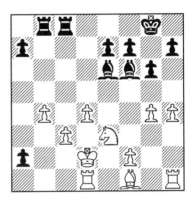

Diagram 19 (B)
Too committal

Diagram 20 (B)
Black to play and win

11...0-0!

A cool move, proving that White is simply not ready to attack on the kingside yet.

12 0-0-0

Trying to pawn-storm the king with 12 g4 is simply met by 12...h5.

12...b5 13 g4 b4 14 Ne4 Qa5 15 Bxf6 Nxf6 16 Nxf6+ Bxf6

Suddenly it is White's king who has problems.

17 Qxc6 Qxa2 18 Qa6 b3

A lovely little move. Now problems start to afflict White.

19 c3 Rfc8 20 Qxa2 bxa2 21 Kd2

White sets out to win the dastardly pawn on a2, but it's not so easy...

21...Rab8 22 b4 (Diagram 20) 22...Rxc3!!

An incredible move, utilizing the theme of overloading.

23 Kxc3 Bxd4+!!

This is the whole point – White simply cannot prevent Black from queening the pawn and regaining material.

24 Kxd4?!

24 Kd2 was more stubborn, although Black's advantage must be sufficient to win.

24...Rd8+ 25 Ke4 Rxd1 26 Nxd1 a1Q 27 Ne3 Qb1+ 28 Kf3 Qxb4 29 Bd3 a5 30 h5 Qc3 31 Be4 Qf6+ 32 Ke2 Qe5 0-1

Game 18
☐ V.Topalov ■ L.Van Wely
Monte Carlo (rapid) 1997

---

1 e4 d5 2 exd5 Qxd5 3 Nc3 Qa5 4 d4 c6 5 Nf3 Nf6 6 Ne5 Be6 7 Bc4 (Diagram 21)

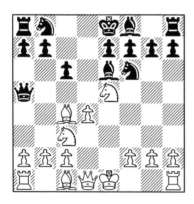
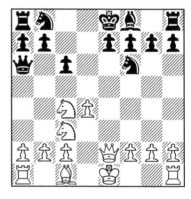

Diagram 21 (B)

Offering a bishop trade

Diagram 22 (B)

Be careful!

Strangely enough, White's best chance to achieve something from the opening may be to trade off the light-squared bishops.

7...Bxc4 8 Nxc4 Qa6

This is actually the easiest way for Black to equalize, although I must admit the position is a little bit dry. Alternatively:

a) Beating a retreat with 8...Qc7 smacks too much of passivity, and White can follow up with the natural 9 Qf3! intending Bf4.

b) 8...Qd8?! is also too passive for my liking: Black has wasted too much time, so the active pawn breaks ...e5 or ...c5 are very difficult to achieve. For example, 9 0-0 e6 10 Bg5! Be7 11 Re1 Nbd7 12 Qf3 and Black's position is still solid but it is a thankless task simply holding on for a draw.

c) 8...Qf5!? (after a trade of bishops, it makes sense for the queen to patrol the light squares) 9 0-0 e6 10 Ne2 (or 10 Re1 Nbd7 11 Ne3 Qh5!, D.Campora-M.Tempone, Sao Paulo 1989 – remember d4-d5 shouldn't be allowed!; or 10 Ne5 h5 – because of his active queen Black can take some liberties in the opening – 11 h3 Nbd7 12 Re1 Rd8 13 Nf3 Be7 14 Ne2 Ne4 15 Nf4 and now instead of 15...g5, 15...Ndf6 would have presented Black with no problems in I.Glek-D.Spinelli, Asti 1997) 10...Nbd7 11 Ng3 Qd5 12 Ne3 Qd6 13 Re1 (if 13 c4 Black should avoid the natural 13...Be7?, as 14 Nef5 would be a shocker!) 13...0-0-0 14 c4 h5 with a double-edged position.

9 Qe2 (Diagram 22) 9...e6!

In N.Grigore-M.Ionescu, Bucharest 2004, Black played the horrific blunder 9...Nbd7?? allowing 10 Nd6+.

10 Bf4

10 0-0 doesn't pose any problems, and 10...Be7 11 Re1 Nbd7 12 Bf4 0-0 13 Rad1 Nd5 14 Bd6 Nxc3 15 bxc3 Rfe8 16 Bxe7 Rxe7 was completely fine for Black in M.Vachier Lagrave-C.Gozzoli, Paris 2002.

10...Nd5 11 Bd6!

The only testing move. 11 Be5 Bb4 12 0-0 0-0 13 Qg4 g6 14 Nd6 Nd7 neutralizes White's attack, and after 15 Qg3 Rad8 16 Nde4 Bxc3 17 bxc3 Nxe5 18 Qxe5 Qa4 19 Rab1 b5 Black is completely safe.

11...Nxc3 12 bxc3 Nd7 13 Bxf8 Kxf8 14 Qd3!

14 0-0?? would be a huge blunder because of 14...Nb6!.

14...Ke7 15 a4 Nb6 16 Ne5 Qxd3 17 cxd3 (Diagram 23)

Black should be fine in this endgame, although White does have a niggling edge which can cause some headaches.

17...Nd7 18 Nf3 Rhc8 19 Kd2 c5 20 Rhb1 Rc7 21 a5 Rac8 22 Ra3 cxd4 23 Nxd4 Nc5 24 Nb3 Nd7

24...Rd7! would have been the correct way to play, and after 25 Nxc5 Rxc5 26 Rab3 Rxa5 27 Rxb7 Rxb7 28 Rxb7+ Kf6 29 c4 Ra2+ 30 Ke3 e5 Black is fine.

25 c4 e5 26 Re1 Kd6 27 f4 f6 28 Kc3 Nc5 29 fxe5+ fxe5 30 Nxc5 Rxc5 31 Re3 Rf8 32 Ra2 Rf6 33 Rg3 g6 34 Rh3 Rf7 35 Kb4 Rcc7 36 Re2 Rf1 37 Rhe3 Rb1+ 38 Kc3 Rc5 39 Ra2 Rc1+ 40 Kd2 Rf1 41 Re2 Rh1 42 h3 Rf1 43 Ke3 Rf7 44 g3 Ke6 45 Reb2 Kd6??

Black doesn't spot the danger.

45...e4! is a great move, as taking the pawn is not possible: 46 Kxe4 Re5+ 47 Kd4 Rd7+ 48 Kc3 Re3 and Black regains the pawn with interest.

46 a6 b6 (Diagram 24) 47 Rxb6+!!

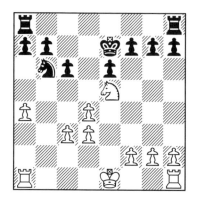 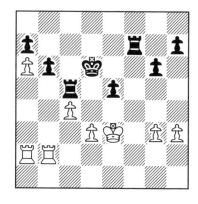

Diagram 23 (B)
Marginally better for White

Diagram 24 (W)
Spot White's next move

Now White gets good practical winning chances – he has a better pawn structure, a better rook and a better king.

47...axb6 48 a7 Rc8 49 a8Q Rxa8 50 Rxa8 Rf1 51 Rd8+ Kc6 52 Rh8 Rg1 53 Kf2 Rd1 54 Ke2 Rg1 55 g4

No draw!

55...Kc5 56 Rxh7 e4 57 Rc7+ Kd6 58 Rg7 Kc5 59 dxe4 Rg3 60 Rc7+ Kd4 61 Rc6 g5 62 Rxb6 Rxh3 63 Rb5 Kxc4 64 Rxg5 Kd4 65 e5 Re3+ 66 Kf2 Rxe5 67 Rg6!

The king is cut off horizontally, so Black is helpless.

67...Kd5 68 Kg3 Re8 69 Kf4 Rf8+ 70 Kg5 Ke5 71 Kh5 Kf4 72 g5 Kf5 73 Rh6 Rf7 74 Rh8 Kf4 75 g6 Rf5+ 76 Kh6 Kg4 77 g7 Rh5+ 78 Kg6 Rg5+ 79 Kf6 1-0

Game 19
☐ **V.Jansa** ■ **T.Polak**
Czech Championship, Brno 2006

---

1 e4 d5 2 exd5 Qxd5 3 Nc3 Qa5 4 d4 Nf6 5 Nf3 c6 6 Ne5 Bf5 7 g4 (Diagram 25)

This is the most critical move. By playing a very early g2-g4, White wishes to advance the pawns on the kingside while placing the light-squared bishop on its optimal diagonal: h1-a8.

Here's a summary of the alternatives:

a) 7 Bc4 transposes to 7 Ne5.

b) 7 Nc4 Qd8 8 Ne3 Bg6 9 h4 h6 10 h5 Bh7 11 d5 cxd5 12 Nexd5 Nc6 13 Bb5 (13 Nxf6+ exf6 doesn't give Black any problems – White is behind in development and Black's pieces are very well placed) 13...Nxd5 14 Qxd5 Qxd5 15 Nxd5 0-0-0 16 Bxc6 bxc6 17 Ne3 e5 and suddenly it is Black who has the advantage: he has the bishop pair and control of the centre, E.Sutovsky-I.Rogers, British League 2005.

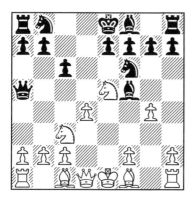
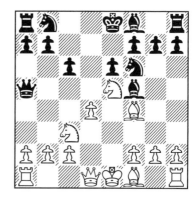

Diagram 25 (B)

The critical move

Diagram 26 (W)

Black should avoid this

c) Despite appearances, 7 Bd2 is not really threatening much. The only thing Black should bear in mind is that until White has forced ...e6 with Bc4, Black should leave that retreat square for the bishop. For example, if 7...e6? there follows 8 g4! Bg6 9 h4! and White has achieved everything he could want from playing Nf3-e5: the bishop will be developed to g2, the knight is superbly placed and he will shortly win the bishop pair. In view of this, Black's best response is 7...Nbd7!.

d) With 7 Bf4!? White hopes to transfer the queen to the kingside and, after an exchange on e5, to establish a vice like grip on d6. Now:

d1) 7...e6?! **(Diagram 26)** neglects our rule and is punished accordingly: 8 g4! Bg6! (or 8...Be4?! 9 Nc4 and after the exchange of pieces White is clearly better: his light-squared bishop can be developed on g2 and he is castling queenside) 9 h4! Bb4 (9...Nd5 10 Bd2 Nxc3 11 Bxc3 Bb4 12 Rh3! again gives White an edge, A.Sidenko-T.Stahl, correspondence 1998) 10 Bd2 Nbd7 11 Nxd7 Kxd7 (11...Nxd7? 12 h5!) 12 h5 Be4 13 f3 Bd5 14 Qe2 and Black must deal with the threat of g4-g5. White will simply play a2-a3 followed by 0-0-0, kicking back the bishop. Please note that ...Bxa3 tricks in these positions fail to Nxd5!.

d2) 7...Nbd7!? 8 Nc4 Qd8 and now:

d21) 9 Qe2 threatening 10 Nd6 mate can be met by 9...Be6 (or the line Wahls gives: 9...e6 10 Nd6+ Bxd6 11 Bxd6 Qa5!) 10 Ne3 g6 11 0-0-0 Nb6 12 Be5 Bg7 13 g4 0-0 14 Rg1 Nbd5 with counterplay, D.Morawietz-M.Ehrke, Bad Wiessee 2006 – Black will simply play for ...b7-b5, and White's attack looks slightly more cumbersome.

d22) The tempting strike 9 d5!? is not dangerous: 9...cxd5 10 Nxd5 e5 11 Nde3 Bxc2! 12 Nxc2 exf4 13 Qe2+ Be7! (the only way to defend) 14 Nd6+ Kf8 15 0-0-0 (D.Morawietz-N.Coenen, German League 2007) and now instead of 15...Qc7 Black could have opened an escape route for his king (and deprived the knight of the f5-square) with 15...g6, and here 16 Nxb7 fails to 16...Qc7.

e) As we have seen previously, often a dangerous plan for White is to exchange the light-squared bishops: 7 Bd3 Bxd3 8 Qxd3 Nbd7 9 Nc4 (9 Nxd7 Nxd7 10 0-0 e6 leads to only a very slight pull for White) 9...Qh5!? (keeping an eye on the light squares with 9...Qa6 is also possible) 10 Bf4 0-0-0 11 0-0 Nc5 12 Qe3 Ne6 13 Bg3 Ng4 14 Qe1 and here 14...Rxd4 is risky but the correct thing for Black to do, resulting in a very sharp position in U.Atakisi-B.Yildiz, Antalya 2004.

7...Be6! (Diagram 27)

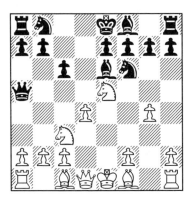

Diagram 27 (W)
The best retreat

Diagram 28 (W)
Hitting g4

7...Bg6?! 8 h4! transposes to a position that can also be reached via the move order 5...Bg4 6 h3 Bh5 7 g4 Bg6 8 Ne5 c6?! (8...e6 is better) 9 h4. After 8...Nbd7 9 Nc4! Qc7 10 h5 Be4 11 Nxe4 Nxe4 12 Qf3 Nd6 13 Bf4 White has a favourable position – it is difficult for Black to develop!

8 Bg2

8 Nc4 Qc7 9 Ne3 Nbd7 is also possible, but the 10 f4 of S.Bogner-R.Almond, Kusadasi 2006, is much too aggressive, and sure enough the tables shortly turned on White after 10...Nb6 11 f5 Bd5 12 Ncxd5 Nfxd5 13 Ng2 0-0-0 14 Bd3 e5!. Now it is

Black's turn! With the white kingside in tatters the advantage is firmly in his hands.

 NOTE: Trying to exchange the Scandinavian bishop with 8 Bc4 does not work well due to 8...Nxg4!. After 9 Bxe6 Nxe5 10 Bc8 Qc7 11 Bxb7 Qxb7 12 dxe5 e6 White's suspect pawn structure gives Black an edge.

8...Nbd7 9 Nxd7 Bxd7! (Diagram 28)

Maintaining the pressure on the g4-pawn. White will at some point or other be forced to make the weakening advance g4-g5.

10 g5

If 10 h3 Black can simply play 10...0-0-0 threatening ...e7-e5.

10...Nd5 11 Bd2 Nxc3 12 bxc3 Qa6

White has overstretched on the kingside, and the only problem for Black is that he is a little underdeveloped.

13 Rb1 Bf5 14 Qf3 Be6 15 Qg3 0-0-0 16 Be4 Bc4 17 Bd3 Bxd3 18 cxd3 Qxa2 19 0-0!

White is worse, so he tries to force a draw...

19...Qxd2

...which Black accepts. The rest of the moves are forced.

19...e6 is probably correct: 20 Bf4 (20 Ra1 Qxd2 21 Rxa7 Bd6 and Black wins, or 20 Qf4 Bd6 21 Qxf7 Rd7) 20...Qd5 21 Bc7 Bd6! and Black is better.

20 Rxb7 Kxb7 21 Rb1+ Kc8 22 Rb8+ Kd7 23 Rxd8+ Kxd8 24 Qb8+ Kd7 25 Qb7+ Kd8 26 Qb8+ ½-½

Summary

Ne5 is perhaps the most overtly aggressive line in the Scandinavian, so please memorize this chapter! White's plan is incredibly crude – occupy e5 and then advance with those kingside pawns while harassing the poor bishop on f5.

White can play Ne5 with the light-squared bishop either on c4 or on f1. The difference between these two options is that with the bishop on f1, Black is not obliged to develop his bishop to f5 but can instead play 6...Be6!? with a relatively comfortable game.

Chapter Five

Modern Move Orders

- White Plays 5 Bc4
- White Plays 5 Bd2

This chapter deals with perhaps one of the most important issues of the 3...Qa5 Scandinavian: modern move orders and transpositions. The subtle points behind these various move orders are incredibly tricky to understand, and it's easy to become confused.

The two most important move orders are closely connected to Shirov's main line, where White aims to achieve the breakthrough d4-d5. The lines in question are 1 e4 d5 2 exd5 Qxd5 3 Nc3 Qa5 4 d4 Nf6 and now either 5 Bc4 or 5 Bd2.

The modern way to manipulate a tempo

Initially the main idea behind 5 Bc4 or 5 Bd2 was to develop the king's knight not to f3 but to g3 via e2, in order to hunt the Scandinavian bishop and to break down Black's pawn structure with the pawn thrust f2-f4-f5. However, recently it has become apparent that White also has at his disposal a more traditional idea.

White still intends to utilize the standard piece set-up seen in Chapter Two, but by delaying the development of the g1-knight, White saves a tempo – a tempo he hopes to use in order to secure the critical d4-d5 pawn break. A fringe benefit of delaying the knight's development is that it makes hunting the Scandinavian bishop with g2-g4 followed by f2-f4 even easier.

Let's now look at 5 Bc4 and 5 Bd2 in turn, including the differences between the two moves.

White Plays 5 Bc4

Should Black continue as "normal", blissfully unaware of the devious point behind 5 Bc4 (or 5 Bd2), he may be caught out and tricked into an unpleasant position. Take a look at the following example:

1 e4 d5 2 exd5 Qxd5 3 Nc3 Qa5 4 d4 Nf6 5 Bc4 c6?! (Diagram 1)

6 Bd2!

6 Nge2 is usually played without committing the bishop to d2, as this gives White the chance to strike with f4-f5 while the black king is still in the centre. For example, 6...Bf5 7 Ng3 and now:

a) 7...Bg6 8 0-0 e6 9 f4 Be7! 10 f5 (10 Qe2 caused Black to panic in the game D.Brandenburg-J.Hawkins, Liverpool 2006, with 10...Kd7, but 10...Qd8 transposes) 10...exf5 11 Qe2 Qd8 12 Nxf5 Bxf5 13 Rxf5 0-0 14 Be3 Nbd7 15 Raf1 Nb6 16 Bd3 Nbd5! and Black's position remains very solid.

b) 7...e6 is also possible. Black reasons that White has gone to such lengths to exchange knight for bishop, so it is better to allow the exchange and enjoy the additional time White has given him. Here 8 Nxf5 Qxf5 9 Bd3 Qa5 10 0-0 Bd6 11 Qe2 Qc7 12 h3 Nbd7 13 Bg5 followed by queenside castling led to a double-edged position in B.Hund-L.Keitlinghaus, German League 2007.

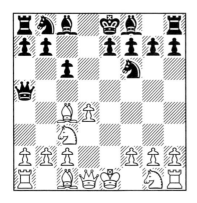

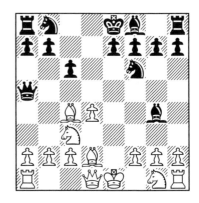

Diagram 1 (W)

Too accommodating?

Diagram 2 (W)

The provocative 6...Bg4

6...Bf5

What about 6...Bg4 **(Diagram 2)** inducing f2-f3? This move has the advantage of provoking a weakness on the kingside. However, the disadvantage is that it actively encourages White to start marching his g- and h-pawns. In addition, because the knight can no longer make use of the e5-square, White should re-route it to the equally annoying f4-square: 7 f3 Bf5 (7...Bd7 is quite passive: 8 Qe2 e6 9 Ne4 Qd8 10 0-0-0 b5 11 Bd3 Na6 was A.Fedorov-S.Mamedyarov, Batumi 2002, and here 12 c3 Be7 13 Nxf6+ Bxf6 14 f4 Nc7 15 g4 gives White a dangerous initiative – Black's king won't be safe wherever it tries to hide) 8 Nge2 e6 9 g4! Bg6 10 Nf4 and now:

a) The queen is not on e2, so 10...Bb4? is a mistake. Black cannot play the opening so carelessly: he cannot give White extra tempi with f2-f3, g2-g4 and then on top of this – the bishop pair! After 11 h4 Bxc3 12 Bxc3 Qc7 13 Qd2 b5 (13...Bxc2 14 Rc1 Ba4 15 b3 b5 16 Be2 wins the bishop, J.Degraeve-P.Verhaeghe, Ghent 2005) 14 Ba5 Qd6 15 Bb3 the threat of h4-h5 was extremely unpleasant in J.Rowson-J.Richardson, British League 2000.

b) After 10...Qb6 White should sacrifice a pawn with 11 Qe2!? Bxc2 (11...Qxd4 is bad because of 12 Bxe6) 12 d5! (as usual we see, where possible, this thematic pawn push!) 12...Qxb2 13 0-0 cxd5 14 Ncxd5 Nxd5 15 Nxd5. Black simply has too many problems with his development, so he must play 15...Nc6 offering some material in order to alleviate his worries. Even so, after 16 Nc7+ Kd7 17 Nxa8 Bc5+ 18 Kh1 Rxa8 19 Rac1 White has the advantage.

c) After 10...Qc7! 11 h4 Bd6 12 h5!? Bxf4 13 hxg6 fxg6 14 Qe2 Nbd7!, taking the pawn is not so convincing: 15 Qxe6+ Kd8 16 Qe2 Re8 17 Ne4 Bxd2+ 18 Kxd2 Qf4+ 19 Qe3 Rxe4 20 fxe4 Nxe4+ 21 Kd3 Nf2+ and Black regains the sacrificed material.

7 Qe2!

 NOTE: White is not yet ready for 7 d5, and Black has no problems after 7...Qc5.

7 Nd5 Qd8 8 Nxf6+ gxf6 **(Diagram 3)** differs from Chapter Two in that White gains the extra option of developing the knight to e2. Indeed, it is probably a better plan for White to establish the knight on f4, where it exerts uncomfortable pressure on e6, and White still menaces a kingside pawn advance. For example, 9 Ne2!? e6 10 Bb3 Bd6 11 Bf4 Bxf4 12 Nxf4 Nd7 (perhaps 12...Qa5+!? 13 c3 Rg8, getting ready to meet Qh5 with ...Rg5) 13 Qh5 with a slight advantage for White, J.Degraeve-C.Daly, Cappelle la Grande 2005.

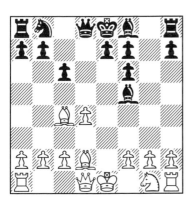

Diagram 3 (W)
Slightly different

Diagram 4 (B)
The whole idea

7...e6?

Black has been playing in a routine manner...

8 d5! (Diagram 4)

...but this is the critical point to White's play.

8...cxd5 9 Nxd5 Qd8 10 Nxf6+ Qxf6!

This is the only move, but the position is so open and Black so under-developed – he can get into deep trouble pretty quickly.

After 10...gxf6?! 11 0-0-0 Qc7 12 g4! another point behind keeping the knight on g1 is revealed: g2-g4 is supported by the queen. Following 12...Bg6 13 f4! White threatens f4-f5, and he has the nice idea of hemming in the light-squared bishop with f4-f5 followed by g4-g5, opening up the kingside should Black's king head there.

11 0-0-0 (Diagram 5)

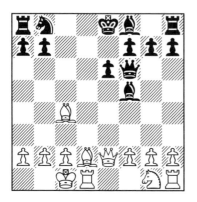
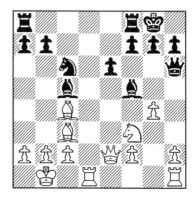

Diagram 5 (B)
Dangerous for Black

Diagram 6 (B)
The pawn is poisoned

Of course not 11 Bc3 Bb4!, but 11 Nf3 is also considered to be good.

11...Nc6!

11...Ba3? is a mistake: 12 c3 Be7 (after 12...Bd6 13 g4! Bg6 14 h4 h5 15 Bg5 Bf4+ 16 Rd2! Bxg5 17 hxg5 Qxg5 White has the stunning 18 Bxe6 after which Black's position is hopeless, while 12...Bc5 13 g4 Bg6 14 Nf3 h6 15 Bb5+ Nc6 16 Ne5 was also overwhelming in A.Feuerstack-J.Kjaergaard Jensen, Kiel 2004) 13 g4! Bg6 14 h4 h6 15 f4 Nc6 16 h5 Bh7 17 Nf3 0-0-0 (or 17...Bd6 18 g5 Qf5 19 g6, J.Koch-J.Kappler, French League 1995) 18 g5 hxg5 19 fxg5 Qf5 20 g6 and the g-pawn is immune from capture so White is winning.

12 Nf3 Bc5 13 Bc3! Qh6+ 14 Kb1 0-0 15 g4! (Diagram 6)

The most important thing here is to open up lines against the enemy king and to seize the initiative. Besides, technically speaking this is not a sacrifice, as 15...Bxg4 16 Rhg1 Bxf3 17 Bxg7 wins after 17...Bxe2 18 Bxh6+ Kh8 19 Bg7+ Kg8 20 Bf6+ Bg4 21 Rxg4 mate.

15...Bg6

White has a great position. The worst problem for Black is that his pieces stand a little clumsily. In particular, his queen is out of the game.

Now let's see what happens if Black employs the same c6/e6 pawn structure but uses a tempo to retreat the queen:

1 e4 d5 2 exd5 Qxd5 3 Nc3 Qa5 4 d4 Nf6 5 Bc4 c6 6 Bd2 Qc7 (Diagram 7)

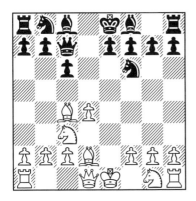

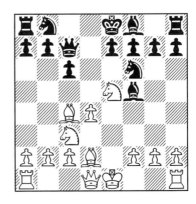

Diagram 7 (W)

Another queen move

Diagram 8 (B)

Activity is the key

> NOTE: This queen retreat flouts one of the guiding rules of the Scandinavian: *don't waste further time.*

By retreating the queen, Black grants White some additional and favourable options. However, I should mention that, because the position is still closed, the e6/c6 pawn structure is still very difficult to break down, especially if d4-d5 is not possible.

Another option is 6...Qb6, which is perhaps preferable to 6...Qc7. The idea is not to capture the b2-pawn immediately, but instead to rely on the nuisance factor of White having to guard d4 and b2: 7 Nf3! (White should ignore the attack on b2) 7...Bf5! (Black must avoid 7...Bg4? 8 Bxf7+, while 7...Qxb2 is a logical consequence of Black's previous play but is extremely risky: after 8 Rb1 Qa3 9 Ne5 e6 10 Rb3 Qd6 11 Bf4 Qd8 in return for the pawn White has pushed Black all the way back to the eighth rank and has some uncomfortable pressure along the b-file) 8 Qe2 e6 9 0-0-0 Nbd7 10 Nh4 (to gain the bishop pair) 10...Bg6 11 Nxg6 hxg6 12 d5 cxd5 13 Nxd5 Nxd5 14 Bxd5, K.Landa-A.Kogan, Paris 2005. White enjoys a pleasant advantage with the bishop pair, but at least here the black queen is on the right side of the board!

7 Nf3 Bf5!?

7...Bg4 8 h3 Bxf3 (or 8...Bh5 9 g4! Bg6 10 Qe2 e6 11 0-0-0) 9 Qxf3 is not the best – Black hands White the bishop pair without extracting a concession. Furthermore, he has no bases for his knights, and should he get pushed back he will be positionally lost. S.Conquest-J.Hodgson, German League 1995, continued 9...e6 10 0-0-0 Nbd7 11 g4! Nb6 12 Bf1, re-routing the bishop to the better diagonal h1-a8.

White stands very well here – he has more space on the kingside and his pieces are well placed.

8 Ne5! (Diagram 8)

Nf3-e5 is generally White's reaction when Black has lost too much time.

8...e6 9 g4

> WARNING: As the position is still semi-closed, White must continue to play actively otherwise Black will have time to consolidate.

9...Bg6!?

9...Be4 10 Nxe4 Nxe4 11 Bf4 was extremely comfortable for White in V.Korchnoi-A.Reshko, Leningrad 1957.

10 Qe2

White is better here. The problem for Black is that he controls very few squares, and worse still there is not much scope for improvement. Black must simply react to White's play. If Black plays normally with 10...Nbd7 11 0-0-0 Bd6, after 12 Rhe1 it becomes apparent that he can no longer hold the tension. He must exchange the powerful knight or grab some space with ...b7-b5, since 12...0-0-0 13 h4 demonstrates the danger.

The correct response

1 e4 d5 2 exd5 Qxd5 3 Nc3 Qa5 4 d4 Nf6 5 Bc4 Bg4!

Usually in the 3...Qa5 Scandinavian, playing ...Bg4 is very double-edged, particularly when White has not yet determined how his pieces will be developed. With 5...Bg4 Black allows White to advance his kingside pawns with tempo. However, Black can argue that these pawn advances are not actually developing moves.

Black will often try to expose the vulnerability of the white king at any cost, including weakening his own pawn structure. Take Diagram 9 for example.

The correct reply there to White's 11 Ne2-f4 is not 11...Bh7 retreating the bishop but 11...Nc6! targeting d4 and preparing to open lines against the enemy king (see note 'd' to White's 8th move in Game 21).

> NOTE: Because Black has not played an early ...c7-c6 to provide an escape route for the queen, he must be very careful not to let his queen get trapped by a nasty Nd5 jump.

Therefore, as soon as White sets up the piece configuration Bc4 and Bd2, threatening Nd5, Black should retreat the queen to b6 where it is safe from harm and furthermore puts pressure on the d4-pawn. For example, after 1 e4 d5 2 exd5 Qxd5 3 Nc3 Qa5 4 d4 Nf6 5 Bc4 Bg4 6 f3 Bf5 7 Bd2 **(Diagram 10)**, or similarly 5 Bd2 Bg4 6 f3 Bf5 7 Bc4, Black plays 7...Qb6! (see Game 22).

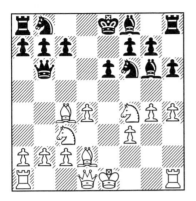

Diagram 9 (B)

Black targets d4

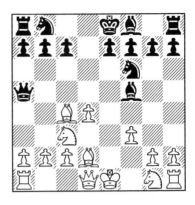

Diagram 10 (B)

The queen must move

Game 20
□ A.Morozevich ■ V.Tkachiev
FIDE World Championship, New Delhi 2000

---

1 e4 d5 2 exd5 Qxd5 3 Nc3 Qa5 4 d4 Nf6 5 Bc4 Bg4! (Diagram 11)

> **NOTE: 5 Nf3 Nc6? is bad due to 6 Bd2! (see Chapter Three). However, with the white bishop committed to c4, here 5...Nc6 is possible. Even so, Black should be aware of the inherent risks involved in cutting off the air supply to the queen.**

5...Nc6 6 Nge2 Bg4 transposes to the game, but White has the extra option of 6 d5. For example, 6...Ne5 (6...Nb4 is a awkward-looking but possible: 7 a3 c6! – to find an escape route for the knight – 8 dxc6 Nxc6 9 Bd2 Qc5 10 Bd3 Bf5 11 Be3 and White was better in M.Parligras-I.Schneider, Thessaloniki 2007) 7 Bb3 Bd7 8 Qe2 Ng6 9 Nf3 0-0-0 10 0-0 and Black still has to fix the problem of developing his dark-squared bishop, Y.Balashov-I.Ruchkin, Vladimir 2008.

6 Nge2

6 Nf3 Nc6! reaches one of the very few situations where the combination of ...Bg4, ...Qa5 and ...Nc6 works especially well: 7 h3 Bxf3 8 Qxf3 0-0-0 (the basic plan is to place as much pressure on the d4-pawn as possible) 9 d5 Ne5 10 Qf5+ Ned7 11 Bd2? (White is careless and allows Black to seize the advantage with...) 11...e6! 12 Qg5 Nb6 13 Bb3 h6 14 Qg3 Nbxd5 (M.Baba-J.Tomczak, Cappelle La Grande 2008)

and here 15 Nxd5 is met by 15...Qxd2+ 16 Kxd2 Ne4+ winning.

6 f3 Bf5 7 g4 is the most principled reaction to 5...Bg4 – White grabs as much space as possible on the kingside: 7...Bg6 8 f4 (relentlessly pursuing the bishop!) 8...e6 (8...Be4 is also possible, although the bishop is slightly vulnerable on e4) 9 f5 (9 Bd2 allows Black to escape with the queen via 9...Qb4 10 Qe2 Nc6! followed by ...0-0-0 and Black is doing very well – there are no problems with discovered attacks as Black always has 11...Qxb2; while 9 Qe2 is met by 9...Nc6!) 9...exf5 10 Qe2+ needn't be feared because of 10...Be7! (instead of having to move the king as in the similar 5 Bd2 line) 11 Bd2 Qb6 12 g5 Bh5!. This is the key move here, and Black is fine after 13 Nf3 Ne4 as 14 Nxe4 is met by 14...Nc6 threatening 15...fxe4 and 15...Nxd4.

6...Nc6 (Diagram 12)

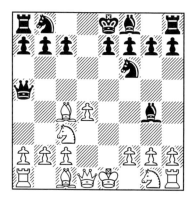 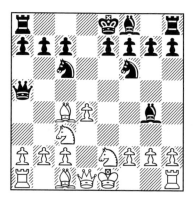

Diagram 11 (W)	**Diagram 12 (W)**
The way to meet 5 Bc4	High-risk strategy

Black employs a high-risk strategy which relies on the "awkwardly placed" knight on e2. He aims to castle rapidly on the queenside and place immense pressure on the d4-pawn. I must stress again that this move is only possible because White has committed his light-squared bishop to c4.

6...e6!? is a more cautious approach, and one that I actually think is more valid. For example, 7 Bd2 (after 7 0-0 Nbd7 8 f3 Bf5 9 Ng3 Bg6 10 Nce4 Be7 11 c3 c6 Black has completed his development with no problems, and after ...c6-c5 he will stand well, L.Vajda-I.Papaioannou, Plovdiv 2008) 7...Qb6! 8 Bb3 Nc6 9 f3 Bf5 10 g4 (this isn't dangerous here) 10...Bg6 11 g5 Nh5 12 Be3 (or 12 d5 Na5! 13 dxe6 fxe6 and Black is sitting pretty) 12...0-0-0 13 Qd2 Bb4 14 a3 (14 d5 is harmless as Black can simply play 14...Qa5) 14...Qa6 15 Kf2 Bc5 and Black's pieces are the better coordinated, S.Ahmed-S.Abu Sufian, Dhaka 2008.

TIP: When Black has not touched the c-pawn, retreating the queen to b6 is entirely valid. Don't get it trapped though!

7 f3! (Diagram 13)

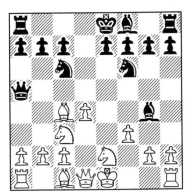

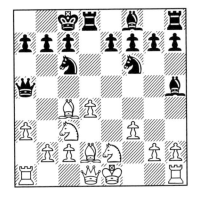

Diagram 13 (B)
White mustn't delay f2-f3

Diagram 14 (B)
No "mouse-hole" trick

The time to drive back the bishop is now!

7 Be3 0-0-0 and only now 8 f3 gives Black the opportunity to play 8...e5!. M.Petursson-H.Danielsen, Reykjavik 2008, continued 9 d5 (9 fxg4 exd4 is better for Black) 9...Be6 10 Bd2 Qc5 (10...Nxd5 11 Nxd5 Qc5 is even stronger) 11 dxe6 Qxc4 12 exf7 Bc5 and White was in some trouble.

7...Bh5

This move is given as dubious by Eric Prié in his excellent articles for *New in Chess Yearbook*, but I am not sure I agree with his assessment. He considers 7...Bf5 8 Bd2 and now:

a) Escaping with 8...Qb4 allows 9 Bb3! 0-0-0 (9...Nxd4 fails to 10 Nd5) 10 d5! Ne5 (10...Na5? 11 Na4 Qh4+ 12 g3 Qh5 13 Nf4 wins) 11 Ng3 Bd7 12 Qe2 Ng6 13 0-0-0 and White was comfortably better in Ye Jiangchuan-Z.Varga, Budapest 1992 – Black's queen sits awkwardly on b4 and the d5-pawn acts as a massive clamp on Black's position.

b) 8...0-0-0 9 a3! cuts out the escape square for the queen, which White is now threatening to win. In order to deal with this threat, Black must give up the exchange with 9...Nxd4 10 Nxd4 Rxd4 11 Nb5 Qb6 12 Nxd4 Qxd4. However, after 13 Bxf7! Qxb2 14 Rb1! Qxc2 (14...Qxa3? is met by 15 Ra1 winning the a-pawn, since 15...Qc5 drops material to 16 Ra5) 15 Qxc2 Bxc2 16 Be6+ Kb8 17 Rc1 Black is not developed enough to warrant compensation for the material.

8 Bd2

 NOTE: Once the knight is committed to c6, White should change tack and play against the awkwardly placed black queen.

8...0-0-0 9 a3! (Diagram 14)

Preventing the "mouse-hole" trick, a term coined by Eric Prié, by denying the queen access to the b4-square.

Here's the "mouse-hole" trick in operation: 9 Nd5 Qa4 (the only square for the queen) 10 Bb3 Qa6 (again the only square) 11 Nxf6 gxf6 12 d5 Na5 13 Nf4 Bg6 14 Qe2 Qxe2+ 15 Kxe2 Nxb3 16 axb3 a6 and Black has equalized, H.Hamdouchi-V.Tkachiev, French League 1999.

9...Nxd4 10 Nb5?!

10 Nxd4! is stronger: 10...Rxd4 (10...Qc5 11 Ne6 fxe6 12 Bxe6+ Kb8 13 Qe2 gives White the advantage) 11 Nb5 Qa6 12 Qe2 Rxc4 (or 12...Rd8 13 0-0-0 and Black's lagging development combined with his queen's horrendous placement gives White a distinct advantage) 13 Qxc4 c6 14 a4 and White is better.

10...Qb6 11 Nbxd4 e5!? (Diagram 15)

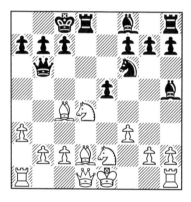

Diagram 15 (W)

A positional sacrifice

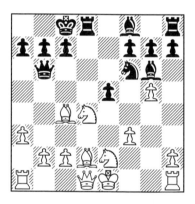

Diagram 16 (B)

Black misses a chance

A purely positional piece sacrifice: Black is banking on the awkward position of White's minor pieces and the fact that White cannot develop easily.

12 g4

If 12 Nf5 Black has the nice reply 12...e4! forcing open the e-file. For example, 13 Neg3 Bc5 (threatening ...e3) 14 b4 Bg1 (if playing a piece a down makes you nervous, there's also 14...Bf2+!? 15 Kf1 e3 regaining the piece) 15 Qe2 exf3 16 Ne7+ Kb8

17 gxf3 Rxd2! 18 Qxd2 (18 Kxd2 loses to 18...Qd4+) 18...Bxf3 19 Rd1! (returning some of his extra material in order to relieve the pressure, as Black was threatening the deadly ...Ng4) 19...Bxd1 20 Kxd1 was M.Palac-V.Tkachiev, Pula 1999. Although White eventually won this game, Black has dangerous compensation for the piece: two pawns and the fact that White's king has no hope of finding a safe home.

12 Nb3 is very risky: 12...e4! 13 Nf4 (or 13 fxe4 Nxe4 and the threat of 14...Qf2 mate leaves White paralyzed) 13...e3 and Black regains his piece.

12...Bg6! 13 g5 (Diagram 16) 13...Nh5?!

Black could have gained the upper hand by regaining some material with 13...Rxd4! 14 Nxd4 Qxd4 15 Qe2 (if White snatches material with 15 gxf6, Black plays 15...Qh4+ winning the bishop) 15...Qxb2 16 0-0 Nd7!. He has two pawns for the exchange, and White's kingside is shaky whereas Black can consolidate with ...Bc5+ followed by ...Bb6.

14 Nb3 Qc6 15 Bd3 Bxd3

15...Qxf3?! allows White to simplify with 16 Ng3.

16 cxd3 Rxd3

The position has become extremely complicated: Black is attacking wildly with three pieces; White has a swarm of pieces surrounding his king but on the flipside they are all incredibly vulnerable.

17 Rc1 Qxf3 18 Rf1 Qe4 19 Qc2 c6 20 Na5 Be7 21 Qc4

White is trying to force the exchange of the queens.

21...Rd4 22 Qb3 Rd7 23 Qh3 Rhd8 24 Nc4

White is slowly consolidating but Black still retains compensation for the piece because of the exposed king.

24...Nf4 25 Bxf4 exf4 26 Rxf4 Qh1+ 27 Rf1 Qd5 28 Rf5 Qe6

Black refuses to repeat moves.

29 Qf1 h6 30 Re5 ½-½

In this complicated position the players agreed a draw, which is not so surprising as it takes a lot of nerve and energy to play these tough tactical positions.

White Plays 5 Bd2

Game 21
□ **C.Koepke** ■ **A.Kislinsky**
Kharkiv 2006

1 e4 d5 2 exd5 Qxd5 3 Nc3 Qa5 4 d4 Nf6 5 Bd2!? (Diagram 17)

With 5 Bd2, trickery is again at work. By delaying the development of the g1-knight, White's intention is still Bc4 and Qe2, and to use the spare tempo to push for d4-d5. However, Black is facing a dilemma over which plan to adopt, as White has not yet committed the bishop to c4.

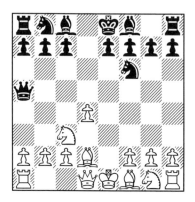

Diagram 17 (B)

A clever sidestep

Diagram 18 (B)

White is winning

5...Bg4

Alternatively:

a) 5...c6 6 Bc4 takes us to back to 5 Bc4 lines.

b) 5...Bf5?! is met by 6 Qf3 and Black is forced to hurry back home with the bishop.

 WARNING: 5...Nc6? does not work at all here. White has not committed the bishop to c4, so naturally he will play 6 Bb5! (Diagram 18) when he is already winning as the threat of d4-d5 or Nd5 is just too unpleasant.

For example, 6...Qb4 (6...a6 7 Nd5!) 7 d5 a6 8 Ba4 b5 9 Nxb5! Qe4+ (or 9...Qxa4 10 Nxc7+ Kd8 11 Nxa8) 10 Qe2 Qxg2 11 Nxc7+ Kd8 12 dxc6. This illustrates an important difference between 5 Bd2 and 5 Bc4.

6 f3

6 Nge2, blocking in the light-squared bishop, is not a good idea: 6...Qb6! (rather than 6...Nc6 7 f3 Bd7 8 a3! preventing "mouse-hole" tricks: after 8...Qb6 at the very least White has a repetition with 9 Na4) 7 h3 Bd7 8 a4 a5 and White cannot develop his kingside army harmoniously without giving up the d4-pawn. J.Hector-L.Milov, Nuremberg 2007, continued 9 Nf4 Qxd4 10 Qf3 Qe5+ 11 Be3 Bc6 12 Bb5 e6 13 Nd3 Qf5 and Black didn't have any problems.

6 Be2?! is the coward's choice, and it simply gives Black a very easy game after

6...Bxe2 (exchanges help Black!) and now:

a) 7 Ngxe2?! Nc6! (with no good hop for the knight on c3, Black is not troubled in any way) 8 Ne4 Qd5 9 Nxf6+ gxf6 was J.Gonzalez Moreno-M.Cornette, La Laguna 2008. Black's queen dominates the whole board and he has the rather straightforward plan of castling and attacking the centre with ...e7-e5.

b) 7 Ncxe2! is the best try for an advantage, because at least White can aim for a pawn storm on the queenside. 7...Qb6 8 Nf3 Nbd7 9 0-0 e6 10 c4! Be7 11 b4!? 0-0 12 a4 c6 13 Qc2 Qc7 was A.Karpov-B.Larsen, Montreal 1979. At first sight the queenside pawn phalanx looks mightily impressive. However, there is a distinct danger that because they are unsupported the pawns may simply become weak. Black should aim for the break ...e6-e5 in order to release his pieces, and also for ...a7-a5.

6...Bf5 7 g4! (Diagram 19)

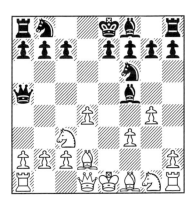

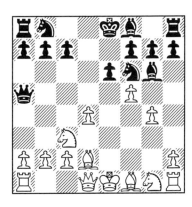

Diagram 19 (B)

The most challenging

Diagram 20 (B)

A strong pawn sacrifice

The only move that "punishes" the ...Bc8-g4 sortie.

7...Bg6

The main move, and one that leads to a rather complicated game which is probably in white's favour.

7...Bd7! is probably safer, even though it does look clumsier. For example:

a) 8 Bc4 Qb6! and now the natural 9 Nge2 fails to 9...Qc6! hitting both the bishop and the f3-pawn, J.Sanchez-E.Prié, Villeneuve Tolosane 2006.

 TIP: Remember, as soon as White plays Bc4 and Bd2 Black should retreat the queen to b6.

b) 8 g5! seizes space but more importantly tries to prove that the knight on h5 will be bad: 8...Nh5! (the natural 8...Nd5 is met by 9 Ne4 Qb6 10 c4 and the knight is trapped in the centre) 9 Nge2 (the immediate 9 f4 doesn't really achieve much after 9...g6 10 Bg2 Qb6 11 Nd5 Qe6+ 12 Qe2 Na6 and Black doesn't have any problems) 9...e6 10 Ne4 (White uses the awkward placement of the black pieces to his advantage) 10...Qb6 11 c4! c5 (moves such as 11...Qxb2 are best left to non-humans with a big processor!) 12 Bc3 (12 d5 looks very tempting but Black can just ignore it and play 12...Na6) 12...cxd4 13 Nxd4 Bb4 14 Qd2 Bxc3 15 Qxc3 0-0 16 0-0-0 Qc7!. Removing the queen from harm's way is vital otherwise White might establish a post on the d6-square. This would be a problem for Black, who must concentrate his efforts on securing play down the d-file.

8 f4!

The best move and the scariest one for Black to face. White is prepared to sacrifice the f-pawn in order to open lines and keep the black king in the centre.

Here's a summary of the alternatives:

a) 8 Ne4? Qb6 9 Nxf6+ Qxf6 and White already has problems with his weakened kingside, J.Gil Martinez-F.Mancebo Ibanez, Mislata 1997.

b) 8 Nge2 is well met by 8...Nc6.

c) 8 g5 Nd5! 9 Bb5+ c6 10 Nxd5 is met by the amazing 10...Qd8 and Black regains his piece.

d) 8 h4 h6 9 Bc4 Qb6! (again the only answer to Bc4 and Bd2) 10 Nge2 e6 (10...Nbd7, following Eric Prié's rule of developing the knight to d7 as quickly as possible, is also possible and leads to very sharp play – after 11 Nf4 0-0-0 Black's plan is to play ...e7-e5!) 11 Nf4 Nc6! (the best move – Black ignores structural disadvantages and instead concentrates on completing his development) 12 d5? (12 Nxg6 fxg6 13 Be3 Qxb2 is the point) 12...Nd4! 13 Nxg6 fxg6 14 Be3 Nxc2+ left Black with no problems in F.Nijboer-L.Milov, Haarlem 2006.

8...e6 9 f5! (Diagram 20)

9 Bg2 is answered by 9...Qa6! protecting the b7-pawn and covering the e2-square. Z.Lanka-E.Bacrot, Linz 1997, continued 10 g5 Nfd7 11 d5 Bd6 (11...Nc5! is also more than good enough) 12 Qe2 Qxe2+ 13 Ngxe2 exd5 14 Nxd5 Nc6. After the exchange of queens the position is balanced, although White has to play carefully because his pawns on the kingside are a little vulnerable.

9...exf5 10 Qe2+!

White continues in an aggressive manner.

10 g5 lets Black off the hook: 10...Ng8 11 h4 h5 12 Bg2 Qa6 13 Qf3 Nc6 14 Qe3+ Nge7 15 Bf1 Nb4! and Black is managing fine, R.Skytte-H.Danielsen, Helsinge 2003.

10...Kd8

This is frightening for Black – he must not only play very precisely but his king is stranded in the centre. It is so dangerous, in fact, that I consider this variation to be the near refutation of 7...Bg6.

I experimented in my analysis with the crazy move 10...Kd7 with the idea that after 11 g5 Black can play 11...Nc6. Without this little trick Black's position would be very bad. However, the resulting positions are just so bizarre that realistically only a computer would be able to play them well!

10...Be7 is the move Black would love to get away with, but 11 g5! **(Diagram 21)** secures White the advantage. For example:

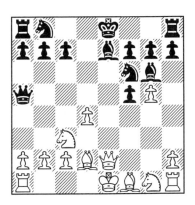

Diagram 21 (B)

Better for White

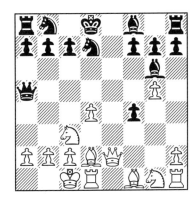

Diagram 22 (W)

Freeing the bishop

a) 11...Nfd7 12 Bg2 Qa6 (12...c6 13 h4 is very unpleasant for Black – White's has perfect development whereas Black's king is stranded in the centre) 13 h4! (a calm move; 13 Qxa6 Nxa6 14 Bxb7 Nb4 was Black's trick) 13...f4 14 0-0-0 Qxe2 15 Ngxe2 Nc6 16 Bxf4 and now the c7-pawn will drop.

b) 11...Nd5 12 Qb5+ Qxb5 13 Bxb5+ c6 14 Nxd5 wins the exchange.

c) 11...Nh5 12 Bg2 Nc6 13 Nd5 Qa4 14 Nxc7+ Kf8 15 Nxa8 Nxd4 and at first it looks as though Black may be generating some counterplay, but White flicks in 16 b3! Qe8 17 Nc7 which is winning.

11 g5 Nfd7 12 0-0-0

E.Levushkina-L.Bensdorp, Plovdiv 2008, continued 12 Bg2 Nc6 13 Nf3 Bb4?! (this just doesn't achieve anything, and 13...Bd6 is the most solid) 14 0-0 Re8 15 Qf2. White will kick back the bishop with a2-a3, and it is very difficult to suggest a good plan for Black.

12...f4! (Diagram 22)

To stand any chance Black must return the pawn in order to free his light-squared bishop.

13 Bg2

13 Bh3! is the most dangerous move according to Eric Prié and it is easy to see why – White targets the weakened light squares around the black king. After 13...Nc6! (13...Bd6?! already runs into 14 Qg4! and Black cannot develop his b8-knight) 14 Bxf4! White has recovered the pawn and his light-squared bishop is well placed on h3. The standard 14...Bb4 (14...Nb4 15 Re1 is devastating) is met by 15 d5 Ne7 16 d6!. This is very convincing for White, and after 16...cxd6 17 Bxd6 Qxg5+ 18 Kb1 his position is overwhelming.

13...Nc6 14 Bxf4 Nb4! 15 Nb5

As Eric Prié points out, chasing away the knight with 15 a3 allows it deep into the heart of the position. After 15...Nxc2! 16 Nb5 Rc8! 17 Bxb7 Black can escape with 17...Nb4! intending 18 Qc4?? (or 18 axb4 Bxb4 19 Be4 Re8 20 Be5 Bxe4 21 Qxe4 Qxb5 with the same result) 18...Na2+! 19 Qxa2 Qxb5 20 Bxc8 Qa4! and Black is winning (21 Kd2 Bb4+).

15...Bd6 (Diagram 23)

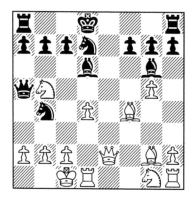

Diagram 23 (W)

White goes wrong

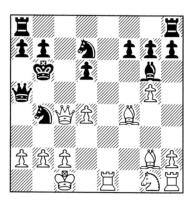

Diagram 24 (W)

...Rc8 is coming next

16 Nxd6?!

White should have continued with 16 Bxd6! cxd6 17 Nxd6 threatening Nxb7+. After 17...Qxa2 18 Nxb7+ Kc7 19 Qf3 (intending 20 Qf4+; Black must cover c6 to give his king a hiding place) 19...Qa4 20 Qf4+ Kb6 21 Qd6+ Nc6 22 b3 Qa1+ 23 Kd2 Qxd4+ 24 Qxd4+ Nxd4 25 Kc3 the fireworks have ended and the game has petered out. Black has recovered the material and after a few accurate moves the position is roughly level: 25...Nb5+ 26 Kb2 Ne5.

16...cxd6 17 Re1?

When one mistake occurs, another one is sure to follow. And here it is!

17 Bxd6 would have kept the game alive: 17...Re8 18 Bxb4 (18 Qd2? loses to 18...Rc8 19 Bc5 Nxc5 20 dxc5+ Nd3+!! – the killer move – 21 cxd3 Rxc5+ and in order to escape checkmate White must give up his queen) 18...Qxb4 19 Qd2 Rc8! and Black stands well. The pressure on c2 is actually very difficult for to meet, and 20 Qxb4 is answered by 20...Rxc2+ 21 Kb1 Rc4+ 22 Ka1 Rxb4.

17...Kc7 18 Qc4+

If 18 Qe7 Black calmly defends with 18...Qb6.

18...Kb6! (Diagram 24)

A fantastic move! Suddenly it is the white queen who is embarrassed! White is completely unable to prevent Black from playing ...Rc8 followed by ...Rxc2.

19 Bd2 Rac8 20 Qxb4+ Qxb4 21 Bxb4 Rxc2+ 22 Kd1 Rxg2

Black's position is overwhelming.

23 Nh3

Or 23 Bc3 Rxg5 and Black wins too many pawns.

23...Rxb2 24 Bc3 Rxa2 25 Nf4 Rc8 26 Nd5+ Kb5 0-1

Game 22
□ **J.Mullon** ■ **E.Prié**
Saint-Affrique 2007

---

1 e4 d5 2 exd5 Qxd5 3 Nc3 Qa5 4 d4 Nf6 5 Bd2!? Bg4 6 f3 Bf5 7 Bc4

In conjunction with g2-g4, this is an alternative way of playing the position. Note that 7 g4 Bg6 8 Bc4 Qb6 would reach the same position.

7...Qb6

Again we see ...Qb6 as a reaction to Bd2 and Bc4.

8 g4

Playing without advancing the kingside pawns doesn't give White an advantage. For example, 8 Nge2 e6 9 0-0 c6 10 Kh1 Be7 11 Bb3 0-0 12 Be3 Nbd7 13 Ng3 Bg6 14 Nce4 Qc7 15 c3 c5 and Black has already equalized, L.Vajda-I.Papaioannou, Plovdiv 2008.

8...Bg6 (Diagram 25) 9 g5?!

This move must be carefully considered by Black on every turn, but here I think it is misguided. Let's look at alternatives:

a) 9 Qe2 is met by the convincing 9...Nc6!.

b) 9 Nge2 isn't challenging enough: 9...Nbd7! (preparing ...e7-e5 should a knight land on f4) 10 Bb3 (10 g5 Nh5 11 Nd5 is bad because of 11...Qc6!) 10...e5! 11 Be3 (11 g5 allows 11...exd4 12 Na4 Qa6 13 gxf6 b5 and Black regains the piece) 11...0-0-0 12 g5 Nh5 13 Bf2 exd4 14 Qxd4 Bc5 15 Qh4 and Black stands a lot better, J.Boudre-

E.Prié, Tallinn 2007.

c) 9 Be3 e6 10 Qd2 Nbd7 11 d5 Bc5 12 Bxc5 Qxc5 13 dxe6 (N.Kirkegaard-P.Holmen, Copenhagen 2006) and here 13...fxe6! looks promising, as after 14 Bxe6 0-0-0 15 0-0-0 Rhe8 16 Bb3 Ne5 Black's lead in development gives him more than ample compensation for the pawn.

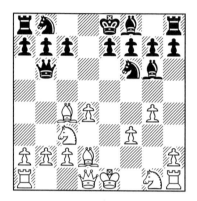

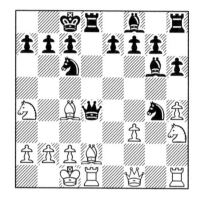

Diagram 25 (W)

A critical moment

Diagram 26 (W)

A stunning resource

d) 9 h4 is a critical move. After 9...h6 White can play:

d1) 10 Nge2 e6 11 Nf4 Nc6 transposes to note 'd' to White's 8th move in Game 21.

d2) 10 Qe2 Nc6 11 Na4 (White is forced to sacrifice a pawn in order to secure some activity) 11...Qxd4 12 0-0-0 0-0-0 13 Nh3 Qe5 14 Be3 e6 15 Rxd8+ Nxd8 was A.Kogan-E.Prié, Spain 2007. Black is a pawn up and although White has some compensation it's not clear how much.

Eric Prié provides some interesting analysis with 14 Qf2 (instead of 14 Be3) 14...Qd4 and now after 15 Qf1 Black has the stunning 15...Nxg4!! **(Diagram 26)**.

As Eric points out, after 16 fxg4 Qe4 White does not have an adequate way of defending against the mate on c2, as 17 Bb3 Nd4 18 Qc4 (running away with 18 Kb1 doesn't help much after 18...Nxb3) 18...b5! 19 Qb4 e5 20 Nc5 Qc6 wins the knight on c5.

9...Qxd4 10 Qe2 Qh4+ 11 Kf1 Nfd7

11...Nh5? was a big mistake in I.Nataf-E.Prié, France 2007 – the knight is needed to help cover the black king in the centre. After 12 Nd5 Kd8 13 f4! (cutting off the black queen) 13...Ng3+ 14 hxg3 Qxh1 15 Qe5 Nd7 16 Qxc7+ Ke8 17 Qxb7 the position was terrible for Black.

Sacrificing a piece with 11...Nc6!? is an idea from Nataf. After 12 gxf6 0-0-0 13 fxe7

Bxe7 Black has some initiative for the sacrificed piece.

12 Nd5 Kd8 (Diagram 27)

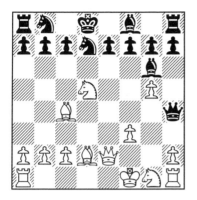

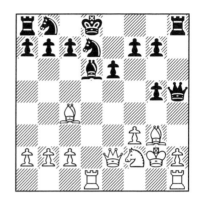

Diagram 27 (W)

Misplaced kings

Diagram 28 (B)

Reciprocal blunders

This position is very complicated. Both sides have misplaced their kings, although Black's is the slightly more vulnerable. Of course Black is a pawn up, but he must consolidate quickly otherwise White's compensation can start to build up.

13 Nf4

With the intention of trapping the queen. 13 f4 does not have the same effect now that the knight is on d7, and Black can simply play 13...h6.

13...e6 14 Ngh3 Bf5!

The only move, as White was planning to trap the queen with Be1.

15 Kg2 Bd6 16 Be1 Bxh3+ 17 Nxh3 Qh5 18 Bg3 h6 19 Rad1 hxg5 20 Nf2 (Diagram 28)

20...Ke7??

Black makes a huge mistake; he had to play 20...Bf4 or 20...Nc6. After the latter it would be a bad idea for White to regain the sacrificed pawn with 21 Bxd6 cxd6 22 Rxd6, as Black has 22...Kc7! and White is too uncoordinated to be able to launch a successful strike on Black's king.

21 Bd5?

Missing 21 Bxd6+! cxd6 22 Qd2 and White has the advantage. Note that 22...d5 fails to 23 Qb4+.

21...Nc6 22 Bxc6 bxc6 23 Qd3 Ne5! 24 Bxe5 Bxe5 25 Qd7+ Kf8 26 Qxc6 Re8 27 Qc5+ Bd6 28 Qxa7 g4! 29 fxg4

29 Nxg4 loses immediately to 29...Bc5 30 Qxc7 Qh3 mate.

29...Qe5 30 Qd4 Rxh2+ 31 Rxh2 Qxh2+ 32 Kf3 e5! 33 Qe4 (Diagram 29)

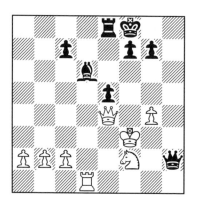

Diagram 29 (B)

Missing a chance

Diagram 30 (B)

White can defend

33...Re6?

As Eric Prié points out, 33...Bc5! was much better, and after 34 Nd3 Rd8! 35 c3 Rd6! White's weaknesses are beginning to tell.

34 g5 Qh5+

Again 34...Bc5! is better.

35 Qg4 e4+ 36 Ke2 Qg6 37 Rd5

37 Rh1 e3 38 Rh8+ Ke7 39 Nd3 gives equal chances.

37...e3 38 Nd3 Qh7 39 Ne1 Qh2+ 40 Qg2 Qh4 41 b3 Bg3?

The final inaccuracy, and now the position is level.

42 Nf3 Qe4 43 Rd3 Bd6 44 Qh3 Kg8 45 a4 (Diagram 30)

White has set up a defence and can begin to force Black's pieces away from his king.

45...Bf8 46 Qh4 Qc6 47 c4 Qb7 48 Qe1 Qe4 49 Qh4 Qb7 50 Qe1 Qe4 51 Qh4 ½-½

Summary

Beware of trickery in the Scandinavian! While the e6/c6 formation is effective against many systems, don't fall into the trap of thinking it is a panacea for everything. When White has delayed developing his king knight, Black must be aware that it is usually for a very good reason. Sometimes it is because White wishes to play for f4-f5 or, rather more dangerously, to secure the blasted d4-d5 pawn break. The variations demonstrated with 5 Bc4 c6 are an indicator of what White has in store if Black goes down the traditional route.

Leading Scandinavian practitioners have developed an alternative mode of development which is based on extracting minor weaknesses from White. Play is very double-edged and readers should be aware of all the nuances involved in delaying pushing the c-pawn. The queen does not have an escape route, and when White indirectly confronts her with Bd2 she must hurry back to b6, out of harm's way. Readers must also be aware that should White choose to commit the bishop to c4 on move 5, then Black has the additional option of playing 5...Nc6!? or 6...Nc6, which led to wild play in Game 20.

5 Bd2 is another dangerous move order with the same ambition of securing d4-d5. This move has the added bonus of not allowing Black the option of 5...Nc6, as White can simply play 6 Bb5!. Both sides should study Games 21-22 carefully.

Chapter Six

Fourth Move Alternatives for White

- White Plays d2-d3
- White Plays 4 g3
- The Mieses Gambit: 4 b4

White Plays d2-d3

This is a vicious little weapon which Eric Prié has named the "Short System" after the English grandmaster Nigel Short. Incidentally, I remember when the idea came into existence. It was during the 1999 European Team Championship in Batumi, when England's top female board IM Harriet Hunt was about to face Natalia Zhukova from the Ukraine, and together Nigel and Harriet refined his idea of d2-d3. It was later used extensively by English juniors, who unleashed it on their unsuspecting opponents.

Why is this little pawn move so dangerous? Well, d2-d3 contains two subtle ideas.

1) The d3-pawn blunts the power of the Scandinavian bishop and limits Black's counterplay on the d-file. This feature gives White's kingside pawn push added venom, as the bishop can no longer use the e4- and c2-squares. Black players should be aware that moves like d2-d3 and h2-h3 are not passive, cautious moves but may be a prelude for a vicious kingside attack.

2) The d4-square is now available for a white knight to use, which could make Black vulnerable to piece sacrifices on e6.

White still retains the option of playing Bd2 followed by Nd5 or Ne4, trying to secure a favourable exchange of pieces; and the e5-square can still be used as a base for White's attack. The main difference between d2-d3 and the d4 main lines is that White's pawn structure is extremely solid.

After having played this variation several times with White, I've realized that there are a few rules that Black must obey:

1) Black mustn't retreat the queen unless absolutely necessary.

2) Shutting in the light-squared bishop with ...e6 is simply too passive. With the bishop stuck on c8, White can always play d3-d4 and reason that the loss of tempo is more than justified.

3) Black must either aim to swap off queens while not allowing White to expand too much on the kingside, *or* induce a weakness on the kingside by playing ...Bg4.

Let's look at the opening moves:

1 e4 d5 2 exd5 Qxd5 3 Nc3 Qa5 4 Bc4

Another option for White is to delay moving the d-pawn until he feels it is the right moment to do so, and 4 Nf3 with this idea is covered in Game 25.

4...Nf6

4...c6 **(Diagram 1)** is probably the most flexible approach against the Short System. For example, 5 d3!? Bf5!? 6 Bd2 e6 7 Qe2 (when the black knight has not been committed to f6, then Nf3 is better) 7...Nd7! 8 h3?! (this is too slow; 8 0-0-0!?, avoiding an exchange of queens, is stronger) 8...Qe5! and Black has equalized already, J.Houska-R.Almond, London (rapid) 2007.

Unfortunately for Black, White is not obliged to play d2-d3. Instead he should revert back to d2-d4 and the set-ups discussed in Chapter Five, where ...c7-c6 does not sit well.

5 d3 (Diagram 2)

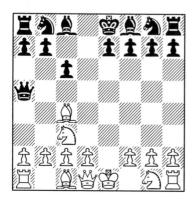

Diagram 1 (W)	**Diagram 2 (B)**
White should play d4	Black has a choice

Now Black must make a decision: 5...c6 is covered in Game 23, while 5...Bg4, which Eric Prié considers to be the best, will be considered in Game 24.

5...a6 did not impress in N.Short-A.Cherniaev, Staunton Memorial, London 2008. After 6 Bd2 c5 7 Nd5 Qd8 8 Nxf6+ gxf6 9 Qh5 e6 10 a4 Black's ruined pawn structure promised White a clear advantage.

Game 23
□ **N.Short** ■ **Liu Dede**
Calvia Olympiad 2004

---

1 e4 d5 2 exd5 Qxd5 3 Nc3 Qa5 4 Bc4 Nf6 5 d3 c6?!

It seems a bit harsh to assess this move as dubious, but that's exactly what I think it is.

> **NOTE:** As we have seen previously, it is wrong to assume that Black's basic set-up of ...Nf6, ...Bf5, ...e6 and ...c6 is a "one size fits all" system. Black cannot afford to be so rigid, especially when White has specifically played to combat this set-up.

6 Bd2! (Diagram 3)

6...Qc7

Bishop moves lead to problems for Black:

a) 6...Bg4 7 f3 Bf5 8 Qe2! (rather than 8 Nd5?! Qd8 9 Nxf6+ exf6! when Black will castle kingside and use his wall of pawns as a barrier against White's attack) 8...Qc7 (8...Nbd7?? is a blunder because of 9 Nb5!) 9 g4 and Black is forced to beat a retreat – see the note on 7...Bg4, below.

b) 6...Bf5?! is also not ideal: 7 Nd5! Qd8 8 Nxf6+ gxf6 9 Ne2! Nd7 10 Ng3 Bg6 11 f4! (forcing Black to lock out his own bishop) 11...f5 12 Bc3 Rg8 13 h4 h6 14 Qf3 e6 15 0-0-0 (E.Mortensen-C.Hansen, Graested 1990), and the bishop on g6 is not what Black usually hopes for when playing the 2...Qxd5 Scandinavian.

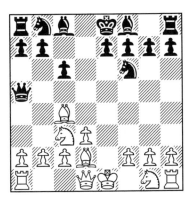

Diagram 3 (B)

Asking the question

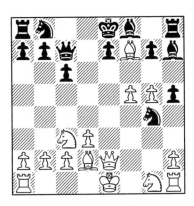

Diagram 4 (B)

A nice trick

7 Qe2

Ng1-f3 is a move which is not particularly effective in d3 systems, and here 7 Nf3 is resoundingly met by 7...Bg4!.

7...Bf5

A beautiful trick in this line is 7...Bg4?! 8 f3 Bf5? 9 g4 Bg6 (consistent, but walking into a devastating pawn storm; 9...Bd7 or even 9...Bc8!? is infinitely stronger) 10 f4! h5 11 f5 Bh7 12 g5 Ng4 13 Bxf7+ **(Diagram 4)** 13...Kxf7 14 g6+ Ke8 (or 14...Bxg6 15 Qe6+ Ke8 16 Qxg6+ Kd8 17 Nf3 – Müller – when Black's future looks bleak) 15 gxh7 Qe5 16 Nf3 Qxe2+ 17 Kxe2 and White has a dominating position, N.Short-A.Reprintsev, Internet (blitz) 2000.

Fianchettoing with 7...g6 doesn't quite work, as Black struggles to find a role for the light-squared bishop. For example, 8 Nf3 Bg7 9 0-0 0-0 10 Rfe1 e6 11 d4 Nbd7 12 a4 Nd5 13 Rad1 b6 14 Qe4 Bb7 15 Qh4 and transferring the queen to the kingside was deadly in J.Houska-B.Yildiz, Gothenburg 2005.

8 h3 e6

I don't believe in 8...h5 one bit. Now that Black has weakened himself with ...h7-h5, it makes sense for White to switch plans with 9 Nf3 Nbd7 10 0-0!, castling kingside and enjoying the fact that Black cannot follow suit. For example, 10...Nb6 11 Bb3 e6 12 a4! a5 and Black will struggle to find a safe haven for his king, P.Potapov-F.Kayser, Dresden 2007. Alternatively, after 10...e6 11 Rfe1! 0-0-0 White simply starts his attack: 12 a4 Bb4 13 a5 a6 (13...Bxa5 is not possible due to 14 Rxa5 Qxa5 15 Nb5 Qb6 16 Nd6+ and Nxf7 winning back the exchange) 14 Ne4 Bxd2 15 Nexd2. White has the advantage here; in particular the b6-square is very sensitive. All he needs to do is to reorganize his pieces so that a queenside pawn-storm is effective. If Black tries to counterattack with 15...Rdg8?! he is immediately stopped by 16 Ng5!.

8...Nbd7 9 g4! Bg6 10 f4! leaves the Scandinavian bishop in trouble, and after 10...h6 11 0-0-0 Nb6 12 Bb3 Nfd5 13 f5 Bh7 **(Diagram 5)**, as played in J.Houska-M.Vasilieva, Chisinau 2005, it is completely shut out.

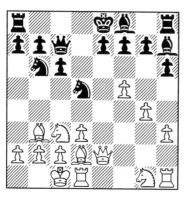

Diagram 5 (W)
Shutting out the bishop

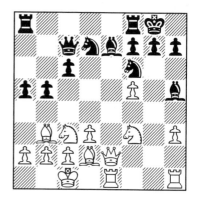

Diagram 6 (W)
Double-edged

Finally, 8...h6 is too slow: 9 Nf3 Nbd7 10 0-0 Nb6 (10...e6! is better) 11 Bb3 e6 12 Nd4! (another dangerous idea for White) 12...Bh7 13 Bxe6 fxe6 14 Nxe6 Qe7 15 Nc7+ and with a rook and two pawns for two minor pieces, White is much better.

9 g4 Bg6 10 f4 Be7 11 Nf3 Nbd7 12 0-0-0

A key point is that Black cannot castle because White simply plays f4-f5 and the bishop on e7 is en prise.

12...Nb6?!

This move is too slow.

Black should probably start a counter-attack, as the position is already incredibly dangerous: 12...b5 13 Bb3 a5! (attacking with pieces is simply too slow: after 13...Nc5 14 Rde1 a5 15 f5 White gets there first, and following 15...exf5 16 Ne5 the point is that 16...a4 loses to 17 Bf4!) 14 f5 (the onslaught begins but Black has a tactical trick up his sleeve...) 14...exf5 15 Rde1 0-0! (this is the point) 16 gxf5 (the e7-bishop is poisoned: 16 Qxe7 Rae8 17 Qa3 b4 18 Qa4 Rxe1+ 19 Rxe1 Nc5 20 Nb5 Nxd3+ wins material) 16...Bh5! **(Diagram 6)** (White is better after 16...Bxf5 17 Nd4 Bg6 18 Qxe7 Rfe8 19 Qa3 b4 20 Qa4 bxc3 21 Bxc3). The position is very double edged after 16...Bh5: both sides have attacking ideas, and both have weaknesses. Black must handle White's attacking potential along the g-file, whereas White must deal with the black pawn phalanx that is steadily advancing towards his king.

13 Rde1! Kf8 14 Bb3 Bd6 15 Ne5 Bxe5 16 Qxe5! (Diagram 7)

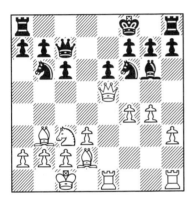

Diagram 7 (B)

Simple and effective

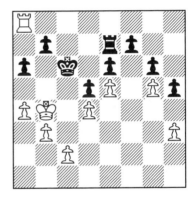

Diagram 8 (B)

White is winning

Nigel considered this to be a good move. He saw that Black's pawns on the kingside could never advance and to him this meant that in the resulting positions he was in effect a pawn up – simple chess!

16...Qxe5 17 fxe5 Nfd7

The rest is a powerful display of endgame technique.

18 Ne4 Kg8 19 d4 h5 20 g5

The kingside is secured.

20...Bxe4 21 Rxe4 Nd5 22 Rf1 g6 23 Bxd5!

Eliminating the knight before it has a chance to re-route itself to f5.

23...cxd5 24 Ref4 Rh7

Black is completely passive now.

25 Bb4 Nb8 26 Bd6 Nc6 27 R1f3 Rd8 28 b3 Rd7 29 Kd2 Ne7 30 Bxe7!

Again a knight is prevented from blocking the f-file.

30...Rxe7 31 Rc3 Kg7 32 Rc8 Rh8 33 Rxh8 Kxh8 34 Rf3 Kg8 35 Rc3 Kf8 36 a4 Ke8 37 Rc8+ Kd7 38 Ra8 a6 39 Kc3 Kc6 40 Kb4 (Diagram 8)

The plan is simply to play c2-c4.

40...Rc7 41 c4 dxc4 42 bxc4 Kd7 43 Rb8 Kc6 44 a5

Preventing any movement of the b-pawn. It's all over now.

44...Kd7 45 d5 exd5 46 cxd5 Rc1 47 Rxb7+ Ke8 48 Ra7 Kf8 49 Rxa6 Rh1 50 Rf6 Rxh3 51 e6 Rg3 52 Rxf7+ Ke8 53 a6 1-0

Game 24
☐ S.Mamedyarov ■ E.Prié
French League 2008

---

1 e4 d5 2 exd5 Qxd5 3 Nc3 Qa5 4 Bc4 Nf6 5 d3 Bg4! (Diagram 9)

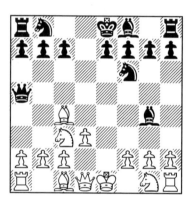
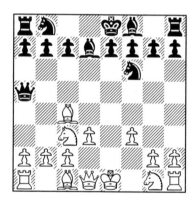

Diagram 9 (W)
A different strategy

Diagram 10 (W)
The best retreat?

As we saw from the previous game, Black cannot develop in the usual way, so instead he adopts a different strategy. His intention, as usual with ...Bg4 attacking the queen, is to provoke the weakening f2-f3. After this move it becomes difficult for White to establish control of the e5-square, so this means that White tends to play only for a kingside pawn advance, something which carries much more risk. Black's strategy is to prove that White will have over-extended himself, and he intends to control the d4-square as a way of highlighting this. Another reason to provoke f2-f3 is that White is no longer able to castle kingside without making some sort of concession, and this allows Black to generate counterplay on the queenside using White's light-squared bishop as a target.

Of course developing the bishop to g4 carries some risk, and there are some factors that Black must be wary of. For example, Black should be reluctant to cut off an escape route for the bishop with an early ...e7-e6. Leaving the bishop somewhat "exposed" outside the pawn chain gives White the opportunity to gain time by continuously making threats against it.

6 f3!

Of course White must rise up to the challenge.

6 Nge2 is possible, but it takes away an important developing square for the queen. This means that f2-f3 followed by g2-g4 will be less effective, as it is more difficult for White to coordinate his minor pieces in a manner that enables easy queenside castling. After 6...c6! (6...Nbd7 cuts out retreat squares for the bishop – not something we wish to do!) 7 f3 Bf5 8 g4 Bc8 (the bishop has done its job and now retires home to safety) 9 Ng3 e6 10 Qe2 Be7 11 Bd2 Qc7 12 g5 Nd5 13 Nh5 0-0 14 0-0-0 b5 15 Bb3 b4 16 Ne4 (menacing Nf6+, which Black takes measures against) 16...Kh8 (S.Satyapragyan-A.Filippov, Hyderabad 2005) the position is very complicated but Black's chances are not worse – ...a7-a5 is going to give him enough counter-chances on the queenside.

6...Bd7! (Diagram 10)

Out of the three possible retreats, this is perhaps the best.

6...Bh5 7 Bd2 c6 8 Qe2 Nbd7? (8...Qc7 must be played, but in any case Black has wasted too much time) 9 Nb5! Qb6 10 Nd6+ gave White a very nice position in P.Velicka-A.Mirzoev, Cairo 2001.

White also stood better after 6...Bf5 7 Bd2! (putting the question to the queen) 7...Qb6 8 Qe2 e6 9 g4! (White starts to seize all the available space) 9...Bg6 10 0-0-0 Nbd7 11 h4 h5 12 Nh3 hxg4 13 fxg4 Rxh4 (the extra pawn is worthless as White soon wins it back, along with gaining the bishop pair) 14 Nf4 Rxh1 15 Rxh1 0-0-0 16 g5 Nd5 17 Nxg6 fxg6 18 Nxd5 exd5 19 Bxd5, in A.Jerez Perez-O.Perez Mitjans, Sitges 2007.

7 Bd2

7 Qe2?! gives Black the time to play 7...Nc6, and 8 Bd2 Nd4! 9 Qd1 Qb6 10 Nge2 Nf5 11 Ne4 e6 12 a4 a5 left Black with the superior position in C.Philippe-E.Prié, Ajaccio 2007.

Black can meet 7 Nge2 with 7...Qb6, beginning to exploit the dark-square weaknesses brought on by White's sixth move. 8 d4 Nc6 9 Be3 e6 10 0-0 0-0-0 11 Kh1 Nb4! 12 a3 Nbd5 13 Bf2 h5 was ambitious play by Black in J.Treguer-E.Prié, Gap 2008. He stands better here: his knights are sitting pretty, and with ...h5-h4 arriving soon it is White who has to worry more about king safety.

7...Qb6 8 Qe2

8 f4 is an interesting try by Nigel Short. Now:

a) 8...Be6! **(Diagram 11)** liquidating some pieces may be the best option, and 9 Bxe6 Qxe6+ 10 Nge2 Nc6 is level. Moving a piece more than once is normally not to be recommended. However, the situation here is rather unique. White has developed his pieces in a compact way, and furthermore he has not staked out an active pawn centre. It is these factors which allow Black the time to play in this way.

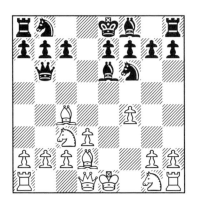

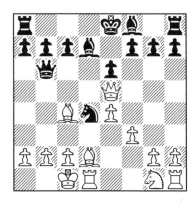

Diagram 11 (W)	Diagram 12 (B)
Another bishop move!	Black is okay

b) 8...e6 is by contrast rather passive. N.Short-E.Prié, Tallinn 2004, went 9 Nf3 Bd6 10 Qe2 0-0 (taking the b-pawn is far too risky: for example, 10...Qxb2 11 Rb1! Qa3 12 Rxb7 Bxf4 13 Bxf4 Qxc3+ 14 Qd2 and White will pick up the c7-pawn) 11 Ne5 Be8 12 g4 c5? (bolstering the d5-square with 12...c6! is considered by Eric Prié to be the best) 13 g5 Nd5 14 Bxd5 exd5 15 Nxd5 Qd8 and here 16 Ng4 Nd7 17 Bc3 would have been catastrophic for Black.

8...Nc6 9 0-0-0

9 Na4 achieves little, as after 9...Qd4 the queen is perfectly at home in the middle of the board. For example, 10 f4 (or 10 0-0-0 0-0-0 11 f4 Qd6) 10...Nb4 11 Bxb4 Bxa4 12 Bc3 Qxf4 13 Nf3 e6 14 0-0 Bc5+ 15 Kh1 0-0 16 Ne5 Qe3 and White does not have sufficient compensation for the pawn.

9...Nd4 10 Qe5 e6 11 Ne4

Against 11 Be3 Black can play the calm 11...Bc5 threatening 12...Nb3+.

11...Nxe4 12 dxe4 (Diagram 12)

12 fxe4 Qd6 13 Qh5 b5 14 Bb3 a5 is promising for Black.

12...Qc5

Eric is critical of this move, and instead prefers 12...f6. After 13 Qh5+ g6 14 Qh4 e5

15 c3 Black can play 15...Bg7!, as 16 cxd4? is bad due to 16...Qc6 17 b3 b5 18 d5 Qc5 regaining the piece. Instead 16 Kb1 Ne6 followed by ...0-0-0 leads to a balanced position.

13 Qxc5 Bxc5 14 Bf4 0-0-0 15 c3 Nc6

This position appears to be level, but there is one serious problem. Black's light-squared bishop is blocked in on d7 and this causes no end of grief.

16 b4 Be7 17 Ne2 Bf6 18 a4 a6 19 Bb3 h5 20 Kc2 h4 21 h3 Be8 22 Ra1 Rh5 23 Be3 e5?!

I don't really like this move as it exposes a weakness on f7.

24 Rad1 Rxd1 25 Rxd1 Bg5 26 Bf2 Ne7 27 c4

White continues to expand on the queenside.

27...Ng6 28 b5 Nf4 29 Nxf4 Bxf4! (Diagram 13)

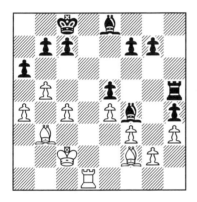

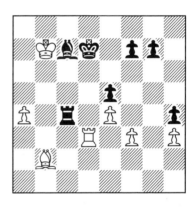

Diagram 13 (W)	Diagram 14 (B)
Targeting the g2 weakness	Black blunders

 TIP: When it comes to weaknesses, one should adopt a "tit for tat" policy – if I have a weakness, I will give you a weakness. This means the opponent can devote less time to attacking your weakness, as he has to protect his own!

30 Kc3 Bg5?

But this is bad. 30...Rh6! is the best – further weaknesses should not be allowed!

31 bxa6 bxa6 32 Kb4 Be7+ 33 c5 Rh6 34 Ka5 Rg6 35 Bc4 Rxg2 36 Bxa6+ Kb8 37 Rb1+ Ka8 38 Be3 c6 39 Bc8 Ra2 40 Rb4 Ra3 41 Bc1

41 Ka6 is another way to play the position, and after 41...Rxe3 42 Bb7+ Kb8 43 Bxc6+ Kc7 44 Bxe8 Rxf3 45 Rb7+ Kd8 46 c6 White is much better.

41...Rc3 42 Bb2 Rxc5+ 43 Ka6 Bd8 44 Bb7+ Kb8 45 Bxc6+ Kc8 46 Bb7+

46 Bxe8?? would be a tremendous mistake, allowing 46...Ra5 mate.

46...Kb8 47 Bc6+ Kc8 48 Bb5 Bc6

48...f6! was stronger, after which it is not so easy for White to make progress.

49 Rb3 Bb7+ 50 Ka7 Bc7 51 Bd7+ Kxd7 52 Kxb7 Rc4 53 Rd3+ (Diagram 14)

53...Ke6?

A decisive mistake. 53...Bd6! holds: 54 Bc3 (54 Ba3 fails to 54...Rd4!, while Black escapes with a draw after 54 Bxe5 Rc7+ 55 Ka6 Rc6+ 56 Kb7 Rc7+) 54...Rc7+ 55 Kb6 Rc6+ 56 Kb5 Rc5+ 57 Kb4 Rc8+ 58 Kb3 Rb8+ 59 Kc2 Kc6 and Black has managed to chase away the king and consolidate his position.

54 Rc3! Rb4+ 55 Kxc7 Rxb2 56 Rc6+ Ke7 57 a5 1-0

The a-pawn cannot be stopped.

Game 25
□ M.Buckley ■ R.Barton
British Championship, Millfield 2000

---

1 e4 d5 2 exd5 Qxd5 3 Nc3 Qa5 4 Nf3 Nf6 5 Be2 (Diagram 15)

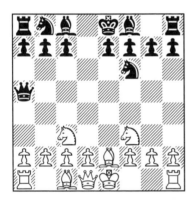

Diagram 15 (B)
Concealed danger for Black

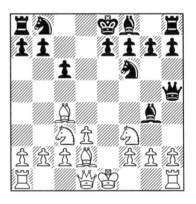

Diagram 16 (W)
Annoying for White

There is a dangerous plan hidden behind this move. White wishes to expand on the queenside with a timely b2-b4, which is normally carried out once Black develops the light-squared bishop.

5 Bc4 can be met by 5...c6 (the knight has committed itself to f3, so it is safe to move the c-pawn). Now:

a) 6 d4 transposes to main lines.

b) 6 0-0?! isn't challenging: 6...Bg4! (since White has castled prematurely, it is more than fine to develop the bishop here) 7 h3 Bh5 8 Re1?! (as Wahls points out, White cannot easily solve the problem of the pin without retreating the bishop, although Bc4-e2 is hardly a try for an advantage) 8...Nbd7 9 d4 e6 10 Bd2 Qc7 11 a4!? (the most logical move; 11 Bg5?! gave White absolutely nothing in L.Fritsche-J.Hickl, Germany League 1994, after 11...Bb4! and 12 g4 Bg6 13 Ne5 Nxe5 14 dxe5 Bxc3! 15 bxc3 Ne4 16 Bf4 Nxc3 picked up a pawn) 11...Bd6 12 a5 0-0 13 Be2 (White must break the pin eventually) 13...b5 14 Ng5 Bg6 and Black has no problems: once he has either secured the d5-square or achieved ...c6-c5 he will stand very well.

c) The combination of Nf3 and d2-d3 is not as potent as Bd2 and d3. However, there is still the annoying idea of the knight hop Nf3-d4, so the best course of action for Black after 6 d3 is 6...Bg4! (6...Bf5 7 Bf4 e6 8 0-0 Nbd7 9 Qe2 Be7 10 Nd4 gave White a slight edge in A.Smith-H.Hunt, British League 1998). For example, 7 Bd2 Qh5! **(Diagram 16)** 8 Qe2 Nbd7 9 Bf4 e6 10 0-0-0 0-0-0 11 h3 Bxf3 12 gxf3 Qf5 and Black did not stand worse in R.Bana-A.Stefanova, Varna 1994. It is true that White has the bishop pair, but Black possesses the strong d5-square and White has weakened his pawn structure – something that will begin to tell in an endgame.

5 h3 is an interesting idea – White takes time out to prevent Black from developing the bishop to its optimum square of g4. A.Filipenko-A.Khalifman, Moscow 1992, continued 5...c6 6 Bc4 (6 Bd3 deprives Black's bishop of the f5-square, but this method of development does not look harmonious, and after 6...Na6 7 0-0 Nb4 8 Bc4 Bf5 9 d3 e6 10 Qe2 Be7! 11 Bd2 Qc7 12 Nd4 Bg6 Black's position is very solid – 13 Bxe6 does not work after 13...fxe6 14 Nxe6 Qd7 15 Bf4 Nxc2!) 6...Bf5 7 d3 e6 8 Bd2 Qc7 9 Qe2 Bc5 (covering d4 so that there are no tricks with Nd4) 10 g4! Bg6 11 Nh4 (11 Ne5 allows Black to liquidate with 11...Nbd7) 11...Nbd7 12 f4 0-0-0 13 0-0-0 Nb6 14 Bb3 Nbd5 and Black was fine: he has good minor pieces and the white bishop is not ideally placed on b3.

5...c6! (Diagram 17)

 WARNING: 5...Bg4?! is famously dubious because of 6 h3 Bh5 7 b4! Qb6 8 0-0 c6 9 Rb1 e6 10 b5!, as played in N.Short-I.Rogers, Tilburg 1992. The point is that White gets in b4-b5 with gain of time.

5...Bf5?! is no better: 6 b4 Qb6 7 Rb1 e6 8 0-0 Nbd7 9 d3 c6 10 Bf4 Nd5? 11 Nxd5 cxd5 12 Nh4, as played in D.Batsanin-S.Grigoriants, St Lorenzo 1995, is very nice for White – he gains the bishop pair and Black has no active squares for his pieces.

6 0-0 Bg4!?

As White has not played actively in the centre, a kingside fianchetto is another reasonable option for Black. For example, 6...g6 7 d4 Bg7 8 Bf4 0-0 9 a3 (attempting to expand on the queenside) and now 9...Nd5! is stronger than 9...Nbd7, which was a little passive in A.Hunt-J.Houska, British League 2000.

7 b4 Qc7

This is the point! By playing ...c6 before ...Bg4, Black gains additional escape squares for the queen so b4-b5 does not come with tempo.

8 h3 Bh5 9 b5 e6 10 Rb1 Be7 11 d4 0-0 12 Ne5 Bxe2 13 Qxe2 Nbd7!? (Diagram 18)

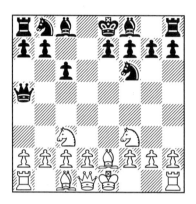

Diagram 17 (W)
A wise choice

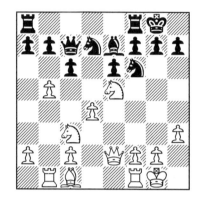

Diagram 18 (W)
Black wants to simplify

I like this simple move, which is much more natural than 13...a6 14 b6 Qd8 15 Rd1 Nbd7 16 Na4 Nd5 17 Nxd7 Qxd7 18 c4 Nf6 19 Bf4 when White is better, A.Hunt-I.Rogers, Gold Coast 2000.

14 Re1?

A mistake. 14 bxc6 bxc6 15 Bf4 Bd6! 16 Nxd7! (16 Rfe1 Nd5! and Black has equalized) 16...Qxd7 17 Be5! would give White a slight advantage due to the wonderful bishop on e5.

14...Nxe5! 15 dxe5 Nd5 16 Nd1 Rfd8 17 a3 cxb5 18 Rxb5 Rac8 19 Qf3 b6 20 Rb2

White's weak pawn islands make life very difficult.

20...Nc3 21 Nxc3 Qxc3 22 Qxc3 Rxc3 23 Ra2 Rd5 24 Kf1 Rcc5 25 f4 Bh4 26 Be3 Bxe1 27 Bxc5 Bd2 28 c4 Rd7 29 Bd6 Bxf4

Black has won one pawn and the rest is relatively easy.

30 Rf2 Bg5 31 Rc2 Be3 32 Ke2 Bd4 33 Kf3 f5 34 a4 a5 35 Rc1 Kf7 36 Rb1 g5 37 Rb5 h5 38 Rb1 h4 39 g3 hxg3 40 Kxg3 Kg6 41 Rb5 Rh7 42 Kg2 f4 43 c5 Bxc5 44 Bxc5 bxc5 45 Rxc5 Ra7 46 Kf3 Kf5 47 Rb5 Rh7 48 Kg2 g4 49 hxg4+ Kxg4 50 Rb8 f3+ 51 Kg1 Kf4 52 Rc8 Rb7 53 Kf2 Rb2+ 54 Kf1 Ra2 0-1

White Plays 4 g3

4 g3 is a very solid move, with White wishing to develop logically but slowly. The special attraction of 4 g3 is that by placing the bishop on the long diagonal White doesn't need to fear it being out of play like it sometimes is on c4.

White is playing with long-term positional aims, and does not try to refute the Scandinavian right from the beginning. This in itself gives Black the unique option of being able to fianchetto his dark-squared bishop too.

Both sides are playing with positional motives throughout the game. Black's strengths lie in the half-open d-file and the strong d5-square. White, on the other hand, intends to utilize the power of his light-squared bishop and the strong e5-square.

Game 26
□ **V.Aveskulov** ■ **A.Kislinsky**
Kharkov 2006

1 e4 d5 2 exd5 Qxd5 3 Nc3 Qa5 4 g3 (Diagram 19)

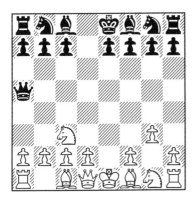

Diagram 19 (B)
White fianchettoes

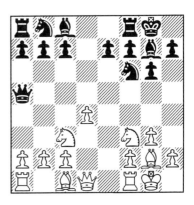

Diagram 20 (B)
The most challenging

4...Nf6 5 Bg2 g6!

5...c6 is the main alternative, and after 6 Nf3 Bg4! 7 h3 Bh5 8 0-0 e6 9 a3 Nbd7 10 Rb1 Be7 11 b4 Qc7 12 d3 Rd8 Black didn't have any problems in A.Vydeslaver-B.Alterman, Israeli League 2008.

6 Nf3

Another way for White to play is to keep the long diagonal unblocked with 6 Nge2. For example, 6...Bg7 7 0-0 0-0 8 d3 c5!? (the most ambitious move, securing a grip on the centre; 8...c6 9 h3 is reasonable for Black but it is difficult for him to establish an active plan, while 8...Nc6 makes it a little bit awkward for the black queen to find a space in the long run) 9 Bf4 (9 Bd2 doesn't really carry a serious threat after 9...Qc7) 9...Nc6 10 a3 Qd8 11 Re1 e5 12 Bg5 h6 13 Be3 Nd4 14 h3 (14 b4 leads to nothing after 14...Ng4 15 bxc5 Nxe3 16 fxe3 Ne6 when Black will regain the pawn and have the bishop pair) 14...Bd7 15 Kh2 Qc8 16 Ne4 and Black stands very well, M.Pasalic-J.Bartholomew, Internet 2008.

6 d3 encouraging ...c7-c6 is probably the most accurate move order, although 6...c6 7 h3 Bg7 8 Bd2 Qd8 9 Qc1 0-0 10 Bh6 (10 Nf3 Be6! reinforces control of the d5-square) 10...Na6 11 Bxg7 Kxg7 12 Nf3 Be6 13 0-0 Qd6 14 b3 Nc7 was level in L.Keitlinghaus-K.Müller, German League 1999.

6...Bg7 7 0-0 0-0 8 d4 (Diagram 20)

This is the critical choice. White aims to swap off the dark-squared bishops and to prevent Black from achieving one of his pawn breaks, ...e7-e5 or ...c7-c5. As with many fianchetto set-ups, White wants to prove that his light-squared bishop is better than its counterpart on c8. Black, in turn, intends to place insurmountable pressure on the d4-pawn, provoking its advance or exchanging it to release some of the tension in the position.

Other possibilities include:

a) 8 d3 Qh5!, as suggested by Karsten Müller, is a good move – it is not easy to chase the black queen away from the kingside. For example, 9 Nd2 Bg4 10 f3 Bh3 and Black is more than fine, S.Tiviakov-P.Ricardi, Buenos Aires 1996.

b) Against the precautionary 8 h3!? Black can gain space with 8...c5! 9 d3 Nc6 10 Be3 Bd7 (D.Pereyra-G.Soppe, Pena City 1996) when the only task left for him is to re-route his queen back into the game.

8...Nc6!? 9 Ne2

The latest way to fend off Black's pressure on d4. If left to consolidate, White will simply play c2-c3 (shutting out the bishop on g7) and try to prevent Black's light-squared bishop from developing to an effective square.

As variations demonstrate, 9 d5 has little effect: 9...Nb4 10 Nd4 (10 Ne5 Rd8!) 10...Bg4 11 Qd2 (11 Qe1?! Rad8! sees Black regain the pawn with a small advantage, M.Kaminski-C.Horvath, Krynica 1998) 11...Rad8 12 a3 Nbxd5 13 Nxd5 and now Karsten Müller's suggestion of 13...Rxd5!? looks interesting, because after 14 Bxd5 Qxd5 15 Nb3 Qc4 White's light-squared weaknesses provide Black with useful compensation for the small material deficit.

9...Bg4! 10 h3 (Diagram 21) 10...Bxf3!

This is Black's worst piece so it makes sense to trade it off for a defender of the d4-pawn.

11 Bxf3 Rad8 12 c4?

12 c3!? is met by 12...Qf5 13 Bg2 (13 Kg2? e5 threatens 14...e4 trapping the bishop) 13...e5 14 Qb3 exd4 15 Nxd4 Nxd4 16 cxd4 Nd5 17 Qxb7 Bxd4 and Black's active pieces compensate for the bishop pair. 12 Be3 e5 13 c3 e4 14 Bg2 Ne5 is also fine for Black.

12...e5! 13 d5 e4! 14 Bg2 Ne5 15 Bd2 Qa6 16 b3 b5?

16...c6! would be very unpleasant for White, especially after 17 dxc6 Qxc6 threatening ...Nf3+.

17 Bf4?! Nf3+!

Now White's position quickly crumbles.

18 Bxf3 exf3 19 Nd4 bxc4 20 Nc6?

20 bxc4 is probably White's best chance, but Black's position is superb anyhow. For example, 20...Qxc4 21 Nc6 Nxd5 22 Rc1 Qe4 23 Nxd8 Nxf4 24 gxf4 Qxf4 (threatening both 25 ...Qg5+ and 25...Be5) 25 Nxf7 Bd4! threatening ...Qg3+ followed by ...Qg2 mate.

20...Nxd5!! (Diagram 22)

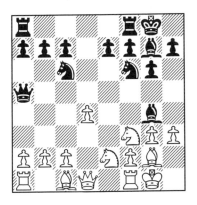

Diagram 21 (B)

Black exchanges his worst piece

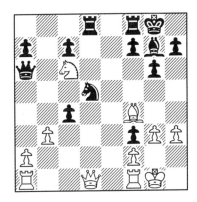

Diagram 22 (W)

This is crushing

A brilliant move, which destroys White.

21 Nxd8 Nxf4 22 gxf4 Bxa1 23 Qxa1 Rxd8 24 bxc4 Qxc4 25 Qc1 Rd4 26 Kh2 Rxf4 27 Kg3 Qxc1 28 Rxc1 Ra4 29 Rxc7 Rxa2 30 Kxf3 Ra3+ 31 Kg2 a5 32 Ra7 a4 33 Kh2 Kg7 34 Ra6 g5 35 Kg2 f6 36 Ra7+ Kg6 37 Ra5 f5 38 Ra6+ Kh5 39 Rf6 f4 40 Ra6 Ra1 41 Kh2 a3 42 Kg2 a2 43 Ra7 Kg6 44 Ra5 Kf6 45 Ra6+ Ke5 46 Ra5+ Ke4 47 Ra4+ Kd3 48 Kf3 Kd2 49 Ra8 h5 50 Ra7 Ke1 51 Kg2 Ke2 52 Re7+ Kd3 53 Rd7+ Kc4 54 Rc7+ Kd5 55 Ra7 g4 56 h4 f3+ 57 Kh2 g3+! 0-1

The Mieses Gambit: 4 b4

This romantic gambit is named after Grandmaster Jacques Mieses, who was a dangerous attacking player. White sacrifices a pawn in order to open up the b-file and gain time by continuously attacking Black's queen.

If played correctly, White can gain some compensation in the form of pressure against b7, which can prove to be a little awkward for Black. However, I don't think White's compensation is worth the sacrificed pawn.

Game 27
□ S.Ivanets ■ V.Minakov
Kiev 2005

1 e4 d5 2 exd5 Qxd5 3 Nc3 Qa5 4 b4 (Diagram 23)

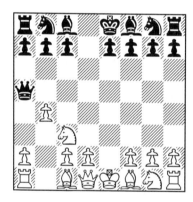

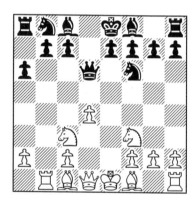

Diagram 23 (B)

The Mieses Gambit

Diagram 24 (W)

The antidote for Black

4 a3 is a way of playing on the wings without sacrificing material. Naturally this shouldn't pose a problem for Black, and 4...c6 5 b4 Qc7 6 Bb2 Nf6 7 d4 Bf5 8 Bd3 Bxd3 9 Qxd3 e6 10 Nf3 Nbd7 11 0-0 was only slightly better for White in E.Najer-A.Shvedchikov, Moscow 1995. Black's position is solid and he should aim for some counterplay along the a-file with ...a7-a5, which might be a bit awkward for White. He also has in reserve the possibility of ...b7-b5 to help control the c4- and d5-squares.

4...Qxb4 5 Rb1 Qd6 6 d4 Nf6 7 Nf3 a6 (Diagram 24)

This move is recognized as the antidote to the Mieses Gambit.

8 g3!

The most promising continuation for White.

According to John Emms, Black should meet 8 Bd3 with 8...g6! to blunt the bishop. After 9 0-0 Bg7 10 Ne5 0-0 11 Bf4 Qxd4 it's difficult for White to prove his compensation.

Against 8 Bc4 Black should really hurry to safety as quickly as possible, and after 8...e6! 9 0-0 Be7 10 Re1 0-0 (Emms) Black is simply a solid pawn up.

8...b6

8...Be6 looks a bit strange. After 9 Bg2 (9 Rxb7 would lose to 9...Qc6) Black must play 9...Qc6 and here 10 Qd2 (10 Bd2 Bc4! cleverly keeps the white king trapped in the middle) 10...Bc4 11 Nh4 is unclear.

9 Bg2 Bb7 10 0-0 e6 11 Ne5 Bxg2 12 Kxg2 Be7 13 Qf3 Ra7 (Diagram 25)

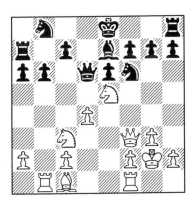

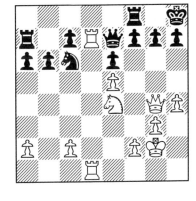

Diagram 25 (W)

Just enough compensation

Diagram 26 (B)

Black goes astray

Because of the misplaced rook on a7, White gets enough compensation to grant him equality, but that is all.

14 Rd1 0-0 15 Bg5 Qd8 16 h4 Nfd7 17 Qg4 Nf6?

Playing for the draw, but Black could have been more ambitious with 17...f5 18 Qf4 Bxg5 19 hxg5 Nxe5 20 dxe5 Qe7 21 Rd3 Nc6 22 Rh1 Raa8 when he is slowly getting his pieces back in order.

18 Bxf6 Bxf6 19 Ne4 Bxe5?

Giving White further compensation: the open d-file and tactical tricks based on Nf6.

20 dxe5 Qe7 21 Rb3 Kh8 22 Rbd3 Nc6 23 Rd7 (Diagram 26)

23...Nxe5?

The losing move. Black had to play 23...Qb4.

24 Rxe7 Nxg4 25 Rxf7! Kg8 26 Re7 Nh6 27 Rdd7 Nf5 28 Rxe6 Raa8 29 Rxc7

Now White is a pawn up with the better pieces, so he should win. Here are the remaining moves.

29...Rae8 30 Rxe8 Rxe8 31 f3 Ne3+ 32 Kf2 Nd5 33 Rc6 a5 34 a3 Rb8 35 c4 Ne7 36 Rc7 Nf5 37 h5 Nd4 38 Nd6 Rd8 39 Ne4 Nc2 40 a4 Rd1 41 c5 bxc5 42 Rxc5 Nb4 43 Rxa5 Ra1 44 Nd6 h6 45 Nf5 Ra2+ 46 Kg1 Nd3 47 Ra7 Ne5 48 f4 Nf3+ 49 Kf1 Rd2 50 Nh4 Nxh4 51 gxh4 Rd4 52 Kf2 Rxf4+ 53 Kg3 Rb4 54 a5 Rb3+ 55 Kg4 Rb4+ 56 Kg3 Rb3+ 57 Kf4 Rb4+ 58 Ke5 Rxh4 59 a6 Rxh5+ 60 Kd6 Ra5 61 Kc6 h5 62 Kb6 Ra2 63 Rc7 Rb2+ 64 Kc6 Kh7 65 a7 Ra2 66 Kb7 Rxa7+ 67 Kxa7 Kh6 68 Kb6 h4 69 Kc5 g5 70 Kd4 Kh5 71 Ke3 Kg4 72 Kf2 Kh3 73 Rc1 Kg4 74 Kg2 Kh5 75 Rc5 Kg4 76 Rc4+ 1-0

Summary

The most critical try for White in this chapter is the "Short System". Game 23 highlights the danger of routine play by Black and also perfectly illustrates the essence of White's strategy. In Game 24 Black demonstrates the best defence, provoking a little weakness with 5...Bg4!. Black should remember that the d4-square becomes a source of counterplay, so ...Nc6 is the way to develop the queen's knight (but also don't forget to answer Bd2 with ...Qb6!).

The notes to Game 25 demonstrate that d2-d3 in conjunction with Nf3 is not dangerous. Against Nf3 with Be2, Black should develop the Scandinavian bishop to g4 rather than f5, preferably after White has castled kingside. He should precede this by playing ...c7-c6, giving the queen an escape route should White play for b2-b4.

The Fianchetto system allows Black the time to mimic White's style with ...g7-g6. Finally, the Mieses Gambit is simply a case of "coffee house" chess. White does gain the b-file and some pressure for the pawn, but maintaining the initiative actually requires rather precise play from White.

Chapter Seven

3...Qd6: Introduction and Main Lines

Introduction to 3...Qd6

1 e4 d5 2 exd5 Qxd5 3 Nc3 Qd6 (Diagram 1)

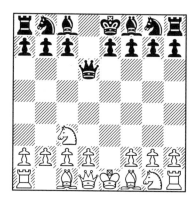

Diagram 1 (W)

3...Qd6

As opening theory developed in the Scandinavian, players turned their attention to lesser-known lines such as 3...Qd6 and 3...Qd8, which were traditionally considered dubious. Whereas 3...Qd8 has never been truly accepted, the popularity of 3...Qd6 has exploded so much that it is almost considered superior to 3...Qa5. In fact, world-class grandmaster Sergei Tiviakov has introduced it into his repertoire and has published several articles celebrating its merits.

First, let's look at the attraction of the ...Qd6 move by itself. We see that the queen is not badly placed on d6 – it is nicely centralized, doesn't interfere with the development of Black's forces and places pressure on the d4-square. It also limits the tactical impact of the dreaded d4-d5 pawn push which is so problematic in the 3...Qa5 section. However, the chief attraction of 3...Qd6 lies in its simplicity. Black has an array of plans that in a typical Scandinavian manner focus chiefly on piece placement. Moreover, the position is not necessarily easy for White to play: as the natural pawn advance d4-d5 may not be particularly effective, an inexperienced player may suddenly find himself in worse position!

Let's now consider Black's possible piece formations:

Set-up A: the ambitious ...a6 and ...b5

Diagram 2 shows Black's most ambitious set-up, and it tends to be his first choice unless White has taken specific measures to deter it. As we can see, Black's pieces are incredibly well placed. Notice the light-squared bishop bearing down on the long diagonal, and the b5-pawn controlling c4 and thus restraining the white pawn centre. Black's pawn breaks are based on ...c7-c5 or, more rarely, ...e7-e5. Should White play passively or aimlessly, then this really is the set-up Black should be playing for.

Because Set-up A is such an effective mode of development, White has developed anti-b5 measures that basically prevent Black from employing it. These anti-b5 measures are usually based around exploiting the weakness of the h1-a8 diagonal *before* Black has consolidated with ...Bb7, or provoking Black to over-extend his queenside pawns.

Diagram 2

Set-up A

Diagram 3

Set-up B

It is because of the harmony of Black's set-up that White simply cannot play in a passive manner. For example, the d3 systems that are so dangerous against 3...Qa5 just don't work well here. Black's light-squared bishop, so often subjected to the dreaded "bishop hunt" in the 3...Qa5 lines, is safely ensconced on b7, and it's Black's strongest minor piece. Indeed, the greatest problem for Black lies in the possibility of its exchange and the potential exposure of the queenside.

The pressure on the d-file is such that if White develops "normally", he may in fact stand slightly worse. Control of the central squares again plays a role: White's strong square is e5 whereas Black has firm control of d5.

Set-up B: putting pressure on d4 with ...a6 and ...Bg4

This set-up **(Diagram 3)** is designed to put as much pressure on the d4 point as possible, making special use of the semi-open d-file. In order to maximize this pressure and to sharpen up the position Black may in fact castle queenside, although this is not necessarily always the case. This set-up is usually played when White has in some way prevented our ideal set-up A.

As a general point on both 3...Qd6 and 3...Qa5, developing the bishop to g4 is especially effective when White is committed to castling kingside, as then it is a major nuisance for him to chase away the bishop. Should the bishop arrive on g4 either (a) when it doesn't threaten anything, or (b) when it is obvious White is intending to castle queenside, I would be a little more sceptical of moving it to that square. There are very few pawn breaks for either side, so the main question then becomes: *who has more space?* As we've already seen, the bishop on g4 can simply act as a target and a way for White to expand on the kingside with moves such as h2-h3, f2-f3 and g2-g4, and this can become very unpleasant for Black.

Set-up C: the Caro-Kann/Slav pawn structure

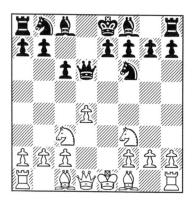

Diagram 4

Set-up C

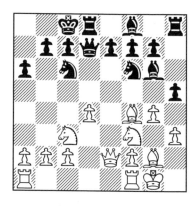

Diagram 5 (W)

Black is crushed

I first knew this as the Pytel Variation (named after the French IM Krzysztof Pytel) and more recently it has also become Sergei Tiviakov's pet system. 5...c6 **(Diagram 4)** is somewhat truer to the Scandinavian concept of developing the light-squared bishop either to f5 or g4, while maintaining the solid Slav/Caro-Kann pawn structure. If Black is allowed to develop his pieces without hindrance then he will reach a pleasant position with no obvious weakness. As usual in the Scandinavian, White must react very aggressively in order to attempt to secure an advantage.

Set-ups A and B will be discussed during the course of the analysed games and variations in this chapter and the following one, whereas set-up C is covered in Chapter Nine.

Crossover themes for White

One of the leading experts on the 3...Qd6 Scandinavian, Sergei Tiviakov, came up with a little rule that effectively summarizes Black's objective: "Black first must develop the light-squared and then the dark-squared [bishop] ... if Black can do this he is rarely worse".

It is White's mission to use this knowledge to his advantage, and to prevent Black from reaching his objectives. Here are some dangerous ideas that White has at his disposal:

A) Pushing back the black queen

This is the first step to pushing Black's whole army back. One of the key ways to achieve this – regardless of the set-up – is either to use the e5-square as a base or to swap off the light-squared bishops. Take this following example **(Diagram 5)**:

Earlier White took the first step by pushing the queen back to d7 with Bf4. Black has just played the reckless 12...h5, and this allows the crushing reply 13 Ne5! (see the notes to Game 31 for further details). This is a typical problem Black may face in this line.

B) Striking with d4-d5

This is not so much of a problem in the 3...Qd6 lines, but Black must not be blasé about it! Take an example from one of my games, P.Varley-J.Houska, British League 1999:

1 e4 d5 2 exd5 Qxd5 3 Nc3 Qd6 4 d4 Nf6 5 Nf3 a6 6 Bc4 Bg4?! (as we shall see in Chapter Eight, 6....b5 is a better choice) **7 0-0 e6 8 h3 Bh5 9 Qe2 Nc6??** **(Diagram 6)**

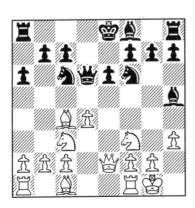

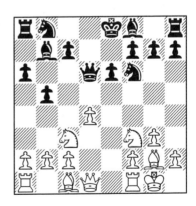

Diagram 6 (W)

Black blunders

Diagram 7 (W)

White plays 9 Ne5!

10 g4! Bg6 11 d5 and Black is struggling.

C) Exchanging the light-squared bishops

The funny thing is that in nearly all lines of the Scandinavian the light-squared bishop never gets left in peace – it is either constantly attacked by white pawns or exchanged to highlight a weakness in Black's position. This latter action is especially true with regards to Set-up A. Take Diagram 7, which arises in Game 28. White plays 9 Ne5!, exchanging off Black's powerful bishop and exposing a whole load of light-square problems on the queenside.

Set-ups for White

In this chapter and the following one I will be discussing set-ups with 5 Nf3. Chapter Nine covers fifth-move alternatives for White, which include the idea of developing the knight to e2, preparing Bf4.

The Main Line: 5 Nf3 a6 6 g3

1 e4 d5 2 exd5 Qxd5 3 Nc3 Qd6 4 d4 Nf6 5 Nf3 a6 (Diagram 8)

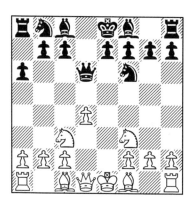

Diagram 8 (W)

Black plays 5...a6

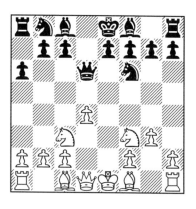

Diagram 9 (B)

The critical 6 g3

5 Nf3 is the most natural development for the g1-knight, and also probably White's most flexible move. After 5...a6 White has a variety of options available to him, of which these are the most testing for Black:

1) The fianchetto system (this chapter);

2) Occupying the centre immediately with 6 Ne5 (Chapter Eight);

3) Playing against the weakness of f7 with 6 Bc4 (Chapter Eight).

6 g3 (Diagram 9)

This is by far the most critical and popular line for White. It is considered to be the best choice and has been recommended by Alexander Khalifman.

As the popularity of 3...Qd6 grew, White players looked at various ways of exploiting the placement of Black's queen, and how to develop his pieces in an easy and simplistic manner. By playing 6 g3 White aims to turn the strength of Black's Set-up A into a weakness. He intends to swap off the light-squared bishops and force Black to over-extend his pawns on the queenside; in particular the b5-pawn.

There are two main ways for Black to meet 6 g3:

♟ Set-up A: 6...b5

♟ Set-up B: 6...Bg4

Of these two options, Set-up B is considered to be the best. (There's a third possibility in the mirror system 6...g6, although this is a minor line.)

The "Refutation" of 6...b5

Unfortunately, 6...b5 is no longer effective against 6 g3. However, it does require some accurate play and a good memory from White, which means that it could still be used as a good surprise weapon!

Game 28
□ **I.Kurnosov** ■ **A.Tzermiadianos**
Warsaw 2005

1 e4 d5 2 exd5 Qxd5 3 Nc3 Qd6 4 d4 Nf6 5 Nf3 a6 6 g3 b5?!

Alternatively:

a) 6...Nc6 7 Bf4!? Qb4 8 a3 Qb6 9 d5 appears very promising for White. However, after 9...Ng4! 10 Qd2 e5! the situation is actually not that clear.

b) 6...Bf5 7 Bg2 c6 8 0-0 e6 9 Bf4 Qd8 10 Qe2 Be7 11 Rad1 0-0 12 Ne5 with a comfortable edge for White, V.Laznicka-P.Jirovsky, Czech League 2004.

c) 6...g6 is solid, but it leaves White with a pleasant position as there are no active pawn breaks for Black. For example, 7 Bg2 Bg7 8 0-0 0-0 9 Bf4 Qd8 10 Qd2 Re8 11 Rfe1 c6 12 a4 a5 13 Rad1 Bg4 14 h3 Bxf3 15 Bxf3 e6, K.Arakhamia-S.Tiviakov, British League 2005.

7 Bg2 Bb7 8 0-0 e6

8...Nbd7 9 Bf4 Qb6 10 a4 b4 11 a5 Qa7 12 Ne2 Nd5 13 c4! Nxf4 14 Nxf4 e6? 15 d5 is absolutely crushing.

9 Ne5! (Diagram 10)

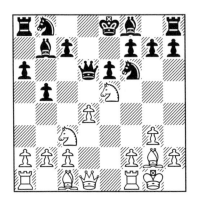

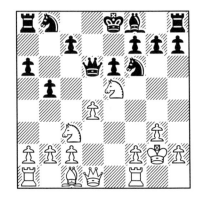

Diagram 10 (B)
The critical test

Diagram 11 (B)
Difficult for Black

This is the move which Greek IM Andreas Tzermiadianos believes refutes Black's whole ...b5 idea.

9 Bf4 is more commonly played, but this gives Black a vital tempo to consolidate. After 9...Qb6 10 a4 Black has the strong reply 10...Bd6!. As Andrew Martin points out, as a general rule for Black, these bishops should be exchanged. The game E.Sutovsky-D.Sermek, Terme Zrece 2003, continued 11 Be3! (11 a5 is premature, as Black is able to block the centre, and 11...Qa7 12 Be3 Nd5 was okay for him in P.Konguvel-D.Milanovic, Moscow 2006) 11...b4 12 a5 Qa7 13 d5 Bc5 14 dxe6 Bxe3 15 exf7+ Kxf7 16 Ne5+ Ke7 17 Bxb7 Qxb7 18 Qd3 bxc3 19 Qxe3 with good compensation.

9...Qb6

Black lost pretty quickly after 9...c6 10 a4 b4 11 Ne4 Qc7?? (11...Nxe4 is forced) 12 Ng5 and 1-0, in A.Ostrovskiy-O.Miljutin, Odessa 2008.

9...Bxg2 10 Kxg2 **(Diagram 11)** is unsatisfactory for Black, as the light-square weaknesses start to tell. For example:

a) 10...Nbd7?! 11 Qf3 Rc8 12 Bf4! Qb6 13 Nxd7 Nxd7 14 d5 is much better for White.

b) 10...b4?! 11 Qf3 c6 12 Bf4! bxc3 (or 12...Nd5 13 Ne4 Qc7 14 Kg1 Nxf4 15 Qxf4 and Black cannot develop a single piece) 13 Nxf7 Qxd4 14 bxc3 and White will win the rook and the game – the weakness on the b-file is too much for Black to handle.

c) 10...Ra7 (given as the best try by John Emms) 11 Qf3 Be7 12 Be3! targeting the black rook. Black's position is very cramped: he cannot develop his knight on b8 as it must guard the c6-square, and the rook on a7 looks faintly ridiculous.

d) 10...Be7 doesn't help much. After 11 Qf3 c6 12 Bf4 Nd5 13 Ne4 Qc7 White has the stunning 14 Bh6!! which clears the path for the queen, and 14...gxh6 15 Qxf7+ Kd8 16 Qxe6 Rf8 17 Nf7+ is winning.

e) 10...c5 is interesting but it doesn't work: 11 Qf3 Ra7 12 Bf4! Qb6 13 dxc5 Bxc5 14 Nd3 and White is much better, for example after 14...Nc6 15 Nxc5 Nd4 16 N5a4 bxa4 17 Be3 0-0 18 Rfd1 e5 19 Nxa4 Qb4 20 Bxd4 exd4 21 b3 (Tzermiadianos).

10 d5! (Diagram 12)

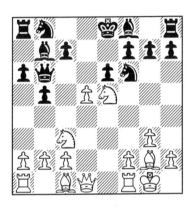

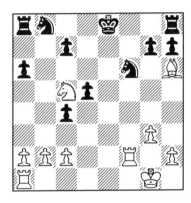

Diagram 12 (B)

Blowing the position open

Diagram 13 (B)

A good endgame for White

White is threatening to win immediately with 11 Be3! followed by dxe6.

10...Bc5

The only move. 10...exd5 is impossible: White is winning after 11 Nxd5 Nxd5 12 Bxd5, and White also wins after 10...Be7 11 Be3 Qd6 12 Nxf7.

11 dxe6 fxe6 12 Nc4!

A great idea, allowing White to liquidate into a superior endgame.

12...bxc4

After 12...Qa7 13 Bxb7 Qxb7 14 Na5 Qb6 15 Qf3 c6 16 Nb3 0-0 17 Ne4 Nxe4 18 Qxe4 Bxf2+ 19 Kg2 e5! 20 Qxe5 Nd7 21 Qe6+ Rf7 22 Bf4 White has a clear edge.

13 Na4 Qa7 14 Bxb7 Bxf2+ 15 Rxf2 Qxb7 16 Nc5 Qd5?

16...Qb6 was stronger, although after 17 Nxe6 Qxe6 18 Re2 Ne4 19 Qd4 0-0 20 Rxe4 Qb6 21 Qxb6 cxb6 22 Rxc4 White is a pawn up.

17 Qxd5 exd5 18 Bh6! (Diagram 13)

18...gxh6

18...0-0 19 Bxg7 wins.

19 Rxf6 Nd7 20 Re6+ Kd8 21 Nxa6

White has a superior endgame and converts it smoothly.

21...Nb6 22 Nb4 Kd7 23 Rxh6 Rae8 24 a4 Re6 25 Rh5 c6 26 a5 Na8 27 b3 cxb3 28 cxb3 Nc7 29 Nd3 Kd6 30 b4 Na6 31 b5 Nc7 32 Nf4 Rf6 33 bxc6 Ra8 34 Rxh7 Ne6 35 Nxe6 Rxe6 36 Rc1 Re2 37 a6 1-0

Black Plays 6...Bg4!

1 e4 d5 2 exd5 Qxd5 3 Nc3 Qd6 4 d4 Nf6 5 Nf3 a6 6 g3 Bg4! (Diagram 14)

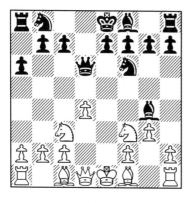

Diagram 14 (W)
Considered best

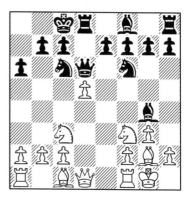

Diagram 15 (B)
The critical move

This set-up is universally considered to be Black's best option against the dangerous 6 g3. Both sides have more than one way to treat the position. Black can play a quick ...Nc6 and castle queenside, placing an incredible amount of pressure on the d4-pawn. The game then becomes incredibly wild so readers are advised to carefully study this variation. An alternative for Black is the more solid ...c6, an idea from Sergei Tiviakov. However illogical this move looks in combination with ...a6, Black's position is still relatively solid.

7 Bg2

White has several choices to make. Firstly, he must decide where to castle: whether he can ignore the pressure on the d4-pawn and head kingside; or play a little more solidly, aiming to retain the central tension by castling queenside.

If White castles kingside, which is the usual choice, there are further questions to consider: should White play d4-d5, and when should he chase the bishop away with h2-h3? Remarkably, the timing of h2-h3 and the possibility of d4-d5 are closely interlinked, as we shall see from the games and analysis below.

White will sooner or later have to play h2-h3, in order to deal with Black's pressure on the centre – the only question is when? The main advantage White obtains from playing 7 h3 is that later on, in the heat of the complications, White can play g3-g4 to keep the knight on f3 controlling the centre. However, there are also some reasons for keeping the bishop on g4, and these are explained below. See Games 31-32 for coverage of 7 h3.

7...Nc6

The more solid option of 7...c6 is covered in Game 33.

8 0-0 0-0-0

Let's take stock of this amazingly complicated position. How does Black intend to play? The answer lies in the centre. Most of his pieces are directly or indirectly fixed upon the d4 point. Left to his own devices, Black will continue with ...e7-e5.

9 d5! (Diagram 15)

This is the key idea behind White's previous play. Black must now play either 9...Ne5 (Game 29) or 9...Nb4 (Game 30), since 9...Nxd5 10 Nxd5 Qxd5 11 Qxd5 Rxd5 12 Ng5! is good for White.

 NOTE: This rather deep idea demonstrates a fundamental difference between 7 h3 and 7 Bg2. This d4-d5 advance is not possible once White has played 7 h3, as the bishop would then be on h5 and the f7-pawn would be defended!

Game 29
□ **P.Mickiewicz** ■ **V.Malaniuk**
Krakow 2008

---

1 e4 d5 2 exd5 Qxd5 3 Nc3 Qd6 4 d4 Nf6 5 Nf3 a6 6 g3 Bg4 7 Bg2 Nc6 8 0-0 0-0-0 9 d5!

9 Be3 can be met by the principled 9...e5! (shameless pawn-hunting is never to be recommended, and 9...Qb4? 10 a3 is playing with fire) 10 dxe5 Nxe5 11 Nxe5! (11 Qxd6 Bxd6 poses absolutely no problems for Black) 11...Bxd1 12 Nxf7 and now 12...Bxc2! 13 Nxd6+ Bxd6 is equal.

9 Bf4 is answered by 9...Qb4! (the standard way to meet this attack) and 10 d5 (10

a3 should be met by 10...Qc4!, while 10 Ne2 Bxf3 11 Bxf3 Nxd4 12 Nxd4 Rxd4 13 Qe2 Rxf4! 14 gxf4 Qxf4 favoured Black in P.Doggers-L.Gofshtein, Ghent 2001) 10...e5! 11 Bd2 Nd4 12 Ne2 Bxf3! 13 Bxb4 Nxe2+ 14 Kh1 Nxg3+ 15 hxg3 Bxd1 16 Bxf8 Rhxf8 17 Raxd1 left Black with a healthy extra pawn in A.Longson-C.Hanley, British Championship 2003.

9...Ne5!

Exchanging pieces. I think that this move is not only the safest but also the best.

At first I preferred 9...Nb4, but that move leads to a very sharp position where Black must proceed with extreme caution (see Game 30).

10 Bf4

10 Nxe5 Bxd1 11 Nxf7 Bxc2 12 Nxd6+ exd6 is slightly better for White.

10...Nxf3+ 11 Bxf3 Bxf3 12 Qxf3 e5! (Diagram 16)

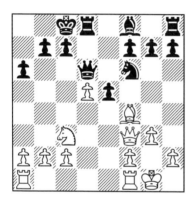

Diagram 16 (W)

Striking back in the centre

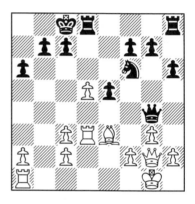

Diagram 17 (B)

White's pawns are a mess

13 Bg5?!

This is a dubious move. White should be opening as many lines as possible, so 13 dxe6! is by far the best continuation. After 13...Qxe6 there's a choice:

a) 14 Bg5 Bd6 15 Rfe1 Be5 16 Ne4 Rhe8 17 Bxf6 gxf6 18 Nc5 Qd5 and a draw was agreed in G.Eleftheriou-A.Nikomanis, Athens 2007.

b) 14 Rfe1 Qf5 15 Re5 Qh3 16 Bg5 Ng4! (16...Bd6 allowed the black queen to get stranded on h3 after 17 Bxf6 gxf6 18 Rf5 and White stood better in D.Larino Nieto-J.Hernando Rodrigo, Mondariz-Balneario 2007) 17 Qf5+ Kb8 18 Bxd8 Qxh2+ 19 Kf1 Bd6 and White must return his material.

c) 14 b4!? is the most direct. White has no regard for material and continues to open up as many lines as possible. Black's defence is based on neutralizing and

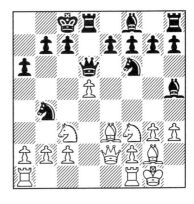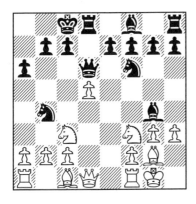

swapping off any white pieces that could be perceived as menacing: 14...Qg4 15 Qg2 (15 Qe3 can be met by 15...Bxb4! because 16 Rab1 Bxc3 17 Qa7 Qf3 defends) 15...Bd6 16 Bxd6 Rxd6 17 b5 axb5 18 Nxb5 Rd2 followed by ...Qe4 and Black is fine.

13...h6! 14 Be3

If 14 Ne4 Nxe4 15 Bxd8 Nd2 16 Qg4+ Qd7 17 Qxd7+ Kxd7 18 Rfd1 Nf3+ 19 Kg2 e4 and the white bishop is trapped!

14...Qd7 15 Rfd1 Qg4 16 Qg2 Bb4 17 Rd3 Bxc3 18 bxc3 (Diagram 17)

Black has managed to cripple White's initiative on the queenside. He will now simply consolidate his king position and play to win the weak d5-pawn.

18...Qc4 19 Rad1 Rd6 20 Qh3+ Kb8 21 Qf5 Re8 22 a4 a5 23 Rb1 b6 24 Rdd1 Kb7 25 Rb5 Qxa4 26 Qd3 Qe4 27 c4 Qxd3 28 cxd3 Ka6 29 Rdb1 Nd7 30 g4 c5 31 Kg2 e4!

After this move Black is completely winning.

32 Bf4 Rf6 33 Bc7 exd3 34 d6 d2 35 Bxb6 Re1 36 Bc7 Rxb1 37 Rxb1 Rf4 0-1

Game 30
□ L.Fressinet ■ Wong Meng Kong
Calvia Olympiad 2004 (variation)

---

1 e4 d5 2 exd5 Qxd5 3 Nc3 Qd6 4 d4 Nf6 5 Nf3 a6 6 g3 Bg4 7 Bg2 Nc6 8 0-0 0-0-0 9 d5! Nb4 10 h3 (Diagram 18)

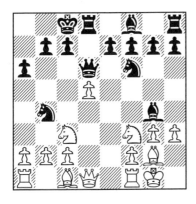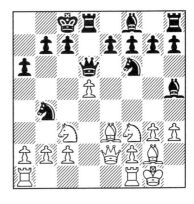

Diagram 18 (B)
Asking the question

Diagram 19 (B)
A dangerous pawn sacrifice

10...Bh5

I am not a big fan of 10...Bxf3? 11 Qxf3 Nbxd5 (not 11...Nxc2? 12 Qf5+) 12 Rd1 e6

13 Nxd5 exd5 14 c4! c6 15 cxd5 Nxd5 (or 15...cxd5? 16 Bf4 and Black is lost) 16 Qxf7 Qd7 when according to Karsten Müller, White keeps a plus due to his bishop pair. I think that practically the position is very tough for Black: the knight is not so stable on d5, as White will be very quick to open lines.

11 Bf4

This can lead to a repetition of moves, but White usually plays this in order to gain the free developing move Be3.

11...Qc5

11...Qd7? runs into 12 Qd4! Bxf3 13 Qa7! Qf5 14 Bxf3 when Black has no good defence to the nasty threat of d5-d6.

12 Be3 Qd6

Avoiding the possibility of a repetition with 12...Qa5? leads to an inferior position: 13 g4! Bg6 (after 13...Nbxd5 14 Nxd5 Rxd5 15 Bd2 Black is forced to give up the exchange, V.Kotronias-M.Godena, Batumi 2002, while in this line 14...Nxd5 15 Bd2 Qc5 16 gxh5 Nf4 17 Re1 leaves Black with insufficient compensation) 14 Nd4! (with the threat of 15 Nb3) 14...Nbxd5 15 Nb3! Qb4 (White wins after either 15...Nxc3 16 Bxb7+ or 15...Nxe3 16 Bxb7+!) 16 Nxd5 Nxd5 17 Bxd5 e6 18 a3 Qb5 (18...Qe7 19 Bxb7+ Kxb7 20 Qf3+ Kb8 21 Na5 wins) 19 c4 Qe8 20 Bxb7+! Kxb7 21 Na5+ Kc8 22 Qf3 and White's attack is decisive, A.Skripchenko-Z.Mamedjarova, Crete 2007.

13 Qe2! (Diagram 19)

Simply giving up the d-pawn, as recommended by Alexander Khalifman.

13 Bf4 is a repetition, and two other moves have been tried:

a) After 13 g4 Bg6 14 Qd4 Nxc2! 15 Qa7 now Black should remove the powerful dark-squared bishop with 15...Nxe3. Once this bishop is exchanged, White's attack disappears, and following 16 fxe3 Qb6 Black's position is at least equal.

 WARNING: Black should avoid 15...Nxa1?? 16 Bc5 Qf4 17 Ne5!! (White throws all his pieces into the attack!) 17...Qxe5 (or 17...Nd7 18 Nc6 bxc6 19 dxc6) 18 f4 when Black's queen is trapped in the middle of the board.

b) 13 Qd4 is answered by the convincing 13...Bxf3! (13...Nxc2 leads to a mass of complications) 14 Bxf3 (14 Bf4 e5!) 14...Nxc2 15 Qa7 Nxe3! and White's attack is stopped.

13...e5!?

I don't think it is wise for Black to take the pawn, as this will simply give White the open d-file down which to attack. For example, 13...Nfxd5? 14 Nxd5 Nxd5 15 Rfd1 Qe6 16 g4 Bg6?? (this natural move loses; after 16...Nxe3 17 Rxd8+ Kxd8 18 Ng5 Qe5 19 Bxb7 the knight is untouchable, as White threatens Rd1+ followed by

Bc6 mate) 17 Ng5 Qe5 18 c4 Nxe3 19 Bxb7+ Kxb7 20 Rxd8 Qxg5 21 Qf3+ c6 22 Rad1 and White wins, M.Huerga Leache-J.Ortega Ruiz, Malaga 2008.

13...Bg6!? attacking c2 is Andrew Martin's recommendation, but the c-pawn cannot really be taken, rendering the whole venture a little pointless: 14 Bf4! Qc5 15 Ne5! Nbxd5 (the c-pawn is taboo: 15...Nxc2 16 Nxg6 Nd4 17 Qe3 and the knight drops due to the nasty pin) 16 Nxd5 Nxd5 17 Rad1!. This is a key move. White is not bothered with material concerns and instead begins to show his strength along the d-file. Now:

a) After 17...e6 White has the strong 18 Bg5! and Black must give up material. The natural 18...Be7 fails to 19 Nxg6 hxg6 20 Rxd5 picking up the loose bishop on e7, while after 18...Rd6 19 Bxd5 Black either falls prey to a mating attack down the d-file, or the back rank is left pitifully weak following 19...exd5 20 Nxg6 Re6 21 Qf3 when White wins the d-pawn and soon the game.

b) 17...c6 fails to the beautiful strike 18 Nxc6! Qxc6 (18...bxc6 19 Qxa6+ Kd7 20 b4! kicks away an important defender of the knight on d5, and Black must give up more material because 20...Qxb4 21 Bxd5 just wins) 19 Qe5 e6 20 c4 Bd6 21 cxd5 Bxe5 22 dxc6 Bxf4 23 cxb7+ Kb8 24 gxf4 and White is better.

c) 17...Nxf4 18 Rxd8+! Kxd8 19 Qd2+ and now:

c1) 19...Qd6 20 Qxf4 f6 (20...Kc8 21 Qf3 c6 22 Nxf7 Bxf7 23 Qxf7 is also very nice for White, as Black's king will not be safe for a very long time) 21 Nxg6 hxg6 22 Qg4 and Black is struggling with his exposed king and the threats along the d-file. After 22...f5 23 Qf3! Qb6 24 Rd1+! Ke8 25 Qxb7 Qxb7 26 Bxb7 a5 27 Bc6+ Kf7 28 Kg2 Black's vulnerable queenside pawns will certainly drop off, leaving White with a won endgame.

c2) 19...Nd5 leads to an equally unpleasant position after 20 Bxd5 e6! (if 20...Qd6 21 Rd1 and the pressure down the d-file becomes insurmountable) 21 Bxe6+ Bd6 22 Nxf7+ Bxf7 23 Bxf7. The presence of opposite-coloured bishops may give Black drawing chances, but with his king so exposed I am a pessimistic about this.

14 dxe6 Qxe6 15 g4 Bg6 16 Nd4 Qe8

This is the only move, as it guards the c6-square.

> **WARNING: 16...Qe7?? is a catastrophic blunder – Black must be very careful about his queenside light squares! After 17 a3 Nbd5 18 Nxd5 Nxd5, 19 Nc6!! is a devastating blow, and 19...bxc6 20 Qxa6+ Kd7 21 c4 Be4 was winning for White in R.Zelcic-D.Sermek, Sibenik 2005.**

17 Rad1! (Diagram 20)

A novelty, and the most accurate move. White's idea is very subtle: there are possibilities of sacrificing on c6, as the d5-square is now a bit more vulnerable.

Fressinet chose the less accurate 17 Rfe1, and the game continued 17...h5!? (Black must try to muddy the waters) 18 Qf3 c6 19 a3 hxg4 20 hxg4 Nbd5 21 Nxd5 Rxd5 (White's problem is that there is no sacrifice on c6, so Black's rooks get active!) 22 g5 Be4 (once the light-squared bishops have been exchanged, the majority of Black's problems disappear) 23 Bh3+?. Here *Rybka* suggests moving the king into the eye of the storm: after 23...Kd8 24 Qg3 Bd6 25 f4 Black has the amazing 25...Rxg5!! 26 Qxg5 Rxh3 27 Nf5 Rh1+ 28 Kf2 Rh2+ 29 Kg1 Qh8 30 Bb6+ Bc7 31 Rad1+ Bd5 with an advantage.

17...h5

Again Black desperately needs to bring his pieces into action, as White was threatening to win with a2-a3. 17...Nbd5 loses to 18 Qf3 c6 19 Bg5 h6 20 Bxf6 Nxf6 21 Rfe1 Qd7 22 Ne6.

18 Qf3 c6 19 g5 Nfd5 20 Rfe1! (Diagram 21)

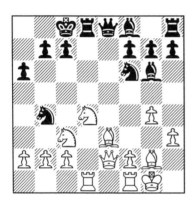

Diagram 20 (B)

The most accurate

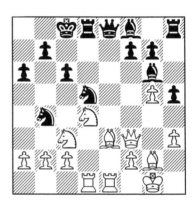

Diagram 21 (B)

Clear advantage for White

Black is in some trouble here:

a) 20...Nxe3 is very bad: 21 Rxe3 Qd7 22 a3 Nd5 23 Nxc6!! (here comes that strike again!) 23...bxc6 24 Nxd5 cxd5 25 Rc3+ Kb8 26 Qe3 d4 27 Qf3 and White wins.

b) The calm 20...Qd7 fails to 21 Nxd5 Nxd5 (21...Qxd5 loses immediately to 22 Ne6 Qxe6 23 Rxd8+ Kxd8 24 Bb6+) 22 Nxc6! bxc6 23 c4 Bb4 24 Rf1 and Black's position is wrecked.

Game 31
□ **F.Caruana** ■ **A.Strikovic**
Lorca 2005

---

1 e4 d5 2 exd5 Qxd5 3 Nc3 Qd6 4 d4 Nf6 5 Nf3 a6 6 g3 Bg4 7 h3

White alleviates the pressure on the d4-pawn but forgoes the possibility of the d4-d5 advance seen in the previous two games.

7...Bh5

7...Bxf3 8 Qxf3 Nc6?! 9 Be3 followed by 0-0-0 (or perhaps just Bg2 and 0-0) is good for White. 8...c6 makes more sense, keeping some control of the d5-square. Even so, playing both ...a6 and ...c6 does look rather clumsy, and 9 Be3 e6 10 0-0-0 Be7 11 g4 Qc7 12 g5 Nd5 13 Ne4 b5 14 h4 Nd7 15 Kb1 was also good for White in E.Sveshnikov-P.Ponkratov, Chelyabinsk 2007.

8 Bg2 Nc6 9 0-0 0-0-0 10 Bf4!? (Diagram 22)

Diagram 22 (B)

...Qb4 or ...Qd7?

Diagram 23 (B)

Drastic measures

10...Qb4!?

This is the most aggressive continuation.

After 10...Qd7!? 11 g4 Bg6 White must deal with Black's pressure on the d-pawn. However, simply sacrificing the pawn to keep the initiative with 12 Qe2 isn't a daft idea. White gains compensation for the pawn because it is difficult for Black to develop his dark-squared bishop quickly:

a) 12...Nxd4 13 Nxd4 Qxd4 14 Be3! Qb4 (14...Qd7 15 Rad1 Qe6 16 Bxb7+ wins) 15 a3! Qa5 16 f4 (depriving the queen of the e5-square) 16...e6 17 b4 and Black is lost.

b) It is too early to counter-attack with 12...h5, because 13 Ne5 Nxd4 14 Qe3 Qe6 15 Rfd1 c5 16 Na4 wins.

c) 12...e6!? is the only move as far as I can see: 13 Ne5 Nxd4 14 Qe3 Qe7 (14...Qe8 15 Rad1 Bc5 16 Nxg6 hxg6 17 g5 Nd5 18 Nxd5 exd5 19 Rxd4 wins) 15 Rad1 Qc5 16 Na4 Qb4 17 b3 and Black is in a quandary as to how to meet c2-c3 without suffering big losses.

11 g4!

It is important for White to ease some of the pressure on the d4-pawn. 11 d5? is unwise, as after 11...e6 Black wins material.

11...Bg6 12 a3! (Diagram 23)

In order to cope with the pressure down the d-file, White is forced to take drastic measures. The ensuing position is extremely complicated. White gets tremendous compensation in the shape of the open b-file, two sweeping bishops pointing at Black's vulnerable king, plus the knight hop into e5.

 TIP: This variation is incredibly risky for Black, so he needs to be very well prepared.

12 Qe2!? Qxb2?? is a mistake now that White's queen can go to an active square, and after 13 Qe3! e6 14 Rab1 Qa3 15 Rb3 Qa5 16 Ne5! White is virtually winning. However, 12...e6! maintains the threat on the d- and b-pawns, and 13 Rab1 Nxd4 14 Nxd4 Qxd4 15 Be5 Qb6 doesn't look like sufficient compensation for White.

12 Ne5 Nxd4 13 a3 Qc5 14 Na4 Qxc2? 15 Nb6+ won for White in I.Nepomniachtchi-V.Gashimov, Internet (blitz) 2006, but Black can play 14...Qa5! reaching an unclear position.

12...Qxb2

12...Qc4?! 13 g5! (13 Ne5!? is an interesting alternative) 13...Nd5! (13...Ne8 is too passive and indeed after 14 Be3 it is difficult to see what Black can play) 14 Nxd5 Rxd5 15 c3!? was played in P.Svidler-S.Tiviakov, Wijk aan Zee 2007, but after 15 Ne5 I'm not convinced Black gets enough compensation for the exchange. I think White is clearly better after 15...Rxe5 16 Bxe5 Nxe5 17 dxe5 e6 18 Qf3! c6 19 Rfd1!. Black's pieces have no real coordination so I don't see how he can claim any form of compensation. For example, 19...Be7 (trying to get activity with 19...h6 20 gxh6 Rxh6 21 Rd2 Bc5 22 Rad1 looks pleasant for White) 20 Qe3 Bxc2 21 Rd4 Qb5 22 Rc1 and White has the better position.

13 Qe1! e6!

The correct choice – Black must complete his development as quickly as possible. I think the pawn-grabbing 13...Bxc2 is going too far: for example, 14 Qe3 Qb3 15 Rfc1 e6 16 Nd2 Qb2 17 Bxc6 bxc6 with advantage to White.

14 Rb1

14 Ne5 should be met by 14...Nd5! blocking the danger on the long diagonal (14...Nxe5 fails to 15 Rb1!). After 15 Nxd5 exd5 16 Nxc6 bxc6 17 Qa5 (17 Rb1 is tempting but not so good, as after 17...Qxc2 18 Qa5 Bd6 19 Qxa6+ Kd7 the king escapes and 20 Rbc1 Ra8! wins) 17...Qb6 (quickly reinforcing the queenside pawns) 18 Qc3 c5! 19 dxc5 Qxc5 I think Black is defending okay, and here 20 Qb2 Qb5 21 Qc3 Qc4 is equal.

14...Qxc2 15 Ne5 (Diagram 24)

Black has to make a choice between blocking the powerful bishop on g2 and developing.

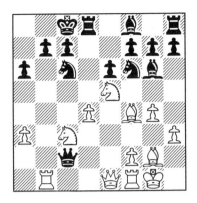

Diagram 24 (B)
A critical moment

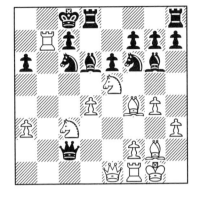

Diagram 25 (B)
A fantastic sacrifice

15...Bd6!?

In his notes to the game, Caruana concluded that 15...Nd5! was the best move – it is imperative to block the long diagonal because White's light-squared bishop is the most dangerous piece: 16 Rc1 Nxf4 (16...Qb2? fails to 17 Nxd5 exd5 18 Nxc6 and Black's position is in tatters) 17 Rxc2 Nxg2 18 Kxg2 Nxe5 "when the position has undergone a remarkable transformation: Black has sacrificed his queen for two bishops and two pawns, but at the same time has rebuffed White's attack and left White with many weaknesses, whilst receiving good control over both the light and dark squares. In fact I feel Black is only very slightly worse at the maximum." – John Watson

16 Rxb7!! (Diagram 25)

A wonderful strike! It should be mentioned that the young Italian GM had to calculate extensively in order to make this work.

16...Kxb7!

16...Bxe5? 17 Bxc6 Bxf4 18 Ra7 Nd7 19 Nd5! Bd6! 20 Nb4! Qc4 21 Qe2! (Watson) wins after 21...Qxe2 22 Bb7+ Kb8 23 Nc6 mate.

17 Nxc6 Kc8 18 Be5! Bxe5?

Stronger was 18...Rde8, making space for the king and intending 19 Na7+ Kd7 20 g5 Nd5.

19 dxe5 Nd5 20 Nxd5 exd5 21 Ne7+

Not blindly taking the material. After this move White gets a huge advantage.

21...Kd7 22 Nxd5 Bd3?! 23 Nb4 Qc4 24 Qd2 Ke8 25 Rc1 Qb3 26 Rxc7 h6 27 Bc6+ Kf8 28 Bd5??

28 Be4 would have won on the spot.

28...Bc4! 29 Rxf7+ Ke8 30 Nc6! Bxd5 31 Re7+ Kf8 32 Qf4+ Kg8 33 Rxg7+ Kxg7 34 Qf6+ Kh7 35 Qf5+ Kg7 36 Qf6+ Kh7 37 Qf5+ Kg7 38 Qf6+ ½-½

Game 32
□ **L.Drabke** ■ **D.Pirrot**
German League 2008

1 e4 d5 2 exd5 Qxd5 3 Nc3 Qd6 4 d4 Nf6 5 Nf3 a6 6 g3 Bg4 7 h3 Bh5 8 Bg2 Nc6 9 Be3?! (Diagram 26)

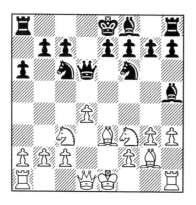
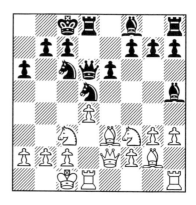

Diagram 26 (B)
Not so threatening

Diagram 27 (W)
Black at least equalizes

This is not the most challenging move, as it allows Black to complete his ideal formation without too many problems.

9 Bf4 Qb4! 10 0-0 0-0 transposes to the previous game. K.Landa-C.Bauer, Nancy 2008, instead continued 10 a3 Qxb2 11 Na4 Qb5 12 c4 (White must sacrifice another pawn to maintain any sort of the initiative) 12...Qxc4 13 Rc1 Qe6+ 14 Be3 Nd5 15 0-0 (15 Nc5 Qc8 16 0-0 e6 17 Qb3 Bxc5 18 Rxc5 0-0 reminds me of Catalan positions where White enjoys substantial pressure on the b- and c-files, but Black's position is very solid and the extra material should begin to count) 15...Nxe3 16 fxe3 Qxe3+ (White has sacrificed three pawns in order to keep his attack going) 17 Kh1 e6 18 g4 (18 d5 loses to 18...0-0-0) 18...Bxg4! 19 hxg4 Qh6+ 20 Kg1 Bxa3 21 Rc3 Bb4 (21...Bd6 may be an improvement) 22 g5 Qh5 when White's exposed king gave Black enough compensation for the piece.

9...0-0-0 10 Qe2

10 0-0 e5 equalizes immediately. For example, 11 dxe5 Nxe5 12 Nxe5 Bxd1 13 Nxf7 Bxc2 (Black has to return the queen, otherwise he is much worse) 14 Nxd6+ Bxd6, E.Van den Doel-S.Tiviakov, Leeuwarden 2005.

10...e6

10...e5 is a mistake, and 11 dxe5 Nxe5 12 g4 Bg6 13 Rd1 Qc6 14 Rxd8+ Kxd8 15 0-0 Nxf3+ 16 Bxf3 Qe6 17 Bxb7 was winning for White in E.Korbut-T.Ivanova, St Petersburg 2004.

11 0-0-0?!

In order to fight for the advantage, White needs to castle kingside and then open lines on the queenside. By castling queenside, White cannot open lines against the black king so easily and so he limits himself to the plan of seizing as much space as possible on the kingside.

11 0-0 is more natural, although 11...Be7 12 a3 Nd5! 13 Ne4 Qd7 14 b4 f5! 15 Nc5 Bxc5 16 bxc5 f4! 17 gxf4 Rhf8 demonstrated an effective way for Black to achieve counterplay in R.Zelcic-D.Sermek, Sibenik 2005.

11...Nd5! (Diagram 27) 12 Nxd5

12 Ne4 is met by 12...Qb4 13 a3 Qa4.

12...Qxd5 13 b3?

13 c4 Qe4 gives Black complete control of the light squares – a typical theme in the Scandinavian – and 14 Qc2 Qxc2+ 15 Kxc2 Bg6+ 16 Kb3 is completely equal.

Unfortunately for White, 13 Kb1 Nb4! is very strong.

13...Qa5 14 Kb1 Nb4 15 a4 Nd5 16 Bd2 Bb4 17 c4? Bxd2 18 cxd5 Bc3 19 dxe6 Rhe8 20 Qe5

20 Qc4 fails to 20...Rxe6 21 Rc1 Rc6.

20...Rd5 21 Qxg7 Qb4 22 Ka2

22 Nd2 Qa3 checkmates.

22...Ra5 0-1

Black was threatening 23...Rxa4+ followed by mate on b2. Here 23 Rd2 doesn't help, as Black simply plays 23...Bg6 renewing the deadly threat.

Game 33
□ **M.Al Modiahki** ■ **S.Tiviakov**
Amsterdam 2006

---

1 e4 d5 2 exd5 Qxd5 3 Nc3 Qd6 4 d4 Nf6 5 Nf3 a6 6 g3 Bg4 7 Bg2 c6!? (Diagram 28)

Black steers the game into calmer waters. Although it does look rather like a luxury to play both ...a6 and ...c6, Sergei Tiviakov's idea is to commit to ...c6 only once White has clarified his system of development. This leaves White unable to play the principled answer to ...c6 – Ne5. The flipside is that Black's position, while solid, is rather passive and it is difficult to win if White doesn't make any unforced errors.

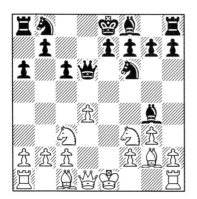

| **Diagram 28 (W)** | **Diagram 29 (B)** |
| The super-solid approach | A promising idea |

8 Bf4

According to Sergei Tiviakov, this move is stronger than 8 0-0. In fact, he is of the opinion that castling kingside ruins White's chances for the advantage altogether! However, I am not so sure. Let's take a look at 8 0-0 e6 and now:

a) 9 a4!? aiming to fix the black pawn structure to its weakest configuration is very interesting: 9...a5?! (the most principled continuation, but Black cannot play the opening just with the pawns! 9...Be7 was stronger) 10 h3 Bxf3 11 Qxf3 Be7 (Black must play 11...Qxd4 and ask White to prove he has compensation, which is far from easy to do) 12 Bf4 with a big advantage, A.Shabalov-R.Gonzalez, Philadelphia 2004. White will simply exchange a pair of knights, centralize the rooks and play d4-d5 when he is ready.

b) 9 Na4 **(Diagram 29)** is a creative way of securing the d4/c4 pawn formation: 9...Qd8 (9...Nbd7 10 Bf4 is a little bit awkward) 10 c4 Nbd7 11 h3 Bxf3 (11...Bh5 12 Qb3 is unpleasant) 12 Qxf3 Bd6 13 b4 0-0 was V.Bologan-I.Saric, Neum 2008. The b-pawn is untouchable and White has a fantastic position: he has space on the queenside, the bishop pair and all the active chances.

8 h3 Bxf3 9 Bxf3 (9 Qxf3 Qxd4) 9...e6 10 Bf4?! is tempting, but I don't think this move achieves that much. Sergei Tiviakov assesses 10...Qd8 as equal, and after 11 Qd3 Bd6! the time White gained with 10 Bf4 is regained by Black!

8...Qd8 9 h3

Black would love to retreat the bishop, but I don't think he can afford this luxury. Once this pair of minor pieces has been exchanged, Black must concentrate on keeping the position semi-closed and reinforcing his control of d5, which is the perfect blockading square for him.

9...Bxf3 10 Qxf3 Qxd4! (Diagram 30)

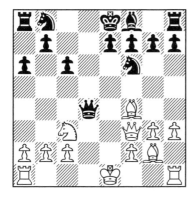
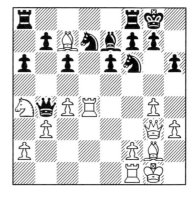

Diagram 30 (W)
Greed pays!

Diagram 31 (W)
Black has consolidated

 TIP: When offered the d4-pawn in a situation like this, it is usually best for Black to take. Otherwise White may get a very pleasant position by centralizing in the centre.

Even so, 10...e6 isn't a bad move here. Sergei Tiviakov accurately summarizes the plans for both sides after 11 0-0-0 Be7. White has a development and space advantage, and moreover the pair of bishops, but it is not easy to gain something special from that. Meanwhile Black's plan is easy: he is going to finish development with ...Nbd7 and ...Nd5, and then start advancing the pawns on the queenside to gain counterplay. White has to advance the kingside pawns to create an attack on the black king. Here's an example: 12 g4 Nbd7 13 Kb1 Nd5 14 Nxd5 (after 14 Bc1!? b5 followed by the advance of the other queenside pawns, Black creates enough counterplay – the position remains very complex with chances for both sides) 14...cxd5 15 c4 Nb6 16 c5 Nc4! 17 Bf1 Na5 18 Qg3 (White is threatening to clamp down on the position with g4-g5, which Black takes strong measures to prevent) 18...Bh4! 19 Qe3 h6 20 Be5 Bf6 21 Bxf6 Qxf6 22 f4 and the game soon fizzled out to a draw in P.Svidler-S.Tiviakov, Turin Olympiad 2006.

11 0-0

11 Rd1 is the obvious candidate but after 11...Qb6 it really isn't obvious how White will continue the attack. Black will play ...Nbd7 followed by ...e6 and his

position is extremely solid. The problem for White is that the light-squared bishop is hitting a wall of granite.

11...e6 12 Rad1

12 Rfd1 Qb6 13 Qd3!? is the most challenging try: 13...Be7! (13...Nbd7 is convincingly met by 14 Ne4) 14 a4 a5 (after 14...0-0?! 15 a5 Qd8 16 Ne4 it is incredibly difficult for Black to develop his queenside) and White should probably bail out for a draw with 15 Be3 Qc7 16 Bf4 Qb6 17 Be3, since Black's position is extremely solid.

12 Bc7 is an interesting move suggested by Sergei Tiviakov, and 12...Nbd7 13 Rfd1 Qa7 14 Rd2 Rc8 15 Bf4 Be7 16 Rad1 Nd5 17 Ne4 0-0 18 c4 Nxf4 19 Rxd7 gives White compensation for the pawn.

12...Qb6 13 Na4?!

Sergei Tiviakov considers this to be dubious, but the alternatives are hardly challenging for Black either. For example, 13 Be3 Qa5 14 Ne4 Nbd7 15 Bd4 Be7 16 Bc3 Qc7 17 Nxf6+ Nxf6 and again Black is holding firm.

13...Qb5 14 b3 Nbd7 15 c4 Qa5 16 g4 h6! 17 Qg3 Rc8 18 Qe3 Ra8

Preventing the queen from penetrating the seventh rank with Qa7.

19 Qg3 Be7 20 Bc7 Qb4 21 Rd4 0-0 (Diagram 31)

It is very difficult to prove something concrete for White here.

22 Rfd1 Nc5 23 Nb6 Rae8 24 f4?

White is so preoccupied with preventing Black from playing ...e6-e5, he doesn't notice the danger. However, it is not clear how White can continue with his initiative.

24 Qe5 is the only move; 24 Qf4? e5! 25 Qxe5 Bd8 is the crafty idea behind Black's play, and here 26 Qg3 Bxc7 27 Qxc7 Ne6 wins.

24...Nce4!?

This is a tactic based on the ...Bc5 pin. However, the stunning 24...e5!! is even stronger. Black wins further material after 25 fxe5 Ne6, and 26 exf6 Nxd4 27 Kh1 Ne2 28 Qf3 Bxf6 29 Nd7 Re6 30 Nxf8 Qxf8 31 Qf2 Nc3 is winning.

25 Bxe4 Bc5 26 a3?

A big mistake in a difficult position. After 26 Qe3 Bxb6 27 Bxb6 Qxb6 Black is a pawn up but the battle continues.

26...Qxa3 27 Bc2 Rd8! 28 Bxd8 Rxd8 29 Kg2 Rxd4 0-1

Summary

This chapter covers the most critical variation of the whole 3...Qd6 Scandinavian. By playing 6 g3, White follows the principled idea of first pushing the queen back and then establishing control of the e5-square. Crucially, White places his light-squared bishop on a fantastic diagonal and, as Game 28 shows, Black cannot challenge White on this diagonal with the dubious 6...b5?!.

Black must adopt Set-up B (bishop to g4, knight to c6 and ...0-0-0), after which White needs to decide whether or not to aim for the pawn push d4-d5. This matter hinges on White's choice on the seventh move: whether to chase away the bishop with 7 h3 or not.

Game 29 demonstrates the correct reaction from Black (9...Ne5!) should White refrain from playing 7 h3, whereas Game 30 demonstrates the dangers associated with 9...Nb4. In my opinion White's best move is 7 h3, and Game 31 with its wild complications is an important one to study. Alternatives for White, including the queenside castling of Game 32, do not work well.

If Black wishes to play in a much more solid way, he can set up a fortress with ...c6. After h2-h3 and an exchange on f3, White can sacrifice the d4-pawn but this was shown to be unclear in Game 33. If White doesn't wish to gambit the pawn and instead plays 10 Bxf3, then Black must do everything in his power to keep the position blocked.

Chapter Eight

3...Qd6: Sixth Move Alternatives

White Plays 6 Ne5

White Plays 6 Bc4

Other Sixth Moves for White

White Plays 6 Ne5

1 e4 d5 2 exd5 Qxd5 3 Nc3 Qd6 4 d4 Nf6 5 Nf3 a6 6 Ne5

This straightforward move was the subject of a comprehensive *New in Chess* survey by Andreas Tzermiadianos. As we have already seen in previous chapters, Nf3-e5 can be a very powerful weapon in the right situation, but here the knight jump looks rather premature.

There are two main ideas behind 6 Ne5:

1) Black cannot achieve the desired Set-up A, as ...b7-b5 falls foul of Qf3. Moreover, Black's light-squared bishop may be difficult to develop effectively unless Black takes radical action.

2) White wishes to develop his pieces with tempo, so Ne5 is usually followed by Bf4 with nasty threats of Ng6 or Nxf7 to push the black queen backwards. For example, 6...e6 7 Bf4 already looks a bit uncomfortable for Black.

6...Nc6! (Diagram 1)

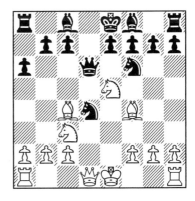

Diagram 1 (W)	Diagram 2 (B)
The principled choice	Not a problem for Black

This is best. Although this involves a further loss of time with the queen, it is useful to exchange pieces. Now 7 Bf4 is covered in Game 34, and 7 Nxc6 in Game 35.

Game 34
□ **E.Mortensen** ■ **D.Bronstein**
Hastings 1995/96

---

1 e4 d5 2 exd5 Qxd5 3 Nc3 Qd6 4 d4 Nf6 5 Nf3 a6 6 Ne5 Nc6! 7 Bf4

White sacrifices a pawn.

7...Nxd4

Black can refuse the pawn, but he must not be idle to White's threats: 7...Bf5 8 Bc4 Nxe5 (8...e6! 9 Qf3 Qxd4 10 Nxc6 Qxc4 11 Ne5 Qb4 12 0-0-0 Bd6 is fine for Black) 9 dxe5 Qc6 10 Qe2 Qxg2 11 0-0-0 Ne4 was K.Arakhamia-I.Mashinskaya, Varna 2002, and here 12 Bd5! would have been very strong.

Kotronias's strong move 7...Ng4!? also gives Black an easy game, as after 8 Be2 Ngxe5 9 dxe5 Nxe5 White still has to prove compensation for the pawn.

8 Bc4 (Diagram 2)

 NOTE: A practical problem for Black is that White can force a repetition of moves here with 8 Ng6 Qe6+ 9 Ne5.

8 Nxf7? doesn't work: 8...Qxf4 9 Nxh8 Bf5 10 Bd3 Qe5+! 11 Ne2 Rd8! and Black's threat of 12...Nxc2+ is impossible to meet.

I think that the best try for White is 8 Bd3!?. Out of Black's possible answers, I would choose 8...Bf5!?. For example, 9 0-0 Bxd3 10 Qxd3 Nc6 11 Qe2 Nxe5 12 Bxe5 Qc6 and Black can concentrate on developing the rest of his army.

8...Be6!

8...Ne6?! is not as good: 9 Qf3 g6 10 Bxe6! Qxe6 11 0-0-0! Bg7 12 Rhe1 is very unpleasant for Black, and here 12...Qf5 loses to 13 g4 Nxg4 14 Nd5.

9 Bxe6!

White must avoid 9 Ng6? **(Diagram 3)**

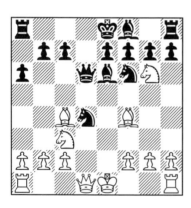

Diagram 3 (B)
Good for Black

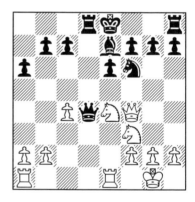

Diagram 4 (B)
Black should play on

9...Qc5 10 Bxe6 hxg6 11 Bb3 0-0-0 12 Qc1 e6, while after 9 Qd3 Nxc2+! 10 Qxc2 Bxc4 11 Rd1 Qe6 12 Ne4 Nxe4 13 Qxe4 Bb5! 14 Qxb7 Rc8! Black has no problems as the white king is stranded in the centre.

9...Nxe6 10 Qf3 Nxf4 11 Qxf4 e6 12 0-0

12 Rd1 fails to 12...Qb4 13 Qf3 when Black can simply grab material: 13...Qxb2 14 0-0 Bb4! (every move Black makes attacks something so he escapes the danger) 15 Qxb7 0-0!.

12...Be7 13 Ne4 Qd5 14 Rfe1 Rd8 15 c4 Qd4 16 Nf3 (Diagram 4)

16...Qd7

Black is much better here, so instead of repeating the position he should continue the game with 16...Qb6. For example, 17 c5 (how else can White mix up the position?) 17...Bxc5 18 Nxf6+ gxf6 19 Qxf6 Bxf2+ 20 Kh1 Rf8 21 Rf1 Bd4 22 Nxd4 Qxd4 with some compensation for White, but it's not worth two pawns.

17 Ne5 Qd4 18 Nf3 Qd7 19 Ne5 Qd4 ½-½

Game 35
☐ **R.Eames** ■ **J.Houska**
London (rapid) 2002

---

1 e4 d5 2 exd5 Qxd5 3 Nc3 Qd6 4 d4 Nf6 5 Nf3 a6 6 Ne5 Nc6! 7 Nxc6

This doesn't present Black with too many problems.

7...Qxc6 8 d5?! (Diagram 5)

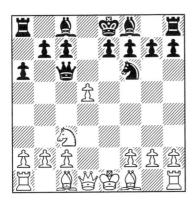

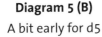

Diagram 5 (B)
A bit early for d5

Diagram 6 (W)
An ideal scenario

This pawn thrust is a tad premature.

I don't believe White gets much in return for the pawn after 8 Be2!? Qxg2 9 Bf3 Qh3 10 Bf4 c6 (10...Qe6+ 11 Be5 gave White some compensation in J.Plaskett-

J.Houska, Islington 1998). For example, 11 Rg1!? g6 12 Na4 Bh6 13 Be5 Be6 14 Rg3 Qh4 15 c4 0-0 and Black was winning in M.Brzeski-V.Malaniuk, Mielno 2006.

8 Bf4 Bg4 9 f3 Be6 10 Qd2 (10 Bd3?! lacks purpose, and 10...g6 11 Qe2 Bg7 12 0-0-0 0-0 13 Kb1 Nd5 is a familiar manoeuvre that equalizes, M.Zelic-C.Horvath, Split 2000) 10...0-0-0 11 Be5 was played in R.Ponomariov-A.Hauchard, Belfort 1998. The Be5 plan is effective against ...g7-g6, but here Hauchard neutralized it with 11...Bc4 12 Bd3 e6 and Black was fine. The immediate 8...Be6!? is also possible, and even 8...Bf5 allowing 9 d5 can be played. It is questionable whether d4-d5 is effective when Black hasn't committed his light-squared bishop to the long diagonal, and 9...Qb6 10 Qd2 e6!? highlights a problem with such an early advance – Black can simply challenge the pawn and White is forced to liquidate the central tension.

8...Qd6!

8...Qb6 is also possible, but not as good.

9 Be2

Alternatively:

a) 9 Be3 b5 (this is effective if White is not ready to meet ...Bc8-b7 with Bf3) 10 Qd4 e5 11 dxe6 Bxe6 12 0-0-0 Qxd4 13 Bxd4 Be7 gave Black absolutely no problems in G.Borgo-D.Bronstein, Ubeda 1996.

b) 9 Qf3?! doesn't really achieve very much: 9...Bg4 10 Qf4 e5 11 Qa4+ (11 dxe6 Qxe6+ liquidates to a very comfortable position for Black) 11...Bd7 12 Qb3 b5 13 Bd3 c5! 14 Ne4 (unfortunately for White the ideal move 14 dxc6 loses to 14...Be6 when White must give up material to avoid losing the queen) 14...Nxe4 15 Bxe4 f5 16 Bf3 c4 17 Qc3 Be7 and Black had an absolutely fantastic position in C.Kilpatrick-N.Povah, British League 2008.

c) 9 Bc4 is designed to prevent ...e7-e6, but it allows 9...b5!. The bishop on b7 will be unchallenged and Black will aim for ...c7-c5. For example, 10 Bb3 Bb7 11 Bg5 c5 12 dxc6 Qxc6 13 f3 e6 **(Diagram 6)** and Black will continue with ...Bc5 and ...Rd8, obtaining lovely coordination for his pieces. Black doesn't bother to defend against Bxf6, as the doubling of the pawns would only give him another avenue down which to attack.

9...e6! (Diagram 7)

This is why I prefer 8...Qd6. Black can simplify into a very comfortable endgame.

I learned from experience that 9...b5?! is dubious. It is consistent with the overall theme of the ...Qd6/...a6 Scandinavian, but in this particular position Black's light-squared bishop is simply useless on the long diagonal: 10 Bf3 (White's whole strategy is based on this idea) 10...Bb7 11 0-0 Rd8 (11...b4?! 12 Ne4 Nxe4 13 Bxe4 g6 was A.Longson-J.Houska, British League 1999, and here 14 c4 would give White a clear advantage) 12 Bg5 g6 13 Qe2 b4 14 Nb5 and White has the initiative, Z.Pavicic-R.Zelcic, Pula 2001.

If you are not in the mood to play an endgame, then 9...Bf5 is a very reasonable alternative. 10 Be3 h5 11 Qd4 e5 12 Qa4+ Bd7 13 Qb3 Qb4 led to a tense queenless middlegame in A.Grobelsek-T.Gruskovnjak, Portoroz 2005. Black will try to establish an advantage on the kingside while White aims to do likewise on the queenside. Alternatively, 10 0-0 0-0-0 11 Qd4 e5! 12 Qa7 Qb6 13 Qxb6 cxb6 14 Bg5 Bb4! left the d5-pawn weak in E.Virnik-A.Dacalor, Patras 1999.

10 dxe6

10 Bf3! is better than the game continuation and leaves the position completely equal.

10...Qxd1+ 11 Bxd1 Bxe6 12 0-0 0-0-0 13 Bg5 h6 14 Bxf6 gxf6 15 Ne4 f5 (Diagram 8)

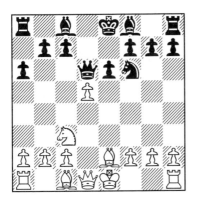

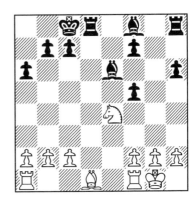

Diagram 7 (W)

Hitting back in the centre

Diagram 8 (W)

Good for Black

The doubled pawns are not a disadvantage for Black, who has the bishop pair in an open position.

16 Ng3 Rd2 17 Rc1 Bc5 18 Be2 f4

18...Bd4! 19 b3 Bb2 20 Rb1 Rxc2 21 Bd3 Rd2 22 Bxf5 is also better for Black, as his rooks are still more active than their counterparts.

19 Ne4 Rxe2 20 Nxc5 Bf5

Now a pawn will drop.

21 Rfe1 Rxc2 22 Rxc2 Bxc2 23 h4 h5 24 Re7 Bg6 25 Kh2 a5 (0-1)

Apologies to the reader, but I don't have the full record of this game as it was played in a rapidplay tournament. Suffice to say that Black has a very good position here, and I later won without any problems by activating the rook on h8.

White Plays 6 Bc4

1 e4 d5 2 exd5 Qxd5 3 Nc3 Qd6 4 d4 Nf6 5 Nf3 a6 6 Bc4

Targeting the f7-pawn. If Black doesn't react well, this move can be very dangerous.

6...b5! (Diagram 9)

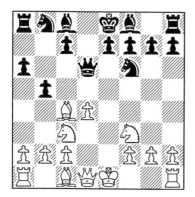

Diagram 9 (W)

Black strikes with ...b5

Diagram 10 (B)

Winning for White

This is consistent with the ...Qd6/...a6 mode of development and the best reply to White's aggressive sixth move.

Other moves do not fare so well for Black. For example, J.Houska-M.Young, Gibraltar 2004, went 6...Bg4 7 h3 Bh5 (7...Bxf3 8 Qxf3 of course gives White a pleasant advantage) 8 Be3!? (I had prepared this move) 8...Nc6 9 Qe2 e6 10 0-0-0 (I was aiming for quick development, a possible sacrifice on e6 and the traditional pawn break d4-d5) 10...b5? (10...Ne7, covering d5, would have been more appropriate) 11 Bb3 Na5 12 d5 Nxb3+ 13 axb3 e5 14 g4 Bg6 with a clear advantage for White.

7 Bb3

With 7 Bd3 White tries to prove that he has provoked a weakness. Then 7...Bb7 8 Qe2 e6 9 Bg5! is perhaps the trickiest, but Black should be able to equalize with 9...Nbd7 10 0-0 Be7 11 a4 b4 12 Ne4 Nxe4 13 Bxe4 Bxe4 14 Qxe4 0-0 15 Bf4 Qb6 – I don't think Black has too many problems here.

7 Bb3 keeps the pressure on the a2-g8 diagonal. Black's main move is 7...Bb7!, which is covered in Game 36.

7...c5!? is an interesting alternative: 8 dxc5 (8 a4!? is more critical) 8...Qxd1+ 9 Nxd1 e6 10 a4 (White cannot hold on to the pawn for long after 10 Be3 Nfd7!, and

11 c3 Nxc5 12 Bc2 Bb7 13 b4 Ne4 was equal in V.Baklan-W.Arencibia, Yerevan 2001) 10...b4 11 a5 Ne4 was fine for Black in H.Stevic-G.Borgo, Leipzig 2002.

 WARNING: 7...Nbd7? is careless, and it allows White to demonstrates the power behind his idea.

For example, 8 0-0 Bb7? (8...e6 is needed, but 9 Ng5! lining up sacrifices on e6 and preparing Qf3 is still very strong) 9 Ng5! **(Diagram 10)** (Black's position is already beyond hope) 9...e6 10 Re1 Be7 (or 10...Nd5? 11 Qh5! g6 12 Qf3 N7f6 13 Nxd5 winning) 11 Nxe6! fxe6 12 Rxe6 Qb4 13 a3 Qa5 14 Bd2 b4 (the only move, as 15 Nd5 trapping the queen was threatened) 15 axb4 Qf5 16 Qe2 Ng8 17 Ra5! Qf8 18 Nd5 with a crushing position for White, R.Ponomariov-L.Fressinet, Batumi 1999.

Game 36
□ **M.Boehnisch** ■ **M.Jirovsky**
German League 2002

---

1 e4 d5 2 exd5 Qxd5 3 Nc3 Qd6 4 d4 Nf6 5 Nf3 a6 6 Bc4 b5! 7 Bb3 Bb7

Black must strive to control the key e4- and d5-squares and, very importantly, get ready to block the a2-g8 diagonal if needed.

8 0-0

8 Ne5 only looks promising. Black simply plays around the knight and targets the d4-pawn. After 8...e6 9 Bf4 c5 White cannot play 10 Ng6? Qxd4 11 Qxd4 cxd4 12 Nxh8 dxc3, as the knight on h8 is trapped. 10 d5 is better, but after 10...Nbd7! White must solve the problem of his knight: 11 Ng6? is a blunder because of 11...e5!; 11 Nxf7 fails after the long sequence 11...Qxf4 12 Nxh8 Qe5+ 13 Kf1 c4 14 dxe6 Qxe6 15 Qe1 Ne5; while 11 Qe2 Nxe5 12 Bxe5 Qb6 13 dxe6 c4 leads to a wild position in which White sacrifices a piece for several pawns.

8...e6 9 Re1 (Diagram 11) 9...c5!?

This is recommended by Andrew Martin on *ChessPublishing.com*. However, Black must be incredibly careful here. The fundamental problem is that he is two moves away from fully completing his development. Should White manage to play d4-d5 while keeping the black king in the centre, then he will have a virtually won position.

9...Be7 runs into 10 Ng5! getting ready to sacrifice on e6. For example, 10...c5 (10...Nd5 11 Qh5 is unpleasant, while 10...0-0? allows 11 Nxe6!) 11 Bxe6 fxe6 12 Nxe6! Kf7 13 Nxc5 when White has three pawns for the piece and a dangerous initiative which makes his position easier to play.

10 a4!

In my opinion this move is absolutely critical.

10...c4

10...b4 lets White strike with 11 d5 bxc3 12 dxe6 Qxd1 13 exf7+ Kd8 14 Rxd1+ (Perez, Mena Crespo) with a chaotic position. My instinct tells me it is perfectly good for White – the f7-pawn is a persistent thorn in Black's side and it will be difficult for Black to coordinate his pieces adequately.

11 Ba2 Qc6

Black should consider 11...Qb6!? 12 Be3 (12 Bf4 Bb4!; or 12 d5 Bc5 13 Be3 0-0 14 Bxc5 Qxc5 15 dxe6 fxe6 16 Rxe6 Nbd7 17 Qe2 Rae8 18 axb5 axb5 and because of the trapped bishop Black has some compensation for the pawn) 12...Qc6 13 Qd2. Here 13...Bb4! is vital, since White was threatening to play d4-d5 followed by Nf3-d4.

11...b4 is just too weakening, and 12 Nb1 Bd5 13 Nbd2 Qc7 14 Ne5 Nc6 15 Ndxc4 wins a pawn.

12 Bg5

12 Re5 aims to win a pawn in an optically unusual way. After 12...Bd6 13 axb5 axb5 14 Rxb5 the rook is in danger of getting trapped, but 14...0-0 (14...Nd5 15 Rb1 indirectly protects the rook and threatens 16 Bxc4) 15 Bd2 Nbd7 16 Bxc4 Ba6 17 Bd3 Bxb5 18 Nxb5, with two pawns for the exchange, is better for White.

12...Nbd7 13 Qe2 Bb4! (Diagram 12)

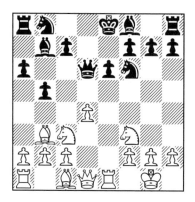

Diagram 11 (B)

Threatening d4-d5

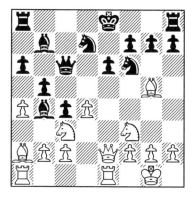

Diagram 12 (W)

...Bb4 is the key move

Again this move is important. Black threatens to lock out the white bishop on a2 with ...Bxc3.

14 Bd2 Nb6 15 axb5 axb5 16 Qe5 Bxc3 17 Bxc3 0-0 18 Bb4 Rfe8

Black is better now, as White has no compensation for the locked-out bishop.

19 c3?

Voluntarily making the bishop on b4 bad is not a good strategy!

19 Bd2 would be met by 19...Nbd7 followed by doubling the rooks on the a-file.

19...Nfd5 20 Ba3 Nxc3! 21 Bb1 Nxb1 22 Raxb1 Nd7 23 Qg3 Qb6 24 Ne5 Nxe5 25 Bc5 Nf3+ 26 gxf3 Qc6 27 Re3 Rad8

Black is a good pawn up. Furthermore, the presence of opposite-coloured bishops makes life harder for White as he cannot defend on the light squares.

28 Rbe1 Rd5 29 Re4 Rf5 30 R1e3 Qa6 31 Rg4 Qa1+ 32 Kg2 g6 33 Qc7 Bd5 34 Qd7 Ra8 35 Qxb5 Qd1 36 Rg3 h5 37 Kh3 Qf1+ 38 Kh4 Qxf2 0-1

Other Sixth Moves for White

1 e4 d5 2 exd5 Qxd5 3 Nc3 Qd6 4 d4 Nf6 5 Nf3 a6

As well as 6 g3, 6 Ne5 and 6 Bc4, White has some further alternatives which we shall look at in this section:

a) During the 1998 Elista Chess Olympiad the late GM Tony Miles told me that, after having seen some of my opening positions, he had decided to look at this "dodgy" 3...Qd6 variation but had dismissed it after 6 Bg5 **(Diagram 13)**.

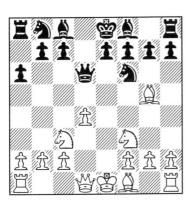
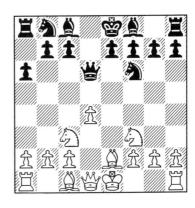

Diagram 13 (B)

A dangerous try

Diagram 14 (B)

Toothless

Black, he declared, had too many weaknesses. In 1998, 3...Qd6 was still in its infancy, but Tony was right about one thing: 6 Bg5 can be very dangerous. So what are White's objectives? Well, firstly he intends to make it difficult for Black to develop the dark-squared bishop on f8, by doubling the f-pawns and then castling queenside. White also still has the aim of playing Nf3-e5 and securing extra space (see Game 37).

b) 6 Be3 was the traditional main line, and probably the move which most players will think up over the board if they don't know the theory. White wishes to push back Black's queen by playing Qd2 and Bf4, obtaining a firm grip on the e5-square and targeting the slightly vulnerable c7 point (see Game 38).

c) 6 Bd3 is an anti-b5/Bb7 move. It also fits in with the idea of controlling the all-important e4-square. The downside is that White leaves d4 a little bit untended (see Game 39).

d) 6 h3 shows that White is worried about Black developing the bishop to g4. However, this precautionary move doesn't cause any trouble. 6...Bf5 and ...e6 is more than satisfactory for Black, but 6...Nc6 intending ...0-0-0 is an exciting option. For example, 7 Be2 Bf5 8 a3 0-0-0 (8...e6 is also perfectly reasonable) 9 Be3 and Black is ideally poised for the central break 9...e5!.

e) The bishop is rather passive after 6 Be2 **(Diagram 14)**. Against this, 6...Bf5 is simple and good enough. For example, 7 0-0 e6 8 Be3 Nc6 9 Nh4 Bg6 10 Bf3 0-0-0 11 Nxg6 hxg6 12 g3 Nxd4 and Black has won a pawn, S.Battesti-C.Bauer, Ajaccio 2007. 6...b5 is not so good, as White can challenge the light-squared bishop with 7 Ne5 followed by 8 Bf3.

Game 37
□ B.Grabarczyk ■ M.Dziuba
Lubniewice 2002

---

1 e4 d5 2 exd5 Qxd5 3 Nc3 Qd6 4 d4 Nf6 5 Nf3 a6 6 Bg5 Nbd7

A very important move – as well as the e4-square, Black should maintain close control of e5.

6...Bg4 is also reasonable, and after 7 Be2 Nbd7 8 Qd2 e6 9 0-0 Be7 10 Rfe1 0-0 11 Ne5 Bxe2 12 Rxe2 Rad8 Black was equal in A.Pornariyasombat-A.Escobar Forero, Dresden Olympiad 2008.

 NOTE: I think that 6...b5 is unwise, and 7 Bd3 Bb7 8 Qe2! is the ideal piece placement for White, keeping a firm grip on e4 and e5. 8...Nbd7 9 a4! b4 10 Ne4 Nxe4 11 Bxe4 Bxe4 12 Qxe4 c6 13 0-0 e6 14 c4 highlighted a major problem for Black in A.Dgebuadze-O.Eismont, German League: his queenside pawn structure is incredibly weak.

7 Qd2

Normal developing moves such as 7 Bd3 should be met by 7...c5!. For example, 8 d5 Nb6! 9 Qe2 (White sacrifices a pawn in order to open lines, but Black's position is sound) 9...Nfxd5 (9...Nbxd5? 10 Nxd5 Qxd5 should be met by 11 0-0-0! as 11...Qxa2 fails to 12 Bxf6 gxf6 13 Bb5+! winning) 10 Nxd5 Qxd5 (Black aims to prevent White from accelerating his development by castling queenside) 11 Be4 (after 11 c4 Qe6 12 Be3 Nd7 13 Ng5 Qb6 14 0-0 g6 Black should be fine, although White does have some pressure for the pawn) 11...Qc4 12 Qe3 Nd5 13 Bxd5 Qxd5 14 0-0 f6 15 Rad1 Qc6 16 Bf4 was S.Rublevsky-L.Gofshtein, Mainz (rapid) 2001. Black's position should be fine as long as he removes some minor pieces from the board, which is why he played 16...Bg4!.

7...b5 (Diagram 15)

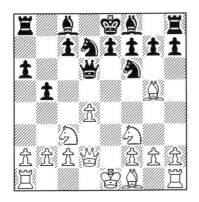

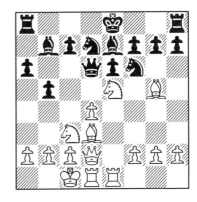

Diagram 15 (W)	Diagram 16 (B)
Black chooses Set-up A	...b4 or not ...b4?

No anti-b5 measures have been taken, so it's Set-up A in operation!

8 0-0-0!

The most logical continuation, and the most dangerous too.

8 Qf4 e6 9 Be2 Bb7 10 0-0 h6 11 Qxd6 Bxd6 12 Be3 doesn't pose Black any problems (C.Parligras-R.Hasangatin, Stare Mesto 2006), and neither does 8 Bf4 Qb6 9 Be2 Bb7 10 0-0 e6 11 Ne5 Rd8 12 Qe3 c5 13 dxc5 Bxc5 14 Qg3 Nxe5 15 Bxe5 Bd6 16 Rad1 Bxe5 17 Rxd8+ (S.Wagman-N.Sulava, Imperia 2002) when 17...Ke7! would have given Black a perfectly good position. Finally, 8 Bd3 Bb7 9 Qe2 is inconsistent. White changes plans but this simply helps Black, and 9...e6 10 0-0-0 Be7 11 Rhe1 Nd5 12 Ne4 Bxg5+ 13 Nfxg5 Qe7 14 Qd2 h6 15 Nf3 Nb4 was fine for him in E.Van den Doel-B.Kurajica, Bugojno 1999.

8...Bb7 9 Bd3 e6 10 Rhe1 Be7 11 Ne5 (Diagram 16) 11...b4!?

I am a little sceptical of this move, as it allows White to control the c5-square, and ...c5 may be one of the ways for Black to open lines against White's king.

The immediate 11...c5 allows 12 Nxd7 Qxd7 13 dxc5 when it's not so easy for Black to recover the pawn. However, I like 11...Rd8!. For example, 12 Bf4 Qb6 13 f3 0-0 14 g4 Nxe5 15 dxe5 Nd5; or 12 Qe3 c5 13 dxc5 Qxe5! 14 Qxe5 Nxe5 15 Rxe5 h6

16 Bxf6 Bxf6 17 Ree1 Bxg2 18 Be4 Bxc3 – in either case Black is fine.

12 Na4 Bd5? (Diagram 17)

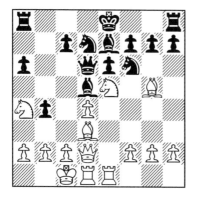

Diagram 17 (W)
The knight wants d5

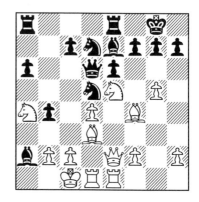

Diagram 18 (W)
White to play and win

 TIP: In lines where White plays Ne5 aiming for Bf4 it is very important for Black to remember to leave the d5-square vacant so that a knight can go there!

12...0-0 is much stronger, although even here I think White retains the better chances as it is not so easy for Black to orchestrate a pawn break or find a satisfactory way to coordinate his pieces for some kind of counter-attack: 13 g4 a5 14 h4 Rad8 15 h5 Bc6 16 Nxc6 Qxc6 17 b3 Nb6 with a very complicated position.

13 Qe2 Bc6

Unfortunately for Black, 13...0-0 looks rather dangerous. White can play 14 Bf4! threatening Ng6 and g2-g4-g5. For example, 14...Rfe8 15 g4! Bxa2? 16 g5 Nd5 **(Diagram 18)** and now White has the stunning and decisive 17 Bxh7+!! Kxh7 18 Qh5+ Kg8 19 Qxf7+.

14 Bxf6 Nxf6 15 Nc5 Bd5 16 g4 g6 17 h4 Qb6 18 g5 Nh5 19 Ned7?

White is too eager. The more restrained 19 Be4 would have swung the game in White's favour. After 19...Bxe4 20 Qxe4 Rd8 21 Qf3 Black has problems defending the f7-pawn, since 21...0-0 22 Ncd7 picks up the exchange.

19...Qd6 20 Qe3 Qf4!

Now the queens will be exchanged and the immediate pressure is off.

21 Kb1 a5 22 Qe5 Qxe5 23 Nxe5 Nf4 24 Bb5+ Kf8 25 Bc6 Bxc6 26 Nxc6 h6! 27 Ne4 Ra6

White is being pushed back so he seizes the opportunity to force a repetition of moves.

28 Nb8 Ra8 29 Nc6 Ra6 30 Nb8 Ra8 31 Nc6 ½-½

Game 38
□ **J.Sanchez** ■ **J.Hernando Rodrigo**
Madrid 2003

---

1 e4 d5 2 exd5 Qxd5 3 Nc3 Qd6 4 d4 Nf6 5 Nf3 a6 6 Be3 (Diagram 19)

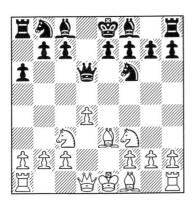
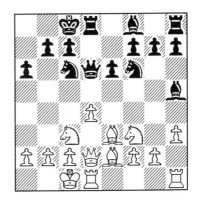

Diagram 19 (B)	**Diagram 20 (W)**
The old main line	Awkward for White

6...b5

6...Nc6 7 Qd2 Bg4 is another popular continuation. Now:

a) 8 Be2 e6 9 h3 Bh5 10 0-0-0 0-0-0 **(Diagram 20)** is logical play from both sides but now comes the tricky part – how to continue? This is particularly awkward for White as he doesn't yet have full control of the e5-square and the d4-d5 pawn break is no longer possible:

a1) To some extent 11 g4 is the natural plan, but 11...Bg6 12 Bf4 Qd7 13 Ne5 Nxe5 14 dxe5 doesn't really promise much.

a2) In S.Grigoriants-L.Galego, Warsaw 2005, White tried to resolve matters through the tactical 11 Ne5, but 11...Bg6 12 h4 Nxe5 13 dxe5 Qxd2+ 14 Rxd2 Rxd2 15 Bxd2 Ne4 was completely level and 11...Bxe2 12 Nxe2 Nxe5 13 dxe5 Qxd2+ 14 Rxd2 Nd5 is also more than okay for Black.

b) 8 Ng5 deals with Black's threat of ...Bxf3, and now:

b1) After 8...Bf5 the battle for control of the e4-square commences: 9 Bc4 e6 10 f3

Be7 11 Nge4 Qb4 12 Bb3 0-0-0 13 a3 Qa5 14 0-0-0 with a slightly better position for White.

b2) 8...e5?! 9 d5 Nb4 10 f3 Bf5 11 Nge4 was better for White in A.Karpov-A.Lutikov, Moscow 1979 – this was the game that ignited the interest in 6 Be3!

b3) 8...e6 is more solid, and 9 f3 Bf5 10 Nge4 Qd7 11 Nxf6+ gxf6 12 Ne4 Be7 13 0-0-0 was at least equal for Black in G.Matjushin-V.Ivannikov, St Petersburg 2000 – as we have seen previously the doubled f-pawns are not a significant problem.

6...Bg4? is a mistake as White has not yet developed his light-squared bishop. This allows him to continue 7 h3 Bh5 8 g4 Bg6 9 Ne5 e6 10 Bg2. This is a key point – White's ability to develop the bishop here makes the position unpleasant for Black. This bishop gets to rule the roost on the long diagonal, and 10...c6 11 h4, as played in S.Zhigalko-T.Novosel, Sibenik 2007, sees White utilizing his advanced kingside pawns.

7 Bd3! (Diagram 21)

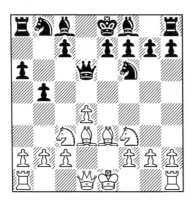

Diagram 21 (B)

To control e4

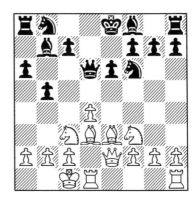

Diagram 22 (B)

Development is best

The best move – White should be aiming to occupy the e4-square, preferably with a knight.

Why is this so important? Well, Black's strength is his bishop sitting powerfully on b7, and White wishes to turn Black's strength against him. By blocking the diagonal, he blunts this bishop and controls the c5-square. Crucially, Back cannot easily exchange the minor pieces, as this would expose some of the holes on the queenside.

7...Bb7 8 Qe2!

8 Qd2 aims to chase the black queen from d6, but I don't think this is as dangerous: White will lose a tempo with Bf4, and b6 isn't necessarily a bad square for the

queen. For example, 8...e6 9 0-0-0 Nbd7 10 Rhe1 Be7 11 Bf4 Qb6. White's plan is based on occupying the e5-square and beginning a kingside pawn attack, but Black has a ready-made attack against the white king. J.Gombac-D.Sermek, Nova Gorica 2007, continued 12 Ne5 Rd8 13 Qe2 and now simplest for Black is 13...0-0! intending 14 Ne4 Nxe4 15 Bxe4 Bxe4 16 Qxe4 Nf6. White must deal with the threat to the d4-pawn and Black's plan is to double on the d-file and strike with ...c7-c5.

There is something to be said for playing it simple with 8 0-0 e6 9 Nd2 aiming to control the e4-square. After 9...Nbd7 10 Nde4 Qc6 11 f3 White is slightly better: he has control of e4 and enough space to begin gradually building up his position.

8...e6

8...Nbd7 9 0-0-0 Nb6 10 Bg5 b4 11 Ne4 Nxe4 12 Bxe4 Bxe4 13 Qxe4 Qd5 14 Qxd5 Nxd5 was a quick draw in D.Baramidze-D.Sermek, Portoroz 2005 – Black equalized easily here.

9 0-0-0 (Diagram 22) 9...Be7

9...b4?! is tempting, but it's premature to release some of the potential on the queenside. 10 Nb1 Nbd7 11 Nbd2 Nb6 12 Nb3 Qd5 13 Kb1 Qh5 14 Rhg1 Na4 15 g4 Qd5 16 Ne5 left White with a clear advantage in A.Morozevich-B.Kurajica, Bled Olympiad 2002, unsurprisingly so given that Black has played too many moves with one piece.

Black must be wary of playing the position too aggressively without having completed his development. White hasn't made any positional concessions and enjoys the natural advantage of the first move, so Black must aim to suppress White's initiative and only then commence a counter-attack.

10 Ng5!?

White reasons that the f3-knight will be better placed to help the kingside attack on e4. On that square it pushes Black back a little bit, discourages the ...c5 pawn-break and at the same time supports the kingside pawn storm.

10 Ne5!? followed by Rh1-g1 and g2-g4-g5 is another standard attacking idea. The downside to this move is that the counter-strike ...c7-c5 will be much more effective than usual. For example, 10...0-0 11 Rhg1 (11 Bf4 Qb6 12 h4 Nbd7 13 h5 c5 14 dxc5 Nxc5 15 h6 g6 with a very double-edged position; or 11 f4 Nbd7 12 Rhg1 b4 13 Na4 Qd5 14 Kb1 Qa5 15 b3 Nxe5 16 dxe5 Nd5 when White must play with caution as Black is threatening ...Bc6) 11...b4 (now that Black has developed he can consider beginning a counter-attack) 12 Na4 Nbd7 13 Bf4 Nd5 14 Bg3 Nxe5 15 Bxe5 Qc6 with equal chances.

10...Nbd7

After 10...0-0 11 Nge4 Nxe4 12 Nxe4 Qc6 13 h4 Nd7 14 h5 f5 15 Ng5 h6 16 Nf3 Qd6 (depriving White's bishop of the f4-square; Black should avoid 16...Bd6 because of 17 d5!! Qxd5 18 c4 and the e-pawn will fall) 17 Kb1 Bd5 **(Diagram 23)** I like Black's position: his pieces are beginning to form some cohesion and although the e6/f5 pawn formation looks ugly it is actually difficult for White to make immediate use of the e5-square.

 WARNING: You should never open lines against your king without a very good reason – so don't even consider 10...Bxg2!

11 h4 Nb6 12 Rhe1 h6 13 Nge4 Nxe4 14 Nxe4 Qd5 15 Kb1 (Diagram 24) 15...Nc4?

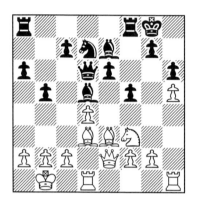

Diagram 23 (W)

Black is well coordinated

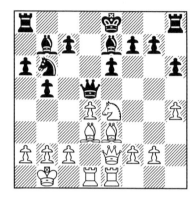

Diagram 24 (B)

Black goes astray

This move doesn't seem to achieve anything, as the black knight really belongs on d5. After 15...0-0 16 Nc3 Qd7 17 Qg4 f5 18 Qg3 Bd6 19 Bf4 Bxf4 20 Qxf4 b4 21 Ne2 Nd5 the knight has finally arrived at its dream destination and all is in order for Black.

16 Bc1 Nd6?

16...0-0 is stronger, although 17 Nc3 Qd6 18 d5 is unpleasant for Black. The queen is cut off from the kingside and White's pieces are perfectly poised in the centre.

17 Qg4 Kf8 18 f3 b4 19 Nc5 Bf6 20 Be4 Nxe4 21 fxe4 Qc6 22 Rf1

Black's position is dire, and he collapses immediately.

22...Kg8? 23 Rxf6 1-0

Game 39
□ **S.B.Hansen** ■ **Wong Meng Kong**
Calvia Olympiad 2004

---

1 e4 d5 2 exd5 Qxd5 3 Nc3 Qd6 4 d4 Nf6 5 Nf3 a6 6 Bd3 Bg4! (Diagram 25)

It is very tricky for White to extricate himself from the pin. The standard freeing manoeuvre h2-h3 and g2-g4 has lost its effectiveness because when the black bishop is chased back to g6 it can simply exchange itself for its counterpart on d3.

6...b5?! would be a mistake in view of 7 a4 b4 8 Ne4.

7 0-0

The immediate 7 Ne4 was played in M.Kobalija-V.Gashimov, Internet (blitz) 2005. After 7...Nxe4 8 Bxe4 Nc6 9 c3 f5 10 Bc2 the time was right for 10...e5, and following 11 dxe5 Qxd1+ 12 Bxd1 0-0-0 13 Bg5 Re8 14 0-0 Bxf3 15 Bxf3 Nxe5 16 Be2 the strong knight on e5 neutralized White's advantage of the two bishops.

7...Nc6

7...e6 is dubious, as 8 Ne4! Nxe4 9 Bxe4 Nc6 10 Re1 0-0-0 11 c3 is better for White.

8 Ne4 Nxe4 9 Bxe4 0-0-0 (Diagram 26)

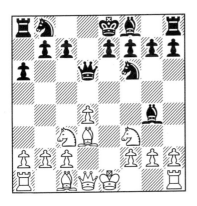

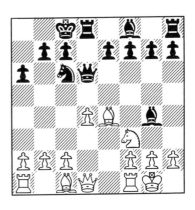

Diagram 25 (W)

...Bg4 is effective here

Diagram 26 (W)

A dynamic choice for Black

9...e6 10 c3 Be7 (10...f5 is better) leaves Black in difficulties. His position is very solid, but the problem is that it is difficult for him to orchestrate a pawn break. As the saying goes, "you cannot win a game without pushing your pawns". 11 Qc2 h6 12 Re1 intending Ne5 is unpleasant for Black, while 11 Qb3!? sets a trap: the natural response 11...Rb8?? loses to 12 Bxc6+ Qxc6 13 Ne5.

9...g6 10 c3 Bg7 11 Qb3 Rb8 12 Bg5 0-0 13 Rfe1 is also very comfortable for White, M.Kobalija-R.Hasangatin, Abu Dhabi 2004.

10 c3

10 Bxc6 Qxc6 11 Ne5 Bxd1 12 Nxc6 bxc6 13 Rxd1 e6 is only a touch better for White because Black can eliminate his doubled c-pawns very easily with ...c6-c5.

10...f5! 11 Bc2 Qd5?

This leads to a forced sequence of moves that gives White the advantage.

11...g6! had to be played. Then 12 h3 (12 b4 is met by the central strike 12...e5) 12...Bh5 13 Qd3 e5 14 Ng5 Rd7 15 Bb3 exd4 16 Be6 (16 Nf7? loses to 16...Rxf7 17 Bxf7 Ne5) 16...Bg7 17 Bxd7+ Qxd7 **(Diagram 27)** reaches a very complicated position, but Black doesn't stand worse: his pieces are active and the white knight on g5 is very awkwardly placed.

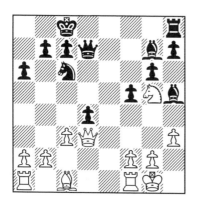

Diagram 27 (W)

A promising exchange sacrifice

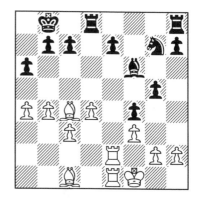

Diagram 28 (W)

White is in total control

12 Bb3 Bxf3 13 Bxd5 Bxd1 14 Be6+ Kb8 15 Rxd1 g6 16 Re1

White's advantage is almost overwhelming: he has a dominating pair of bishops, control of the open files and extra space.

16...Bg7 17 b4

Sune plays the endgame instructively, grabbing space for his army all over the board.

17...Bf6 18 a4 Na7 19 Ra3 Nc8 20 Kf1 Nd6 21 f3 Ne8 22 Ra2 Ng7 23 Bc4 g5 24 Rae2

The secret to playing these positions is to use all parts of the board, pushing and prodding for weaknesses.

24...f4? (Diagram 28)

Another concession – now the light-squared bishop can roam free.

25 Kf2 Nf5 26 Bd3 Nd6 27 Bc2 b5 28 Bb3 c6 29 Re6 Kc7 30 g3!

Opening up the position further.

30...fxg3+ 31 hxg3 h5 32 Kg2 Rh7 33 Bc2 Rg7 34 Rh1 Rh8 35 g4 Kd7 36 Re2 h4 37 Rhe1 Ra8 38 a5 Rh8 39 Kh3!

Now all that is left is to secure f3-f4.

39...Kd8 40 Re6 Kd7 41 f4 Ne8 42 Bf5 Kc7 43 Be4 Nd6 44 fxg5 Rxg5

Black sacrifices an exchange to gain some activity, but the position is beyond salvation. 44...Bxg5 45 Bxg5 Rxg5 46 Rxe7+ is hopeless too.

45 Bxg5 Bxg5 46 Bg2 Kd7 47 R6e5 Nf7 48 Rc5 Bd2 49 Rf1 Ng5+ 50 Kh2 Rh6 51 Rcf5 Rg6 52 d5 e6 53 dxe6+ Nxe6 54 Rf7+

54 Rd1 would have won a piece, but I am guessing that both sides were in time trouble.

54...Ke8 55 R7f5 Nd8 56 Rf6 Rxf6 57 Rxf6 Bxc3 58 Bxc6+ Ke7 59 Rg6 Bxb4 60 Bd5 Bxa5 61 Rxa6 Bd2 62 Kh3 Bg5 63 Rg6 Bf6 64 g5 Bc3 65 Kxh4 Nf7 66 Bxf7 Kxf7 67 Rb6 b4 68 Kh5 Bd2 69 Rb7+ Kf8 70 Kg6 Bc3 71 Kh7 1-0

Summary

In this chapter we have looked at alternatives to 6 g3 after 5 Nf3 a6. We have seen that 6 Ne5 has been successfully neutralized by 6...Nc6!, and Black experienced few problems in Games 34 and 35.

Of all the continuations in this chapter, 6 Bc4 (see Game 36) is the most dangerous primarily because White rapidly targets the vulnerable f7/e6 points. 6...b5 is the critical reaction, and Black must control the d5-square in order to arrange a quick ...c7-c5. The downside to 6...b5 is that White can and should undermine the queenside with a2-a4.

6 Bg5 (see Game 37) is another important continuation. Black must first protect the critical e5-square and then utilize Set-up A (...b7-b5). If play becomes sharp Black must remember to keep the d5-square available for the knight, to meet Bf4 with ...Nd5.

Other lines for White are not threatening, as long as Black abides by the following rule: if White reinforces the e4-square (for example with 6 Bd3 preparing Ne4! to take control of the a8-h1 diagonal) then Black should adopt Set-up B; but if no steps are taken to control this diagonal, Set-up A is the optimal one for Black.

Chapter Nine

3...Qd6: Fifth Move Alternatives

- 5 Nf3: Black Plays 5...c6
- Fifth Move Alternatives for White

5 Nf3: Black Plays 5...c6

1 e4 d5 2 exd5 Qxd5 3 Nc3 Qd6 4 d4 Nf6 5 Nf3 c6 (Diagram 1)

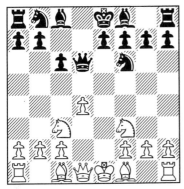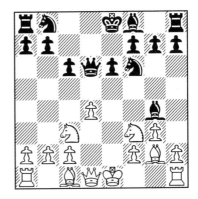

Diagram 1 (W)

Black plays 5...c6

Diagram 2 (W)

Kingside or queenside castling?

As I mentioned in Chapter Seven, in the introduction to 3...Qd6, White must react in an aggressive manner against 5...c6 otherwise Black could easily reach a comfortable position with ...Bf5 or ...Bg4 followed by typical Scandinavian development.

The first thing to notice is that by playing ...c7-c6 Black has taken the c6-square away from the b8-knight. This means that White can and should play:

6 Ne5!

 NOTE: A fundamental difference between 5...c6 and 5...a6 is that after 5...a6 6 Ne5 Black can neutralize the knight jump with 6...Nc6!, whereas after 5...c6 he no longer has this option.

Recently Black has been experimenting with delaying the development of the king's knight, by playing 4...c6 5 Nf3 Bg4, in order to resolve this issue of Ne5. This line is covered in Game 43.

Here are two alternatives to 6 Ne5:

a) 6 g3!? is a quieter variation, but White still aims to push back the black queen. Play continues 6...Bg4 7 Bg2 e6 **(Diagram 2)** and now:

a1) After 8 0-0 Be7 9 h3 Bxf3 10 Bxf3 0-0 11 Bf4 Qd8 Black is happy to play with less space, relying on his technical skills to outplay the opponent in the middlegame and endgame stages. B.Socko-S.Tiviakov, German League 2008, continued

12 Qd3 Nbd7 13 Ne2 Re8 14 Rfd1 Bf8 15 Bg2 Qc8 16 c4 e5 and Black's piece activity compensated for White's bishop pair.

a2) 8 Bf4 Qd8 9 Qd2 is a more accurate move order, as White can now put his space advantage on the kingside to good use: 9...Bxf3 10 Bxf3 Bd6! (exchanging bishops is critical to Black's plan) 11 0-0-0 Bxf4 12 Qxf4 Na6 13 Ne4! (now it's just a case of bishop vs knight) 13...Nxe4 14 Bxe4 Nb4 15 Kb1 Nd5 16 Qd2 Nf6 17 Bf3 Qc7 18 Rhe1 0-0-0 19 h4 led to a pleasant space advantage for White in W.Spoelman-S.Tiviakov, Liverpool 2008.

b) 6 Bd3 is a move which shouldn't worry Black, but he should be aware of the following trick: 6...Bg4 7 h3!? Bxf3 8 Qxf3 Qxd4 (the natural follow up, but a risky one) 9 Be3 Qb4 10 a3 Qxb2? (10...Qa5 with an unclear position was called for) 11 Kd2! and White wins, G.Salem-H.Aryanejad, Abu Dhabi 2003.

6...Nbd7! (Diagram 3)

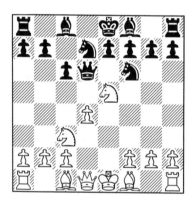

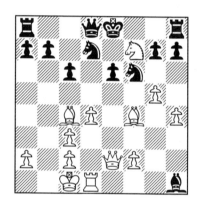

Diagram 3 (W)	**Diagram 4 (W)**
Challenging the knight	A crushing attack

 NOTE: Black again follows our little rule: when a knight lands on e5, challenge it as soon as you can!

White managed to achieve a very easy advantage after 6...Be6 7 Bf4 Qd8 8 Be2 Nbd7 9 0-0 g6 10 Nxd7 Qxd7 11 Be5 Bg7 12 Ne4 Bd5 13 Nc5 Qc8 14 c4 Be6 15 Qb3 b6 16 Nxe6 Qxe6 17 Bf3 in I.Nataf-K.Pytel, Aubervilliers 2001.

6...Bf5 is a very risky move, as the bishop may become a target: 7 Bc4 (7 Bf4 is a promising alternative) 7...e6 8 Bf4 Qd8?! (8...Nbd7 is a better option, as 9 Ng6? fails to 9...Qb4) 9 g4! Bg6 10 h4 Nbd7 11 Qe2 Bb4 12 0-0-0 Bxc3 13 bxc3 Be4 14 g5! Bxh1 15 Nxf7! **(Diagram 4)** and White soon won in R.Schuermans-K.Pytel, Le Touquet 2006.

Returning to 6...Nbd7, there are two main options for White and both aim to exploit the vulnerable position of the black queen: 7 Bf4 is covered in Game 40, and 7 Nc4 in Game 41. Finally, there's the relatively new idea of 7 f4, which is the subject of Game 42.

Game 40
☐ **K.Szabo** ■ **L.Kernazhitsky**
Zalakarosi 2008

---

1 e4 d5 2 exd5 Qxd5 3 Nc3 Qd6 4 d4 Nf6 5 Nf3 c6 6 Ne5! Nbd7! 7 Bf4 Nd5!? (Diagram 5)

Diagram 5 (W)

Offering further exchanges

Diagram 6 (B)

The most challenging

Black cannot solve his opening problems by exchanging on e5: 7...Nxe5 8 Bxe5 (8 dxe5 is also good) 8...Qd8 9 Bc4 Bg4 10 f3 Bf5 11 g4! (this is the whole point – Black will really struggle with his lack of space on the kingside) 11...Bg6 12 Qe2 e6 13 0-0-0 with a clear plus for White, B.Grabarczyk-H.Alber, Offenbach 2005.

8 Nxd5

After 8 Bg3 Nxe5 9 Bxe5 Nxc3 10 bxc3 Black should play 10...Qg6! reaching a good position, rather than 10...Qa3 11 Qd2 when White should be prepared to sacrifice the a-pawn in order to further his attack.

8...Qxd5

8...Nxe5 was tried by Sergei Tiviakov, but without success: 9 Ne3! Nd3+ 10 Qxd3 Qxf4 11 d5! (Black has the advantage of the bishop pair, so White should strike before Black can consolidate) 11...Qb4+ (11...cxd5? 12 Qxd5 e6 13 Bb5+ was absolutely foul for Black in V.Gashimov-S.Tiviakov, Reggio Emilia 2008, but this check

189

looks playable) 12 c3 Qxb2 13 Rd1 Qb5 (13...Bd7? is bad because after 14 Nc4 Qxa2 15 Ne5! it's very difficult for Black to meet the attack on the bishop satisfactorily; while 13...Qb6 looks risky, and here 14 Be2 g6 15 dxc6 bxc6 16 Nd5! is very strong) 14 Qxb5 cxb5 15 Bxb5+ Bd7 16 Bxd7+ Kxd7 17 Rb1 b6 and Black's chances are not worse in the endgame.

9 Be2!? (Diagram 6)

White must sacrifice material in order to maintain his initiative.

9 Nf3 Nb6! makes it difficult for White to play c2-c4 and looks perfectly fine for Black. For example, 10 Be2 Bf5 11 c3 (11 0-0? Qe4 wins a pawn) 11...e6 12 0-0 Be7 13 Re1 0-0 14 Ne5 Rac8 15 a4 Qd8 16 a5 Nd5 17 Bg3 Bg5, X.Vila Gazquez-S.Tiviakov, Benidorm 2008. Black has been making excellent use of the space available to him. The resulting position is very much a game of cat and mouse, with both sides patiently improving their pieces and trying to control the d-file.

The easiest way to equalize against 9 Qd3 is 9...g5. Here 10 Bg3 Nxe5 11 dxe5 was agreed drawn in E.Inarkiev-A.Dreev, Ermioni 2006.

9...Nxe5 10 Bxe5

10 dxe5 doesn't seem to give White too much for the pawn: 10...Qxg2 11 Bf3 Qh3 12 Qe2 g6 13 0-0-0 Bh6 14 Bxh6 Qxh6+ 15 Kb1 Bh3 16 Bg4 e6 17 Bxh3 Qxh3 18 Rd3 Qg2 19 Re1 (M.Llaneza Vega-M.Calzetta, Pamplona 2007), and here Black should play 19...0-0 when White doesn't have enough compensation.

10...Qxg2! (Diagram 7)

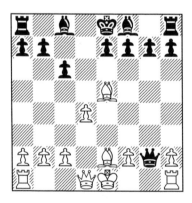 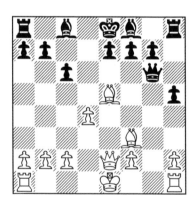

Diagram 7 (W)	**Diagram 8 (W)**
Black grabs the offer	Aiming for ...Bg4

Of course Black must rise to the bait.

11 Bf3 Qg6

The only real move for Black, who can exploit a tactical possibility after 12 d5.

11...Qh3 is weaker, and after 12 d5 cxd5 13 Qxd5 f6 (13...Qe6 fails to 14 Qxe6! and Black must return the pawn since 14...fxe6 loses to 15 Bh5+) White has the devastating 14 Bxf6!! blowing open the position. White is winning here: 14...exf6 15 0-0-0 Be7 16 Rhe1 Bd7 17 Rd3 Bc6 18 Rxe7+ Kxe7 19 Re3+ Kf8 20 Qc5+ Kf7 21 Bd5+; 14...Qe6+ 15 Qxe6 Bxe6 16 Bxb7 Rb8 17 Bc6+; or 14...gxf6 15 Bh5+.

12 Qe2!

12 d5 strives to open up the position, but this allows Black to liquidate some pieces. The ensuing position is still very complex but I don't think it is worse for Black. V.Anand-S.Tiviakov, Wijk aan Zee 2006, continued 12...Bg4! (this is Sergei Tiviakov's point! – it is very important to exchange off a pair of bishops and relieve some of the pressure) 13 dxc6 bxc6 14 Qe2 Bxf3 15 Qxf3 Rd8 16 Rd1 Qe6 (Black is not in a hurry to return the material in order to simplify the position; after 16...Rxd1+!? 17 Kxd1 Qe6 18 Re1 Qd5+ 19 Qxd5 cxd5 20 Bd4 a6 21 Re3 e6 22 Rb3 Bd6 23 Rb6 Kd7 the chances should be about equal) 17 0-0 Rxd1 18 Rxd1 h5! 19 Qd3 Qc8. The black king is quite safe in the middle, and the rook comes into play via h6 – the point of 18...h5.

12...h5 (Diagram 8)

Trying to exchange those light-squared bishops.

If 12...Bf5 13 0-0-0! Rd8 14 Kb1 White continues to have an incredible amount of play for the pawn: the open g- and e-files provide avenues down which to attack; Black's development is lagging; and to make matters worse, Black's queenside pawns are vulnerable to a double attack.

12...Qe6 doesn't work on account of 13 d5 cxd5 14 0-0-0 f6 and now not 15 Rxd5? which allowed Black to wriggle out in S.Ivanets-I.Smirnov, Ilyichevsk 2007, but 15 Bxd5! Qxe5 16 Qc4 e6 17 Rhe1 when Black must give back his material.

13 h3

13 0-0-0?!, as played in F.Caruana-D.Milanovic, Budva 2009, simply allows Black to achieve his objective with 13...Bg4!.

13...f6!

Things are very dangerous for Black, so he must proceed with great care.

13...Qh6 prevents White from castling, but 14 d5! tears Black's position apart. After 14...Bd7 15 Rg1! Rc8 16 Rd1 cxd5 17 Bxd5 f6 18 Bh2 White's active pieces provide him with strong compensation.

An attempt to solidify with 13...e6 doesn't work either, as White plays 14 d5! cxd5 15 Bxd5 and Black will be struggling for a long time.

14 Bh2! (Diagram 9)

14 Bc7 was played recently in a rapidplay match between Sophie Milliet and Alexandra Kosteniuk (Corsica 2009). Black played 14...Qf7 guarding d5, and now:

a) Milliet blundered with 15 0-0-0? and the game ended 15...Qxa2! 16 d5 (16 Bxh5+ Kd7 17 Bg3 Qa1+ 18 Kd2 Qa5+ wins) 16...g6! 17 dxc6?? allowing 17...Bh6+ 18 Rd2 Qa1 mate.

b) 15 d5! is stronger:

b1) 15...e5 (this leads to a draw) 16 dxc6 Qxc7 17 cxb7 Bxb7 18 Qb5+ Ke7! (keeping on the dark squares to avoid any annoying bishop checks) 19 Bxb7 Rb8 20 Qb4+ Ke6 21 Qb3+ with a perpetual check.

b2) 15...cxd5 is also possible. The natural 16 Qb5+ would be a mistake, as after 16...Bd7 17 Qxb7 Qe6+ 18 Kf1 Bc6 Black emerges with a superior position. 16 0-0-0 is best, when Black's centre looks solid but 16...e6 17 Ba5 Be7 18 Rhe1 still leaves him with problems over his development.

14...Qf7?

Too passive – Black had to play 14...Bxh3!. It's not a case of simple greed; Black really must swap off those light-squared bishops after 15 d5 Bg4!.

15 d5!

This is the basic idea of the whole variation: get developed and then play d4-d5! After this move Black is struggling.

15...Bd7 16 0-0-0 g6 17 Kb1 Bh6 18 Rhg1 Kf8 19 dxc6 Bxc6 20 Bxc6 bxc6 21 Rd7 (Diagram 10)

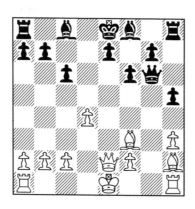

Diagram 9 (B)

A critical moment

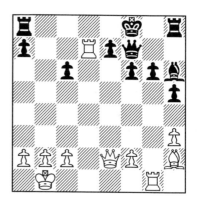

Diagram 10 (B)

White dominates

Completely tying Black down.

21...Re8 22 Rxa7 Qd5 23 Rd1 Qg2 24 Rxe7! Rxe7 25 Bd6 Rhh7 26 Re1

26 Qe6 would have won more easily.

26...Rhf7 27 Bxe7+ Kg7 28 Bc5 Qxh3 29 a4

Black is helpless against the march of the queenside pawns.

29...Qf5 30 b4 Bf4 31 a5 Be5 32 a6 h4 33 Qe4 Qc8 34 Rg1 g5 35 f4 Bxf4 36 Qxf4 Qxa6 37 Qxh4 Rb7 38 Qd4 Kf7 39 Rh1 Qa8 40 Qe4 Kg8 41 Qg6+ 1-0

Game 41
☐ **E.Hossain** ◼ **S.Tiviakov**
Turin Olympiad 2006

---

1 e4 d5 2 exd5 Qxd5 3 Nc3 Qd6 4 d4 Nf6 5 Nf3 c6 6 Ne5 Nbd7 7 Nc4

This is somewhat safer in the sense that White is not gambiting a pawn.

7...Qc7 8 Qf3! (Diagram 11)

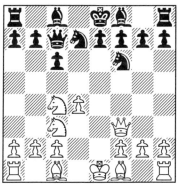 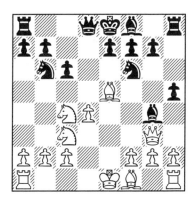

Diagram 11 (B)

Intending Bf4

Diagram 12 (W)

The most ambitious move

Again White aims to push back Black's queen.

8 g3 allows Black an easy game after 8...Nb6 9 Ne5 Be6 10 Bg2 g6 11 Bf4 Qd8 12 Ne2 Bg7 13 0-0 0-0 14 a4 a5; Black has a cramped but solid position.

8...Nb6!

Black must attempt to relieve some of his space worries by exchanging pieces.

9 Bf4 Qd8

9...Qd7 is Sergei Tiviakov's latest try: 10 Nxb6 axb6 11 Be5?! (11 0-0-0! is stronger) 11...Qf5 12 Qxf5 Bxf5 13 0-0-0 Nd7 14 Bc7 e6 15 Bd3 Bxd3 16 Rxd3 b5 and Black has a great position, K.Lahno-S.Tiviakov, Benidorm 2008: all of Black's pieces have excellent potential and his doubled b-pawns, far from being weak, are extremely effective! If White isn't careful, he will find himself saddled with a weak pawn on a2.

10 Be5 Bg4

The only move – Black must play very carefully just in order not to emerge from the opening with a significantly worse position.

At first sight 10...Nbd5 looks logical, but after this move Black cannot really challenge White's control of the e5-square. With the pawn structure fixed, this creates huge problems. For example, 11 Nxd5 cxd5 12 Ne3! e6 13 Bd3 Bd7 14 0-0 Be7 15 Rae1 0-0? (Black gets into even more trouble after this move) 16 Ng4 Nxg4 17 Qxg4 g6 18 Re3 and through a series of natural moves White has built up a very dangerous initiative, J.Emms-A.Ledger, Southend 2006.

11 Qg3 h5 (Diagram 12)

 NOTE: 11...h5 is an ambitious move, and one with significant long-term consequences. From now on Black is committed to active play in order to ensure that the h5-pawn doesn't become a weakness.

11...Be6 12 Nxb6 axb6 13 Bd3 g6 is also possible. Black will try to exchange pieces and make the a2-pawn a target. White will naturally aim to prevent this and try to deprive Black of any productive counterplay.

12 h3

12 f3 was played in A.Grischuk-S.Tiviakov, Sochi 2006, but this is not the best way to kick back the bishop because the white queen becomes a bit cut off on g3. That game continued 12...Be6 13 Ne3 Nbd5 14 Ncxd5 Nxd5 15 Nxd5 Qxd5 16 Bd3 f6 17 Bb8?! (according to Tiviakov, 17 Bc7 is the best) 17...h4! 18 Qc7 Kf7! **(Diagram 13)** 19 Qxb7 c5! 20 Qxd5 Bxd5 21 c4 (otherwise Black will simply capture on d4 winning back the pawn) and here 21...Bb7 22 Bc7 cxd4 23 Ke2 e5 would have led to a double-edged endgame in which Black's chances are by no means worse.

12...h4 13 Qf4 Be6 14 Ne3 Nbd5 15 Nexd5 Nxd5 16 Qd2

16 Nxd5 Qxd5 leaves the queen and dark-squared bishop awkwardly placed, and Black can play à la Grischuk-Tiviakov with a well timed ...f6: 17 Bd3 f6 (17...Qxg2 is impossible because of 18 Be4) 18 Bc7 g5 19 Qe3 Bh6! 20 Qe2 g4!? 21 c4 (intending 21 hxg4 Qxg2!) 21...Qd7 22 hxg4 Bxg4 23 Bg6+ Kf8 24 f3 Qxc7 25 fxg4 Qg3+ and Black has the preferable position.

16...Nxc3

Another new idea from Sergei Tiviakov. Previously 16...Bf5 17 Bd3 Bxd3 18 Qxd3 e6 19 0-0 Ne7 was better for White in N.Kosintseva-I.Nikolaidis, Moscow 2005: the h-pawn is more of a liability than an asset.

17 Qxc3 Bd5 18 Qd2

After 18 0-0-0 e6 19 Kb1 b5 Black has a superbly placed bishop on d5 and his position is extremely solid.

18...e6 19 c4 Be4 20 f3 Bf5 21 a3 Rh5 (Diagram 14)

A rather creative move with some aesthetic appeal. Black wishes to solve his development problems by either exchanging pieces via the g5-square or by kicking back the bishop and using the rook's power along the fourth rank. Chasing away the bishop with 21...f6 22 Bf4 g5 23 Be3 Qc7 followed by queenside castling and exchanging the dark-squared bishops is also perfectly acceptable.

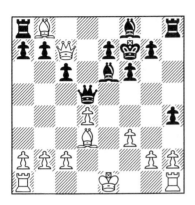

Diagram 13 (W)

Scurrying from the danger

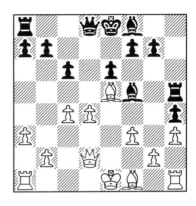

Diagram 14 (W)

An imaginative idea

22 Rd1 Bd6 23 Qe3 f6 24 Bxd6 Qxd6 25 f4 Kf8

25...0-0-0!? was a more logical choice, and after 26 Be2 Rh6 27 0-0 Kb8 the game becomes rather double-edged. Let's look a little bit further: 28 b4 Rg6 29 Rf3 (some defence is needed; 29 b5 cxb5 30 cxb5 Rg3 31 Rf3 g5 would turn the tables on White) 29...Qc7 and the position is level.

26 Be2 Rh6 27 0-0 a5 28 Bd3

Aiming to exchange the light-squared bishops in order to exploit the e6 weakness.

28...Bxd3 29 Qxd3 Rd8 30 Kh1 Rh5!? 31 Qg6 Rf5 32 Qg4 b5!

Undermining the c4/d4 pawn front.

33 c5 Qd7 34 Qxh4 Rd5

The h5-pawn has fallen, but it has not been lost in vain and Black has incredible pressure on d4. White must devote all his strength to defending this pawn, and in effect some kind of deadlock is reached.

35 Qe1 a4 36 Qe4 Kg8 37 Rd3 Kf7 38 Re1 Rh8 39 Ree3 Rh4 40 Rf3 Rf5 41 Rde3 ½-½

Despite the material deficit the position is completely gridlocked, so the players agreed a draw.

Game 42
□ **S.Kudrin** ■ **J.Stopa**
Richardson 2008

1 e4 d5 2 exd5 Qxd5 3 Nc3 Qd6 4 d4 Nf6 5 Nf3 c6 6 Ne5 Nbd7 7 f4!?

This is a relatively new idea developed by Shirov. White's intention is clearly to seize as much space as possible. However, there is a positional downside to this move: there may be some long-term repercussions over the weakness of e4, and White has in effect shut in his own bishop. Of course the game has only just begun so these factors shouldn't bother White for a while at least.

7...Nb6

 WARNING: Black should not abandon his control of e4 without being forced to. 7...Nd5? is premature as it helps White in the battle for space. After 8 Ne4 Qc7 9 c4 the knight simply gets pushed back, and 9...Nxe5 10 fxe5 Nb6 left White with a nice advantage in J.Krivec-K.Novak, Ljubljana 2008.

8 g4 (Diagram 15)

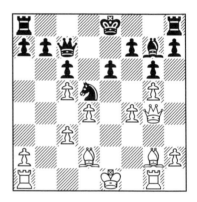

Diagram 15 (B)
Aggressive stuff from White!

Diagram 16 (W)
A superb knight

The slower 8 Be2 shouldn't lead to any problems after 8...g6 9 g4 Bg7 10 g5 Nfd5 11 Ne4 Qd8 12 a3 0-0 13 c4 Nc7 14 Be3 f6, E.Szalanczy-E.Vegh, Budapest 2007.

8...Nbd5

Alternatively:

a) 8...Be6 9 Bg2 g6! 10 0-0 Bg7 11 f5 gxf5 12 gxf5 Bc4 13 Nxc4 Nxc4 and White's attack has run out of steam – all that is left are weaknesses. A.Shirov-S.Tiviakov, Benidorm (rapid) 2008, continued 14 Qd3 Ng4 15 Rf4 (15 Bf4 loses to 15...Qxd4+) 15...Nxb2!! 16 Qg3 Bxd4+ 17 Kh1 and here 17...Bxc3! 18 Qxc3 Rg8 19 Qxb2 Qd1+ 20 Bf1 (20 Rf1 loses to 20...Qxf1+! 21 Bxf1 Nf2 mate) 20...Ne3 leaves White facing the deadly threat of ...Qd5+.

b) 8...g6 9 g5 Nfd5 10 Ne4 Qd8 11 c4 Nc7 12 Qe2 Bg7 13 c5 and Black is forced to give up his knight for two pawns: 13...Ne6 (13...Nbd5 loses to 14 Nd6+ exd6 15 Nxc6+) 14 cxb6 Nxd4 15 Qf2 Bxe5 16 fxe5 Qd5! 17 Bg2 Qc4 18 b3 Qd3 19 Qd2 Nc2+ 20 Kf2 Qxd2+ 21 Bxd2 Nxa1 22 Rxa1 axb6 23 Be3 and White was better in A.Shirov-L.Nisipeanu, Foros 2007.

9 g5 Nxc3 10 bxc3 Qd5 11 Rg1 Nd7 12 Ng4

After 12 Bc4 Qe4+ 13 Qe2 Qxe2+ 14 Kxe2 Nxe5 15 fxe5 Bf5 16 Rb1 b6 Black does not have any problems. His plan should be to consolidate on the kingside with ...e7-e6 followed by opening up the h-file with ...g7-g6 and ...h7-h6.

12...g6 13 c4 Qa5+ 14 Bd2 Qc7 15 c3 Bg7 16 Qe2 Nb6 17 c5

After 17 Ne5 Be6 18 c5 Nd7 Black's position is very compact. Rather like a coiled spring, there remains a lot of tension in the position. For instance, if 19 h4 Nxe5 20 fxe5 b6! and the tables are turning on White.

17...Bxg4 18 Qxg4 Nd5 19 Bg2 e6 (Diagram 16)

Note that White cannot knock back the knight on d5 without weakening his pawn on d4.

20 h4 h5 21 Qf3 0-0 22 Qe4 Ne7 23 Kd1 Rfd8 24 Kc2 Nf5 25 Be1 Rd7 26 Bf2 Ne7 27 Rgb1 b6 28 Rb3 bxc5 29 dxc5 Rad8 30 Be1 Qa5 31 Qb4 Qa6 32 Qe4 Rd5 33 Qe3 Nf5 34 Qf2 Rxc5!

It's all over, since 35 Qxc5 loses on the spot to 35...Qe2+ and Black checkmates.

35 Kb2 Qa5 36 Rc1 Rc4 37 Bf1 Ra4 38 Kb1 Qd5 39 Kb2 Nd4 40 Rd1 Rxa2+ 0-1

Game 43
□ **D.Sadvakasov** ■ **S.Tiviakov**
Calicut 2007

---

1 e4 d5 2 exd5 Qxd5 3 Nc3 Qd6 4 d4 c6 5 Nf3 Bg4!? (Diagram 17)

It has recently become fashionable to delay the development of the g8-knight in order to meet 5 Nf3 with 5...Bg4, thus preventing Ne5 (5...Nf6 transposes to 4...Nf6 5 Nf3 c6).

6 Be3

6 h3!? offering the d4-pawn is the most principled continuation: 6...Bxf3 (6...Bh5 7 g4!? Bg6 8 Ne5 would be interesting, for example 8...Nd7 9 Nc4!? Qc7 10 Qf3) 7 Qxf3 Qxd4!? (after 7...e6 White can simply enjoy the bishop pair and expand on

the kingside – after 8 Bf4 Qd8 9 0-0-0 Nf6 10 g4 White had a pleasant advantage in A.Rasmussen-S.B.Hansen, Aalborg 2007, although the d5-square will still give Black some counterplay) 8 Be3 Qd8 9 Rd1 Qc7 10 Bc4 Nf6 11 g4 h6 (11...e6 is a very logical way for Black to defend) 12 0-0 Nbd7 13 Bf4 e5 14 Bg3 Be7 15 h4 Rf8 16 Rfe1 0-0-0 17 a3 with a double-edged position, S.Maze-P.Benkovic, Biel 2008.

6...Nf6 7 h3 Bh5 8 g4 Bg6 9 Ne5 Nbd7

9...Nd5 10 Nxd5 Qxd5 11 Rg1 Nd7 12 Nxg6 hxg6 13 Qd2 e6 14 c4 Qd6 15 0-0-0 Qb4 16 Qc2 Qa5 17 Kb1 led to a nice advantage for White in N.Sedlak-M.Kristovic, Croatia 2005: now White has established the c4/d4 pawn front, it is very difficult for Black to find a base for his knight, particularly after f2-f4.

10 Qe2

The alternative is 10 Nxg6 hxg6 11 Qf3, and 11...e6 12 0-0-0 Qc7 13 Kb1 Bb4 14 Ne4 Nxe4 15 Qxe4 Nf6 16 Qf3 Nd5 17 Bc1 b5 18 h4 0-0-0 19 h5 gxh5 20 gxh5 was slightly better for White in L.Fressinet-C.Bauer, Pau 2008.

10...Nd5 11 Bg2 (Diagram 18) 11...Nxe3

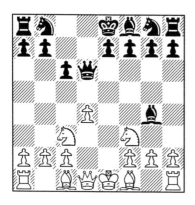
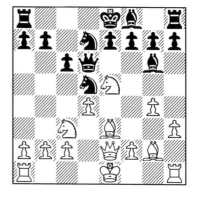

Diagram 17 (W)

Preventing Ne5

Diagram 18 (B)

Which capture?

11...Nxc3 12 bxc3 Nxe5 13 dxe5 Qxe5 might be better, although White clearly has compensation after 14 0-0 intending f2-f4.

12 Qxe3 e6 13 0-0-0 Nxe5 14 dxe5 Qc7 15 f4 Bb4 16 a3 Bxc3 17 Qxc3 h5 18 Rhf1 hxg4 19 hxg4 Rd8

Black's position has quickly fallen apart.

20 Rde1 Qe7 21 Kb1 Rh2 22 f5 exf5 23 gxf5 Bxf5 24 Rxf5 Rxg2 25 e6 fxe6 26 Qh3 Rdd2? 27 Qh8+ Kd7 28 Qb8 Rge2 29 Rxe2 Rxe2 30 Qxb7+ Kd6 31 Qb8+ Qc7 32 Qb4+ c5 33 Qf4+ e5 34 Qg3 Qa5 35 Qxg7 Kd5 36 Qd7+ Ke4 37 Qd3 mate (1-0)

Fifth Move Alternatives for White

1 e4 d5 2 exd5 Qxd5 3 Nc3 Qd6 4 d4 Nf6

We finish off our coverage of 3...Qd6 by looking at various fifth-move alternatives for White:

a) 5 Bc4 is usually played in conjunction with Nge2 and Bf4, attacking the queen (see Game 44).

b) 5 Bd3 is a tricky move. It prevents ...Bf5 and tries to provoke Black into playing ...Bg4. The downside of 5 Bd3 is that it leaves the d4-pawn just that little bit more vulnerable (see Game 45).

c) With 5 Be3 White simply wishes to accelerate his development by castling long, with the intention of breaking quickly with d4-d5 or attacking the queen with Be3-f4 (see Game 46).

d) 5 Be2 is, in the words of Andrew Martin, "just a 'normal' developing move" (see Game 47).

Game 44
□ **A.Rodriguez Vila** ■ **L.Galego**
Sao Paulo 2005

---

1 e4 d5 2 exd5 Qxd5 3 Nc3 Qd6 4 d4 Nf6 5 Bc4 a6 6 Nge2

With 6 Bb3?! White wishes to develop the knight to e2 without allowing Black to win a pawn with ...Qc6. However, White's time-consuming manoeuvre allows Black to equalize with 6...Nc6 7 Nge2 e5!.

6 Nf3 transposes to 5 Nf3 a6 6 Bc4 (see Chapter Eight).

6...Qc6!? (Diagram 19)

 TIP: 6...Qc6 carries some risk, so players choosing this move should make sure they are well prepared.

The easiest approach is to reject the pawn offer with 6...b5! 7 Bb3 Bb7 8 Bf4 and now Black should play the lesser-known 8...Qd7!. This move was shown to me by IM Gary Lane, and I played it in a world junior championship. I remember being very happy because Black's moves are incredibly straightforward, and after a few moves my opponent was very nearly losing: 9 0-0 (blocking the bishop with 9 d5 is not dangerous, as after 9...c5 White is forced to exchange pawns anyhow, and 10 dxc6 Qxc6 11 f3 Nbd7 12 Qd2 e5 13 Be3 Nc5 forced White to give up the bishop pair in A.Ardeleanu-V.Malaniuk, Arad 2006) 9...e6! (the idea is to play ...c5 and to develop an initiative based on the two bishops pointing dangerously towards the white king) 10 Re1? (10 a4 b4 11 Nb1 was A.Rodriguez Vila-J.Ryan, Sants 2006, and here Black is doing very well after 11...c5! 12 Nd2 Nc6 13 dxc5) 10...c5 11 dxc5 Qc6 12 f3 Bxc5+ 13 Nd4 (this is forced, since 13 Kh1 is met by 13...Qxf3 and the queen is immune from capture) 13...Qb6 14 Nce2 Nc6 15 c3 0-0 16 Kh1 (I.Werner-J.Houska, Calicut 1998) and now the simple 16...Rfd8, with the idea of inflicting White with an isolated pawn, would have given Black a positional advantage.

7 Qd3

7 Bb3! is a very dangerous alternative, and I think that it is White's best choice. For example, 7...Qxg2 8 Rg1 Qh3 9 Bf4 Qd7 (to defend the c7-pawn) 10 Qd3 Nc6 11 a3 (depriving the black knight of b4, so now d4-d5 is a strong positional threat) 11...Na5 12 Ba2 b5 13 0-0-0 Bb7 14 d5! (seizing as much space as possible) 14...g6 15 Ng3 Bg7 16 Nce4 (threatening the unpleasant 17 Nc5) 16...Nc4 17 Nxf6+ Bxf6 18 Bxc4 bxc4 19 Qxc4 0-0 20 Ne4 and White has a promising position, D.Gormally-J.Plaskett, London 2005.

7...Qxg2 8 Rg1 (Diagram 20) 8...Qh3

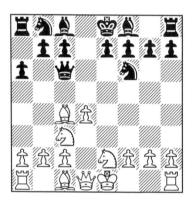

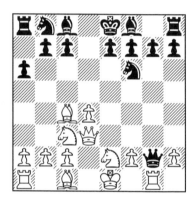

Diagram 19 (W)

Boldly grabbing a pawn

Diagram 20 (B)

Greed doesn't pay here

Greed is usually a sin during the opening phase, and in this particular case it comes with a tremendous amount of risk: 8...Qxh2 9 Bf4 Qh3 10 Qd2 Qd7 (Black holds on to his extra material for dear life, but 10...Bf5 returning a pawn may be a wiser choice) 11 0-0-0 e6 12 Be5 Nc6 13 Bxf6 gxf6 14 Ne4 and White has a very strong initiative for the two pawns. It is difficult for Black to defend f6 without allowing d4-d5 or Qd2-h6. For instance, if Black plays 14...Be7 15 Qh6 f5, then 16 d5 is crushing.

9 Qxh3!

9 Be3 is a more combative option, but it looks as though Black should be holding on as the dark-squared bishop is not particularly well placed on e3. After 9...Bf5 10

Qd2 the most accurate move may be 10...Nc6!. Black must be ready to meet d4-d5 with ...Ne5 hitting the bishop on c4 and threatening the crushing ...Nf3+. The game I.Madl-G.Feher, Hungarian League 1997, continued 11 0-0-0 e6 (Black's plan is simply to castle queenside and ensure that the queen sitting precariously on h3 doesn't get trapped!) 12 Nf4 Qh4 and here 13 d5 0-0-0 14 Qe2 would threaten the tactical shot Bxa6.

9...Bxh3 10 Nf4 Bf5 11 Nfd5 (Diagram 21)

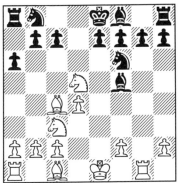

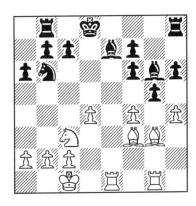

Diagram 21 (B)

Black must defend c7

Diagram 22 (B)

Black is more than okay

11...Kd8!

After 11...Nxd5 12 Nxd5 Kd7 13 Bf4 Nc6 14 0-0-0 (if 14 Bxc7 Rc8 and the c2-pawn hangs) 14...Rc8 15 Ne3 Bg6 16 Be2 the fundamental problem for Black is that he is unable to develop his kingside pieces because 16...e6 loses to 17 d5 exd5 18 Bg4+.

12 Nxf6?!

12 Bf4! is perhaps a better option, and here 12...Ne8 13 Ne3 Bg6 14 0-0-0 Nd6 15 Be2 Nd7 16 h4 h5 17 Bg5 leaves Black very cramped.

12...exf6 13 Bf4 g5 14 Bg3 Nd7

14...Bxc2 looks rather risky to me.

15 0-0-0 Bg6 16 h4 h6 17 f4 Nb6 18 Be2 Be7 19 Bf3 Rb8 20 Rde1 (Diagram 22)

Black's extra pawn is doubled, but his position is very solid: his pieces have good squares and he has the superior pawn structure. Once the black rooks get into the game Black will stand much better, even if White wins the f7-pawn.

20...Re8 21 h5 Bf5 22 Nd5 Nxd5 23 Bxd5 Bd6 24 Bxf7 Rxe1+ 25 Rxe1 Kd7

Black has the advantage here.

26 Rf1 Bh3 27 Rf2 Rf8 28 Bg6 f5 29 Kd2 Bg4 30 Bh2 Bxf4+ 31 Bxf4 gxf4 32 Rxf4

Ke6 33 Ke3 Kf6 34 c4 Kg5 35 d5 b6 36 b4 Bxh5 37 Bxh5 Kxh5 38 c5!

White must establish some form of counterplay otherwise Black would simply be winning.

38...Kg5 39 Rd4 Re8+ 40 Kf3 bxc5 41 bxc5 Rd8 42 d6 cxd6 43 c6 h5

43...d5! ensures that the a6-pawn isn't a target, and 44 Ra4 (or 44 c7 Rc8) 44...Ra8 45 Ke3 h5 46 Kd4 h4 47 Kxd5 h3 48 Rb4 h2 49 Rb1 Rh8 50 c7 Kg4 wins for Black.

44 Ra4 Ra8 45 Rd4 Rc8 46 Rxd6

Now it's a draw.

46...h4 47 a4 a5 48 Re6 h3 49 Kg3 Rh8 50 Kh2 Kf4 51 c7 Rc8 52 Rc6 Kf3 53 Rc3+ Kg4 54 Rg3+ Kf4 55 Rc3 Ke5 56 Kxh3 Kd6 57 Kg3 Rxc7 58 Rxc7 Kxc7 59 Kf4 Kd6 60 Kxf5 Kc5 61 Ke4 Kb4 62 Kd3 Kxa4 63 Kc2 ½-½

Game 45
☐ **Nay Oo Kyaw Tun** ■ **Goh Koong Jong**
Bangkok 2005

---

1 e4 d5 2 exd5 Qxd5 3 Nc3 Qd6 4 d4 Nf6 5 Bd3 Nc6!?

This is perhaps the easiest way to equalize, although the position may end up a little dry.

5...Bg4 is also possible. As we know, playing an early ...Bg4 in the Scandinavian is usually doubled-edged, and even more so when White has not yet played Ng1-f3 because ...Bg4 allows White to expand with tempo by playing f2-f3 and g2-g4. Scandinavian players must always remember that White's most aggressive and dangerous plan is to castle queenside and steal as much kingside space as possible.

Let's see what happens after 6 f3 Bh5 7 Nge2 a6 8 Bf4 and now:

a) 8...Qd7 is convincingly answered by 9 d5! making it tricky for Black to develop:

a1) After 9...Bg6 10 Qd2 White's extra space gave him the advantage in G.Kasparov-I.Rogers, Batumi (rapid) 2001.

a2) 9...Nxd5 is bad because of 10 Bf5! e6 (10...Qxf5 11 Nxd5) 11 Nxd5 Qxd5 12 Qxd5 exd5 13 0-0-0! and Black must return the pawn, as 13...c6 14 Rhe1 is crushing – 14...Be7 loses a piece to 15 Ng3.

b) Against 8...Qb6, harassing the queen with 9 Na4 seems very good, and 9...Qc6 10 c4 e6 11 0-0 Be7 12 Nec3 0-0 13 d5 exd5 14 Nxd5 Nxd5 15 cxd5 looks the most sensible way for White to play.

6 Nge2 e5! (Diagram 23) 7 Nb5

7 dxe5 leads to an ending in which Black has absolutely no problems: 7...Nxe5 8 Bb5+ c6 9 Qxd6 Bxd6 10 Ba4 b5 11 Bb3 a5 12 a4 b4 13 Nd1 Ba6 and Black later squeezed out a win in I.Manolov-V.Panbukchian, Sunny Beach 2004.

Sacrificing a pawn with 7 0-0 is probably White's best bet. After 7...Nxd4 8 Nxd4 Qxd4 9 Re1 (if 9 Nb5 Qd8 10 Qe2 Bd6 11 Bf4 Nd7 12 Rae1 0-0 Black should be fine) 9...Bd6 10 Bg5 Be6 11 Qf3 0-0-0 12 Bxf6 gxf6 13 Qxf6, as played in A.Sokolov-I.Nikolaidis, Athens 2005, White has regained the pawn but Black is fine – he has the bishop pair and an open g-file that could cause White problems.

7...Qe7 8 0-0

8 dxe5 Nxe5 9 Bf4 c6 10 Nbd4 Bg4 11 f3 Bd7 12 Qd2 0-0-0 13 0-0-0 Nd5 was very comfortable for Black in S.Macak-E.Kovacik, Slovakian League 2003. White must exchange one of his bishops for the strong knight on e5, and this will give Black a slight advantage.

8...a6 9 dxe5 Nxe5 10 Nbd4 g6!

Black must not waste any further time; he should develop his pieces at once.

11 Bg5

White isn't quick enough to take advantage of Black's clumsy piece configuration on the e-file: 11 Re1 Bg7 12 Bf4 (12 f4 Nxd3 followed by ...0-0 only weakens White's position) 12...0-0 13 Ng3 Nfd7 reaches an equal position. However, White should be aware that 14 Bxe5 would simply be a mistake, as after 14...Nxe5 15 f4 Black can play 15...Qc5!.

11...Bg7 12 Nc3 0-0 13 Re1 Qd6! 14 Nf3 Nfg4 15 Bf4?

After 15 Nxe5 Bxe5 16 Ne4! (16 h3? Bxc3!) 16...Bxh2+? 17 Kh1 Black must lose some material, but 16...Qb6! is stronger.

15...Nxf2! (Diagram 24)

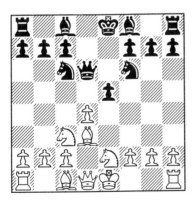

Diagram 23 (W)

The most straightforward

Diagram 24 (W)

Winning a pawn

This neat tactic nets Black a pawn.

16 Kxf2 Nxd3+ 17 Qxd3 Qxf4 18 Nd5 Qa4

With a material disadvantage and up against the bishop pair, White has no hope.

19 c3 Be6 20 Red1 Rfd8 21 c4 Bf5 22 Qb3 Qxb3 23 axb3 Bc2 24 Re1 Bxb3 25 Rac1 Bf8 26 Nf6+ Kg7 27 Ne4 Ba4 28 Nc3 Bc6 29 Ne5 Rd2+ 30 Re2 Bc5+ 31 Kf1 Rxe2 32 Nxe2 Bxg2+ 33 Kxg2 Re8 34 Nd7 Rxe2+ 35 Kf3 Re3+ 36 Kf4 Bd4 37 Rd1 c5 38 b4 Rc3 39 bxc5 Bxc5! 40 Nxc5 Rxc4+ 41 Ne4 f5 42 Rd7+ Kh6 0-1

Game 46
☐ **T.Wedberg** ■ **J.Fries Nielsen**
Stockholm 2003

---

1 e4 d5 2 exd5 Qxd5 3 Nc3 Qd6 4 d4 Nf6 5 Be3 a6 6 Qd2

6 g3 looks a little bizarre now that White has already committed to playing Be3. It looks like the time is right for 6...Bg4!, and after 7 Qd2 Nc6 8 Bg2 0-0-0 9 h3 Bh5 10 g4 Bg6 11 f4 e6 12 0-0-0 Nb4 Black has firm control of the blockading square d5.

6...b5 (Diagram 25)

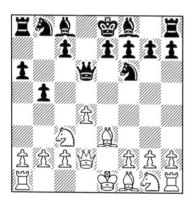

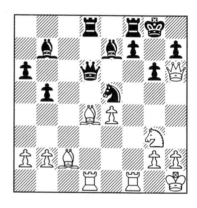

Diagram 25 (W)
Set-up A in operation

Diagram 26 (B)
White begins to create threats

6...Nc6 7 0-0-0 Bf5 8 Nf3 e6 9 Nh4 Bg6 10 Nxg6 hxg6 11 Bf4 Qd7 12 d5 gives White an advantage due to the bishop pair, M.Gongora Reyes-O.Almeida Quintana, Santa Clara 2005.

7 f3!

> **NOTE: When Black adopts the ...b5 set-up, the key square for White to control and occupy is e4 so this move is absolutely instrumental.**

7...Bb7 8 Bd3 Nbd7 9 Nge2 e6 10 Ne4

The most dangerous idea – White uses the awkward placement of Black's queen to establish a pawn centre.

The somewhat slow 10 0-0 is met by 10...c5 11 Rad1 and now:

a) 11...Be7? blunders a pawn to 12 dxc5 Qc7 (12...Nxc5 fails after 13 Bxb5+) 13 b4, S.Haslinger-C.Hanley, Halifax (rapid) 2003.

b) 11...Qc7! 12 Bf4 Qb6 gives Black complete equality (but 12...Bd6? fails to 13 Bxb5).

10...Nxe4 11 fxe4 c5 12 c3 Be7 13 0-0

13 e5 is not possible because of 13...Qc6 14 Nf4 Rd8 with the threat of ...Nxe5 and ...c5-c4.

13...0-0

13...f6 may be the best move, taking preventative action against White's threat of e4-e5 – a move which in effect cuts the board in two for Black. Although this position on balance is probably slightly better for White, it is not easy for him to arrange an attack towards Black's Achilles' heel – the h7-square. Bc2/Qd3 plans can be met easily by ...c5-c4, and rook lifts leave White's army somewhat disjointed.

14 Rad1

After 14 e5 Qc7 15 Nf4 Rad8 16 Qe2 g6 17 a4 White's position is preferable. It is not easy for Black to coordinate his knight and dark-squared bishop, and furthermore Black's kingside is particularly vulnerable to an attack on the dark squares.

14...cxd4 15 cxd4 e5 16 Bc2 Rad8 17 Ng3 g6 18 Kh1 exd4 19 Bxd4 Ne5 20 Qh6! (Diagram 26)

Suddenly both the black queen and the black king become vulnerable, and White's attack gathers momentum.

20...f6 21 Bb3+ Kh8 22 Rf4 Qc7 23 Rh4 Bd6?

A costly mistake. Better is 23...Bb4, when 24 Bxe5 Rxd1+ 25 Bxd1 fxe5 26 Qxg6 gives White a material advantage but Black has the bishop pair and active pieces.

24 Bb6! Qe7 25 Bxd8 Rxd8 26 Rf4 Bc5 27 Rff1 Nd3 28 Rd2 Bb4 29 Re2

Black has generated some counterplay for the material deficit, but it is insufficient.

29...Qe5 30 Bd5! Bc8 31 a3 Bf8 32 Qd2 Nc5 33 Qa5 Be7 34 Rc2 Rf8 35 Rfc1 Qd4 36 Qc7 1-0

Game 47
□ D.Rosandic ■ R.Zelcic
Bosnjaci 2003

1 e4 d5 2 exd5 Qxd5 3 Nc3 Qd6 4 d4 Nf6 5 Be2 a6

With 5 Be2 White has no ambition of immediately chasing the queen away from d6 through the most logical means (Nge2/Bf4 or g3/Bf4). Furthermore, by delaying Nf3 White postpones the start of the fight for the e5-square, which is one of fundamental issues in the 5 Nf3 c6 variation. In view of this, even 5...c6 is entirely viable here. For example, 6 Bg5 Bf5 7 Qd2 Nbd7! (now Black has firm control of the e5-square) 8 Nf3 e6 (against 8...Nb6 I think White should play the principled 9 Ne5 e6 10 g4!) 9 0-0 Qc7 10 Nh4 Bg6 11 Rfe1 Bd6 12 g3 was only slightly better for White in F.Nijboer-S.Tiviakov, Hilversum 2006.

6 Bf3

6 Nf3 Bf5 was covered under the move order 5 Nf3 a6 6 Be2 Bf5.

6...Nc6 7 Nge2 Bf5! (Diagram 27)

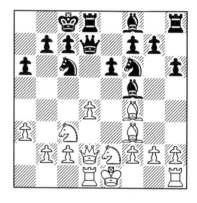

Diagram 27 (W)
The best development

Diagram 28 (W)
The race begins

7...e6 is undesirable, as it leaves Black with a problematic light-squared bishop.

7...e5?! is dubious: after 8 Bxc6+ Qxc6 9 dxe5 Ng4 10 0-0 White holds on to the pawn, as 10...Nxe5 fails to 11 Re1!.

The best alternative is 7...Bg4!?, although this does lead to forcing play: 8 Bxg4 Nxg4 9 d5 Nce5 10 Bf4 Qb6 11 0-0 g5! (Black is forced to take active measures in order to untangle the knights) 12 Bg3 Bg7 ½-½ D.Baramidze-A.Karpatchev, Kiel 2001.

8 Bf4!

The only move, as after 8 0-0 Black can seize the initiative: 8...0-0-0 9 Bf4?! (or 9 Be3 e5!) 9...e5! 10 dxe5 Nxe5 11 Ng3 (11 Qxd6 Nxf3+!) 11...Qb4 12 Qc1 Nxf3+ 13 gxf3 and Black has a structural advantage, V.Kupreichik-F.Grafl, German League 2004.

8...Qd7!

Black must maintain pressure on the d4-pawn in order to tie down White's pieces to its defence.

9 Qd2 0-0-0 10 Rd1?!

White reacts aggressively, making it clear that the game will develop as an attacking race. However, the white pieces are not well enough placed to merit this aggression.

10...e6 11 a3 h6! (Diagram 28)

Suddenly the game becomes a race to see who can advance on the wings first. White must take time out to deal with Black's threat of ...g7-g5-g4 hitting the bishop on f3.

12 h3 g5 13 Bg3 Bd6 14 Bxd6 Qxd6 15 Bxc6 Qxc6 16 0-0 Ne4?!

This is tempting but dubious. I like 16...Rhg8 instead. After 17 Ng3 Bh7 18 b4 h5 Black has a very strong attack, and 17 b4 g4 18 h4 Ne4 also looks very good for Black.

17 Nxe4 Bxe4 18 f3 Bf5 19 c3 h5 20 Qxg5 Bxh3! 21 Qc5 Qxc5 22 dxc5

This endgame is equal.

22...Bf5 23 Nd4 Bg6 24 f4 Rd5! 25 b4 h4 26 Kh2 h3

Black sacrifices a pawn in return for pressure.

27 gxh3

In principle weakening the pawn structure is not to be advised, but in this case White is fine as the weaknesses are easily defended – and a pawn is a pawn!

27...Bh5 28 Rde1 Bg4! 29 Kg3! Bxh3 30 Rh1 Rdh5?

A big mistake; 30...Rg8+ is better.

31 Re5! Rg8+ 32 Rg5

This is the clever point: White forces off a set of rooks which is to his advantage, as his pieces are more active.

32...Rhxg5+ 33 fxg5 Bf5 34 Kf4

Now the pawn on g5 is invaluable, and White is doing very well here.

34...Bg6 35 Ke5 Rd8 36 Kf6 Be4 37 Re1 Bd5??

Black makes a big mistake, presumably in time trouble.

38 g6??

White could have won with 38 Kxf7 e5+ 39 Ne6 Kd7 40 Rxe5, attacking the bishop.

38...fxg6 39 Kxg6 Rg8+ 40 Kf6 Rg3

Now the black rook gets active.

41 Ke7?

White should play 41 Nxe6, although 41...Bxe6 42 Rxe6 Rxc3 43 a4 Rc4 is still advantageous for Black.

41...Rxc3 42 Rg1 e5 43 Rf1 Kb8 0-1

Summary

After 5 Nf3, the move 5...c6 is somehow truer to the "Scandinavian" concept of establishing a favourable Caro-Kann with the e6/c6 pawn formation. As we have seen, the key feature here is that White can play 6 Ne5 without being hassled by 6...Nc6. After 6 Ne5 Nbd7 play can become very sharp, especially if White chooses 7 Bf4 and the pawn sacrifice 9 Be2!? (Game 40), although White does have a safer option in 7 Nc4 (Game 41). Recently White has been experimenting with 7 f4, but this doesn't look too convincing. As Game 42 shows, Black must react with 7...Nb6 followed by 8...Nbd5 to exchange the important c3-knight. It has also become fashionable for Black to delay the development of his king's knight in order to meet 5 Nf3 with 5...Bg4, but Game 43 shows that Black has still got a long way to go in this line.

Despite its early popularity, 5 Bc4 does not promise much of an advantage to White. In Game 44 White sacrifices a pawn early in the opening to gain some play along the g-file. Black can certainly accept this offer, but in my opinion declining the sacrifice with 6...b5!? is more than good enough.

Game 45 demonstrates how Black can play in a forcing manner should White handle the opening slowly. Game 46 sees a much more critical try for White, with Nge2, f2-f3 and an attempt to gain full control of the e4-square. Finally, in Game 47 White plays the strange Be2-Bf3 manoeuvre, but with no real control over e5 and no threat of d4-d5, Black is able to deal with this in a straightforward manner.

Third Move Alternatives

3 Nc3 Qd8

1 e4 d5 2 exd5 Qxd5 3 Nc3 Qd8 (Diagram 1)

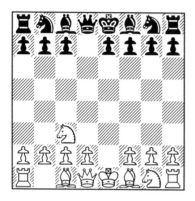

Diagram 1 (W)	Diagram 2 (W)
The Banker variation	The Patzer variation

3...Qd8 is nicknamed the Banker variation, although I must admit I am not too sure why. I would guess it's because it's a move, to put it politely, "that doesn't thrill the soul". By retreating the queen right back to its original square, Black wishes to secure all the advantages of extracting 3 Nc3 from White but without exposing his queen to any form of harassment. The onus shifts to White to prove that this retreat is not justified.

3...Qe5+ **(Diagram 2)** is an alternative with another nickname! The so-called Patzer variation gets its nickname from the saying "Patzer sees a check, patzer plays a check." Even though this move cannot be refuted, it's not to be entirely recommended either! For example, 4 Be2 c6 (this is the whole point – Black can still adopt the Scandinavian structure) 5 Nf3 Qc7 6 d4 Nf6 7 Ne5 (this typical reaction is, of course, the most critical against 3...Qe5+) 7...Bf5 8 Bf4 Qa5?! (with this natural move, Black wastes more time) 9 0-0 e6 (9...Be6 10 Qd2 g6 11 Rfe1 Qd8 12 d5! Nxd5 13 Nxd5 Bxd5 14 Rad1 Qc8 15 Qc3 Be6 16 Nxf7 crushed Black in M.Yarmysty-I.Shkuro, Rodatychi 2006) 10 g4 (White can exploit Black's loss of tempo to lash out) 10...Bg6 11 h4 Nd5 (or 11...Be4 12 Re1 Be7 13 Nxf7!! Kxf7 14 Nxe4 Nxe4 15 Bc4 and Black must return the piece, as 15...Nf6 loses to 16 Qe2) 12 Nxd5 cxd5 13 c4 Be7 14 Qb3 and White has an extremely strong initiative.

4 d4

White can also play 4 Nf3 c6 5 Bc4 Bf5 6 d3 blunting the bishop, but this is not too dangerous as the black queen – so often a target after 3...Qa5 – is safely ensconced on d8. A.Cosovic-I.Plivcevic, Neum 2005, continued 6...e6 7 Bf4 Nf6 8 Qd2 Bd6 9 0-0-0 and since there is no tension in the centre, Black can act on the queenside with 9...b5 10 Bb3 a5 reaching a double-edged position: White must react to the threat of ...a5-a4 and at the same time create some counterplay.

4...Nf6

4...g6 asks too much from the Black position, as the former World Champion Robert Fischer effectively demonstrated: 5 Bf4! (the idea of this move – followed by 6 Qd2 – is to prevent Black's knight manoeuvre to f5 via h6) 5...Bg7 (by covering e5 Black gets ready to play 6...Nh6) 6 Qd2! Nf6 (after 6...Qxd4 7 Qxd4 Bxd4 8 Nb5 Bb6 9 Nxc7+ Bxc7 10 Bxc7 White has the long-term advantage of the bishop pair and a queenside pawn majority; 6...Bxd4? is even worse for Black after 7 0-0-0 Nc6 8 Bb5 Bd7 9 Nd5! e5 10 Nf3 – following 10...exf4 White can play the cool 11 Qxf4 threatening both the c7-pawn and the bishop) 7 0-0-0 c6 8 Bh6 0-0? (8...Bxh6 had to be played) 9 h4 Qa5 10 h5! **(Diagram 3)** and Black is practically lost. If 10...Nxh5 11 Be2 Nf6 12 Bxg7 Kxg7 13 Qh6+ Kg8 14 g4! there's the deadly threat of g4-g5.

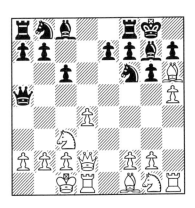

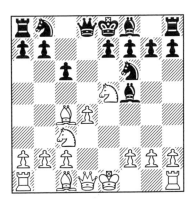

Diagram 3 (B)
Fischer busts 4...g6

Diagram 4 (B)
The most challenging

5 Nf3 c6

As usual, 5...Bg4 6 h3 Bxf3 (6...Bh5 allows White to expand on the kingside when he so chooses) 7 Qxf3 gives White a small advantage, although Back's position remains very solid.

6 Bc4 Bf5

6...b5!? is a speciality of IM Zdravko Vuckovic. The idea is to use b7 as an outlet for the light-squared bishop. Given time, Black will play ...e7-e6, ...Bb7 and ...a7-a6 followed by the freeing ...c6-c5. For example, 7 Bb3 (7 Bd3 may be more in keeping with what the position demands) 7...e6 8 Bg5! Be7 and now:

a) 9 a4 b4 10 Bxf6 gxf6 11 Ne2 Na6 12 Qd2 h5 13 0-0-0 Nc7 14 Ne1 Nd5 15 Nd3 Qa5 16 f4 f5 17 Ne5 was A.Shirov-E.Dizdarevic, Calvia Olympiad 2004. White holds the trump card – the strong knight on e5 – but the position is still pretty unclear as it is not obvious how White should make progress.

b) 9 Ne5 looks the most logical: 9...a5 10 a3 0-0 11 0-0 Bb7 (D.Svetushkin-E.Dizdarevic, Calvia Olympiad 2004) 12 Qd3! Nbd7 13 f4 h6 14 Bxf6 Bxf6 15 Ne4 with an initiative.

7 Ne5! (Diagram 4)

As mentioned throughout the book, this is White's principled reaction should Black "waste" more time in the opening. The intention is clear: White wishes not only to embed a mighty piece in the centre but also to hunt the bishop with g2-g4 and h2-h4. Players on the White side, take note; players on the Black side, be warned! This position is covered in Games 48-49.

Game 48
□ E.Prokopchuk ■ J.Lopez-Martinez
Moscow 2005

---

1 e4 d5 2 exd5 Qxd5 3 Nc3 Qd8 4 d4 Nf6 5 Nf3 c6 6 Bc4 Bf5 7 Ne5 e6 8 g4

This position resembles the 7 Ne5 line in Chapter Four, except the queen is back on its original square. Because the queen is no longer pinning the c3-knight, White is able to swap off the Scandinavian bishop for this knight.

8...Bg6

In Chapter Four we saw that it was beneficial for Black to provoke h2-h4 as it weakens White's kingside and makes it easier for Black to undermine the position. The same is true here. After 8...Be4 White simply plays 9 Nxe4 Nxe4 10 Qf3 Nd6 11 Bb3 with the advantage.

9 h4 Bb4 (Diagram 5)

9...Nbd7 is covered in the next game.

10 f3

Depriving the bishop of the e4-square is the most ambitious try, although 10 h5 is also playable. For example, 10...Be4 (according to Ponomariov, the tempting 10...Bxc2? is a mistake: 11 Qxc2 Qxd4 12 f4 Ne4 13 Bd2 Qf2+ 14 Kd1 Bxc3 15 bxc3 Ng3 16 Re1 0-0 17 Be3 and White is winning) 11 0-0 Bxc3 12 bxc3 b5!? 13 Bb3 Bd5 14 Ba3 Ne4 (Black must play actively, not only to compensate for the weakened dark squares around his king but in order to exploit the weaknesses surrounding White's king) 15 Bxd5 (T.Ernst-V.Okhotnik, French League 2004) and here 15...cxd5 is more logical than Black's choice of 15...Qxd5. Capturing with the c-pawn makes the c3-pawn even more prone to attack, and if 16 Re1 Nd7 17 f3 Black can safely play 17...Nxc3 18 Qd2 Qa5 19 Bb2 Nxe5 20 Rxe5 Rc8 and the knight is in no danger.

10...Nd5

This is the critical move.

10...Bxc2 11 Qxc2 Qxd4 leads to a very murky position where it is not clear whether Black has enough compensation for the piece:

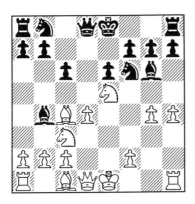

Diagram 5 (W)	**Diagram 6 (B)**
The sharpest continuation	This looks promising

a) 12 Qe2 Bxc3+ (12...b5? allows 13 Nxf7!) 13 bxc3 Qxc3+ 14 Kf2 Qxa1 is very unclear. Black has managed to regain more than his sacrificed material, but his pieces lack harmony and development. The game T.Huesmann-D.Martinez Pelaez, Donostia 2008, continued 15 Kg2 Qd4 16 Rd1 Qc5? 17 Nxf7! 0-0 18 Qxe6 Nbd7?? (18...Na6 still saves the day) 19 Ne5+ Kh8 20 Nxd7 Nxd7 21 Rxd7 Rae8 and here White won with the stunning 22 Bb2!!.

b) 12 f4 Nbd7 (or 12...Nxg4 13 Nxg4 Qxc4 14 Bd2 and once White has castled he will stand better) 13 Nxd7 Nxg4! (the initiative is in Black's hands and he must keep it at any cost; 13...Kxd7 allows White to simplify with 14 Qd2) 14 Bf1! (White must keep this bishop) 14...Qxd7 15 Be2 h5 16 Bd2 0-0-0 17 Bxg4 hxg4 18 0-0-0 was C.Lupulescu-V.Barnaure, Romania 2002. Even though Black has three pawns for the piece, he stands worse, although if he keeps his pieces active he has chances to hold the game.

10...0-0 11 h5! and only then 11...Bxc2 doesn't work. After 12 Qxc2 Qxd4 13 f4! Nxg4 14 Nxg4 Qxc4 15 Bd2 White's king can reach safety.

11 Bxd5!?

White plays forcefully to keep h4-h5 as a threat. However, I am not sure what Black has against the simple 11 Bd2!? **(Diagram 6)**.

For example, 11...Qb6 is met by 12 Qe2 intending 12...Qxd4? 13 Bxd5 cxd5 14 Qb5+; or 11...Nb6 12 Qe2 Qxd4 13 0-0-0 and Black's bishop on g6 is in real trouble, as 13...Nxc4 loses on the spot to 14 Bg5; finally there's 11...Bxc3 12 bxc3 f6, but White is comfortably better here.

11...cxd5

After 11...Qxd5 12 h5! Black must sacrifice a piece to remain in the game: 12...f6 13 hxg6 fxe5 14 Bd2 Qxd4 15 Qe2 h6 16 0-0-0 gives White a lethal attack along the d-file, but after 12...Bxc2 13 Qxc2 f6 14 Nd3 Qxf3 Black's compensation isn't convincing.

11...exd5 12 h5 is clearly bad for Black.

12 h5

The more restrained 12 Qe2 should be met by 12...Qa5 13 Bd2 Nc6 14 Nxc6 bxc6 15 0-0-0 h5 with a very unclear game.

12...f6 (Diagram 7)

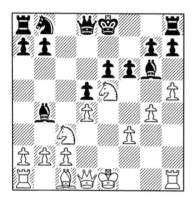

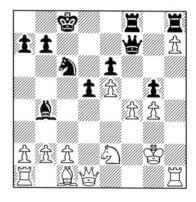

Diagram 7 (W)
White misses a chance

Diagram 8 (W)
Seizing the initiative

13 hxg6

13 Nxg6! is a good try for the advantage. After 13...hxg6 14 Qd3 Bxc3+ 15 bxc3 f5 the problem is that not only are the dark squares incredibly weak but there is also no safe haven for the black king. Following 16 Rb1 Qd7 17 Bf4 gxh5 18 gxh5 Nc6 19 Kf2 Kf7 20 Rbg1 Rh7 21 Rg5 Rg8 White will pile up on the g-file and force Black into complete passivity, C.Carmaciu-G.Ardelean, Bucharest 2002. In this line 19...0-0-0 is more dangerous than it appears, as White gains a vicious attack down the b-file: for example, 20 a4 Rh7 21 Rb5 b6 22 a5!.

13...fxe5 14 gxh7

14 dxe5 looks harmless, and Black is okay after 14...d4 15 a3 Ba5 16 b4 dxc3 17 Rxh7 Qxd1+ 18 Kxd1 0-0 19 bxa5 Nc6 20 f4 Ne7.

14...Qe7

14...Qc7! 15 Bd2 Nc6! 16 dxe5 0-0-0 (it is vital for Black to gets his king to safety as quickly as possible) 17 Nb5 Qxe5+ 18 Qe2 Bxd2+ 19 Kxd2 Qf4+ 20 Kd1 e5 is probably a tad better Black, as White's pieces are very awkwardly placed.

15 dxe5 Nc6 16 Kf2?

This gives Black counterplay along the f-file. After 16 Bd2 Nxe5 17 Qe2 Nc4 18 0-0-0 the advantage of the h-pawn may begin to tell.

16...0-0-0 17 Ne2 Rdf8 18 Kg2 Qf7 19 f4 g5! (Diagram 8) 20 Nd4 Rxh7 21 Nxc6 bxc6 22 Rxh7 Qxh7 23 Qd3 Qh4 24 Qg3

24 Qa6+?? Kb8 leaves White with no defence.

24...Qh6 25 fxg5 Qg6 26 Qd3 Qf7 27 Qe2 Qh7

Planning a deadly pile-up on the h-file. White wisely secures a repetition.

28 Qd3 Qf7 29 Qe2 Qh7 30 Qd3 Qf7 ½-½

Game 49
□ **T.Oral** ■ **D.Paunovic**
Ourense 2007

---

1 e4 d5 2 exd5 Qxd5 3 Nc3 Qd8 4 d4 Nf6 5 Nf3 Bf5 6 Ne5 c6 7 Bc4 e6 8 g4 Bg6 9 h4 Nbd7

Challenging the knight on e5 is the more "solid" choice, although this is only relative to 9...Bb4 – the positions are still wild. White still hunts the g6-bishop, but the main difference is that Black forces White to resolve the issue of the e5-knight before embarking on active operations.

10 Qe2

White has a few alternatives here:

a) 10 Nxg6? simply solves Black's biggest problem – where to hide the g6-bishop!

b) After 10 h5, the point of 9...Nbd7 is revealed and the resulting endgame following 10...Nxe5 11 dxe5 Qxd1+ 12 Kxd1 Be4 13 Nxe4 Nxe4 14 Be3 0-0-0+ 15 Ke2 Bc5 is equal.

c) 10 f3 (preventing ...Be4 and so threatening 11 h5) 10...Qc7 11 Bf4? Bd6 12 Qd2 0-0 13 h5? was C.Philippe-G.Mateuta, St Lorrain 2003, and here Black could have played 13...Nxe5! 14 dxe5 Bxe5 15 Bxe5 Qxe5+ 16 Kf1 Rad8 17 Qg2 (17 Qf2 h6 18 hxg6 Nxg4 leaves White's king rather exposed) 17...Qf4 18 Bb3 Be4 when he has avoided losing the bishop and has emerged with the superior position.

d) 10 Nxd7 is recommended by Alexander Khalifman and is a solid try for the advantage. White banks on the bishop pair and the kingside space advantage to give him a safe and enduring advantage. P.Svidler-M.Adams, Frankfurt 1999, continued 10...Qxd7 11 h5 Be4 12 Nxe4 Nxe4 13 c3 0-0-0 14 Qe2 Nf6 15 Bd2 with an edge for White.

10...Bb4 (Diagram 9)

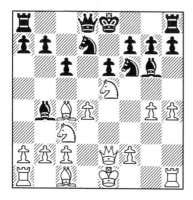

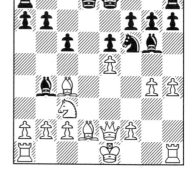

Diagram 9 (W)

Preparing ...Be4

Diagram 10 (B)

Black makes a mistake

11 Bd2

11 Rh3 performs some useful horizontal functions. E.Inarkiev-A.Kogan, Moscow 2002, continued 11...Nb6 12 h5 Be4 13 Bf4! Nxc4 (13...Qxd4 14 Rd1 Qc5 15 a3 Bxc3+ 16 Rxc3 gives White compensation) 14 Nxc4 Bxc2?! (this pawn grab is very risky, and 14...b5 is perhaps wiser) 15 Be5! Ba4 16 h6 Rg8 17 hxg7 Rxg7 and White has very good compensation for the pawn.

After 11 f3 Nxe5 12 dxe5 Nd5 13 Bxd5 (or 13 Bd2 Nxc3 14 bxc3 Be7 simultaneously attacking h4 and c2) 13...Qxd5! 14 h5 Black must sacrifice the bishop, but he gets ample compensation: 14...Bxc2 15 Qxc2 Qxf3 16 Rg1 (Z.Borosova-I.Plivcevic, Herceg Novi 2005) and here 16...0-0-0! would have left White's king stranded in the centre.

11...Nxe5

After 11...Bxc3 12 Bxc3 Be4 13 Rh3 Bd5 14 Bd3 Nxe5 15 Qxe5 Qb8 16 Bb4 Qxe5+ 17 dxe5 Nxg4 18 Bd6! (C.Lupulescu-G.Ardelean, Bucharest 2003) White has some compensation for the pawn: the bishop on d6 is a powerful piece which cripples Black.

12 dxe5 (Diagram 10) 12...Ne4??

Black gets into trouble after this move. Perhaps 12...Nd7!? is better: 13 h5 (13 0-0-0 h5) 13...Bxc2 14 Rc1 Bxc3 15 Bxc3 Ba4 16 b3 Bb5 17 Bxb5 cxb5 18 Rd1 Qc7 19 Rh3 was R.Soltanici-G.Ardelean, Bucharest 2003, and here I don't see why Black cannot play 19...0-0-0! with the idea of getting the king to safety and then re-routing the knight to d5.

13 Rd1! Qd4

13...Nxc3 14 Bxc3 Bxc3+ 15 bxc3 Qa5 16 h5 Qxc3+ 17 Kf1 Bxc2 18 Rc1 wins.

14 h5 0-0-0

Black cannot escape the fact that he must lose a piece. 14...Nxf2 15 Qxf2 Qxe5+ 16 Qe3 Qxe3+ 17 Bxe3 Bxc2 18 Rd2 Bxc3 19 bxc3 Be4 is another way of giving it up.

15 hxg6 Nxc3 16 bxc3 Bxc3 17 Rxh7 Bxd2+ 18 Rxd2 Qa1+

Black gets a couple of spite checks, but that's about all he can show for the piece.

19 Qd1 Qxe5+ 20 Kf1 Qf4 21 Rxd8+ Rxd8 22 Bd3 fxg6 23 Rxg7 Qh6 24 Rf7 Qh3+ 25 Ke1

White's king calmly runs away.

25...Qh1+ 26 Ke2 Qg2 27 Ke3! Qd5 28 Qf3 Qxa2 29 Rf8 a5 30 Rxd8+ Kxd8 31 Qf6+ Kc7 32 Qxg6 a4 33 Qg7+ Kb6 34 Qd4+ Kc7 35 Qf4+ Kb6 36 Qd4+ Kc7 37 g5 a3 38 g6 Qb1 39 g7 Qe1+ 40 Be2 Qc1+ 41 Qd2 Qxd2+ 42 Kxd2 a2 43 g8Q a1Q 44 Qg3+ Kd7 45 Qd3+ Kc7 46 Qg3+ Kd7 47 Qd3+ Kc7 48 Qc3 Qg1 49 Qf6 1-0

White Plays 3 Nf3

1 e4 d5 2 exd5 Qxd5 3 Nf3 (Diagram 11)

Diagram 11 (W)

White plays 3 Nf3

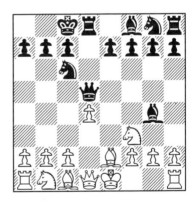

Diagram 12 (W)

A sharp battle is expected

Of all the moves I've faced when playing the Scandinavian, I've always been a bit wary of this one – why? Because White is aiming for something that the whole

2...Qxd5 Scandinavian is designed to prevent: a d4/c4 pawn centre. There are two main choices for Black here: he can grant White the d4/c4 centre or he can play a bit more riskily and meet the challenge head on.

3 d4 is well known to be insufficient: 3...Nc6 4 Nf3 e5 5 Nc3 (White gains nothing from 5 dxe5 Qxd1+ 6 Kxd1 Bg4) 5...Bb4 6 Bd2 Bxc3 7 Bxc3 e4 8 Ne5 Nxe5 9 dxe5 Ne7 10 Qxd5 Nxd5 11 Ba5 Be6 12 0-0-0 0-0-0 and Black is fine, D.Svetushkin-A.Zajarnyi, Kishnev 2001.

3...Bg4 4 Be2 Nc6

Both parties have marked out their plans. By developing the knight to c6 in front of his pawns, Black has committed himself to playing actively with ...0-0-0 and only has the ...e7-e5 pawn break after d2-d4.

 NOTE: 4...Nc6 is exciting but can be a difficult line to play. For those with a nervous disposition there is the more solid (if a little bit more passive) 4...Nf6 5 d4 transposing to the Portuguese Variation (see Chapter Fourteen).

5 d4!

Playing passively with 5 0-0 0-0-0 6 d3 plays into Black's hands. After 6...e5 Black intends ...Nf6 followed by ...e5-e4 removing some of the tension in the position.

5 h3 Bxf3! 6 Bxf3 Qe6+ 7 Qe2 (7 Kf1 was suggested by Jonathan Rowson but I don't see the problem for Black – it's better for White to try to nurture his bishop-pair advantage through to the endgame) 7...Qxe2+ 8 Bxe2 0-0-0 9 0-0 e5! (taking as much space as possible to combat the bishop pair) 10 d3 Nf6 11 Nd2 Nd5 12 a3 Be7 13 Nc4 was I.Efimov-E.Relange, Nice 1994. Here Black must play for space with 13...Bf6 and then ...g7-g6, ...Bg7 followed by ...f7-f5.

5...0-0-0 (Diagram 12)

Now there are two main moves for White: 6 c4 is covered in Game 50, and 6 Be3 in Game 51.

After 6 Nc3 Qh5 7 0-0 Nf6 8 h3 Nxd4! 9 Nxd4 Bxe2 10 Ncxe2 e5 11 Be3 Qg6 12 Qe1 exd4 13 Nxd4 Bd6 Black's chances are not worse.

Game 50
□ C.D'Amore ■ E.Prié
European Union Championship, Arvier 2007

---

1 e4 d5 2 exd5 Qxd5 3 Nf3 Bg4 4 Be2 Nc6 5 d4 0-0-0 6 c4 Qf5 7 Be3 (Diagram 13) 7...Bxf3!?

This is very interesting but incredibly sharp, and Black must tread carefully to maintain the balance.

7...e5!? is also possible. Black must continue actively with this pawn break either now or on next move, otherwise he may find himself in big trouble fighting with no space: 8 d5 Nf6 9 0-0 e4 10 Nd4 (10 Nh4 leaves the knight misplaced, and after 10...Qh5 followed by an exchange of light-squared bishops the d3-square will be very strong for Black) 10...Nxd4 11 Bxd4 Bd6 12 Nc3 Rhe8 13 c5? **(Diagram 14)** 13...Bxh2+ 14 Kxh2 Qh5+ 15 Kg1 Bxe2 16 Nxe2 Ng4 with a dangerous attack for Black, M.Bueno Abalo-A.Stefanova, Mondariz 1999.

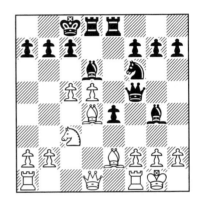

Diagram 13 (B)

More than one option

Diagram 14 (B)

A bad mistake

7...Nf6 has been the main line: 8 Nbd2 (indirectly defending the d4-pawn) 8...e5!? (8...e6 is too passive, and 9 a3 Bh5 10 h3 Bg6 11 Rc1 h5 12 b4 gave White a fantastic initiative in J.Borisek-V.Nevednichy, Nova Gorica 2007) 9 d5! (9 dxe5 Nxe5 is fine for Black, while 9 Nxe5? just loses after 9...Bxe2 10 Qxe2 Nxd4) 9...Nb4 10 Rc1! Nxa2 (10...e4!? is a very interesting move; after 11 Nd4 Qg6 12 0-0 Nd3! 13 Rc3 Bh3 14 g3 Black should probably not take the exchange but instead concentrate on developing his initiative) 11 Ra1 Nb4 12 0-0 a6 13 Ra4! Nd3 14 Bxd3 Qxd3 15 Qa1 Re8 16 b4 and b4-b5 soon came with devastating effect in G.Sax-J.Waitzkin, Pula 1997.

8 Bxf3 Nxd4 9 Bxd4

9 Bg4 Nc2+ is the whole point, and here 10 Qxc2 Qxg4 11 0-0 e6! is the best. Now:

a) Grabbing the pawn with 12 Bxa7?! is I guess the acid test. Although the black king becomes more exposed, the white bishop does get locked in and following 12...b6 13 Qa4 Kb7 14 Nc3 Nf6 15 Rad1 Bc5! it looks doomed.

b) 12 Qa4 is probably wiser. After 12...a6 13 Nd2 Nf6 14 b4 Black has the sly move 14...Rd3 intending to meet 15 b5 with 15...Ra3!.

9...Qe6+ 10 Be2 Qe4 (Diagram 15) 11 0-0 Qxd4 12 Qa4 e6! 13 Nc3

13 Rd1 Qxb2 14 Nd2 (14 Nc3! is an improvement) 14...Nf6 (14...Qa3! is much stronger) 15 Rab1 Qa3 16 Qb5 Qa6 17 Qxa6 bxa6 18 c5 and after ...Rd4 Black is fine, M.Lyell-D.Calvert, Hastings 2008/09.

13...Bd6!

White was a bit better in D.Brandenburg-S.Tiviakov, Hilversum 2008, after 13...Qb6 14 Rad1 Rxd1 15 Rxd1 Nf6 16 b4! Bxb4 (it is too dangerous to let the pawns march, so Black decides to take the offered material in exchange for his queen) 17 Rb1 a5 18 a3 Bxc3 19 Rxb6 cxb6, although here White was content to force a draw with 20 c5 bxc5 21 Ba6 bxa6 22 Qc6+ Kb8 23 Qb6+.

14 Nb5 Qe5 15 Nxd6+

After 15 Nxa7+?? Kb8 White loses the bishop on e2.

15...cxd6 16 Bf3 Kb8 (Diagram 16)

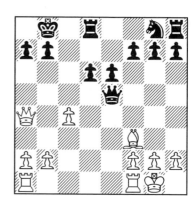

Diagram 15 (B)

Black regains the piece

Diagram 16 (W)

Good compensation

Black is a pawn up, but White has a strong bishop which gives him good compensation. Like in many games with opposite-side castling, dynamic play is the most important feature.

17 Rfe1

White cannot open files easily with 17 b4 Ne7 18 b5, as Black can ward off the initiative with 18...Rc8 19 Rab1 Qc5 20 Rfc1 Qb6 (blockading the b5-pawn) 21 Qb4 Nf5 (heading for d4) 22 a4 Qc5.

17...Qc5 18 b4 Qc7

18...Qxc4? is playing with fire, and 19 Bxb7! Kxb7 20 Rac1 Qd5 21 Rc7+! wins.

19 Rac1 Ne7 20 Re3 Qd7 21 Qd1 Rc8 22 c5 Rhd8 23 Rd3 Qc7 24 Qa4 dxc5 25 Rxd8 Rxd8 26 bxc5 Nc6 27 Rb1 Rd4 28 Qc2

Black has defended accurately, and all that remains is to grind out the advantage.

28...Rh4 29 Bxc6 Qxc6 30 g3 Rh5 31 Qd3 Kc8 32 Qa3 a6 33 Rc1 Rf5 34 Qc3 f6 35 Qe3 h5 36 h4 Kb8 37 Qd4 Rd5 38 Qe3 Ka7 39 Qa3 g5 40 Qb4 Re5 41 hxg5 fxg5 42 Qd4 Rd5 43 Qe3 h4 44 g4 Ka8 45 Qc3 e5 46 Qe3 Rd4 47 f3 Rf4 48 Rc3 e4 49 Rc4 Rxf3 50 Qxg5 Qd7 51 Rc1 Qd4+ 52 Kh1 Qd3 53 Qg8+ Ka7 54 Qb3 Rh3+ 55 Kg2 Rg3+ 56 Kh1 Qd2 57 Qc2 Rh3+ 58 Kg1 Qe3+ 0-1

Game 51
□ **A.Areshchenko** ■ **R.Almond**
Port Erin 2007

---

1 e4 d5 2 exd5 Qxd5 3 Nf3 Bg4 4 Be2 Nc6 5 d4! 0-0-0 6 Be3!?

White secures the d4-pawn before challenging the bishop with h2-h3 or the queen with c2-c4. This is an incredibly sharp line.

6...e5!?

6...Nf6 transposes into the Portuguese Variation (see Game 65).

7 c4 Qa5+ 8 Bd2 Bb4 9 d5 Bxf3

9...e4 doesn't quite work out after 10 Ng5! Bxe2 11 Qxe2 Nd4 12 Qd1! (12 Qxe4 Bxd2+ 13 Nxd2 Nb3 14 Rd1 Nxd2 15 Rxd2 Nf6 gives Black great compensation) 12...Bxd2+ 13 Nxd2 Nh6 14 0-0 and Black cannot defend the e4-pawn adequately.

10 Bxf3 (Diagram 17)

 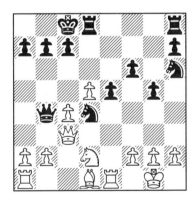

Diagram 17 (B)
A major choice for Black

Diagram 18 (B)
Offering an endgame

10...Bxd2+

10...Nd4 11 Nc3 Qc5?! 12 Be2 Nf6 13 0-0 c6 was recommended Wahls, but after 14

Bg5! Movsesian claims that White is significantly better, and following 14...Qa5 15 Bg4+ Kb8 16 Rc1 Black has a strong knight on d4 but nothing much else to write home about. S.Movsesian-I.Papaioannou, Bled Olympiad 2002, continued 16...h5 17 Bh3 Ne6 18 Qe2! Nxg5 19 Qxe5+ Qc7 20 Qxg5 Bxc3 21 bxc3 cxd5 22 Qxg7! Ng4 23 g3 dxc4 (Black was forced to take on c4 with the pawn to keep f7 protected, but now the white bishop moves to the long diagonal with decisive effect) 24 Rb1 Ne5 25 Bg2 and White had a very strong attack.

11...Qa6!? (instead of 11...Qc5) may be Black's option. For example, 12 Be2 Nf6 13 0-0 (13 Bd3 e4!) 13...Bxc3 14 Bxc3 Nxe2+ (after 14...Rxd5!? 15 cxd5 Nxe2+ 16 Kh1 Rd8 17 Re1 Nxc3 18 bxc3 Rxd5 Black has two pawns for the exchange so he shouldn't stand worse) 15 Qxe2 Rxd5 was fine for Black in F.Cheverry-D.Berges, French League 2001.

11 Nxd2 Nd4 12 0-0 Qb4 13 Re1 f6

13...Nf6! is the positional approach: 14 Qc1 (defending c4 and b2; White can't really play 14 Rxe5 as 14...Nxf3+ is a little awkward) 14...Rhe8 15 Bd1 (15 a3 Qd6 16 b4?! is tempting but wrong: 16...Nxf3+ 17 Nxf3 e4 18 Nd4 Ng4 and Black has seized the initiative) 15...Kb8 16 a3 Qd6 17 b4 h5 18 Nb3 Nxb3 19 Bxb3 e4 20 c5 Qe5 and Black will soon follow up with ...Ng4.

14 Qc1 Nh6 15 Bd1 g5 16 Qc3! (Diagram 18) 16...Qxc3?

This is probably the losing mistake. Despite initial appearances the endgame is bad for Black: the doubled c-pawns can advance quickly and effectively, and furthermore the open b-file gives White tremendous pressure against the b7-pawn.

16...Qd6 had to be played, although the position favours White as Black's attack is pretty cumbersome.

17 bxc3 Ndf5 18 Ne4 Rhf8 19 Bb3 Ng8 20 c5 Nge7 21 Red1 Ng7 22 Bc4 h6 23 c6!

This was White's plan when offering to take the position into the endgame. Now Black is completely lost!

23...b6 24 Ba6+ Kb8 25 c4 f5 26 Nc3 Ne8 27 a4

The pawns are marching down the board and Black is simply powerless to do anything about them.

27...Nd6 28 a5 e4 29 c5 Ndc8 30 axb6 cxb6 31 Nb5 Rxd5 32 c7+ Ka8 33 Rxd5 Nxd5 34 c6 Nxc7 35 Nxc7+ Kb8 36 Nb5 f4 37 c7+ Ka8 38 Bxc8 1-0

Summary

In this chapter we've looked at two variations with nicknames: the Patzer (3...Qe5+) and the Banker (3...Qd8). White deals with both of these variations in a highly principled way – occupying the centre with Ne5 followed by a pawn storm on the kingside! Naturally, the main games in this chapter deal with the more reputable Banker variation. Theory begins on move nine, where Black has a choice between 9...Bb4 (Game 48) and 9...Nbd7 (Game 49). However, as the resulting positions show, the situation is none too pleasant for Black.

A universal system not to be underestimated is 3 Nf3. The aim is to refute the basic 2...Qxd5 premise by managing to establish the d4/c4 pawn centre. Black can react in two ways: the principled ...Bg4 followed by ...Nc6 contesting White's intentions; or ...Nf6, transposing to the Portuguese Variation and allowing the two-pawn centre (see Chapter Fourteen). Of these two approaches, the first is preferable. However, the positions become incredibly wild, and Games 50-51 show that Black must proceed in a radical and dynamic manner.

Chapter Eleven

Introduction to 2...Nf6

- Can White win a Pawn?
- Black's Options
- A Potential Problem with 3 d4
- Nf3 before Nc3

1 e4 d5 2 exd5 Nf6 (Diagram 1)

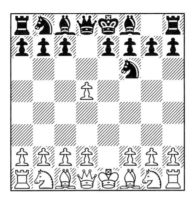

Diagram 1 (W)

The 2...Nf6 Scandinavian

It is surprising how one move can change the whole nature of the Scandinavian, and this is certainly true of 2...Nf6. By refusing to capture the d5-pawn with the queen, Black takes the game into something Nimzowitsch would call "hypermodern" territory. Rather like in the Grünfeld and the Alekhine defences, Black freely allows White to establish a pawn centre. His aim is to first restrain and then pressure the centre, followed by a timely pawn break (...e7-e5 or ...c7-c5).

 TIP: When White has chased away the knight with c2-c4, the pawn break tends to be ...e7-e5. If the knight is left on d5 then ...c7-c5 becomes the main consideration (as long as White has not actively prevented it!).

The 2...Nf6 Scandinavian is not so popular at the highest levels, but it has featured in the opening repertoires of grandmasters David Bronstein, Bent Larsen, Gata Kamsky and Roman Dzindzichashvili to name just a few.

The attraction of 2...Nf6 lies in its simplicity. The core idea for Black is to place a tremendous amount of pressure on the d4-pawn. Black hopes that this pressure forces White to either overextend in the centre, allowing Black to open the position, or to make some form of positional concession in order to maintain the tension. If White takes some preventative measures, this often gives Black enough time to achieve his ideal pawn breaks.

Can White win a Pawn?

I must point out that White cannot just play **3 c4** and sit back, content in the knowledge that he has won a pawn. Black has two options available to him: he can play the sharp Icelandic Gambit with 3...e6; or he can play the more reliable 3...c6. While things are undoubtedly messy in the Icelandic Gambit, objectively Black probably doesn't have sufficient compensation for the pawn – although he may have a lot of fun! Meanwhile, 3...c6 is such a dangerous gambit that White would do best to reject it and instead transpose to the Caro-Kann Panov-Botvinnik Attack with 4 d4, although even here Black's chances are acknowledged to be fine.

After much consideration I have decided not to focus on the Panov-Botvinnik for two reasons. Firstly, space does not permit me to summarize concisely a complicated system that deserves a book on its own. Secondly, and more importantly, I don't believe that 3 c4 necessarily gives White an advantage, and I am of the opinion that either 3 Nf3 or 3 d4 is the best move. 3 c4 is covered in Chapter Fifteen, along with 3 Bb5+.

Black's Options

If White chooses to develop with d2-d4 and Nf3, Black can choose between two set-ups:

Set-up A: the fianchetto system

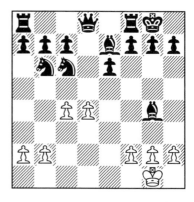

Diagram 2	**Diagram 3**
Set-up A	Set-up B

Diagram 2 shows Set-up A in its purest form (please note that White's c-pawn may be on c2, in which case the black knight would be on d5). Whenever I look at this set-up I am always struck by how alike it is to the Grünfeld. However, there is one fundamental difference: Black is playing for the ...e7-e5 pawn break rather than ...c7-c5 (as mentioned earlier, ...c7-c5 is traditionally seen in lines where White refrains from playing c2-c4).

The ...e7-e5 pawn break is in fact Black's fundamental aim. All the black pieces are geared for this purpose and if White for some reason is able to prevent it, Black will be positionally lost. However, if Black plays accurately then White should not be able to deal with the pressure on the d4/c4 pawn centre *and* prevent ...e7-e5.

 NOTE: White should aim to swap off Black's dark-squared bishop. This bishop adds vital pressure to the centre, and it is certainly Black's strongest minor piece.

This brings me on to an important point: the attraction of the fianchetto system is the long-term advantage of the bishop on g7. In endgames this piece has tremendous long-range power. If you combine this with the possibility of a minority attack on the queenside, it's easy to see that Black's position has tremendous potential.

Set-up B: ...Bg4 and ...e6

Diagram 3 shows the set-up that Black is aiming for (again please bear in mind that the black knight may be on d5 and the white pawn on c2).

Set-up B is somewhat more solid than Set-up A, primarily because Black restrains the centre not just with pieces but with the e6-pawn as well. Black is banking on easy development and long-term pressure on d4, and if allowed he will play ...Be7-f6, ...Qd8-e7 and a rook to d8. Black's position is very solid and not easy to refute. However, there is one weakness in Black's position which White may choose to play on, and this is that the knight on b6 is out of play.

There is a third set-up for Black, in which he doesn't even bother to recapture the pawn and instead concentrates on developing his pieces at maximum speed, and this leads us to the following topic:

A Potential Problem with 3 d4

A possible problem with **3 d4** is that it allows Black to play the Portuguese Variation, **3...Bg4 (Diagram 4)**, which was popularized by Portuguese GM Luis Galego and IM Rui Damaso. This fiery little move is a true gambit in every sense of the word. Black is not bothered with material; all he is interested in is active piece play and pressure along the open e-file.

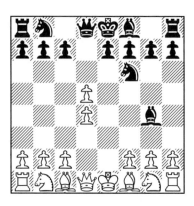

Diagram 4 (W)
The Portuguese Variation

However, a major practical problem for Black is that White can play 3 Nf3 followed by 4 d4, rather than the other way round. This is a well-known move-order trick White can use to bypass the Portuguese Variation; not necessarily because it is dangerous, but because choosing 3 Nf3 avoids the hassle of having to memorize an antidote to 3 d4 Bg4. The Portuguese Variation and the 3 Nf3 antidote are covered in Chapter Fourteen.

Nf3 before Nc3

Should Black decide after 3 d4 that the Portuguese Variation is not for him, and he goes into the main lines with 3...Nxd5, there is one point that both sides should be very much aware of. After **1 e4 d5 2 exd5 Nf6 3 d4 Nxd5 4 c4 Nb6** (4...Nb4 is a move for blitz or if you are looking for a quick victory against a beginner; Black threatens 5...Qxd4 but after 5 a3 the black knight must hop back), it is incredibly important that White plays **5 Nf3!**, as 5 Nc3 allows 5...e5!. This is known to be fine for Black: for example, 6 dxe5 Qxd1+ 7 Nxd1 Nc6 8 f4 Be6 9 b3 0–0–0 10 Ne3 Bc5 11 a3 Rhe8 12 Nf3 f6 13 Be2 fxe5 14 fxe5 Nxe5 15 Nxe5 Bd4 and Black had the superior position in the famous game K.Treybal-E.Bogoljubow, Bad Pistyan 1922.

Chapter Twelve

The Fianchetto Variation

- **White Plays 5 c4**
- **The Aggressive 7 c5**
- **The Old Main Line**
- **Playing without c2-c4**

1 e4 d5 2 exd5 Nf6 3 Nf3 Nxd5 4 d4 g6 (Diagram 1)

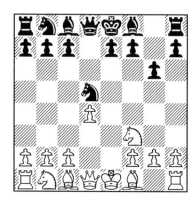

Diagram 1 (W)
Black plays 4...g6

The fianchetto is currently the most popular set-up in the 2...Nf6 Scandinavian. As mentioned in the previous chapter, Black's plan is fairly straightforward. Everything is focused on restraining the white centre and then breaking with ...e7-e5 or ...c7-c5 at the right moment.

White has several different methods of dealing with Black's set-up, and they can be split into two categories. White can advance with an early c2-c4, or he can play more solidly by leaving the pawn on c2 and maintaining the option of c2-c3. We will look at each of these in turn.

White Plays 5 c4

1 e4 d5 2 exd5 Nf6 3 Nf3 Nxd5 4 d4 g6 5 c4 Nb6 6 Nc3 Bg7 (Diagram 2)

This is by far the most popular and principled continuation. Not only does White kick back the well-placed knight but he also stakes a big claim for the centre. However White decides to continue the game, his play is normally based on one or many of the following factors:

♟ depriving Black of space (c4-c5 systems)

♟ depriving Black of the ...e7-e5 pawn break and adequate counterplay (c4-c5 and the old main line); and

♟ depriving Black's light-squared bishop of a good square. This is usually achieved either by denying it the g4-square or by tying it down to the defence of the b7-pawn.

The Aggressive 7 c5

1 e4 d5 2 exd5 Nf6 3 Nf3 Nxd5 4 d4 g6 5 c4 Nb6 6 Nc3 Bg7 7 c5 (Diagram 3)

This is the most aggressive answer to the Fianchetto Variation. It's the scariest line for Black to face, and a near-refutation of 4...g6. Since it has been recommended by Alexander Khalifman in his *Opening for White according to Anand* series, 7 c5 has increased in popularity.

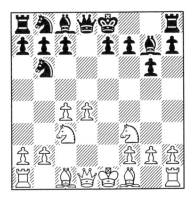

Diagram 2 (W)	Diagram 3 (B)
An early c2-c4	The aggressive 7 c5

At first sight this pawn advance seems very strange – White not only concedes the d5-square but chases the knight back to the centre! However, White's logic is based on some deep ideas:

1) White compromises his pawn structure but in return gains considerable piece activity. In addition, Black's queenside is suffering from a case of overpopulation.

2) White intends to tie up Black's forces to the defence of the knight on d5. If we look at the position a little further, we see that Black cannot develop the bishop to e6 without worrying about a knight jump to g5; nor can he develop the b8-knight to d7 without first resolving the issue of the knight on d5.

3) White wishes to use his active pieces to target three "soft" points in Black's position: the e7-pawn, which will come under heavy pressure down the half-open e-file; the f7-pawn; and the b7-pawn. White's aim is to place insurmountable pressure along the a2-g8 diagonal and down the e-file.

There are three main defensive tries:

1) Black can support the strong knight on d5 with ...c7-c6, and aim to break White's bind with ...b7-b6 or ...b7-b5.

2) Black can liquidate into an endgame very quickly by playing ...Be6. This is very much a drawing attempt, with Black accepting a slightly worse position.

3) Black can exchange knights with a quick ...Nxc3, followed by breaking the pawn chain with ...b7-b6.

Game 52
☐ A.Greet ■ H.Stefansson
World Mind Sports, Beijing (rapid) 2008

---

1 e4 d5 2 exd5 Nf6 3 Nf3 Nxd5 4 d4 g6 5 c4 Nb6 6 Nc3 Bg7

 WARNING: Combining systems with 6...Bg4 is not to be recommended, on account of 7 c5! Nd5 8 Qb3 when Black already has problems. P.Svidler-F.Berend, Vilnius 1995, continued 8...Nxc3 9 bxc3 Bxf3 10 gxf3 b6 11 Bc4 e6, and here 12 d5! looks strong.

7 c5 Nd5

7...N6d7 is just far too passive – Black will not be developing his pieces in a hurry after this.

8 Bc4 c6 (Diagram 4)

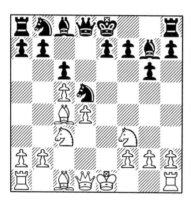
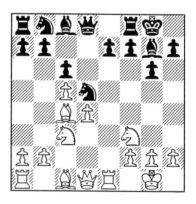

Diagram 4 (W)
Supporting the knight

Diagram B (W)
Black is under pressure

8...Nxc3 is covered in the next game.

9 0-0!

An important move – White gets ready to create pressure down the e-file.

9 Qb3 is not the best move, as Black can gambit a pawn with 9...0-0!. It is simply

too risky for White to accept, as after 10 Nxd5 cxd5 11 Bxd5 Nc6 he is in an awkward position: Black threatens both 12...Na5 and 12...Nxd4, and following 12 Bd2 Bg4!? White must either return the pawn or give up the bishop pair, when the extra d4-pawn doesn't count for anything.

9...0-0

9...Be6!? is interesting, but probably only enough to offer chances for a draw. Black has the following idea in mind: 10 Ng5 Nxc3 11 Nxe6 Nxd1! 12 Nxd8 Nxb2! 13 Bxb2 Kxd8 14 Bxf7 Na6!? 15 Rab1 Rf8 16 Bc4 Nc7 17 Rfe1 Bf6 18 Re3 b5 (I.Saric-J.Tomczak, Szeged 2008) and after 19 Bb3 a5 20 Rh3 Rh8 Black's position is a tough nut to crack.

10 Re1 (Diagram 5)

White's plan is simply to place as much pressure on e7 and d5 as possible, in the process extracting further concessions from Black.

I don't like 10 Qb3 as much, primarily because it allows Black to relieve the pressure on the queenside with 10...Nxc3 11 bxc3 b5, and after 12 cxb6 axb6 13 Re1 Ba6 Black gets some activity.

10...Nxc3

Alternatively:

a) 10...b6 11 Bg5! induces further weaknesses: 11...f6 (11...Re8 fails to 12 Qb3 Be6 13 Nxd5 cxd5 14 Bb5! forcing Black back, and after 14...Rf8 15 cxb6 axb6 16 Qb4 Ra7 17 a4 White's position is overwhelming; while 11...Be6 12 Nxd5 cxd5 13 Bxe7 Qxe7 14 Bxd5 is a neat trick, and 14...Na6 15 Bxa8 Rxa8 16 d5 Rd8 17 Qe2 is much better for White – Emms; finally, White also has a clear plus after 11...Bf6 12 Nxd5 cxd5 13 Bxf6 exf6 14 Bb5) 12 Bd2 bxc5 13 Qb3 e6 14 dxc5 and Black's pieces are stuck on the back rank whereas White's are simply dominating, A.Hauchard-P.Aveline, Cappelle la Grande 2003.

b) 10...Bg4 11 Bg5! f6 (if 11...Re8 12 Qb3 Bxf3 13 gxf3 and White is winning – it is irrelevant that he has weakened his own kingside, as Black hasn't developed many of his pieces) 12 Bd2 Bc8 13 Qb3 e6 14 Nxd5 exd5 15 Bd3 b6 16 Bf4 (Khalifman). Black's lack of development and his bad bishop on g7 make this position very bad for him.

c) 10...Be6 11 Qb3! b6 was J.Houska-A.Muzychuk, Gothenburg 2005, and here I should have played 12 Ng5!. The reply I was afraid of was 12...b5 (12...Bxd4? loses to 13 Rxe6! fxe6 14 Nxe6 Bxf2+ 15 Kh1) but I had missed the stunning 13 Bxb5!!. White must sacrifice an exchange but his position is wonderful after 13...Nc7 (13...cxb5 14 Nxe6 fxe6 15 Rxe6 and White regains the piece since 15...Nxc3 loses to 16 Rd6+!; or 13...Nxc3 14 Nxe6 fxe6 15 bxc3 cxb5 16 Rxe6 Kh8 17 Bg5 Bf6 18 Bxf6+ Rxf6 19 Rxf6 exf6 20 Qxb5 when Black's extra piece is no match for the passed pawns) 14 Nxe6 Nxe6 15 Rxe6 fxe6 16 Be2 Bxd4 17 Be3 Bxe3 18 Qxe6+ Kh8 19 Qe5+ Rf6 20 Qxe3. Note that Black cannot play 20...Nd7, as 21 Rd1 Qe8 22 Qd4 wins.

d) 10...h6 prevents Bg5, but after 11 Ne5! e6 12 Ne4 the d6-square is an inviting outpost.

11 bxc3 b5 12 Bb3 Bg4 13 Bg5 (Diagram 6)

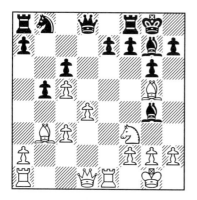

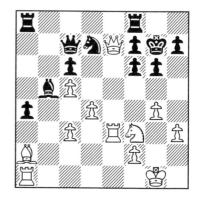

Diagram 6 (B)	Diagram 7 (W)
Focussing on e7	White has a decisive advantage

Accurate play by Andrew Greet, zooming in on the weak e7 point.

13...Bf6 14 Bxf6

Andrew chooses the "no-risk" approach, but 14 Bh6 Re8 (or 14...Bg7 15 Bxg7 Kxg7 16 a4 Nd7 17 axb5 cxb5 18 h3) 15 h3 Bc8 16 a4 is also dismal for Black.

14...exf6 15 h3 Bf5 16 a4 a5

White has a devastating position, although from here he begins to lose the thread a little.

17 Qe2 bxa4 18 Rxa4 Qc7 19 Qe7 Nd7 20 g4 Bd3 21 Re3 Bb5 22 Ra1 a4 23 Ba2 Kg7 (Diagram 7) 24 Qd6?

24 Be6 is crushing: for example, 24...Ra7 (24...Rad8 25 c4 wins) 25 c4 Ba6 26 Qxd7 Qxd7 27 Bxd7 Rxd7 28 Rxa4 is an easy win.

24...Qxd6 25 cxd6 Nb6 26 Nd2 Nd5 27 Rf3 Be2 28 Rg3 Nf4 29 Kh2 Rab8 30 Bc4 Rb2 31 Bxe2 Nxe2 32 Rd3 Nf4 33 Rf3 Nxh3 34 Kxh3 Rxd2 35 Rxa4 Rd8 36 Kg3 Rxd6 37 Re3

Due to White's inaccurate play, his advantage has petered out and it should be a draw, although when there are four rooks on the board the position is always dangerous.

37...Rd7 38 Rc4 Rc7 39 Rc5 Kf8 40 Re1 Ra2 41 f3 Ra6 42 Rh1 Kg7 43 Rb1 Rd7 44 Re1 Rd5 45 Rxd5 cxd5 46 Rb1 Rc6 47 Rb5 Rxc3 48 Rxd5 Ra3 49 Rd8 Rd3 50 Kf4 g5+ 51 Ke4 Ra3 52 d5 Ra4+ 53 Ke3 f5 54 gxf5 Kf6 55 d6 Ra6 56 Ke4 h5 57 d7 Ra4+ 58

Kd5 Ke7 59 Rf8 Kxd7 60 Rxf7+ Ke8 61 Rh7 Ra5+ 62 Ke6 Ra6+ 63 Ke5 h4 64 f6 Ra3
65 Ke6 Ra6+??

A big blunder: 65...Re3+ 66 Kf5 Rxf3+ 67 Kxg5 is an easy draw.

66 Kf5 Ra3 67 Kg6 Rxf3 68 Rh8+ Kd7 69 f7 h3 70 f8Q Rxf8 71 Rxf8 g4 72 Rh8 Ke6
73 Kg5 Kd5 1-0

Although this was a rapidplay game, the opening is very instructive.

Game 53
□ **I.Nataf** ■ **L.Galego**
Andorra 1999

---

1 e4 d5 2 exd5 Nf6 3 Nf3 Nxd5 4 d4 g6 5 c4 Nb6 6 Nc3 Bg7 7 c5!? Nd5 8 Bc4 Nxc3 9
bxc3 (Diagram 8)

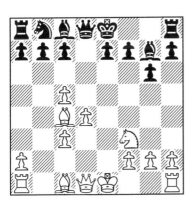

Diagram 8 (B)

A strong pawn formation

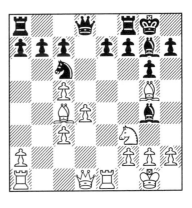

Diagram 9 (B)

Difficult for Black

Black can try to break White's pawn formation in two ways: by challenging the c5-pawn with ...b7-b6, or by playing ...Nc6 and then ...e7-e5.

9...0-0 10 0-0

10 h4!?, as John Emms points out, looks very scary, but Black should be able to hold the position. A critical line runs 10...Bg4! (Black doesn't want to allow White an easy attack along the h-file, but 10...h5 conceding the g5-square is not advisable) 11 h5 Bxh5 12 Rxh5 gxh5. White's attack may only lead to a draw, even though 13 Ng5 looks menacing. After 13...h6 14 Nxf7 Rxf7 15 Bxf7+ Kxf7 16 Qxh5+ Kg8 17 Bxh6 Bxh6 18 Qxh6 Nd7 White can take a perpetual check or play on with 19 0-0-0 Nf6 20 Qg6+ Kf8 21 Rh1, but Black can defend here with 21...Qd5 reaching a complicated position.

10...b6

This doesn't solve all of Black's problems, but I think it is the best move.

10...Nc6 is the main alternative, and the main line here is 11 Re1! Bg4 12 Bg5! **(Diagram 9)**.

It is difficult for Black to simply defend the e7-pawn with the rook, as this in turn makes f7 vulnerable. Therefore Black is obliged to make some positional concessions (remember, pawns cannot move backwards!). Now:

a) 12...Qd7 13 h3! (13 d5 is bad due to 13...Na5! 14 Rxe7 Qf5) 13...Bxf3 14 Qxf3 e5 (or 14...e6 15 Rab1 Rab8 16 h4 h6 17 Bf6 and White has a clear plus – Khalifman) 15 Rad1! and White has the advantage of the bishop pair and firm control of the centre.

b) 12...h6 13 Bh4 g5 takes direct action to break the uncomfortable pressure on e7: 14 Bg3 e5 (14...e6 is passive, and 15 Qe2 Na5 16 Bd3 b6 17 Rad1 Qe7 18 cxb6 axb6 19 h3 Bh5 20 Be5 is better for White, D.Arngrimsson-T.Thorhallsson, Reykjavik 2007; White also has the advantage after 14...b6 15 h3 Bh5 16 Be2 bxc5 17 Qa4 Nb8 18 Rad1, as indicated by Emms and De Firmian – after Be5 it will be difficult for Black to develop his knight) 15 d5! (this natural advance destroys the coordination between Black's pieces) 15...Na5 16 Bf1! c6 was played in D.Lima-E.Scarella, Buenos Aires 2005. 16...c6 allows White to establish a powerful-looking passed pawn. Black's logic behind such an unusual move is to freeze the g3-bishop out of the game by forming a dark-square pawn blockade with g5/f6/e5. It is for this reason that White cannot leave the knight on f3 unguarded. Black wishes to regroup his pieces to undermine White's powerful d6- and c5-pawns. Although ambitious, this plan is incredibly risky. The game continued 17 d6 f6! 18 h3 Bd7 (18...Bh5!? also deserves attention; for instance 19 Be2 b6 20 Qd3 Bf7 21 Qf5 Re8) 19 h4 (trying to weaken Black's kingside) 19...b6!. As GM Michael Roiz points out, it's important to liberate the knight as soon as possible. Overall White has the better chances because of the weak light squares around the black king. However, White's dark-squared bishop remains restricted and the position is very complicated.

11 Re1!

White concentrates on developing his initiative along the e-file rather than worrying about pawn structure.

11...Bb7

Black must tread carefully. 11...Nd7 12 Bg5 Nf6 13 Ne5 bxc5 14 Qf3 Be6 15 Nc6 Qd6 was Zhang Zhong-G.West, Sydney 1999, and here 16 Bf4 Qd7 17 d5 Bg4 18 Nxe7+ Qxe7 19 Rxe7 Bxf3 20 gxf3 would give White an unquestionable edge, as indicated by John Emms.

12 Bg5! Bf6

The only move.

13 Bxf6

13 Bh6!? Re8 14 Qe2 threatening Bxf7+ is also very interesting. For example, 14...e6 15 Ne5 (threatening Nxf7) 15...Bd5 16 Bb5 c6 17 Bd3 Nd7 18 c4 bxc5, and now 19 Rab1 (after 19 cxd5 exd5 Black is only slightly worse) 19...cxd4 20 Nxd7 Qxd7 21 cxd5 exd5 22 Qc2 is the best way for White to obtain a piece for three pawns.

13...exf6 14 d5!?

True to his typical attacking style, Igor Nataf is prepared to sacrifice a pawn in order to prevent Black from developing his pieces.

14...bxc5 15 Rb1 Bc8 16 d6! (Diagram 10)

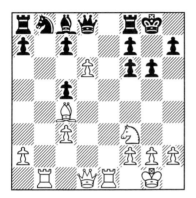

Diagram 10 (B)

Releasing the bishop

Diagram 11 (W)

White's minor pieces dominate

16...Nc6?

Black "loses" two pieces for a rook and two pawns, but don't be fooled by the material equality. White's two pieces will be superior, and furthermore one of the extra pawns is doubled and virtually useless.

16...Bf5! saves Black, and 17 Rb7 Qxd6 18 Qxd6 cxd6 19 Ree7 Nc6 20 Rxf7 Rxf7 21 Rxf7 d5! 22 Bxd5 Rd8 23 Rd7+ Kf8 24 Rxd8+ Nxd8 reaches a completely equal ending.

17 Qd5! Qxd6

Black loses material after 17...Qd7 18 Bb5 Bb7 19 Ba4!

18 Qxd6 cxd6 19 Bd5 Bd7 20 Rb7 Rad8 21 Rxd7 Rxd7 22 Bxc6 Rc7 23 Bd5 Rb8 (Diagram 11) 24 h4!? Rb2 25 Rd1!!

A key move, overprotecting the bishop while at the same time planning to target the d6-pawn.

25...Rc2

25...Re7! is the best try, and 26 Nd2! f5! 27 a4 Rc2 should be okay for Black.

26 Nd2! f5 27 Bb3! Rxc3 28 Nb1 Rxb3 29 axb3 Rb7?

After 29...c4 30 Rc1!? d5 31 Kf1 Kf8 32 Na3 a5 33 bxc4 dxc4 34 Nxc4 a4 35 Ke2 White is winning.

30 Nd2! d5 31 Nf3! d4?

Now White can safely blockade the black pawns and the extra piece soon begins to tell.

32 Rc1 Rb5 33 Nd2! Kf8 34 Ra1! a5 35 Kf1 Ke7 36 Ke2 Ke6 37 Kd3 Kd5 38 Kc2! h5 39 Nc4 Rb8 40 Rxa5 Re8 41 Kd3 Rb8 42 Nd2 1-0

The Old Main Line

1 e4 d5 2 exd5 Nf6 3 Nf3 Nxd5 4 d4 g6 5 c4 Nb6 6 Nc3 Bg7

Maintaining the centre with the d4/c4 pawn front is one of the most logical plans for White. This pawn front contains a lot of potential energy. Not only does it control all those important central squares, but it also acts as a clamp on the black pieces.

Having obtained this pawn structure rather easily White now takes steps to protect it, by aiming to squash any Black counterplay or by advancing one of the pawns when it can be adequately supported.

As far as Black is concerned, playing with the pieces in front of the pawns carries great risk, so he must play as actively and purposefully as possible. He must stay focused on his plans of restraining, pressurizing and breaking the centre. Most importantly, he must not drift and start playing random moves! Everything should be geared towards a pawn break (usually...e7-e5, but sometimes ...c7-c5), or pressurizing the d4-pawn with ...Bg4. White has two main options to counter these ideas: h2-h3 preventing ...Bg4, or logical play with Be2 and Be3.

TIP: Exchanging minor pieces is usually a good idea for Black (not the dark-squared bishop, though!).

Game 54
☐ **H.Jonkman** ■ **T.Krnan**
Kapuskasing 2003

1 e4 d5 2 exd5 Nf6 3 d4 Nxd5 4 Nf3 g6 5 c4 Nb6 6 Nc3 Bg7 7 h3 (Diagram 12)

White prevents Black from playing the key move ...Bg4, but this allows Black to crash through in the centre with ...e7-e5.

7...0-0 8 Be3 Nc6 9 Qd2!

The best move – White must already confront Black's idea of ...e7-e5.

9 Be2 is unwise. After 9...e5! 10 d5 Ne7, the only good move is 11 g4! as 11 0-0 allows Black to play 11...h6 followed by ...Nf5 or ...f7-f5.

9...e5

The most principled continuation.

10 d5 (Diagram 13) 10...Na5!?

This allows Black to play ...f7-f5 without any problems. However, the knight on a5 is seriously misplaced and it may be problematic to get it back into play.

10...Ne7!? is positionally the best move, but it does allow White to play 11 g4!. It is clear from the pawn structures that the position will become very sharp. The kings are headed for opposite-side castling so it becomes important for both sides to disturb each other's intentions:

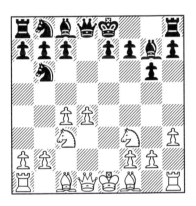

Diagram 12 (B)

The preventative 7 h3

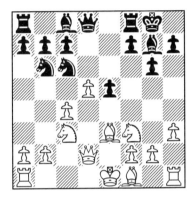

Diagram 13 (B)

...Na5 or ...Ne7?

a) The pawn sacrifice 11...e4 leads to a very complicated game, although I think that White has the upper hand: 12 Nxe4 f5 13 Nc5 (opening lines against your own king is never a good idea, and 13 gxf5 is simply too risky for White: for example, 13...Nxf5 14 0-0-0 Qe8 15 Neg5 Nxe3 16 fxe3 h6 and Black wins) 13...fxg4 14 Ng5! g3!! (a magnificent try, although it's not clear whether it works) 15 fxg3 Rxf1+ (this is the point – Black removes the defender of the c4-pawn) 16 Rxf1 Nxc4 17 Qe2 Nxe3 18 Qxe3 Nf5! and the position is very unclear.

b) 11...f5 12 0-0-0 e4 (the tempting 12...fxg4 does not work so well after 13 Ng5 with the threat of c4-c5) 13 Ng5 h6 14 Ne6 Bxe6 15 dxe6 Qxd2+ 16 Bxd2 with a preferable endgame for White: not only does he have the bishop pair and – for the moment – control of the d-file, but Black's b6-knight is misplaced.

11 b3 e4

Against 11...f5!? John Emms considers 12 Bh6 to be the most logical, as it removes a defender from Black's already weakened kingside, and after 12...e4 13 Bxg7 Kxg7 14 Nd4 c5 15 Nc2 Nd7 the position is very double-edged.

However, 12 Bg5!? **(Diagram 14)** might be better. For example, 12...Qd7! (after 12...Bf6 13 Bxf6 Qxf6 14 c5 Black has big problems with his knight stranded on a5) 13 Rd1! (overprotecting the d-pawn without exposing the king too much; 13 c5!? e4 14 Nh4 Nxd5 15 Nxd5 Bxa1 16 Qxa5 c6 is less clear, while I fear that the dark squares around White's king may become exposed after 13 0-0-0) 13...Re8 (Black gets ready with some potential ...e5-e4-e3 strikes; White should concentrate on completing his development in the knowledge that the knight on a5 is a sitting duck) 14 Be2 e4 15 Nd4 c6 16 0-0! and White is slowly building up his advantage. Here 16...cxd5 17 cxd5 Nxd5 18 Bb5 wins.

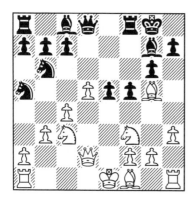

Diagram 14 (B)
Difficult to meet

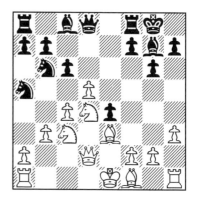

Diagram 15 (W)
Black's best option

 NOTE: White should bear in mind that the over-excitable 12 c5 does not win material, due to 12...f4!.

12 Nd4 f5

12...c6! **(Diagram 15)** is the best move. 13 dxc6 resolves the tension far too easily and doesn't give Black any problems: 13...Nxc6 14 Rd1 (14 Nxc6 Qxd2+ 15 Kxd2 bxc6 is level) 14...Qe7 (Black should not be in a hurry to exchange pieces, as in the resulting endgame White has the queenside pawn majority and Black's pieces are somewhat misplaced – after 14...Nxd4 15 Bxd4 Bxd4 16 Qxd4 Qxd4 17 Rxd4 it is not easy to defend the e4-pawn in a satisfactory manner) 15 g3 Be6 and Black has a good position: he has nice play along the d-file and his pieces are actively placed. 13 Rd1 is the most uncompromising answer to 12...c6, although Black doesn't seem to have too many problems after 13...cxd5 14 Ncb5 Nc6 15 Be2 dxc4 16 bxc4 Ne5.

On the other hand, 12...c5 has not worked out too well for Black. It may kick back the white knight on d4, but Black is not challenging White's pawn structure so consequently White has the easier game. For example, 13 Nc2 Nd7 14 Nxe4 (White sacrifices the exchange for a pawn and an initiative on the dark squares) 14...Bxa1 15 Nxa1 b6 16 Nc2 Nb7 17 Be2 Re8 18 Nc3 Nd6 19 g4 with long-lasting compensation, K.Aseev-P.Svidler, St Petersburg 1996.

13 g3! (Diagram 16)

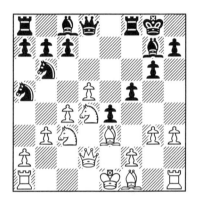

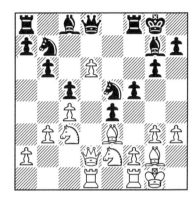

Diagram 16 (B)

A strong move

Diagram 17 (B)

Preventing a blockade

This is by far the best move, and I couldn't find a decent response for Black.

13 Nce2 has led to some wild games where Black gets the initiative after 13...c5! 14 Qxa5 f4! 15 Qxc5 fxe3 16 fxe3 Qg5.

13 Bg5 Qe8 14 0-0-0 c5! 15 Nde2 Naxc4 16 bxc4 Nxc4 17 Qc2 Ne5! 18 d6! c4 (after 18...Nd3+? 19 Rxd3 exd3 20 Qxd3 White retains the better chances due to the strength of the d-pawn and Black's lack of mobile pieces, A.Grischuk-V.Malakhov, Lausanne 2000) 19 Nf4 Nd3+ 20 Bxd3 exd3 21 Qa4! was D.Gumula-J.Tomczak, Koszalin 2005, and here 21...Qxa4! 22 Nxa4 Be5 23 Nb2 Bd7!? 24 Nd5 b5 would reach an unclear position.

13...c5 14 Nde2 Nd7?!

This gives White time to consolidate his position. As the game turned out very badly for Black, perhaps he needs to consider radical means to disrupt White's position. For example, after 14...Nbxc4 15 bxc4 Nxc4 16 Qc2 Qa5 17 Bg2 Nxe3 18 fxe3 b5 19 Rc1 b4 20 Qa4 Qb6 21 Nd1 Ba6 Black has some play for the piece.

15 Bg2 Ne5 16 0-0 b6 17 Rad1 Nb7

17...a6 18 Nf4 Qd6 looks the most solid. But as Nimzowitsch once remarked, the queen is a poor blockader because when attacked she must move!

18 d6! (Diagram 17)

This is the critical move – White does not let Black establish the perfect blockade. The rest of the game features exemplary play by Harmen Jonkman.

18...Be6 19 Nb5 Qd7 20 Bg5 Nd3 21 Nf4 Nxf4 22 Qxf4 Nd8 23 f3 Nc6 24 fxe4 Nd4 25 Nxd4 Bxd4+ 26 Rxd4 cxd4 27 e5 Rac8 28 Qxd4 Rc5 29 Bd5 Re8 30 b4 Rcc8 31 c5 bxc5 32 bxc5 Kf7 33 g4 Kg8 34 gxf5 gxf5 35 Bf6 Bxd5 36 Qxd5+ Re6 37 Kh2 1-0

Game 55
□ **G.Baches Garcia** ■ **A.Mirzoev**
Balaguer 2006

---

1 e4 d5 2 exd5 Nf6 3 d4 Nxd5 4 Nf3 g6 5 c4 Nb6 6 Nc3 Bg7 7 Be2

White does not bother taking the time out to prevent ...Bg4.

7...0-0 8 0-0 (Diagram 18)

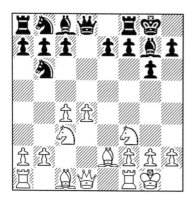

Diagram 18 (B)

Black has a choice

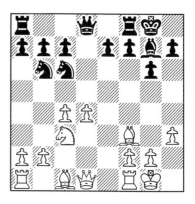

Diagram 19 (W)

Pressure on c4 and d4

8...Nc6

Black can also play the immediate 8...Bg4 and now:

a) 9 c5 Nd5 10 h3 Bxf3 11 Bxf3 e6 12 Re1! (trying to exploit the weak d5- and b7-pawns backfired spectacularly on White in P.Nielsen-E.Maljutin, Forli 1992: 12 Nxd5 exd5 13 Qb3 Nc6! 14 Qxb7 Nxd4 15 Qxd5 Qxd5 16 Bxd5 Rab8 17 Rb1? – White must return the material – 17...Ne2+ 18 Kh1 Nc3 and Black soon won) 12...Nc6 13 Nxd5 exd5 14 Be3 Qd7 15 Qd2 and White has only a very slight advantage, P.Nunn-J.Houska, British League 1996. White's bishop is tied down to the defence of the d4-pawn, and here Black should play 15...a5 to prevent White from achieving positional dominance on the queenside.

b) 9 h3 Bxf3! 10 Bxf3 Nc6 **(Diagram 19)** 11 c5 Nc4 12 Be2 (if 12 Bxc6 bxc6 13 Ne2 e5 14 Qa4, Black has the nice idea 14...exd4! 15 Qxc4 d3 and ...d3-d2 winning back the piece) 12...N4a5 13 d5 Nd4 14 Bd3 b6 15 c6 e6 and White's position was over-extended in J.Gdanski-J.Tomczak, Warsaw 2006.

NOTE: When Black plays ...Bg4 in conjunction with a kingside fi-anchetto, he must exchange the bishop in order to continue exert-ing pressure on the d4/c4 pawn front.

9 Be3

9 d5 is covered in the next game.

9...Bg4! 10 d5

10 c5 doesn't make too much sense, and 10...Nd5 11 Qb3 Nxe3 12 fxe3 Bh6! in-creases the pressure on White's centre.

Trying to maintain the tension with 10 b3 works in Black's favour after 10...Bxf3 11 Bxf3 Nxd4 12 Bxb7 Rb8. For example, 13 Be4 c5 (the most popular move, but John Emms's suggestion of 13...f5! looks promising) 14 Rc1 e6 15 f4 Qe7 16 Qe1 Rbd8 gave Black easy equality in D.Moskovic-J.Rogers, British League 2008.

10...Bxf3 11 Bxf3

11 gxf3!? **(Diagram 20)** is more dangerous than it appears.

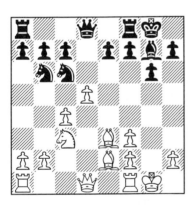

Diagram 20 (B)

...Na5 or ...Ne5?

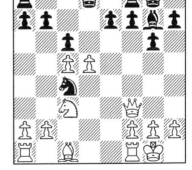

Diagram 21 (W)

Attacking the d5-pawn

It was first played against me by a young Luke McShane, and I remember being crushed in that game. 11...Na5! is a very important move, as White must not be given a tempo to transfer his bishop to the kingside so easily via f3-f4 and Be2-f3.

243

For example, 11...Ne5? 12 c5 Nc8? (12...Nbc4 13 Bc1 was the move I was afraid of – it goes to show that Black's knight is not necessarily better placed on e5) 13 f4 Nd7 14 Bf3 was good for White in G.Lee-J.Houska, British Championship 1997.

After 11...Na5, K.Janetschek-B.Larsen, Copenhagen 1977, continued 12 c5 Nbc4 13 Bf4 (13 Qc2 Nxe3 14 fxe3 e6 is also good for Black, because against 15 b4 there's the strong reply 15...Qg5+ 16 Kh1 Qxe3 hitting the knight) 13...e6! (Black should seek to break up the restrictive white centre pawns) 14 dxe6 fxe6 15 Qxd8 Raxd8 16 Bxc7 Rd2 with a very pleasant ending for Black.

11...Ne5! 12 c5 Nxf3+

This move, although viable, is somewhat beneficial for White as the exchange of minor pieces frees his queen's movement. 12...Nbc4 is safer, and after 13 Bc1 c6! 14 Be2 cxd5 15 Nxd5 e6 16 Ne3 Nxe3 17 Bxe3 Qc7 a draw was agreed in J.Nunn-J.Palkovi, German League 1995.

13 Qxf3 Nc4 14 Bc1?!

14 Bg5 looks more active, and White is better following 14...Re8 (14...Nxb2 15 Rfe1 Re8 16 Rab1 Nc4 17 Rxb7 is very nice for White) 15 Rfe1 h6 16 Bh4 Qd7 (16...b6? 17 Rxe7! Rxe7 18 d6) 17 Re2 Rad8 18 Rae1.

14...c6! (Diagram 21)

Once the white pawn wedge has been removed, it is only Black who can stand better as the bishop on g7 is a magnificent piece.

15 dxc6 Ne5 16 Qe4 Nxc6 17 Be3 Qa5 18 Rfc1 Rfd8 19 a3 Qa6 20 Rab1 Qd3 21 Qa4 Qf5 22 Ne2 a6 23 b4 h5

Now the white queen is cut off on the queenside, so it is a good idea for Black to commence action on the kingside.

24 h3 Qe4! 25 Rd1 Qc4 26 Kf1?

This is incomprehensible.

26...Ne5 27 Qa5 Nd3 28 Rd2 e5 29 Rc1 Qe6 30 Rcd1 e4 31 Nf4 Qc4 32 Kg1 Bc3 33 Rc2 Qb3 34 Rcc1 Rd7 35 Rb1 Qc4 36 Ne2 Be5! 37 b5? Bc7!

Forcing White to overstretch the queenside pawns.

38 b6 Be5

The threat is 39...Rc8 picking up the c5-pawn. White panics in time trouble.

39 Rbc1?? Nxc1 40 Rxd7 Nxe2+ 41 Kh1 Nd4 42 Kg1 Qd3 0-1

Game 56
☐ **J.Van Mil** ■ **H.Oswald**
German League 2000

---

1 e4 d5 2 exd5 Nf6 3 d4 Nxd5 4 Nf3 g6 5 c4 Nb6 6 Nc3 Bg7 7 Be2 0-0 8 0-0 Nc6 9 d5 (Diagram 22)

Instead of defending with 9 Be3, White lashes out in the centre. I have always had a soft spot for this variation, in particular because I always seemed to struggle against it as Black.

9...Ne5

Judit Polgar gives 9...Na5 10 c5! Bxc3 11 cxb6 Bg7 12 Bf4 Bxb2 (or 12...axb6 13 b4 Bxa1 14 Qxa1 Nb3 15 Qb2! and the knight has nowhere to run) 13 bxc7 as good for White, an assessment which is hard to dispute.

10 Nxe5!?

10 c5 also leads to a mass of complications. By provoking the advance of the white pawn centre Black makes his pawn breaks of ...e6, ...c6 and ...b6 even easier to achieve, and once the position opens, Black's development problems will be solved: 10...Nbd7 (after 10...Nbc4? 11 Nd4! Black's knight on c4 is in a mess, while 10...Nxf3+ usually transposes to 10...Nbd7) 11 Be3 Nxf3+ 12 Bxf3 Ne5 13 Be2 (13 Be4 allows 13...f5!) 13...c6 (or 13...b6 14 c6 f6 15 f4 Nf7 and Black is very cramped, B.Lepelletier-L.Pecot, Gonfreville 1999) 14 f4 Nd7 15 Bf3 **(Diagram 23)** and now:

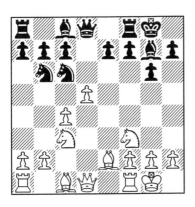

Diagram 22 (B)
White lashes out

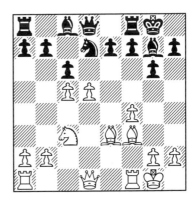

Diagram 23 (B)
Black must be careful

a) 15...Qa5? 16 dxc6 Nxc5 17 Nd5! led to a quick win for White in M.Brodsky-E.Maljutin, Moscow 1991.

b) 15...cxd5 16 Qxd5 opens the game in White's favour. In A.Koglin-J.Houska, Dresden 1998, I tried to grab some activity with 16...e5? (the patient 16...Qc7 was wiser, but White's position is still much more preferable) but after 17 Rad1 Qc7 18 Qd6 Qxd6 19 cxd6 exf4 20 Bxf4 Rd8 21 Nd5 Ne5 22 Ne7+ Kh8 23 Nxc8 White was practically winning.

c) 15...Qc7 is the only realistic try for Black. Now:

c1) Volzhin suggests 16 d6!?. Then 16...exd6 17 cxd6 Qd8 18 Qb3?! (the prophylactic 18 Qd2 would give White the slightly better position, although it is far from easy for him to make considerable progress) 18...Nb6 (now Back can develop his pieces with tempo) 19 Rad1 Be6 20 Qb4 Nc4! 21 Bf2! b6! 22 Bxc6 Rc8 23 Bb7 Nxb2!! 24 Bxc8 Nxd1 25 Nxd1 Qxc8 and Black has emerged from his experiences unscathed.

c2) 16 Rc1 Nf6 17 Qe2 (17 dxc6 bxc6 18 Nb5 Qd7 19 Qxd7 Bxd7 20 Nd4 Rfc8 21 h3 e6 22 Kf2 Nd5 was A.Evdokimov-E.Alekseev, St Petersburg 1998 – as John Emms indicates, Black's inferior pawn structure is compensated by the strong positioning of the knight on the d5 outpost) 17...Bd7! was S.Solovjov-E.Alekseev, St Petersburg 1999. Black has successfully coordinated his forces and now plans to exchange twice on d5 and play ...Bc6. White probably has no more than equality here.

10...Bxe5 11 Bh6

11 Bg5!? c6! 12 dxc6 bxc6 (12...Qc7? 13 c5) 13 Qxd8 Rxd8 14 Rfd1 Be6 is equal, P.Dukaczewski-W.Sapis, Krakow 1999.

11 Be3 Bg7 12 Qd2 c6 13 Rfd1 Qc7 14 Rac1 Rd8 15 Bg5 Be5 16 h3 Bf5 was better for White in K.Jurkiewicz-J.Houska, European Girls Championship 1998. Striking in the centre with 11...c6!? looks the best – Black cannot hope for much if he doesn't try to challenge White's spatial advantage.

11...Re8!

This is the best move: 11...Bg7? 12 Bxg7 Kxg7 13 Qd4+ f6 14 c5 e5 15 Qd2 Nd7 16 b4 gave White a clear plus in J.Polgar-H.Stefansson, Egilsstadir 1988.

12 f4!? (Diagram 24)

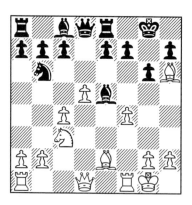

Diagram 24 (B)
Danger!

Diagram 25 (B)
More danger!

White throws everything into an attack.

12 Qd2 offers little: for example, 12...e6 (12...c6 is also playable) 13 Rad1 exd5 14 cxd5 Bd7 15 Rfe1 Nc8! 16 Bg5 Bf6 with equality, Dmitriev-A.Volzhin, Russia 1990.

12...Bh8

 TIP: Remember that swapping off the dark-squared bishops would be a positional mistake, so Black must avoid 12...Bg7.

After 12...Bf6! White must sacrifice even more material to keep the attack going. L.Fressinet-M.Somalo Fernandez, Creon 1997, continued 13 Ne4 Bxb2 14 Rb1 Bh8 15 f5 Bxf5 16 Rxf5 gxf5 17 Bh5 Bf6 (17...e6! is better: 18 Rb3 Be5 19 Bg5 f6 and Black defends) 18 Ng5 Bxg5? 19 Bxf7+! Kh8 20 Bxg5 Rf8 21 Qd4+ and Black resigned.

13 f5! (Diagram 25)

This very dangerous pawn sacrifice was brought to prominence by the Dutch IM Van Mil.

13...Bxf5 14 Qd2! Qd6!

This is the best way to deal with the threat of Rxf5. After 14...Bg7? 15 Bxg7 Kxg7 16 c5 Nc8 17 Rad1 White has an overwhelming position; 14...e6? loses a piece to 15 g4!; and finally 14...Bc8 15 Qf4 f5 16 Rad1 Qd6 17 Nb5! was good for White in J.Van Mil-T.Thorhallsson, Reykjavik 1993.

15 Rxf5!! gxf5 16 Nb5! Qf6

After 16...Qg6?! 17 Nxc7 Bxb2 18 Rd1 Bd4+ 19 Qxd4 Qxh6 20 Nxe8 Rxe8 21 Bf3 Nd7 22 c5 Black has big problems even though he is a pawn up. His pieces lack coordination, whereas White enjoys a massive space advantage and has a potentially very dangerous passed c-pawn.

16...Qc5+ 17 Kh1 Bf6 18 Qf4 was J.Van Mil-Shrentzel, Groningen 1992. White will win back the sacrificed exchange and pawn, but as compensation Black will have a passed pawn which should pose White some problems: 18...e6 19 Nxc7 Qd4 20 Nxe8 Rxe8 21 dxe6 fxe6 22 Qxd4 (if White chooses to keep the queens on with 22 Qg3+ Kh8 23 Rb1 Nxc4 24 Rd1 Qe4 25 Bf3 Qe5 Black is holding the position) 22...Bxd4 looks as though it should be roughly equal.

17 Nxc7 Qd4+ 18 Qxd4 Bxd4+ 19 Kf1 Bxb2 20 Rd1 (Diagram 26) 20...Rec8

Or 20...Be5 21 Nxe8 Rxe8 22 c5 (C.Cobb-M.Simons, British League 1998) and according to John Emms Black still has some problems to solve.

21 Nxa8 Nxa8 22 Rb1 Bg7 23 Bg5

White preserves the bishop-pair advantage: 23 Bxg7 Kxg7 24 Rxb7 Rc7 is not so easy for him.

23...f6 24 Be3 Nb6

After 24...b6 25 Bd3 Kf7 26 Ke2 Black's minor pieces are completely restricted. White will win the f5-pawn, so Black won't even have an extra pawn for his woes.

25 Bxb6 axb6 26 Rxb6 (Diagram 27)

Now that White has regained the pawn, he has a clear advantage. The problem for Black is that his bishop is locked in.

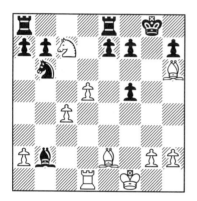

Diagram 26 (B)
Excellent compensation

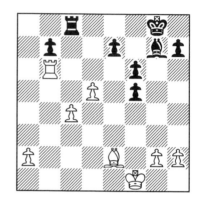

Diagram 27 (B)
Clear advantage for White

26...Rc7 27 Kf2 Bh6 28 Kf3 Bc1 29 Bd3 Ba3 30 Bxf5 Rxc4 31 Rxb7 Bd6 32 g3

White is a pawn up. All that is needed is to advance the a-pawn and destroy the black blockade.

32...Ra4 33 Rb2 Kg7 34 Bc2 Ra8 35 a4 h5 36 Ra2 Ra5 37 Bb3 Kh6 38 h4 Bb4 39 Rc2 Ra7 40 Rc8 Kg7 41 g4 hxg4+ 42 Kxg4

Now an extra passed pawn has been created and Black is doomed.

42...Rb7 43 Bc4 Be1 44 Bb5 Ra7 45 h5 Bb4 46 Kf5 Kh6 47 Rg8 Bd6 48 Kg4 Bb4 49 Rg6+ Kh7 50 Kf5 Ra8 51 Ke6 Bc5 52 Bd3 f5 53 Bxf5 Ra6+ 54 Kf7 1-0

Playing without c2-c4

1 e4 d5 2 exd5 Nf6 3 Nf3 Nxd5 4 d4 g6 5 Be2 (Diagram 28) (or 5 Bc4)

White takes a slower approach, preferring to complete his development before choosing whether to play c2-c4 or the super-solid c2-c3. This is not a naïve system, and in fact it contains some danger for Black if he is not awake.

White's plan is to play a controlled c4, when the time is right and when Black is not equipped to deal with the resulting problems. Think of "catching someone on the wrong foot!" However, initially the emphasis is on developing pieces and denying Black any of the usual central pressure that normally results from playing an early c2-c4.

If White plays very quietly and does not bolster the centre with c2-c3, then contrary to the usual ...Nb8-c6 followed by ...e5, Black should instead play dynamically with ...c7-c5. This is seen in Game 57, where Black reacts to the slow 7 Re1 with 7...c5 **(Diagram 29)**.

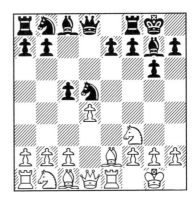

Diagram 28 (B)

The solid approach

Diagram 29 (W)

Challenging the centre

White can also develop the bishop more actively to the c4-square, and 5 Bc4 is covered in Game 58.

Game 57
□ **K.Mokry** ■ **M.Zurek**
Olomouc 1998

---

1 e4 d5 2 exd5 Nf6 3 d4 Nxd5 4 Nf3 g6 5 Be2 Bg7 6 0-0 0-0 (Diagram 30) 7 Re1

Alternatively:

a) Black can equalize against the slower 7 h3 with 7...Nc6 (or 7...c5 as in the game, since h2-h3 isn't really a useful move here) 8 Re1 Nb6! 9 c3 e5.

b) With 7 Na3 White wishes to control the centre with pieces. In particular White intends Nc4 clamping down on the e5-square. However, this idea is not so dangerous for Black, as he can retaliate with a timely ...c7-c5. For example, 7...Nd7 8 Nc4 c5 9 c3 a6 10 a4 b6 11 Re1 Bb7 and Black has completed development without any problems, A.Shaabani-V.Gaprindashvili, Teheran 2006.

c) 7 c3 is a critical try, bolstering the centre and hoping to deter Black from playing ...c7-c5. Now:

c1) 7...Nd7 8 Re1 c5 9 Na3, when instead of the unnecessary 9...a6?! which led to an unpleasant position for Black after 10 Bg5 h6 11 Bh4 cxd4 12 Nxd4 N7f6 13 Bf3 in E.Sutovsky-H.Olafsson, Reykjavik 2006, I think Black should play 9...cxd4 10

Nxd4 N7b6 followed by ...e7-e5 gaining space.

c2) Black can also play the bold 7...c5!?, and after 8 dxc5 Na6 9 Bxa6 bxa6 10 Na3 Bb7 11 Nd4 Qc7 12 c6 Bxc6 13 Nxc6 Qxc6 14 Nc2 e5 his piece activity more than compensates for the pawn weakness, S.Erenburg-T.Thorhallsson, Reykjavik 2006.

7...c5

Black meets White's rather quiet play with this dynamic strike.

7...Nc6 8 c3 a6 9 a4 Bg4 10 h3 Bxf3 11 Bxf3 e6 12 a5 Rb8 13 Qb3 Nce7 14 Nd2 Nf5 15 Ne4! left White with a very easy position to play in M.Al Modiahki-U.Adianto, Doha 2006. This is a model game for White, who can play very simple moves whereas Black is struggling to find a plan.

7...c6 looks like a reasonable move if Black wants to play quietly: 8 c4 Nf6 9 Nc3 Bg4 10 h3 Bxf3 11 Bxf3 e6 12 Bg5 Qb6 13 Qd2 Nbd7 14 Rad1 with a minimal advantage for White, N.Short-M.Adams, Brussels (rapid) 1992.

8 dxc5 (Diagram 31)

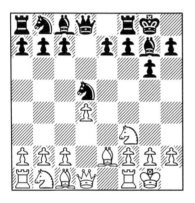
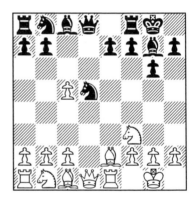

Diagram 30 (W)	Diagram 31 (B)
White has some options	White accepts the offer

White should decline the pawn offer with 8 c4 Nb6 and now 9 d5! (9 dxc5?! Qxd1 10 Rxd1 Na4! is fine for Black) 9...Bg4 10 Qb3 e6 11 Bg5 Qc8 12 Nc3, when White's space advantage gives him a very pleasant position, E.Safarli-M.Muzychuk, Pardubice 2007.

8...Nb4!?

After 8...Na6 9 Bxa6 bxa6 Black has sacrificed a pawn and ruined his queenside structure in return for the bishop pair and control of the light squares. However, it is very unclear whether Black has adequate compensation. For example, 10 a3!? (preventing ...Nb4 in order to be able to play c2-c4 in peace) 10...Be6 11 Nd4! Nc7

12 c3 Bd5 (G.Al Sulaiti-T.Thorhallsson, Turin Olympiad 2006) and here 13 Bf4 contains a neat little trick: if Black plays a move like 13...Re8, then 14 Nf5! is very good for White.

9 Na3

9 a3 N4a6 wins back the c5-pawn.

9...N4a6 (Diagram 32)

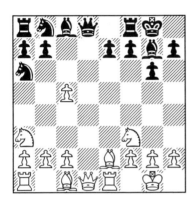

Diagram 32 (W)	**Diagram 33 (B)**
Regaining the pawn	Slight advantage for White

9...N8c6? is a mistake, and after 10 c3 Na6 11 Be3 Black cannot win back the pawn.

10 c3 Nxc5 11 Be3 Nbd7

11...Qxd1 is premature, as Black is not ready to challenge the d-file. 12 Raxd1 Na4 13 Rd2 Nc6 14 Nb5 a6 15 Nbd4 Nxd4 16 Bxd4 Bxd4 17 Nxd4 e5 18 Nf3 was agreed drawn in R.Reinaldo Castineira-J.Ivanov, Mondariz 2000, but White has the advantage in this final position.

12 Qd2 a6 13 Rad1 Qc7 14 Bh6 Ne4 15 Qe3 Ndf6

15...Bxh6 16 Qxh6 Ndf6 forces White to retreat the queen, as Black is threatening ...Nxf2 followed by ...Ng4 forking the king and queen. The position is completely equal after 17 Qh4 Be6 18 Bd3 Nc5 19 Ng5 Rfd8.

16 Bf4?

A mistake. White should eliminate Black's strongest piece, so 16 Bxg7! is the best.

16...Qc5 17 Qxc5 Nxc5 18 Nc4 (Diagram 33)

White still has the better chances here: he has blunted the g7-bishop, and c4 is an excellent location for the knight.

18...Na4 19 Bc1

This looks passive, but the active 19 Nfe5 is not convincing either: 19...Be6! 20 Bf3 Rac8! 21 Bxb7 Rb8 22 Bxa6 Nd5 23 Bg3 (23 Bc1 Nc7 wins the bishop) 23...Nxb2 24 Rd2 Ra8! 25 Bb5 Nxc4 26 Bxc4 Nxc3 27 Bxe6 fxe6 and Black should be able to hold.

19...b5 20 Na5 Bf5

The position is now level. Black's pieces are well placed but White has some good squares available to him, which makes for a complicated struggle.

21 Nd4 Be4 22 Bf1 e6 23 a3 Rfc8 24 f3 Bd5 25 Nc2 Nb6?

This is incorrect: the knight was okay on the rim, as it tied down the white bishop. 25...Bf8!, taking control of the dark squares, would have been stronger.

26 Nb4 Bc4 27 Rd6 Nfd5 28 Nxd5 Nxd5 29 Bxc4 bxc4 30 Rc6 Nxc3!

A neat tactic to preserve the material balance.

31 Rxc4 Nb5 32 Nc6

A very risky move. Self-pinning like this requires a great deal of calculation, something which brings about White's downfall.

32...Kf8 33 b3 Nd6 34 Rc2 Rc7?

This works out well in the game, but it is a mistake.

35 Bf4! e5!

Black sacrifices a pawn in order to hunt bigger fish, but he misses a trick.

36 Bxe5 Bxe5 37 Rxe5 Rac8 38 Rec5 Nb5?

38...Nb7 was better.

39 R5c4?

39 Ne5 would have been better for White.

39...Nxa3 40 Na7 Rxc4 41 bxc4 Rxc4 42 Rb2 Rc1+ 43 Kf2 Rc2+ 44 Rxc2 Nxc2

> **NOTE: Knight and pawn endgames are to some extent very similar to king and pawn endgames – passed pawns and piece activity count for a lot!**

45 Nc6 f5 46 Ke2 f4 47 g3 Kf7 48 Kd3 Ne1+ 49 Ke4 fxg3 50 hxg3 Ke6 51 f4 Kd6 52 Ne5 Kc5 53 g4 Nc2 54 f5 gxf5+ 55 gxf5 Kd6 56 Nc4+ Ke7 57 Ke5 Nb4 58 f6+ Kf7 59 Nd6+ Kf8 0-1

White probably lost on time here.

Game 58
□ **M.Chierici** ■ **Z.Gregorova**
World Girls Championship, Istanbul 2005

---

1 e4 d5 2 exd5 Nf6 3 d4 Nxd5 4 Nf3 g6 5 Bc4 (Diagram 34) 5...Bg7 6 0-0

WARNING: 6 h3 0-0 7 0-0 Nc6? shows us the danger Black may face if he chooses to play without any pawn breaks. After 8 c3 Bf5 9 Re1 a6 10 Nbd2 Re8 11 Ne4 h6 12 Ng3 Bc8 Black is slowly being pushed back, Myint Han-M.Al Modiahki, Genting Highlands 1998.

Instead of 7...Nc6, Black should play 7...Nb6! 8 Bb3 Nc6. Only now that the white bishop is offside should the knight be developed to c6, and after 9 d5 (9 c3 allows 9...e5 10 d5 Na5) 9...Na5 Black will manage to exchange a pair of minor pieces.

6...0-0

6...Nb6 7 Bb3 c5? does not work: 8 dxc5 Qxd1 9 Rxd1 N6d7 10 Ng5! 0-0 11 Bc4!, as played in Y.Kruppa-Z.Sturua, Podolsk 1989, prevents Black from playing 11...Na6 in view of 12 c6!, while against 11...Nxc5 White has the resounding 12 Nxf7!.

7 c3

If 7 Re1, then 7...Nb6 8 Bb3 c5 is now possible.

With 7 Bb3 **(Diagram 35)** White wants to achieve c2-c4 in a controlled manner, but the downside is that White's idea of pushing for c4-c5 never quite works as he can never quite manage to take full control of the d5-square: 7...Nc6 8 c4 Nb6 9 c5 (9 d5 fails to 9...Na5) 9...Nd5 10 Nc3 Be6! 11 Re1 Qd7 and White cannot in the immediate future dislodge the knight from d5. Although there remains a lot of tension in the position, Black has no positional weaknesses and White is continually tied down to the defence of the d4-pawn.

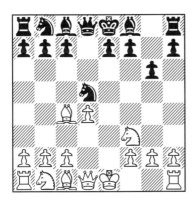

Diagram 34 (B)

Active development to c4

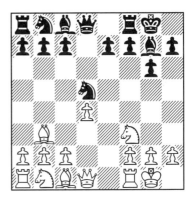

Diagram 35 (B)

Planning c2-c4-c5

7...c6!

As White has played incredibly solidly, Black should not react wildly. True, White has not adopted the most aggressive of approaches, yet cautious play does not equate to passive play and White has great potential to expand. If Black does not play with some purpose, White will time his advance to catch Black out, just when he is least expecting it.

As I have already mentioned many times, playing with the minor pieces in front of the pawns is risky, and when White has played ultra-solidly I don't think there is much point in banking everything on ...e7-e5. Chess is more sophisticated than that! After 7...Nc6 8 Re1 Nb6 9 Bb3 Bg4 (Black must play this move in order to secure ...e7-e5) 10 h3! Bxf3 11 Qxf3 e5 (Black has achieved his break, but at what cost?) 12 dxe5 Nxe5 13 Qxb7 a5 14 Na3 a4 15 Bc2 Rb8 16 Qa6 Ra8 17 Qe2 White was simply a pawn up in A.Morozevich-L.Comas Fabrego, Pamplona 1994.

8 Re1 Nd7

After 8...h6 9 Nbd2 Be6 10 Bb3 a5 11 Ne5 Bf5 12 Nf1 b5 13 Ng3 Bc8 White had a very promising initiative in G.Hitzgerova-J.Jackova, Ostrava 1997.

 TIP: When fianchettoing the bishop, think very carefully before playing ...h7-h6, as it may become a serious weakness in the long run.

9 Qe2

After 9 Bb3 N7b6 10 c4 Nf6 11 h3 Bf5 12 Nc3 Qc7 13 Be3 a5 14 Ne5! (ambitiously aiming for Bf4 to disturb the black queen) 14...Be6 (tying White to the c4-pawn) 15 Bf4 Qd8 16 Re2 Nfd7 17 c5 White has achieved an advantage in space.

9...e6 (Diagram 36)

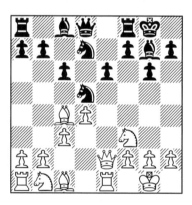

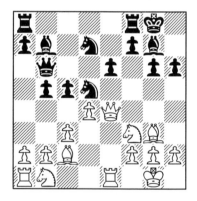

Diagram 36 (W)	**Diagram 37 (W)**
Black plans ...b5 and...c5	The bishop comes to life

The best move. Although Black has shut in the light-squared bishop for the time being, he wishes to release it through ...b7-b5 and ...c6-c5. If Black achieves this, he will stand better.

10 Bg5 Qc7 11 Qe4 b5 12 Bb3?

12 Bd3 h6 13 Bh4 e5 is a risky try for the advantage, but it is possible to play it safe with 13...Bb7 14 Bg3 Qb6 followed by ...c6-c5.

12...h6!

This move is forced, as White was planning to transfer the queen to h4 and swap off the dark-squared bishops.

13 Bh4 Bb7 14 Bg3 Qb6 15 Bc2 c5! (Diagram 37)

Black has secured the release of the bishop and now stands fine.

16 Qe2 a6?

16...cxd4 17 Nxd4 b4 would have put White's position under pressure.

17 Ne5 Rad8 18 dxc5 Nxc5 19 Nd2 Nf6 20 h3 Ba8?

It looks as though Black is a little bit lost as to how to gain the upper hand. 20...Bd5! prevents 21 Rad1 because of 21...Bxa2 22 b3 Nd5 23 Qf3 Nd7 piling the pressure on the c3-pawn.

21 Rad1 Bd5 22 c4 bxc4 23 Ndxc4 Qb7 24 f3 Nfd7 25 b3 Nxe5 26 Nxe5 Qb5 27 Nd3 Rc8 28 Kh1 Nb7 29 Nf4 Qxe2 30 Rxe2 Bc6 31 Bb1 Rfd8 32 Rc1 Bb5 33 Rxc8 Rxc8 34 Bd3??

In a slightly worse position, White blunders a piece.

34...e5 35 Nxg6 Rc1+ 36 Re1 Rxe1+ 37 Bxe1 Bxd3 38 Ne7+ Kf8 39 Nc6 Bb5 40 Nb4 a5 41 Nd5 Bc6 42 Ne3 Ke7 43 a4 Ke6 44 Kh2 Bf8 45 Nc2 f5 46 Kg3 Bd5 47 b4 axb4 48 Nxb4 Bb3 49 a5 Nxa5 50 Nd3 Nc4 51 Bf2 Bc2 52 Nc1 Be7 53 Ne2 Ba4 54 Nc3 Bc6 55 Ne2 Bb4 56 Bg1 Kf6 0-1

Summary

In this chapter we have covered the most common set-up for Black after 2...Nf6 3 Nf3 Nxd5 4 d4: the fianchetto system with 4...g6, in which Black intends to utilize the long-term advantage of the dark-squared bishop and place tremendous pressure on the d4-pawn. As Games 52-53 demonstrate, White's most critical response is to play 7 c5, grabbing as much space as possible and turning Black's source of strength – the d5-square – against him.

Before 7 c5 rose to prominence, playing in a classical manner was very popular. White either prevents the bishop foray to g4 with 7 h3 (as in Game 54) or develops his pieces before lunging with d4-d5 (as in Games 55-56). Game 55 is complicated but Black should be fine as long as he is prepared to surrender the bishop pair and occupy the centre with his knights. Game 56 shows a more dangerous version with White pushing in the centre before committing the dark-squared bishop, allowing him to play Bh6 in one go. This line is very pleasant for White.

Delaying c2-c4 in favour of a quiet Be2, 0-0 and Re1 allows Black to strike first with ...c7-c5, and Game 57 is a highly instructive encounter. Developing the bishop to c4 and aiming to play a controlled c2-c4 does not trouble Black too much either (see Game 58).

Chapter Thirteen

The 4...Bg4 Variation

- White Plays c4-c5
- White Plays Be2
- White Plays g2-g4

1 e4 d5 2 exd5 Nf6 3 Nf3 Nxd5 4 d4 Bg4 (Diagram 1)

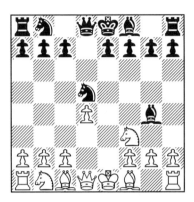

Diagram 1 (W)
Black plays 4...Bg4

Black develops the light-squared bishop with the aim of targeting the d4-pawn. Black's intention is *not* to fianchetto the dark-squared bishop. Instead his plan is to restrain and then pressurize the white pawn centre with both pieces and pawns. It is for this reason that 4...Bg4 is regarded as a more solid continuation for Black, but the disadvantage to this approach is that once the natural developing moves have been completed it is not so easy for Black to continue. Furthermore, if Black plays carelessly or without purpose he can very quickly find himself in an uncomfortable position. This in effect means that every move by Black should be aimed at breaking down the d4-pawn and taking control of the d-file.

In response, White has a variety of options: he can play aggressively with c2-c4 followed by c4-c5, or h2-h3 followed by g2-g4; he can play positionally by "locking" one of the black knights out of play; or he can delay c2-c4, preferring to play it only when Black is unable to generate counterplay.

White Plays c4-c5

1 e4 d5 2 exd5 Nf6 3 Nf3 Nxd5 4 d4 Bg4

4...Bf5 is another possibility. I remember when I faced this a few years ago I reacted with a2-a3 intending to kick back the knight with c2-c4. However, more to the point is 5 Nh4: for example, 5...Bc8 6 g3 g6 7 Bg2 Bg7 8 0-0 0-0 9 Re1 Na6 10 c3 Be6 (E.Sutovsky-S.Krivoshey, Internet 2004) and now instead of the ambitious 11 Rxe6, 11 c4 is a very convincing move.

5 c4 Nb6

> **NOTE: 1 e4 d5 2 exd5 Nf6 3 d4 Nxd5 4 c4 Nb6 5 Nf3 Bg4 is another common move order to reach the same position.**

5...Nf6 is a little bit illogical, and after 6 Be2 e6 7 Nc3 Be7 8 Be3 c6 9 0-0 Nbd7 10 h3 Bxf3 11 Bxf3 0-0 12 Bf4 Qb6 13 a3 Rfd8 14 b4 White has a pleasant space advantage, G.Arias Duval-H.Cordoba, correspondence 2003.

6 c5!? (Diagram 2)

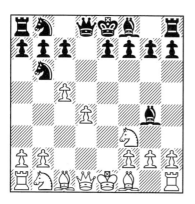

Diagram 2 (B)

Another dangerous c4-c5

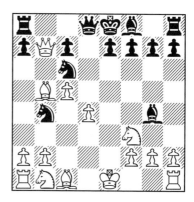

Diagram 3 (B)

Better for White

Rather like the dangerous 7 c5 against the fianchetto system, White aims for a long-term spatial advantage, and heavy pressure along the a2-g8 diagonal and against the b7-pawn.

6 Be2 is likely to transpose to 5 Be2.

6...N6d7!

The two alternatives are inferior:

a) 6...Nd5 7 Qb3! Nc6 (or 7...Bxf3 8 Qxb7 Be4 9 Nd2 and White wins back the piece) 8 Qxb7 Ndb4 9 Bb5! **(Diagram 3)** 9...Bd7 10 d5! Nc2+ (10...Rb8 fails to 11 dxc6) 11 Kd1 N6b4 (after 11...Rb8 White again has the marvellous 12 dxc6 Bxc6+ 13 Kxc2 winning) 12 Bxd7+ Kxd7 13 Bf4 Rb8 14 c6+ Ke8 15 Qxc7 Qxd5+ (or 15...Qxc7 16 Bxc7 Rc8 17 Ba5 and White is much better) 16 Nbd2 Rd8 17 Rc1 and White has the advantage in this complicated position.

b) 6...Bxf3 7 Qxf3 Nd5 8 Qb3! (making sure that it is not easy for Black to establish a light-square blockade) 8...b6 9 Bg5 Qd7 10 Nc3 e6 (or 10...Nxc3 11 bxc3 e6 12 Be2 and White has control of the light squares, M.Mathias-J.Majewski, correspondence 1995) 11 Nxd5 Qxd5 12 Qxd5 exd5 13 c6! with a tremendous spatial advantage for

White, not to mention the bishop pair, A.Suetin-L.Shamkovich, Kiev 1964.

Returning to 6...N6d7, the next two games examine White's options.

Game 59
□ R.Felgaer ■ D.Lima
Sao Paulo 2005

---

1 e4 d5 2 exd5 Nf6 3 d4 Nxd5 4 c4 Nb6 5 Nf3 Bg4 6 c5!? N6d7! 7 Be2!

This is the most logical try. White wishes to transpose to a line that is unfavourable for Black.

7 Bc4 is discussed in the next game, and alternatives include the following:

a) 7 Qb3 is dangerous for the unprepared, but it doesn't lead to anything for White after 7...Nc6! **(Diagram 4)**

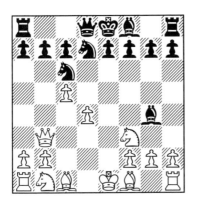

Diagram 4 (W)

Black gets counterplay

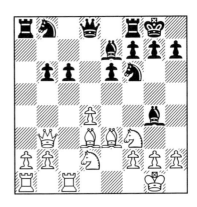

Diagram 5 (B)

Nice for White

and now:

a) 8 d5 Bxf3 9 Qxf3 Nd4 10 Qe4 e5! and Black gains a huge lead in development after the forced 11 dxe6 Nxe6.

b) 8 Nbd2 e5! 9 Bc4 Nxd4! (an important trick to remember) 10 Nxd4 (or 10 Bxf7+ Ke7 11 Nxd4 Nxc5 and Black is better) 10...Nxc5 11 Qb5+ Bd7 12 Bxf7+ Kxf7 13 Qc4+ Ke8 and Black is a pawn up.

c) 8 Be3 Bxf3 9 gxf3 e5!? 10 Bc4 (after 10 Qxb7 Nxd4 11 Bxd4 exd4 12 Bb5 Rb8 13 Bxd7+ Kxd7 Black need not fear for the safety of his king just yet: firstly, White is only attacking with his queen; and secondly, White does not have a safe haven for his king either) 10...Be7! (a great move, completely ignoring White's threat; White is better after 10...Qf6 because of 11 Bxf7+) 11 Bxf7+ Kf8 12 Bh5 (12 dxe5! looks best) 12...g6 13 Bg4 (C.Conrady Janssen-H.Wietor, Luxembourg 1992) and here Black should simply capture the pawn with 13...Nxd4 when he is fine.

7 Nc3 can be met aggressively with 7...e5!: for example, 8 dxe5 Bxc5 9 Bf4 Nc6 10 Be2 0-0 and Black has equalized, L.Butkiewicz-J.Tomczak, Polanica Zdroj 2007.

7 h3?! allows Black to come alive after 7...Bxf3! 8 Qxf3 Nc6! 9 Be3 e5!. This advance is justified because of White's misplaced queen and the crucial fact that Black will win the c5-pawn. After 10 dxe5 Bxc5 11 Bxc5 (or 11 e6 Bb4+ 12 Nc3 fxe6) 11...Nxc5 12 Bb5 0-0 Black was doing well in D.Schuh-J.Gehres, Böblingen 2004.

7...e6

After 7...c6 8 0-0 Nf6 9 Qb3 Bxf3 10 Bxf3 Qd7 11 Bg5 Black was already in big trouble in G.Kaidanov-S.Grubbs, Dallas 1999.

8 Qb3 b6 9 Be3 c6 10 0-0 Be7 11 cxb6 axb6 12 Nbd2

It is important for the knight to be here, as it allows White to extricate himself from the pin.

12...0-0 13 Rfc1 Nf6 14 Bd3! (Diagram 5)

White has escaped the pin and now intends to jump into the centre with 15 Ne5. Black has some problems here because he still cannot develop the b8-knight.

14...Bxf3?

By giving White the bishop pair, this move really cements White's advantage.

After 14...Nd5 15 Ne5 Bh5 16 Nxc6 Nxc6 17 Rxc6 Nb4 18 Rcc1 Nxd3 19 Qxd3 Black has some compensation for the pawn due to the weakness of the isolated queen's pawn and the presence of the bishop pair.

15 Nxf3 Nd5 16 Be4 Ra5 17 Bd2 Rb5 18 Qc2 Nf6 19 a4 Rh5 20 Bxc6 Qd6 21 Bb5

White has picked up a pawn and with it the game.

21...Nd5 22 Bf1 g5??

Desperation, but Black was already losing.

23 g3 f6 24 Qe4 Nd7 25 Re1 Kf7 26 Rac1 f5 27 Ne5+ Kg8 28 Qe2

This game has been a disaster for Black, and now to make matters worse he loses even more material.

28...g4

28...Rh6 29 Rc6 wins a piece.

29 Nc4 1-0

Game 60
□ **S.Rublevsky** ■ **A.Dreev**
Russian Championship, Elista 1996

---

1 e4 d5 2 exd5 Nf6 3 d4 Nxd5 4 c4 Nb6 5 Nf3 Bg4 6 c5!? N6d7! 7 Bc4 (Diagram 6)

This is considered to be White's main move. There are a couple of general guidelines that are useful to know:

1) Black should not castle too early. If he is hasty with his king, White may unleash a potent initiative with g2-g4 using the Scandinavian bishop as a target.

2) It is generally inadvisable for Black to play ...Bxf3 *unless* he is able to play ...Nc6 with tempo and ...Qf6 encouraging an exchange of queens.

One additional note: White is threatening to play the obvious 8 Bxf7!+ followed by Ng5+ winning the bishop.

7...e6 8 Nc3

8 Be3 Be7 9 0-0 is different to the game, with White choosing to play quietly and castle kingside. After 9...0-0 10 Nc3 Nc6 11 Bb5 the natural strike 11...e5! is very powerful. Ye Ling Feng-J.Tomczak, Vung Tau City 2008, continued 12 d5? (tempting, but this is a mistake; after 12 Bxc6 bxc6 13 h3 exd4 14 Bxd4 Be6 Black has the bishop pair as compensation for his weak queenside pawn structure) 12...Nd4!, which gave Black a slight advantage that increased after 13 Bxd4 exd4 14 d6 dxc3! 15 dxe7 Qxe7.

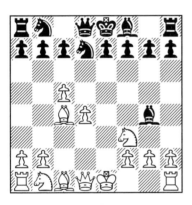

Diagram 6 (B)

The main move

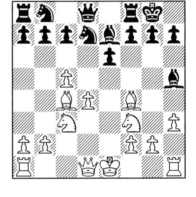

Diagram 7 (W)

Castling too soon?

After 8 h3 it is possible for Black to exchange on f3, because he can develop the queen to f6 with tempo: 8...Bxf3! (having studied the alternative, I think this is the best response for Black: after 8...Bh5 9 Be3 Be7 10 Nbd2! – defending his brother on f3 – 10...a6 11 Qb3 the absence of the light-squared bishop as a defender can be felt on the queenside) 9 Qxf3 Nc6 10 Be3 Qf6 11 Nc3 (if White keeps the queens on the board with 11 Qd1 Black can then increase the pressure on d4 with 11...0-0-0) 11...0-0-0 12 Qe4 Qg6 (Black is insistent on swapping the queens off) 13 0-0-0 Qxe4 14 Nxe4 and the position is equal, D.Szoen-Z.Pakleza, Karpacz 2008.

8...Be7 9 h3 Bh5

Black no longer has the option of ...Qf6, but the exchange on f3 is still playable: 9...Bxf3!? 10 Qxf3 Nc6 11 Be3 0-0 12 0-0 e5! 13 Rad1! exd4 14 Bxd4 Nxd4 15 Rxd4 Bxc5 16 Rdd1 Bd6 and Black was probably okay in D.Popovic-Mamuzic, Serbia 2003.

10 Be3

> WARNING: 10 Bf4 0-0? (Diagram 7) neglects a vital rule in this position – don't castle too early! After 11 g4 Bg6 12 Qe2 Nf6 13 0-0-0 Nd5 14 Bxd5 exd5 15 h4 Re8 16 h5 Be4 17 Nxe4 dxe4 18 Qxe4 Nc6 White was simply a pawn up in V.Yemelin-E.Maahs, Hamburg 2000.

10...Nc6

10...b6 is possible but I am a little bit sceptical, as Black must be able to confront the immediate 11 d5! and I am not sure he is able to do this. After 11...Nxc5 12 Bb5+ Kf8 13 0-0 exd5 14 Nxd5 Bd6 15 Nf4 Bg6 16 Nxg6+ hxg6 17 Ng5 Black is losing because he cannot protect the f7 point or the h1-a8 diagonal adequately.

11 Qe2! (Diagram 8)

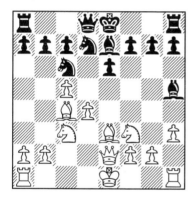

Diagram 8 (B)

A menacing move

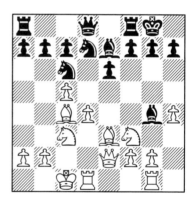

Diagram 9 (W)

Subtle bishop moves

Getting ready to castle queenside, as recommended by John Emms, is the most dangerous move Black can face.

11 a3?! aims to expand on the queenside, but now White has made his intentions clear Black can commit to 11...0-0!?. Here 12 g4 no longer works, as Black gets too much pressure against the d4-pawn, and 12...Bg6 13 Qe2 e5 14 0-0-0 exd4 15 Nxd4 Nxd4 16 Bxd4 Re8 is fine for him.

Black has also played the radical 11...e5 (instead of 11...0-0) and here the main line runs 12 d5! Bxf3 (12...Nd4? is tempting but leaves Black worse after 13 g4 Nxf3+ 14 Qxf3 Bg6 15 d6 cxd6 16 cxd6 Bxd6 17 Qxb7, since 17...0-0 18 Rd1 picks up some material) 13 Qxf3 Nd4 14 Bxd4 exd4 15 d6! Ne5! 16 Qxb7 Nxc4 17 Nd5 Bxd6 18 cxd6 0-0 19 dxc7 Re8+ 20 Kf1 Qd7 21 Rd1 Qe6 22 Kg1 Rac8 23 Kh2 with an advantage for White, J.Percze-J.Bibens, correspondence 2003.

11...0-0

11...e5?! is refuted by 12 g4! Bg6 13 0-0-0 exd4 14 Nxd4 0-0 15 Ne6! and White wins a pawn, M.Santo Roman-R.Goldenberg, French League 1992.

12 0-0-0!

This is an incredibly dangerous position for Black. With opposite-side castling, both sides need to get on with things and attack. However, it is not so easy for Black to (a) gain squares for his knights, or (b) open lines for the heavy pieces.

12...Bg6!?

Removing this hook from White's attack works out well in the game. Note that 12...b6 fails to 13 d5.

13 h4?!

This allows Black to set up an effective blockade. The direct 13 g4! is best, and following 13...Na5! 14 h4! Nxc4 15 Qxc4 White has a fierce attack.

13...Bh5 14 Rhg1 Bg4! (Diagram 9)

This equalizes. The main purpose of all these bishop moves has been to prevent White from establishing an attack.

15 d5 exd5 16 Nxd5

Against 16 Bxd5 Black should play 16...Qc8 removing the queen from the d-file and defending the bishop on g4. After 17 Qc4 Nf6 both sides must play in the centre. Because White is better developed for the moment, Black must seek to make some favourable exchanges along the d-file.

16...Bxc5

A bold move, and a good one too.

17 Bxc5 Nxc5 18 Qe3

18 Nb6 doesn't work because of 18...Nd4 19 Qe3 cxb6 20 Rxd4 Qc8 21 Kb1 Qf5+ and Black is simply a pawn up.

18...Nd7

The only move, as 18...Ne6 fails to 19 Nb6.

19 Qf4 Bxf3

Played to neutralize White's initiative in the centre.

20 gxf3 Nce5! 21 Rg5 Re8 22 Rdg1 Ng6

22...g6 allows White to go on the offensive with 23 h5 intending 23...h6?? (23...Kh8 gives an unclear position) 24 Rxg6+ Nxg6 25 Rxg6+ fxg6 26 Ne7+ Kh8 27 Qxh6 mate.

23 Qg3

After 23 Rxg6 hxg6 24 Nxc7 Ne5 25 Nxa8 Qc8 26 Kb1 Qxc4 27 Qxc4 Nxc4 Black is winning due to White's terrible pawn structure.

23...Nde5 24 Bb3 c6 25 Nc3 Qf6 26 h5 Nxf3 27 hxg6 Qxg5+ 28 Qxg5 Nxg5 29 Rxg5 hxg6 30 Rxg6 Rad8

This endgame is practically winning for Black. He has an extra pawn on both sides of the board which means as soon as he exchanges rooks, the two minor pieces cannot work well together to prevent the advance of the pawns.

31 Rg4 Kf8 32 Rf4 Re7 33 a4 g6 34 Kc2 Kg7 35 Bc4 Rd6 36 Rg4 Re5 37 Bd3 Rh5 38 Rb4 b6 39 Be2 Rh2 40 f3 f5 41 Rc4 g5 42 b4 Rh4

Now it is easy!

43 Kb3 Kf6 44 Nb1 Rxc4 45 Kxc4 Ke5 46 Bd3 Kf4 47 Nd2 b5+ 48 axb5 cxb5+ 49 Kc3 Rd5 50 Nb3 Ke3 51 Bc2 g4 52 fxg4 fxg4 0-1

White Plays Be2

By playing 5 Be2 White can use his extra space to deny Black any counterplay without having to risk anything. 5 Be2 is a reliable move, and it gives White the flexibility to play the position with c2-c4 (as in Game 62) or without this advance (as in Game 61).

Game 61
□ **H.Hunt** ■ **A.Muzychuk**
Stockholm 2008

1 e4 d5 2 exd5 Nf6 3 d4 Nxd5 4 Nf3 Bg4 5 Be2 (Diagram 10) 5...e6 6 0-0

White can also try to eliminate one or two Black options by playing Ne5 a move earlier: 6 Ne5 Bxe2 7 Qxe2 Nd7 (7...Nc6 is possible, but Black has to accept a structural disadvantage) 8 0-0 Be7 and Black has a solid, if a little passive, position.

The question after 6 0-0 is whether or not Black should allow White to exchange the light-squared bishops with Ne5. If Black allows this exchange, White will have made his position a little easier because he will have removed Black's most active piece.

6...Nc6!? (Diagram 11)

Here's a summary of the alternatives:

a) 6...Be7? allows 7 Ne5! and is a strategic mistake. For example, 7...Bxe2 8 Qxe2 0-0 9 Rd1 Nd7 10 c4 N5f6 (10...N5b6 11 Nc3 c6? is a big error, as now Black has the weakness of d6 to worry about after 12 Bf4) 11 Bf4 c6? (again this is a mistake) 12 Nc3 Re8 13 Rd3 (this rook can become a powerful attacker on the kingside) 13...Nf8 14 Rad1 Qa5 15 a3 Ng6 16 Bg3 Rac8 was played in P.Leko-G.Kamsky, Groningen 1995. Here Leko recommends 17 h4! when White's attack is very dangerous.

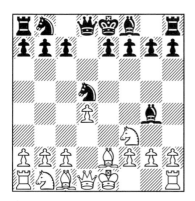

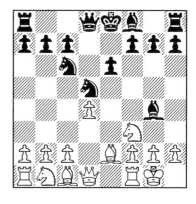

Diagram 10 (B)	Diagram 11 (W)
The solid 5 Be2	Preventing Ne5

b) 6...Nd7 7 c4 N5f6! 8 Nc3 Be7 9 h3 Bh5 10 Qb3 makes it awkward for Black to defend the b7-pawn. Ideally Black wants to have flicked in ...c7-c6, but sadly this is not possible.

 NOTE: Once Black has committed a knight to d7, the d5-knight has no place on b6 – it is out of the game. So 7...N5b6? is a mistake, and after 8 Nc3 Be7 9 c5! Black is forced to play the undesirable 9...Nc8 because 9...Nd5 10 Nxd5 exd5 11 Qb3 attacks b7 and d5.

c) 6...Bd6!? 7 Ne5 (the principled continuation; 7 Re1 is insufficient for an advantage after 7...0-0 8 c4 Nf4, and the same goes for 7 c4 Nf4 8 c5 Nxe2+ 9 Qxe2 Be7 10 Qb5+ Nc6 11 Ne5 a6 12 Qxb7 Nxe5 13 dxe5 0-0 with reasonable compensation for the pawn, S.Kerr-B.Littleboy, correspondence 2001) 7...Bxe2 8 Qxe2 0-0 (now that Black has adequate control of the d6-square, 8...Bxe5 is also possible although Black must be prepared to accept a space deficit) 9 c4 Ne7 10 Rd1 Nf5 11 Nc3 Nd7 12 f4 Nxe5 13 dxe5 (13 fxe5 was much, much better although Black still gains equality after retreating the bishop to e7) 13...Bc5+ 14 Kh1 Qh4 and once Black challenges White on the d-file he will stand better, M.Simeonov-G.Simovski, Struga 2005.

7 c3!? Be7?!

This is wrong, as Black must establish some control over the e5-square. 7...Bd6! 8 Ne5? (simplifying seems to benefit Black; given that Black doesn't exert any pressure on d4, perhaps White should consider losing a tempo with 8 c4 Nf6 9 Nc3 0-0 10 Be3 Qd7 11 h3, keeping a very slight advantage) 8...Bxe2 9 Qxe2 Bxe5 10 dxe5 Qh4 11 Nd2 Nf4 12 Qe4 Qg4 13 Re1 h5! left Black reasonably placed in J.Aagaard-D.Bryson, Rotherham 1997.

8 h3 Bh5 9 Re1 0-0 10 Nbd2 Qd7

Harriet later called this move an inaccuracy, preferring 10...a6. This little pawn move actually fights for control of the e5-square by preventing Bb5, which can often be annoying for Black, and here 11 Ne4 Bg6 12 Bd3 h6 13 Bd2 Qd7 14 Qc2 Rad8 led to equality in the old game P.Benko-K.Rogoff, Pasadena 1978.

11 Nc4 (Diagram 12)

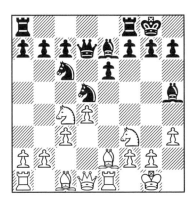

Diagram 12 (B)

Should Black exchange?

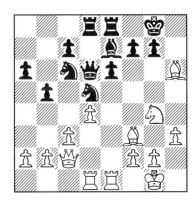

Diagram 13 (B)

A winning tactic

11...Bxf3

As Harriet pointed out, her opponent was worried by the possibility of Ne5. However, this fear is unfounded, as after 11...Rfd8 12 Nce5 Nxe5 13 Nxe5 Bxe2 14 Qxe2 Qe8 Black doesn't stand too badly following the favourable exchanges.

12 Bxf3 Rad8 13 Qb3 b6

13...b5 is possible because after 14 Qxb5? Nxd4 15 Qxd7 Nxf3+ Black stands better. Instead 14 Ne3! Na5 15 Qc2 Nxe3 16 Bxe3 Nc4 17 Bf4 Nb6 leaves Black with firm control of the d5-square which offsets White's advantage of the bishop pair.

14 Bd2 Rfe8 15 Rad1 b5 16 Ne3 a6

16...Na5 is better.

17 Qc2 h6 18 Ng4!

It's no surprise that White is manoeuvring towards the h6-pawn.

18...Qd6??

18...Bg5 is the only move that doesn't lose.

19 Bxh6! (Diagram 13) 19...f5

Anna was banking on this move, but it falls short.

20 Bxd5! Qxd5

20...exd5 21 Qxf5 gxh6 22 Re6 is devastating.

21 Ne3 Qd6 22 d5! gxh6 23 dxc6 Qc5 24 Qb3 Bd6 25 Nc2

Zooming in on the e6 point.

25...Kf7 26 Nd4 Qc4 27 Qc2 b4 28 Rxe6!!

A stunning tactic, but it's not surprising that it exists.

28...Rxe6 29 Qxf5+ Ke7 30 Qh7+ Ke8 31 Qg8+ Ke7 32 Nf5+ Kf6 33 Qg7+ Kxf5 34 g4+ Kf4 35 Qf7+ 1-0

Checkmate will soon follow – a beautiful finish!

Game 62
☐ **S.Bogdanovich** ■ **R.Khaetsky**
Kiev 2008

---

1 e4 d5 2 exd5 Nf6 3 Nf3 Nxd5 4 d4 Bg4 5 Be2 e6

The more enterprising 5...Nc6 puts pressure on the centre, but by not protecting d5 Black encourages complications resulting from an early c2-c4 and d4-d5: 6 c4 (entering into a complicated mess is by no means forced, and White can play 6 0-0! when 6...e6 could transpose to the main game) 6...Nb6 7 d5 Bxf3 and now:

a) 8 Bxf3 is the move White would ideally like to play, but he is not well placed to deal with the undermining moves ...e6 or ...c6: 8...Ne5 9 Be2 c6 (or 9...e6) 10 Qd4 Ng6 11 Nc3 e5 and Black is fine, F.Hellers-R.Dzindzichashvili, New York 1987.

b) 8 gxf3! Ne5 9 f4 Ned7 10 Nc3! **(Diagram 14)** gets ready to play Be3 and c4-c5, pushing Black's knights all the way back, and to take charge of the light squares with a well-timed Bf3. Now:

b1) 10...e6! (breaking up White's pawn centre in this manner has the advantage of freeing the f8-bishop) 11 dxe6 fxe6 12 Be3 Bc5! 13 h4 Qe7 14 Qc2 0-0-0 15 0-0-0 Bxe3+ 16 fxe3 e5 17 Qe4 Rhe8 18 Qxh7 exf4 19 exf4 (M.Versili-T.Strand, correspondence 2002) and here Black should play 19...Na4!, when his pieces are very active. White's c4-, f4- and h4-pawns are targets and overall Black has compensation for the sacrificed pawn.

b2) 10...c6 is very risky because Black still hasn't made any room for his dark-squared bishop. 11 dxc6 bxc6 12 Be3 e6 was played in V.Anand-G.Kamsky, Sanghi

Nagar 1994, and here 13 Rg1! would be my choice. Although it gives Black time to play 13...Nf6 and swap off queens (Black gets into trouble after 13...g6 14 Qd4 Nf6 15 Bf3), following 14 Qxd8+ Rxd8 15 Bf3 Nxc4 16 Bxc6+ Nd7 17 Bxa7 White definitely has the advantage, with the two bishops and a passed a-pawn.

6 c4

I've called this set-up with Be2 and c2-c4 the "Classical Variation" because the moves are so natural and logical that anyone could think of them over the board.

6...Nb6 7 0-0 Be7 8 Nc3 0-0 9 Be3 Nc6 10 b3 (Diagram 15)

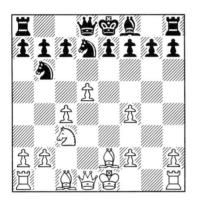

Diagram 14 (B)

...e6 or ...c6?

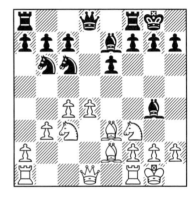

Diagram 15 (B)

A potential problem

As a teenager I was shown this line by FM Graham Lee. At the time I was pretty blasé about it. However, a few years later, after encountering it in a tournament, I began to realize that there were some problems that were not so easy for Black to solve. So this became my favourite set-up as White!

White's aim is simple: he just wants to keep the knight on b6 out of play, deprive Black of space and eventually play d4-d5. Black must find a purpose for his pieces and get to grips with his lack of space.

10 d5 exd5 11 cxd5 Bxf3 12 Bxf3 Ne5 13 Be2 Bf6 14 Bd4 Ned7 (R.Mamedov-V.Alexandrova, Moscow 1997) isn't a problem for Black. His pawn on c7 is vulnerable but so is the one on d5, and knights make excellent blockaders!

10...Qd7?!

Black is playing on only one factor – the pressure down the d-file. At the minute White holds the trumps in space and piece activity, and this means he can deal with this pressure relatively easily. In addition, the black queen is cut off from the kingside, which makes any White offensive on the kingside very dangerous for Black.

What Black must do is to either distract White from his goal or transfer the dark-squared bishop to the long diagonal *without* letting it get swapped off. Here are a few alternatives:

a) 10...a5!? obtains counterplay along the a-file and secures the b4-square: 11 Qd2 a4! (switching plans with 11...Bf5? is not a good idea, and after 12 Rfd1 Bf6 13 Rac1 Qe7 14 d5 White was comfortably better in A.Weng-J.Houska, Dresden 1998) 12 Rfd1 axb3 13 axb3 Bb4 and Black is fine. The open a-file provides activity for both players, while the d4-pawn may become a long-term weakness.

b) 10...Bf6?! allows White an easy game: 11 Ne4 h6 12 Qd2 Qe7 13 Rad1 Rad8 14 Nxf6+ Qxf6 15 Qb2 Rd7 16 Rd2 Rfd8 17 Rfd1 Nc8 (J.Houska-M.Lambshire, Bourne End 2000) and now 18 Ne5 would have won.

 TIP: Black must not let White exchange a knight for the dark-squared bishop without good reason.

c) 10...Bf5!? preparing 11 ...Bf6 is a viable alternative: 11 Qd2 Bf6 12 Rac1 Qe7 13 Rfd1 Rfd8 14 Qe1 Rd7 15 c5 Nd5 16 Nxd5 exd5 17 b4 Nd8 was agreed drawn in D.Mastrovasilis-A.Gurevich, Tallinn 1997.

11 Qd2

11 Ne5! **(Diagram 16)** enables White to transfer the queen to the kingside,

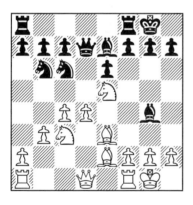 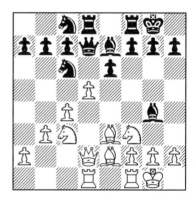

Diagram 16 (B)	**Diagram 17 (B)**
More forcing	You go backwards; I go forwards!

and 11...Nxe5 12 Bxg4 Nxg4 13 Qxg4 Rad8 14 Rad1 Bb4 15 Ne2 Kh8 16 Rd3 Nc8 17 Qh5 Kg8 18 Rfd1 reached a very uncomfortable position for Black in G.Voss-S.Williams, correspondence 2000. He is entirely on the defensive, whereas White has a very easy plan of playing either in the centre with d4-d5 or transferring the rook on d3 to the kingside to extract further concessions.

11...Rad8 12 Rad1 Nc8?

12...Bf5 was a better option.

13 d5! (Diagram 17) 13...exd5 14 Nxd5 Nd6 15 Qc1 b6??

A big mistake: the opening of the c-file is disastrous for Black and causes him to lose material.

After 15...Rfe8 16 c5 Nf5 17 h3 Bxf3 18 Bxf3 Nxe3 19 Nf6+ Bxf6 20 Rxd7 Rxd7 21 fxe3 White has the advantage.

16 c5! bxc5 17 Qxc5 Rfe8??

In a bad position, Black makes a further mistake.

18 Nxe7+ Rxe7 19 Bb5

Black must lose a piece, and even the opening of White's kingside does not help.

19...Bxf3 20 gxf3 Qh3 21 Bxc6 1-0

After 21...Re6, 22 Kh1 calmly defends everything.

White Plays g2-g4

Advancing with h2-h3 and g2-g4 is an aggressive way for White to play. The light-squared bishop reaches its optimal diagonal (h1-a8), where it is ideally placed to support the centre and also the light squares around the white king.

Game 63
□ **M.Meszaros** ■ **R.Ekstroem**
Brno 2006

1 e4 d5 2 exd5 Nf6 3 Nf3 Nxd5 4 d4 Bg4 5 h3 Bh5

5...Bxf3 just gives White the long-term advantage of the bishop pair – not the best thing to do if the pawn structure has not yet been determined.

6 c4

Or 6 g4 Bg6 7 Bg2 e6 8 0-0 and now:

a) 8...c6 (this is simply too passive) 9 c4 Nf6 10 Nc3 Be7 11 Ne5 Nfd7 12 Nxg6 hxg6 13 d5 exd5 14 cxd5 0-0 15 Bf4 and Black was really struggling in E.Rozentalis-J.Orzechowski, Ustron 2006.

b) 8...Nc6! controlling e5 is critical. 9 c4 Nb6 10 Nc3 is not scary because Black can play 10...Nxc4! 11 d5 exd5 12 Re1+ Be7 13 Nxd5 Nb6! 14 Nxe7, and here 14...Qxd1! saves the day and reaches an equal endgame.

6...Nb6 7 Nc3!

The most flexible move.

7...e6

7...Nc6? was convincingly refuted in E.Van den Doel-D.Meijer, Leiden 2007, after 8 c5 Bxf3 (8...Nd5!? is the best) 9 Qxf3 Nd7 (or 9...Nxd4 10 Qe4 f5 – all other moves lose – 11 Qd3 Nc4 12 Be3 Nxe3 13 fxe3 Nc6 14 Qxf5 when White has regained the pawn and still has a massive attack) 10 Bc4 e6 11 Be3 Be7 and White has everything he could possibly want from the opening: the bishop pair and many dynamic possibilities.

8 g4

8 Be2 Be7 takes us back into the realms of the Classical Variation.

8...Bg6 9 Ne5

9 Qb3 is also interesting, and after 9...Qc8 10 Ne5 White has the better position.

9...c5! (Diagram 18)

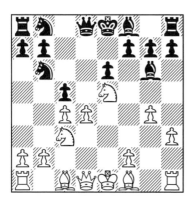

Diagram 18 (W)
Striking out

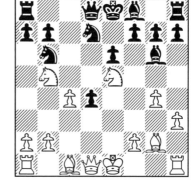

Diagram 19 (W)
White makes a mistake

9...N6d7? makes too many moves with one piece, and furthermore Black will struggle to find a good square for the other knight on b8. After 10 Nxg6 hxg6 11 Bg2! c6 12 0-0 Be7 13 d5! we have transposed to the Rozentalis-Orzechowski game, above.

After 9...N8d7 10 Nxg6 hxg6 11 Qe2 Be7!, Black's main task is to re-route the b6-knight or to make it useful, but this is not so easy to do. Here 12 Bg2 c6 13 Bf4! (a wait-and-see move) 13...0-0 14 h4 Bxh4 15 Ne4 looks dangerous for Black.

10 Bg2 cxd4 11 Nb5

11 Bxb7 would be a mistake in view of 11...Qc7.

11...N8d7 (Diagram 19)

12 Bf4?

A big mistake. 12 Nxg6 was the only move, although after 12...hxg6 13 Bxb7 Rb8 14 Bc6 Bb4+ 15 Bd2 Bxd2+ 16 Qxd2 Nxc4 17 Qxd4 Rxb5! 18 Qxc4 (18 Bxb5 fails to 18...Qa5+) 18...Qa5+ 19 Kf1 Rc5 20 Qa4 Qc7 21 Bxd7+ Qxd7 Black has the edge because his pieces are the more active.

12...Bb4+ 13 Kf1 Nxe5 14 Bxe5 0-0 15 Bxb7?

Another mistake – 15 Qxd4 had to be played.

15...Nxc4! 16 Bc7 Qd7 17 Qa4 a5 18 Bxa8 Rxa8 19 Kg1 Be4

Black is winning, as his pieces dominate the whole board.

20 a3 Qd5 21 f3 Bxf3 22 Rh2 Bc5 23 Bg3 Nb6 24 Nc7 Nxa4 25 Nxd5 Bxd5 26 Rc1 d3+ 27 Kf1 Be3 28 Rd1 Bb3 0-1

Summary

As an alternative to the Fianchetto Variation, Black may adopt a more solid set-up by developing the bishop to g4 and then restraining the white pawn centre before placing pressure on d4. White may attempt to refute the system immediately with the promising c4-c5 (Games 59-60) or chase away the bishop with h2-h3 and g2-g4 (Game 63). If White wants to plays more slowly, he may decide to lock the b6-knight out of the game with the classical formation seen in Game 61. He may also delay c2-c4 or simply refrain from playing it altogether, as in Game 62.

Chapter Fourteen

The Portuguese Variation

- The Danger White Faces
- The Main Line
- 3 Nf3: Avoiding the Portuguese

1 e4 d5 2 exd5 Nf6 3 d4 Bg4 (Diagram 1)

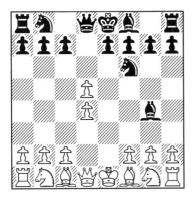

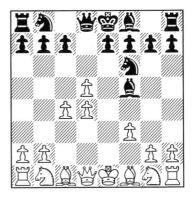

Diagram 1 (W)	**Diagram 2 (B)**
The Portuguese Variation	Too brave?

This chapter deals with the repercussions of White playing 3 d4 and allowing the Portuguese Variation. Like the Icelandic Gambit, which is covered in the next chapter, Black sacrifices material in order to open lines against the white king. Black is relying on his fast development and the considerable time White spends securing his extra material to achieve very quick counterplay, and the resulting positions are usually very messy. Unfortunately for Black, White can avoid the Portuguese Variation by simply playing 3 Nf3 first, intending to reach the 2...Nf6 main lines after 3...Nxd5 4 d4 (see the final section of the chapter).

The Danger White Faces

We begin with a demonstration of why the Portuguese Variation can be such a perilous opening to face:

1 e4 d5 2 exd5 Nf6 3 d4 Bg4 4 f3 Bf5 5 c4?! (Diagram 2)

NOTE: Holding on to the extra pawn in this simple way just allows Black to accelerate his development even further by uncorking a second pawn sacrifice.

5...e6! 6 dxe6 Nc6!

This kind of activity can often make White feel more than a little bit uneasy, especially as Black now threatens 7...Nb4!.

7 Be3!

There are several alternatives for White, but none of them are fully satisfactory. For example:

a) 7 d5? Nb4 8 Na3 fxe6 and Black is fully developed.

b) 7 exf7+? Kxf7 is much too greedy. White desperately needs the e-pawn as a shield on the e-file. With the pawn missing and an extra development tempo for Black, White is in deep trouble. For example, 8 Be3 Bb4+! 9 Nc3 Re8 10 Kf2 Rxe3 11 Kxe3 Bc2 and White resigned in F.Halwick jr-R.Pe Ang, correspondence 1997, as Black wins after 12 Qd2 Ng4+ 13 fxg4 Qg5+ 14 Ke2 Re8+.

7...Bb4+

7...Qe7!?, aiming to win a pawn with a timely ...Qb4+ hitting c4 and b2, is a very good alternative. Black was much better after 8 Nc3 0-0-0 9 Kf2 Qb4 10 Nge2 (10 exf7 is met by 10...Nxd4!) 10...Qxc4 11 exf7 Qxf7 12 Kg1 Bc5 13 Qa4 Qe7 14 Bf2 Nxd4 15 Nxd4 Rxd4 in I.Sudakova-A.Muzychuk, Zlatibor 2007. Note here that 16 Bxd4?? is not possible due to 16...Qe3+ mating.

8 Nc3

8 Nd2!? is analysed in depth by Selby Anderson in his book *Center Counter Defense: The Portuguese Variation*. He recommends 8...0-0!? and now:

a) 9 a3 is met by the dynamic 9...Nxd4! 10 axb4 (10 Bxd4 Qxd4 11 axb4 Qxb2 is good for Black) 10...Nc2+ 11 Kf2 Re8! 12 Ra3 Rxe6 reaching a very complicated position. Black has compensation for the piece in the shape of White's exposed king and lack of development, which makes the situation very tricky for White.

b) 9 d5 Re8!! is an excellent try by Black. Now 10 dxc6? is bad: 10...Rxe6 11 Kf2 Rxe3! 12 Kxe3 Bc5+ 13 Ke2 Qe7+ 14 Ne4 Nxe4 15 fxe4 Qxe4+ 16 Kd2 Qe3 mate.

8...Qe7 9 Bd3! (Diagram 3)

9 d5? 0-0-0! led to a decisive attack for Black in Wang Zili-R.Damaso, Macau 1996: 10 Qa4 Nxd5! 11 cxd5 Qh4+ 12 Kd1? (12 Ke2 is more resilient but still loses after 12...Nd4+ 13 Bxd4 Qxd4 14 Qb3 Bc5 – Anderson) 12...Rxd5+ 13 Nxd5 Qe1 mate.

9...fxe6!

After 9...Bxe6 10 Qd2 0-0-0 11 Nge2 Rhe8 12 Bf2 Bc5 13 0-0-0 Nxd4 14 Nxd4 Bxd4 15 Bxd4 Rxd4 White was very slightly better in T.Ernst-F.Bentivegna, Cutro 2004.

10 Nge2 0-0-0 11 Bb1!

11 0-0 is met by 11...Bxd3 12 Qxd3 Ne5! and 13...Nxc4.

11...Nxd4! (Diagram 4)

A radical way to keep the initiative.

12 Nxd4 c5 13 a3 cxd4 14 axb4 dxe3

C.Herbrechtsmeier-A.Pereira, correspondence 1996, continued 14...dxc3 15 Qb3 Bxb1 16 Rxb1 Ne4 17 0-0 Nd2 18 Bxd2 cxd2 19 Rfd1 and the players agreed a draw in this unclear position.

15 Qb3! Bxb1 16 Nxb1!

John Emms assesses this as good for White, but in this dynamic position I think both sides have good attacking chances. For example, 16...Ne4 (with the unpleasant threat of 17...Qh4+) 17 0-0 (17 fxe4 loses to 17...Qh4+ 18 g3 Qxe4 19 Rf1 e2 20 Rf2 Rd1+) 17...e2 18 Re1 Rd1 19 Rxd1?? Qxb4!! and Black wins.

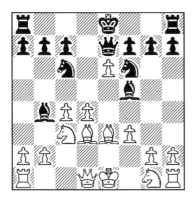

Diagram 3 (B)	Diagram 4 (W)
White must get developed	Keeping the initiative

The Main Line

1 e4 d5 2 exd5 Nf6 3 d4 Bg4 4 f3

With 4 f3, White accepts a weakness in order to gain time on the bishop and keep his extra pawn.

4 Nf3 Qxd5 5 Be2 can also be reached via the move order 1 e4 d5 2 exd5 Qxd5 3 Nf3!? Bg4 4 Be2 Nf6 5 d4. Black has two options here: the aggressive 5...Nc6 is covered in Game 65, while the more solid 5...e6 is looked at in Game 66. 4 Be2 is a low-risk option, but the downside is that White cannot expect to claim a huge advantage from the opening (see Game 67).

4...Bf5 5 Bb5+! (Diagram 5)

4 f3 followed by 5 Bb5+ is the only good way for White to hold on to the pawn. In fact, I would even go so far as to say that Black is struggling after this move to achieve compensation. As long as White follows the golden rule of not allowing his bishop to get locked out of play, then he will be fine.

5...Nbd7

5...c6 is quite clearly insufficient, and after 6 dxc6 Nxc6 7 Ne2 Qb6 8 Nbc3 0-0-0 9 Bxc6 Qxc6 10 Bf4 it is not clear how Black can keep the initiative.

6 c4 e6

> **NOTE: As a general rule, as soon as White plays c2-c4 Black will break with ...e7-e6.**

6...a6!? is another critical try, but 7 Ba4 b5 8 cxb5 Nxd5 9 bxa6 Rxa6 10 Ne2 e6 11 0-0 Be7 12 Nbc3 Nxc3 13 Nxc3 was good for White in S.Tiviakov-M.Goodger, Port Erin 2001.

7 dxe6 Bxe6 8 d5! (Diagram 6)

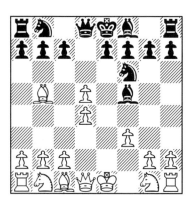

Diagram 5 (B)	Diagram 6 (B)
The best move	Hitting the bishop again

Conceding the d5-square with 8 c5?! is not as effective. After 8...c6 9 Ba4 Nd5 10 Nc3 N7f6 11 Nge2 Qc7 12 0-0 0-0-0 13 Nxd5 Nxd5 14 Bd2 Be7 15 b4 Bf6 16 b5 Ne7 things weren't easy for White in J.Dworakowska-M.Muzychuk, Dresden 2007.

8 Nc3 allows 8...c6, restricting the pawn on d4 and making it a target rather than a strength.

8...Bf5

Now:

a) 9 Be3 gives Black too much time to develop his pieces. 9...Bb4+ 10 Nc3 0-0 11 Nge2 Ne5! 12 0-0 a6 13 Qd4 was V.Balint-G.Acs, Hungarian League 2004, when instead of 13...Nd3 Black can play 13...Qe7! 14 Ng3 Bg6 15 Ba4 Nxc4! recovering the pawn with the superior position.

b) The main line runs 9 Nc3 Bb4 10 Nge2 0-0, and this position is discussed in Game 64, below. If Black chooses 9...Bc5 instead of 9...Bb4, White should play the awkward 10 Qe2+. Following 10...Qe7 11 Bg5 0-0-0 12 g4 Bg6 13 Qxe7 Bxe7 it's wise to play 14 Bxd7+!. White has a gaping hole on d3, so we better get rid of the beast that may infiltrate it one day!

Game 64
□ R.Eames ■ S.Lalic
British League 2008

1 e4 d5 2 exd5 Nf6 3 d4 Bg4 4 f3 Bf5 5 Bb5+! Nbd7 6 c4 e6 7 dxe6 Bxe6 8 d5! Bf5 9 Nc3 Bb4 10 Nge2 0-0 (Diagram 7)

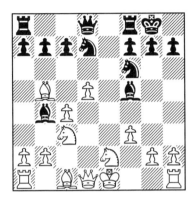

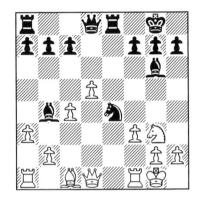

Diagram 7 (W)	Diagram 8 (W)
An important moment	Which piece to capture?

11 Bxd7!

> **NOTE: White must make sure that his bishop on b5 is not "locked out". Often the best thing to do is to exchange the bishop for the knight on d7.**

11 0-0 can be met by 11...Ne5!, eyeing the d3-square and also aiming for ...c7-c6. For example, 12 Bg5?! (12 Nd4! is the strongest move, and after 12...a6 13 Nxf5 axb5 14 Nxb5 Nxc4 15 b3 White still stands slightly better) 12...a6 13 Ba4 h6 14 Bh4 Nxc4 15 Qd4 b5 16 Ne4 Bxe4 17 fxe4 Qd6! (Black escapes the unpleasant pin with this crafty move, threatening 18...Bc5) 18 Rxf6 gxf6 19 Kh1 Qe5 20 Bc2 Bd6 and Black was much better in R.Eames-G.Buckley, British League 2005.

11...Nxd7

If 11...Qxd7 12 0-0 c6, White has the irritating 13 Bg5.

12 0-0 Re8

12...Qh4 is convincingly answered by 13 Ng3 Bg6 14 Nce4 threatening to win the queen with 15 Bg5, and here 14...h6 15 Bd2 Bc5+ 16 Kh1 Bd4 allows the little trick 17 Nf5 Bxf5 18 Be1 with a clear plus for White, J.Smeets-D.Smerdon, Kochin 2004.

12...Ne5 13 Ng3! Bd7 14 Qd4! Qe7 (threatening 15...Bc5) 15 Nge4 c5 16 dxc6 Nxc6 17 Qe3 f5 18 Nd5 Qd8 19 Nc5 Re8 20 Qf2 (U.Haug-M.Ibar, correspondence 2002) also looks good for White – Black doesn't have enough for the pawn.

13 Ng3 Bg6 14 Nce4 Nc5!

This is Susan Lalic's improvement over her husband Graeme Buckley's play in a previous game: 14...a5 15 Kh1 f5? (Black lashes out too quickly) 16 Ng5 Nf8 17 Nh3 Qf6 18 Qb3 Nd7 19 Bg5 Qf7 20 Bf4 Nc5 21 Qc2 a4 (otherwise the dark-squared bishop is in danger of being trapped) 22 Rad1 a3 23 b3 h6 24 Qf2 Qe7 25 d6 and White had a distinct advantage in R.Berzinsh-G.Buckley, British League 2005.

15 a3 Nxe4 (Diagram 8) 16 Nxe4

Here White should play 16 axb4!, which guarantees a very slight advantage after 16...Nxg3 17 hxg3 Qd6 18 Qd4 Qxb4 (if 18...Qxg3 19 Qf4 Qxf4 20 Bxf4 it is difficult for Black to defend the c7-pawn in a satisfactory manner) 19 Bd2 Qb6 20 c5 Qb5.

16...Bf8 17 Qd4 b6 18 Kh1 Qh4 19 Qf2 Qxf2 20 Nxf2 Bd6 21 Bd2 Be5 22 Bc3 Bxc3 23 bxc3 Re2

Black's activity provides more than sufficient compensation for the pawn deficit, and in any case the doubled pawns on the c-file are about as useful as only one pawn.

24 a4 a5 25 Kg1 Rae8 26 Rad1 Rc2 27 Rfe1 Rxe1+ 28 Rxe1 Kf8 29 Ng4 Rxc3 30 Ne5 Bf5 31 g4 f6 32 Nc6 Bd7 33 Re4 Bxc6?

33...Rxf3 would give Black a clear advantage.

34 dxc6 Rxf3 35 Rd4 Re3 36 Rd7 Re7 37 Rd8+ Kf7 38 Kf2 Kg6 39 Rd7 Kf7 40 Rd5 Ke8 41 Kf3 g5 42 c5

After this move Black's advantage disappears.

42...bxc5 43 Rxc5 Re6 44 Rxa5 Rxc6 45 Ra8+ Kf7 46 a5 Rc2 47 a6 Rxh2 48 Rh8 Rh3+ 49 Kf2 Ra3 50 Rxh7+ Ke6 51 Rxc7 Rxa6 52 Rc5 Ra3 53 Rb5 Rd3 54 Ra5 Rd5 55 Ra4 Ke5 56 Ke3 Rb5 57 Re4+ Kd5 58 Re8 Rb3+ 59 Kf2 Rb6 60 Kf3 Rb3+ 61 Kf2 Ra3 62 Re7 Kd6 63 Re8 Ra5 64 Kf3 Re5 65 Ra8 Ke6 ½-½

Game 65
□ **A.Kolev** ■ **D.Laylo**
Chicago 2008

1 e4 d5 2 exd5 Nf6 3 d4 Bg4 4 Nf3 Qxd5 5 Be2 Nc6!? (Diagram 9) 6 Be3!

This move, overprotecting the d4-pawn, is considered to be White's best choice, but there are alternatives:

a) 6 Nc3 is considered inaccurate because of 6...Qh5!.

b) 6 h3 Bxf3! (since Black has not restricted White's pawn centre, he should exchange on f3) 7 Bxf3 Qd7 8 c3 (8 Be3?! is inferior because of 8...0-0-0 9 c3 and now the vital pawn break 9...e5!) 8...0-0-0 9 0-0 e5 10 Qb3 e4 11 Be2 Nd5 12 Qc2 f5 13 Nd2 Nf4 14 Nc4 g5 and Black has a strong initiative, R.Webb-N.Povah, British League 2004.

c) 6 c4 is critical:

c1) 6...Qh5 7 Be3 0-0-0 8 Nbd2! e5 9 d5 Nd4 10 Nxd4 exd4 11 Bxd4 Re8! 12 f3 Bf5 13 0-0 Bd6 14 g3 Qg6 (all of Black's moves create a threat) 15 Rf2 Bc2 was double-edged in C.Nanu-Z.Vukovic, Bucharest 1998.

c2) 6...Qd7! is preferable, and 7 Be3 e6 8 Nbd2 Bf5 (planning to release some of the tension with ...Ne4) 9 Ne5 Nxe5 10 dxe5 Ne4 11 Nb3 Bb4+ 12 Kf1 Qe7 was very satisfactory for Black in S.Solomon-I.Rogers, Melbourne 1998.

6...0-0-0 7 Nbd2 Qf5 8 c4 e5! (Diagram 10) 9 dxe5 Nxe5 10 Qa4 a6 11 0-0-0 Nd3+ 12 Bxd3 Rxd3 13 h3 Bxf3 14 Nxf3 Rxd1+ 15 Rxd1 Bc5

Diagram 9 (W)	Diagram 10 (W)
The sharpest try	The equalizing move

The position is completely level. With everything virtually symmetrical, Black has a very easy game.

16 Nd4 Qe4 17 b4!?

White plays very aggressively, trying to force a mistake.

17...Bxd4 18 Rxd4 Qe6 19 b5 Rd8!

Calm defence – Black simply eliminates one of the attackers. Now the game peters out to a draw, despite White's efforts.

20 bxa6 bxa6 21 Rxd8+ Kxd8 22 Qd1+ Kc8 23 Qd4 Qc6 24 Qc5 Qe6 25 Kb2 Nd7 26 Qd4 g6 27 Kb3 h5 28 Kc3 Nb6 29 Qf4 Qe7 30 Kb3 Qd7 31 Bxb6 cxb6 32 Qf3 Kc7 33 Qf4+ Kb7 34 Qf3+ Kc7 35 Qf4+ Kb7 36 Qf3+ ½-½

Game 66
☐ O.Korneev ■ S.Tiviakov
FIDE World Cup, Khanty Mansiysk 2005

1 e4 d5 2 exd5 Qxd5 3 Nf3 Bg4 4 Be2 Nf6 5 d4

The Portuguese move order is 1 e4 d5 2 exd5 Nf6 3 d4 Bg4 4 Nf3 Qxd5 5 Be2.

5...e6 (Diagram 11)

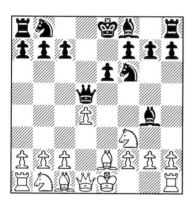

Diagram 11 (W)	**Diagram 12 (B)**
The solid 5...e6	A challenging idea

6 0-0

The aggressive option for White is to chase away the bishop with the aim of attacking it even further by g2-g4: 6 h3 Bh5 7 c4 Qd8 8 Qb3 Qc8 9 Nc3 Be7 (White is better after 9...Nc6 10 Be3 Bd6 11 d5 exd5 12 cxd5 Bxf3 13 Bxf3 Ne5 14 Be2 0-0 15 0-0), and now 10 g4 Bg6 11 Ne5! **(Diagram 12)** is the most dangerous line for Black to face. White establishes a very strong base for the knight and prepares to castle long. Black has a big problem because it isn't an easy job to shift the piece from its square. For example:

a) 11...Nfd7 12 Nxg6 hxg6 13 Bf3 Nc6 14 Be3 Rb8 15 0-0-0 and White has a very pleasant position, L.Dominguez-J.Alvarez, Cuba 1999.

b) 11...Nbd7? fails to 12 g5 Ng8 13 Nxd7 when to avoid material loss Black must capture the knight with the king!

c) 11...c5 12 d5 0-0 13 g5 Nfd7 14 Nxg6 hxg6 15 Be3 exd5 16 cxd5 a6 17 h4 with a strong initiative for White, L.Bruzon Bautista-T.Willemze, Oropesa del Mar 1998.

6...c6 7 h3 Bh5 8 c4 Qd8

This structure is reminiscent of a Slav-type position where White has broken in the centre with e3-e4. However, there is one crucial difference in that the light-squared bishops have not been exchanged. As long as Black plays carefully and doesn't allow White to expand on the queenside then he can hold the position.

9 Nc3 Be7 (Diagram 13)

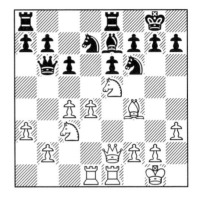

Diagram 13 (W)

The correct bishop development

Diagram 14 (B)

A space advantage for White

 NOTE: It is very important to develop the bishop on e7, even though ...Bd6 looks more natural. The point is that 9...Bd6 10 Bg5! makes it is very difficult for Black to break the pin, and this can inconvenience him greatly.

For example, 10...h6 (10...Be7! is the only move that makes sense, although after 11 Qd2 0-0 12 Rad1 Nbd7 13 Ne5 Bxe2 14 Qxe2 White has a pleasant space advantage) 11 Bxf6 Qxf6 (11...gxf6? 12 d5 was much better for White in G.Kaidanov-A.Zatonskih, San Diego 2006) 12 Qb3 b6 13 Ne4 Qf4 14 Nxd6+ Qxd6 15 c5!. The c4-c5 advance is a common motif in this type of position. White concedes the d5-square but gains extra space and, more importantly, will destroy Black's pawn structure. Finkel's analysis here is very convincing: 15...Qc7 16 Qe3 0-0 17 g4 Bg6 18 Ne5 Bh7 19 Bf3 Rc8 20 Rfc1, after which the c6-pawn is immeasurably weakened and Black has tremendous problems developing his pieces.

10 Bf4 0-0 11 a3

Getting ready to expand on the queenside – a common theme in positions with this pawn structure.

11...Nbd7

Unfortunately for Black, the natural 11...a5 is a bit too weakening, and after 12 Qb3! b6 13 Rfe1 Nbd7 14 Ne5! Black is very cramped.

12 Ne5

After 12 Qd2?! Black can equalize with 12...Bxf3! 13 Bxf3 e5 14 dxe5 Nxe5, while 12 b4 a5 gives Black counterplay along the a-file.

12...Bxe2 13 Qxe2 Re8

Without control of the d5-square, Black should not play 13...Nxe5? 14 dxe5 which would leave him struggling to maintain control of d6.

14 Rad1 Qb6 15 Rfe1 (Diagram 14) 15...Qa6?!

A prophylactic move designed to prevent b2-b4. However, I am not so sure it is necessary.

15...Rad8! looks the most natural. For example, 16 b4 Qa6! 17 Qd3 Nxe5 (the a-pawn is taboo: if 17...Qxa3 18 Ra1 Qxb4 19 Reb1 Qd6 20 Qe3 Nh5 21 Bh2 and the queen just cannot escape from the discovered attack) 18 Bxe5 Rd7 19 Rb1 Red8 20 a4 b6 and with ...c6-c5 coming Black doesn't have any problems.

16 g4!?

An interesting strike, now that the black queen is offside. However, 16 Nxd7! Nxd7 17 d5! is the best option. After 17...cxd5 18 cxd5 e5 19 Qxa6 bxa6 White has a distinct advantage, while 18...Qxe2 19 Rxe2 exd5 20 Nxd5 Bf8 21 Ne7+ Bxe7 22 Rxd7 is practically winning.

16...Nf8 17 g5 N6d7 18 Nxd7 Nxd7 19 d5! e5?!

As Sergei Tiviakov suggests, 19...Bf8 was perhaps a better option. It's true that 20 d6 gives White an almighty pawn but it is adequately blockaded by the knight, and if it is not bolstered properly then it may become a liability.

20 d6 Bf8 21 Be3 b6 22 Ne4 Re6

22...c5 is met by 23 b4 when 23...Rac8 24 b5 leaves Black suffering due to a lack of space, while 23...Qxa3?? gets the queen trapped after 24 Ra1 Qxb4 25 Reb1.

23 c5?

Now the position becomes unclear. 23 b4 (Tiviakov) would have maintained a clear advantage.

23...Qxe2 24 Rxe2 f5! 25 gxf6 gxf6 26 b4 f5 27 Nc3 ½-½

After 27...bxc5 28 Bxc5 (or 28 bxc5 Rb8 threatening ...Rb3) 28...Rg6+ 29 Kh2 Black has generated more than enough compensation for White's advanced pawn.

Game 67
□ **P.Sowray** ■ **G.Buckley**
Coulsdon 2005

---

1 e4 d5 2 exd5 Nf6 3 d4 Bg4 4 Be2 Bxe2 5 Qxe2

5 Nxe2 isn't challenging at all, as the white knight belongs on f3. Now the d4-

pawn is sure to come under heavy fire: 5...Qxd5 6 0-0 Nc6! (here we go!) 7 Nbc3 Qf5 8 Be3 e6 9 Ng3 Qg6 10 Qe2 0-0-0 11 Rad1 h5 12 Qd3 (O.Cooley-N.Povah, British League 2008) and now instead of the dubious 12...Qg4, Black should have chosen 12...Qxd3! 13 Rxd3 h4 14 Nge2 Rh5 with no problems.

5...Qxd5 6 Nf3 e6! (Diagram 15)

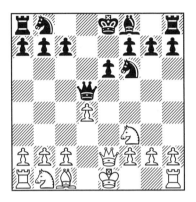 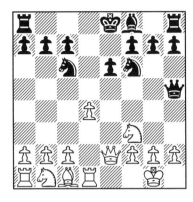

Diagram 15 (W)

6...e6 is accurate

Diagram 16 (W)

Well placed on h5

6...Nc6 treads a fine line as Black is making no effort to restrain White's central pawns. After 7 c4 Qf5 (7...Qe4 is safer) 8 0-0 0-0-0 9 d5! Nb4 10 a3! (this leads to a series of forced moves) 10...Nd3 (10...Nc2 11 Ra2 simply gets the knight trapped) 11 Be3 e6 (Black must try to break up White's centre) 12 Nd4 Qg6 13 Rd1 Ne5 14 dxe6 c5 15 Nb5 Rxd1+ 16 Qxd1 White has a clear advantage.

 TIP: Control central squares as much as possible. Failing that, restrain enemy pawns!

7 c4

7 0-0 may be a little premature, as this gives Black the option of opposite-side castling: 7...Nc6 8 Rd1 Qh5! **(Diagram 16)** (the active queen makes life a little bit unpleasant for White) 9 c4 0-0-0 10 Nc3 Rg8 11 Be3 g5 12 d5 g4 13 dxc6 gxf3! 14 Rxd8+ Kxd8 15 Qd3+. In this position 15...Bd6 is only possible because after the natural 16 cxb7? Rxg2+ 17 Kf1 Black has the stunning 17...Rg1+!! and mates. Instead 16 g3 bxc6 17 Rd1 Ke7 leads to a very unclear position in which Black is not worse, as White's king will be constantly under threat.

7...Bb4+!?

Alternatively:

a) 7...Qh5 is a little bit risky: 8 Nc3! Bd6 (8...Be7 9 Bf4 and only now 9...Bd6 fails to

10 Bxd6 cxd6 11 Nb5 when Black must use his king to defend d6) 9 c5 Be7 10 Qb5+ wins.

b) 7...Qf5!? is stronger than 7...Qh5, as the queen and knight coordinate better: 8 0-0 Nc6 9 d5 Nb4 10 Nd4 Qd3 11 Qxd3 Nxd3 12 dxe6 0-0-0 and Black is fine, as he will kick back the knight and regain the pawn.

c) 7...Qe4!? aims for an endgame where the d4-pawn will prove a weakness and the half-open d-file a strength: 8 Be3! (of course White should prevent Black from getting his wish!) 8...Bb4+ 9 Nbd2 Bxd2+ 10 Qxd2 Ng4 11 0-0 Nxe3 12 fxe3 f6 13 Qa5 (provoking a weakness...) 13...b6 14 Qh5+ (...and another one) 14...g6 15 Qb5+ Nd7 16 Rfe1 and White has the advantage, L.Aroshidze-A.Hamad, Adana 2006.

8 Bd2

8 Nbd2! is the best move. After 8...Qh5 9 a3 Be7 10 Nf1 Nc6 11 Ng3 Qg6 12 b4 0-0-0 13 Be3 Ng4 14 b5 Na5 15 0-0 h5 16 h3 h4 17 Nh1 Nxe3 18 fxe3 (J.Aagaard-D.Bryson, Oban 2005) White has the advantage – the black knight is somewhat stranded on a5, whereas the white knight on h1 will rejoin the action via f2 and g4. A safer option for Black is to force an endgame with 8...Qe4 so that White's edge in the centre cannot harm the safety of the black king.

8...Bxd2+ 9 Nbxd2 Qa5

9...Qh5 places the queen out of harm's way and is the safest reply. After 10 0-0 0-0 11 Ne4 Nbd7 12 Rad1 Rad8 13 Rd3 Nxe4 14 Qxe4 Qg6 15 Qe3 Rfe8, a draw was agreed in V.Arjun-S.Bromberger, Budapest 2007.

10 0-0?!

10 b4! is the most challenging move: 10...Qf5 (Black should probably refuse the offer: if 10...Qxb4 11 Rb1 White wins back the pawn with extras, and after 11...Qc3 12 0-0 b6 White has 13 Ne4! when an exchange of knights followed by d4-d5 will give him a huge initiative) 11 Nb3 0-0 12 0-0 c6 13 Nc5 b6 14 Nd3 with a space advantage for White.

10...0-0 11 Ne5

Again 11 b4! looks promising.

11...Nbd7 (Diagram 17)

> NOTE: Black follows an old adage: when a knight arrives on e5, challenge it!

12 Nxd7 Nxd7 13 Ne4 Rad8

13...Qf5 is dead level: for example, 14 Rfd1 Nf6 15 Nxf6+ Qxf6 16 Rd3 Rad8 17 Rad1 Rd7 18 Qe5 Rfd8 and Black has a very reasonable position.

14 Rfd1 Rfe8 15 Qf3

Objectively the position is level. However, the problem Black must solve is what to do with the knight on d7, which is interfering with the scope of the rooks.

15...h6 16 a3 Qa6 17 Rac1 f5!?

Black solves the problem through radical means, but this is a very risky approach which could easily backfire.

18 Ng3 Nf6 19 d5! Qb6 20 b4 exd5 21 cxd5!?

21 Nxf5 doesn't quite work as it's meant to, as after 21...dxc4 22 Qg3 Rxd1+ 23 Rxd1 Nh5! 24 Qh4 Qe6 25 Ne3 Nf6 26 Qxc4 the position is level.

21...g6 22 Qf4 Rxd5 23 Rxd5 Nxd5 24 Qxh6

Black's king is perfectly safe despite the menacing position of White's queen, and the position is still equal.

24...Qf6 25 Qd2 Qe5 26 Nf1 c6 27 a4 a6 (Diagram 18) 28 Rd1??

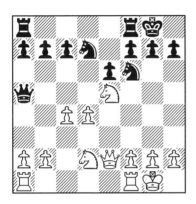

Diagram 17 (W)

Black challenges the knight

Diagram 18 (W)

White blunders

A careless mistake.

28...Nc3

Now White does not have a good square for his rook.

29 f4 Ne2+ 30 Kh1 Nxf4 31 Ng3 Nd5 32 b5

White tries hard to create something, but the damage has been done.

32...axb5 33 axb5 cxb5! 34 Kg1 Nf6 35 Rb1 f4 36 Nf1 Ne4 37 Qb4 Rc8 38 h3

38 Qxb5 is impossible because of 38...Qd4+, checkmating.

38...Nc3 39 Rb2 Ne2+ 40 Kf2 Nc1 41 Kg1 Ne2+ 42 Kf2 Ng3

Now Black gets there!

43 Rb1 Rc4 44 Qxb5 Rc2+ 45 Kf3 Qe4+ 46 Kg4 Nf5 47 g3 fxg3+ 48 Kg5 Qh4+ 49 Kxg6 Ne7 mate (0-1)

3 Nf3: Avoiding the Portuguese

1 e4 d5 2 exd5 Nf6 3 Nf3 (Diagram 19)

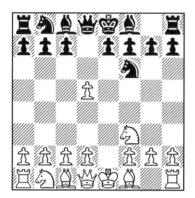

Diagram 19 (B)

The anti-Portuguese move

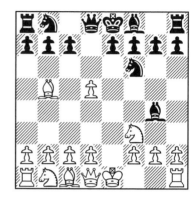

Diagram 20 (B)

The antidote

Normally 3 Nf3 just transposes to main lines considered elsewhere in this book, but what happens if Black insists on playing in gambit style?

3...Bg4

The difference here is that bishop doesn't hit anything, which gives White the time to play 4 Bb5+.

In practice Black normally captures on d5:

a) 3...Nxd5 4 d4 transposes to the main lines of 2...Nf6.

b) Should Black try to confuse matters with 3...Qxd5 White can transpose to the 2...Qxd5 main lines with 4 Nc3, albeit those where White is committed to Nf3. 4...Qa5 and 4...Qd6 lead to positions discussed in previous chapters. 4...Qh5 is the only independent try but this is unsatisfactory for Black, who stands worse after 5 Be2! Bg4 6 0-0 Nc6 7 h3. White also has the option of 4 d4, transposing back to the Portuguese Variation after 4...Bg4.

4 Bb5+! (Diagram 20)

4 Be2 Qxd5 5 d4 transposes back to the Portuguese Variation, while 4 h3, simply aiming for the bishop pair and a slight advantage, is another possibility.

4...Nbd7

4...Bd7 5 Bc4 Bg4 6 h3 Bf5 7 Nc3 Nbd7 8 d3 (this is the point – Black doesn't get to kick back the bishop with tempo) 8...Nb6 9 0-0 Nfxd5 10 Nxd5 Nxd5 11 Nd4 Bc8 (Black is forced to play this move, as 11...Bg6 loses to 12 Bb5+) 12 Re1 c6 13 Qf3 e6

14 Nf5 looks incredibly good for White.

5 h3!

It is worth flicking in this move to drive the bishop back to an inferior square.

5...Bh5!

After 5...a6?! 6 Be2 Bxf3 (or 6...Bh5 7 c4 Bxf3 8 Bxf3 Ne5 9 Be2 e6 10 d4 Ng6 11 dxe6 fxe6 and Black was simply a pawn down in F.Hindermann-H.Kongevold, Dresden 2007) 7 Bxf3 Ne5 8 Nc3 Qd7 (if Black plays 8...Qd6 the queen becomes a target, and following 9 d4 Nxf3+ 10 Qxf3 0-0-0 11 Bf4 Qd7 12 Be5 Black's pieces are all tied up) 9 d3 0-0-0 10 Be3 Nxf3+ 11 Qxf3 the problem for Black is that if he regains the d5-pawn he loses the one on f7.

6 c4!?

Of course the most principled choice is to hold on to the pawn. However, 6 Nc3 is also a very reasonable continuation, and 6...a6 7 Be2 Nb6 8 d4 Nfxd5 9 Nxd5 Qxd5 10 0-0 e6 11 b3 followed by c2-c4 left White with a space advantage in B.Macieja-A.Gershon, Paget Parish 2001.

6...a6 7 Ba4 b5 8 cxb5!

8 g4 Bg6 **(Diagram 21)** gives Black considerable compensation for the pawn, as it is no longer so safe for White to castle kingside. E.Sutovsky-A.Gershon, Israeli Championship 2000, continued 9 cxb5 Nxd5 10 Nc3 and here Black would be doing very well after 10...Nb4! (10...N5b6? 11 bxa6 Rxa6 12 Bb5 was good for White in the game) 11 0-0 axb5 12 Bxb5 c6 13 Bc4 h5.

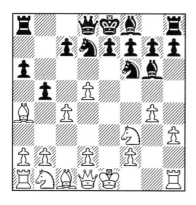

Diagram 21 (W)
Compensation for Black

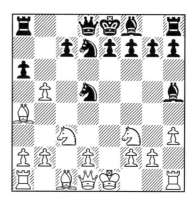

Diagram 22 (B)
White develops with tempo

8...Nxd5 9 Nc3! (Diagram 22)

Taking another pawn with 9 bxa6 Rxa6 is extremely risky. The threat is 10...Bxf3 when White cannot recapture with the queen as the bishop on a4 is hanging, so White will have to make another concession – to either accept doubled pawns or expose his king even further.

Black also gets a lot of compensation after 9 d4 e6 10 g4 Bg6 11 Nc3 Bb4 (A.Pecori-D.Smerdon, Melbourne 2004); he enjoys easy access to important squares and White has an exposed king.

9...N5b6

9...Nb4 is calmly refuted by 10 0-0 axb5 11 Bxb5 c6 12 Be2 when Black has no compensation whatsoever.

10 Bc2 axb5

Now:

a) 11 g4 Bg6 12 Nxb5 was played in L.Kritz-K.Deng, Las Vegas 2006, and here 12...c6! seems to be better than the game's 12...Ra5. After 13 Nc3 e6 14 d4 Nd5 Black has good long-term compensation for the pawn: he has a well-placed knight on d5 and pressure along the a-and b-files (rather in the style of the Benko gambit), and White doesn't have a safe place for his king.

b) There doesn't seem to be a problem with 11 Nxb5!. For example, 11...e6 12 Be4 Nd5 13 Bxd5 exd5 14 0-0 Be7 15 Qb3 with advantage. 11...c6 isn't much better: 12 Nbd4 Qc7 13 0-0 e6 (or 13...Ne5 14 Re1 and Black must move away or exchange on f3) 14 b3 c5 15 Nb5. Here Black should play 15...Qb7, because if 15...Qc6 White plays 16 a4 and Black cannot take advantage of the pin on f3.

Summary

In this chapter we have looked at the potential perils of playing 3 d4 and allowing the Portuguese Variation. Game 64 shows how White can accept the pawn and achieve an advantage with 4 f3 and 5 Bb5+, but he must play accurately in order to do so. White should avoid the natural 5 c4?!, which hands over the initiative to Black.

White can also choose to let go of his extra material with either 4 Nf3 (Games 65-66) or 4 Be2 (Game 67). However, Black does not seem too troubled by these quieter moves – the acid test for the Portuguese Variation is to grab the pawn!

Finally, White can play 3 Nf3, which avoids the Portuguese Variation altogether. Black should transpose to the main lines here, as 3...Bg4 isn't very convincing.

Chapter Fifteen

3 c4 and 3 Bb5+

This chapter deals with variations where White tries to hang on to the d5-pawn. He can do this by playing 3 c4, or with the slightly disruptive 3 Bb5+ intending to displace Black's pieces.

White Plays 3 c4

1 e4 d5 2 exd5 Nf6 3 c4?! (Diagram 1)

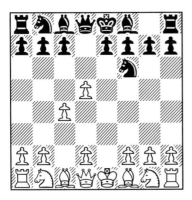

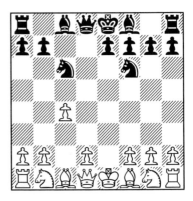

Diagram 1 (B)
White plays 3 c4

Diagram 2 (W)
An excellent gambit for Black

This move isn't bad, as long as it's followed up correctly; in fact White has chances of gaining an advantage. However, I have a firm belief that the main lines are simply much more promising.

3...c6!

3...e6 is the Icelandic Gambit. This is a true gambit where Black gives up a pawn in return for fast development, a possible clamp on the d4-square and chances to exploit an open e-file against the white king. See Game 69 for further details.

4 dxc6?!

> **WARNING: Accepting this gambit is just too risky. Black gets so much play for the pawn, so White should steer clear!**

4 d4! cxd5 takes us into the realms of the Caro-Kann Panov-Botvinnik Attack, a major subject which lies outside the scope of this book. After 5 Nc3 Black has the following options:

a) 5...Nc6 6 Nf3 (6 Bg5 avoids the endgame but I believe that after the solid 6...e6 or 6...dxc4 Black has no problems) 6...Bg4 7 cxd5 Nxd5 8 Qb3 Bxf3 9 gxf3 e6 (9...Nb6 is a tricky line) 10 Qxb7 Nxd4 11 Bb5+ Nxb5 12 Qc6+ Ke7 13 Qxb5 Qd7 14 Nxd5+ Qxd5 15 Qxd5 exd5 reaches one of the most double-edged endgames around. Black tries to prove that White's kingside pawns are terribly weak and that the passed d-pawn is an asset. On the other hand, White sets out to prove that his lead in development and Black's exposed king will give him tremendous attacking potential!

b) 5...g6 6 Qb3 Bg7 7 cxd5 0-0 gives up a pawn in order to secure freedom of movement. Black will try to put the doubled d5-pawn under heavy pressure, and should it fall Black will stand positionally better.

c) 5...e6 6 Nf3 Bb4 (or the more solid 6...Be7) 7 cxd5 (or 7 Bd3 dxc4 8 Bxc4) 7...Nxd5 reaches an incredibly complex isolated queen's pawn (IQP) position. Everything hinges on whether White will be able to use the dynamic potential of his pieces, or whether Black is able to defuse the attack and enjoy the static advantages of his position.

4...Nxc6 (Diagram 2)

This gambit has a great reputation, and for good reason. Black enjoys long-term compensation along the d-file, a great outpost on d4 and very active pieces.

5 Nc3 is covered in Game 68. If 5 Nf3 e5 6 d3 Black has the option of simplifying into a favourable endgame with 6...e4 7 dxe4 Qxd1+ 8 Kxd1 Nxe4 9 Be3 Bf5, as played in M.Chandler-M.Adams, Hastings 1989/90. That game continued 10 Nh4 0-0-0+ 11 Kc1 Be6 12 Nc3 (if 12 f3 Bc5 13 Bxc5 Nxc5 Black has an edge, as the c4-pawn will fall) 12...Nxc3 13 bxc3 b6 and it was Black who was slightly better, due to the weak doubled c-pawns.

Game 68
□ B.Savchenko ■ K.Asrian
Moscow 2007

---

1 e4 d5 2 exd5 Nf6 3 c4?! c6! 4 dxc6?! Nxc6 5 Nc3 e5! (Diagram 3) 6 d3 Bf5

Black's plan is clear: to establish firm control of the d4-square while at the same time putting the d3-pawn under tremendous pressure. As White is tied to the defence of d3, he has very limited space which makes life uncomfortable. Furthermore, White must always be wary of the ...e5-e4 break.

7 Nf3

7 Bg5, aiming to occupy d5, can be met by 7...Bb4. If 8 a3 Bxc3+ 9 bxc3 h6 10 Bh4 0-0 White's position is far from easy to play; the d3-pawn is especially vulnerable to ideas such as ...Qd6 and ...Rd8.

7...e4!

The critical idea – after this move White soon finds himself in trouble.

8 dxe4 Nxe4 9 Be2

After 9 Qxd8+ Rxd8 10 Nxe4 Bxe4 11 a3 (White cannot allow ...Nb4) 11...Be7 12 Be2 Bf6! Black has tremendous compensation for the pawn – White just cannot get developed!

9...Bb4 10 Bd2 Nxd2 11 Nxd2 Nd4 12 Rc1

The threat on c2 is extremely unpleasant for White. If 12 0-0 Bc2! the queen is forced to an inferior square, and after 13 Qe1 0-0 (threatening ...Re8) 14 Bf3 Bd3 Black picks up an exchange.

12...0-0 (Diagram 4) 13 Nf1

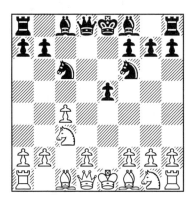

Diagram 3 (W)

Establishing a big clamp

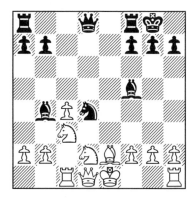

Diagram 4 (W)

White can't castle

Grovelling around on the first rank cannot be a pleasant experience for White. He can't play 13 0-0 because of 13...Nxe2+ 14 Qxe2 Bd3.

13...Qg5 14 Ne3 Rad8

The threats begin to mount.

15 h4 Qf4?

After 15...Qh6 White would have been in serious trouble, as 16 0-0 Nxe2+ 17 Qxe2 Bd3 again wins the exchange.

16 0-0 Bxc3 17 Rxc3 Nb5 18 cxb5 Rxd1 19 Rxd1

Now White's position is very tough for Black to break down.

19...Be6 20 Ra3 Qb8 21 Ra4 g6 22 Bc4 Bxc4 23 Rxc4 Qe5 24 a4 Qxb2 25 g3 Re8 26 Rcd4 Re7 27 R1d2 Qb1+ 28 Kg2 h5 29 Rc4 Kg7 30 Rcd4 Rc7 31 Rd1 Rc1 32 Rxc1 Qxc1 33 Rf4

White has achieved a fortress, and despite his attempts Black cannot make any progress.

33...Qc5 34 Kh2 Kg8 35 Rc4 Qd6 36 Rf4 Qe6 37 Kg2 Kg7 38 Rc4 Qd7 39 Kg1 Qd6 40 Kg2 Qe6 41 Kg1 a6 42 bxa6 Qxa6 43 Rb4 Qc6 44 Rc4 Qd6 45 Kg2 Qa3 46 Kg1 Qb3 47 Kg2 Kf8 48 Kg1 Kg7 ½-½

Game 69
□ **A.Dgebuadze** ■ **E.Taylor**
Liverpool 2007

---

1 e4 d5 2 exd5 Nf6 3 c4?! e6!? 4 dxe6 Bxe6 **(Diagram 5)**

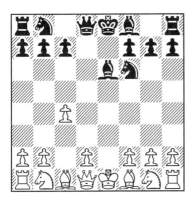

Diagram 5 (W)

The Icelandic Gambit

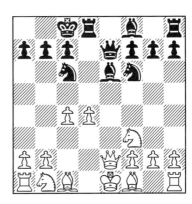

Diagram 6 (W)

Dangerous, but unsound?

The Icelandic Gambit first became popular in the 1990s and for a while it was hot stuff! It's particularly fun to play against an unprepared opponent, as White tends to get lured into making natural but bad moves.

5 Nf3!

White shouldn't allow Black to develop with tempo, and for this reason 5 d4?! is dubious because of 5...Bb4+.

5...Nc6

The objective with 5...Nc6 is to establish complete control of the d4-square, and if Black succeeds in this aim he will be guaranteed long-term positional compensation.

However, 5...Qe7 is probably a better try. Play continues 6 Qe2 (the only way for White to prevent ...Bxc4) 6...Nc6 7 d4 and now:

a) 7...0-0-0 **(Diagram 6)** looks like it can be refuted, although I'm sure it will provide a headache for an unsuspecting opponent! Play continues 8 d5 Qb4+ 9 Nc3

Bxd5! (the only chance to confuse matters; 9...Bf5 allows White to grab material with 10 dxc6 Bc5 11 Be3 Bd3 12 a3! Qb3 13 Qd1) 10 cxd5 Nxd5 11 a3 (kicking back the queen is important, as White needs to be able to develop the dark-squared bishop without having to worry about the b2-pawn) 11...Qa5 12 Bd2!. This is the ideal defensive location for the bishop, and now Black is just lost: for example, 12...Bb4 13 Nxd5 Rxd5 14 0-0-0 Rhd8 15 g3 Qc5+ 16 Kb1 Bxa3 17 Bh3+ Kb8 18 Bc3.

b) 7...Bg4! 8 Be3! (after 8 Qxe7+?! Bxe7 9 Be3 0-0-0 10 d5 Nb4 11 Na3 Rhe8 Black's advantage in development and his strong knight on b4 grants him some compensation, A.Tate-D.Bryson, Oban 2005) 8...0-0-0 9 d5 Ne4!? (after 9...Ne5 10 Nc3 Nfd7 11 0-0-0 Qf6 12 h3 White stands much better – he is prepared to return the pawn in order to gain the bishop pair, the centre and a space advantage) 10 dxc6 Qb4+ 11 Nbd2 Nxd2 (11...Qxb2 fails to 12 Rb1!) 12 0-0-0 Nxf1 13 Rxd8+ Kxd8 14 Rxf1 with an advantage for White.

5...c5 tries to secure long-term pressure down the d-file, and I think 6 d4! is the only move that challenges Black: 6...cxd4 7 Nxd4 Bc5 (7...Bb4+ 8 Nc3 Ne4 should be met by 9 Nxe6! giving White an advantage) 8 Be3 Qb6 (or 8...Ng4 9 Nxe6 Qxd1+ 10 Kxd1 Bxe3 11 Nxg7+ Kf8 12 fxe3 Kxg7 13 Ke2 Re8 14 Nc3 and although Black wins back one of his pawns, I don't think he has enough compensation) 9 Nxe6! Qxe6 (or 9...Bxe3 10 Nxg7+ Kf8 11 fxe3) 10 Qe2 Bxe3 11 Qxe3 Qxe3+ 12 fxe3 0-0 13 Na3 Re8 14 Nc2 and White is better. Although the e-pawn is very weak and will probably fall, Black has to devote a lot of energy to win it. In addition White enjoys a small but long-term advantage in the queenside pawn majority, and – if a pair of knights are traded – the better minor piece.

6 Be2 Bc5 7 0-0 Qd7 8 b4!? (Diagram 7)

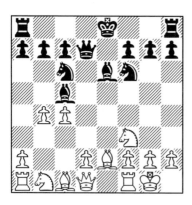

Diagram 7 (B)

Fighting for the centre

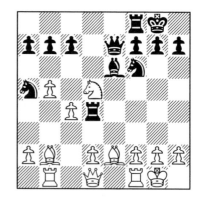

Diagram 8 (B)

White is winning

I really like this move. White returns the pawn to regain control of the centre. Indeed, Black has some problems to solve after 8...Bxb4 9 d4. The d4-d5 advance is threatened and there is no way to prevent it. All Black can do is get his pieces out of harm's way, but after 9...Bg4 10 d5 Bxf3 11 Bxf3 Ne5 12 Bb2 Nxf3+ 13 Qxf3 0-0-0 14 Bxf6 gxf6 15 Nc3 White gains a strong attack down the b-file rather quickly, R.Weston-D.Bryson, Scottish League 1994.

8...Bd4 9 Nc3 0-0 10 Bb2 Rad8

Taking the pawn again leads to problems: 10...Nxb4 11 Nxd4 Qxd4 12 Qb3 Qd6 13 d4 and Black's pieces are completely lacking in coordination.

11 Rb1 Qe7?

Black completely misses the threat! 11...a6 had to be played, although White is still considerably better after 12 b5 axb5 13 Nxb5 Bxb2 14 Rxb2.

12 b5 Na5?

In order to stay alive, 12...Bxc3 had to be played.

13 Nxd4 Rxd4 14 Nd5 (Diagram 8)

Now it is all over.

14...Rxd5 15 cxd5 Bxd5 16 Bf3 c6 17 Bxd5 Nxd5 18 Qa4 Qc7 19 Qd4 f6 20 Rfe1 Nb6 21 Rbc1 Qf7 22 Ba3 Re8 23 Rxe8+ Qxe8 24 bxc6 Nxc6 25 Qe3 Qf7 26 h3 h6 27 Bc5 Nd5 28 Qb3 Kh8 29 Bxa7! Nxa7 30 Rc5 1-0

White Plays 3 Bb5+

1 e4 d5 2 exd5 Nf6 3 Bb5+ (Diagram 9)

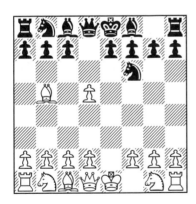

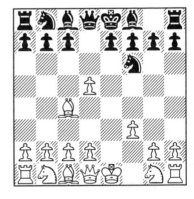

Diagram 9 (B)	Diagram 10 (W)
3 Bb5+	All the way back

I have always believed that 3 Bb5+ is not the most problematic move for Black to face. By trying to preserve the pawn on d5, White will have to make some positional concessions, and even then he doesn't always end up keeping the pawn.

3...Bd7

Here White has a choice:

a) 4 Bc4 tries to hold on to the pawn, and this move is covered in Game 70.

b) 4 Be2 is the most modern way to play 3 Bb5+, and this is the subject of Game 71.

Game 70
☐ **O.Girya** ■ **A.Muzychuk**
Moscow 2008

---

1 e4 d5 2 exd5 Nf6 3 Bb5+ Bd7 4 Bc4 Bg4! 5 f3

 NOTE: 5 Bb5+ Bd7 repeats the position, but White can and should play for an advantage.

5...Bc8! (Diagram 10)

This is the move I favour. The bishop has done its job in provoking f2-f3 and now it should clear out of the way so that Black can regain the d5-pawn.

I don't like 5...Bf5 simply because the bishop on f5 can become a target for White's kingside pawns. I remember losing a disastrous game with 5...Bf5, which put me off this move. I was simply overrun on the kingside and I never regained the pawn on d5!

Play continues 6 Nc3 (of course White should hold on to the pawn for dear life) 6...Nbd7 7 g4! Nb6! (the only move; after 7...Bg6? 8 h4 h5 9 g5 Nb6 10 Bb5+ Nfd7 11 Nh3 a6 12 Be2 Black is in danger of being overwhelmed) 8 Bb3 Bc8 9 d4 (strangely White's early kingside pawn thrust doesn't necessarily harm his chances at all; on the contrary, after queenside castling this pawn front will become a powerful weapon) 9...g6 10 Qe2 Bg7 11 Bg5 0-0 12 0-0-0 Nbxd5 13 Nxd5 Nxd5 14 h4 h6 15 Bd2 a5 16 a3 a4 17 Ba2 with a double-edged position, I.Rogers-A.Gipslis, German League 1998.

6 Nc3 Nbd7 7 Nge2

7 d4 Nb6 8 Qd3 Nfxd5 9 Nxd5 Nxd5 10 Bg5 Qd6 11 0-0-0 Be6 12 Kb1 0-0-0 13 Ne2 Nb4 14 Qb3 Bxc4 15 Qxc4 Qd5 16 Qxd5 Nxd5 17 c4 h6 18 Bd2 Nb6 was M.Borriss-S.Krivoshey, German League 2005. This position is slightly better for White, but I must stress that the evaluation is in a state of flux because of the strength and weakness of the d4-pawn. Given time Black will simply double on the d-file, fianchetto his bishop and exert intolerable pressure on d4, in which case Black would stand better. However, if the strength of the d4-pawn – the space it gives White – is utilized, then maybe it will be White who has the slight advantage.

7...Nb6 8 Bb3 a5! (Diagram 11)

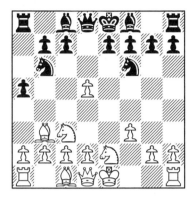

Diagram 11 (W)

Gaining space

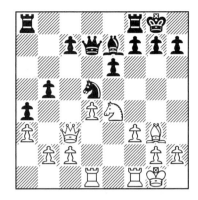

Diagram 12 (W)

A strong knight on d5

Before recapturing the pawn, Black seeks to extract as much as possible from the position.

9 a3

9 a4 might be a better choice.

9...a4 10 Ba2 Nbxd5 11 d4 e6 12 0-0 Be7 13 Ne4 b5!

Perfect strategy on the light squares! Black secures a strong knight on d5 before commencing further action.

14 Nf4 Bb7 15 Qd3

Ideally White would like to play 15 Nd3 heading for c5, but unfortunately 15...Nxe4 16 fxe4 Nf6 costs White a pawn. 15 c3 0-0 and only then 16 Nd3 is probably the best try.

15...0-0

Although the position is objectively equal, it is very difficult for White to establish an effective plan.

16 Bd2 Nxf4!

Anna frees up her game by exchanging knights.

17 Bxf4 Bd5! 18 Bxd5

18 Qxb5 of course doesn't work because of 18...Bxa2 19 Rxa2 Qxd4+ and Black has a massive advantage.

18...Nxd5 19 Bg3 Qd7 20 Rad1 Nb6 21 Qc3 Nd5 (Diagram 12)

I think that Black enjoys the slightly better long-term chances, due to a well-placed knight and space on the queenside.

22 Qe1? Qc6 23 Qe2 Nb6 24 Nc3? Bxa3! 25 bxa3 Qxc3 26 Qxb5 Qxa3 27 Bxc7 Nd5

White has badly miscalculated and now Black has a much superior position. The a-pawn is simply too strong.

28 Bg3 Rfc8 29 Ra1 Qb4 30 Qd3 Qc4 31 Rf2 Qxd3 32 cxd3 Rc3 33 Rfa2 a3 34 Bd6 Rxd3 35 Rxa3 Raxa3 36 Rxa3 Rd1+ 37 Kf2 h5

White has managed to get rid of the a-pawn, but Black is still much better. As we all know, a knight is superior to a bishop when the pawns are all on one side of the board.

38 Bc5 Rd2+ 39 Kf1 h4 40 Ra8+?

This spite check only helps Black's king reach its destination.

40...Kh7 41 Rf8 Kg6 42 Rh8 Ne3+ 43 Ke1 Rc2 44 g3 Rxh2 45 gxh4 Nf5 46 h5+ Rxh5 47 Rxh5 Kxh5

This endgame is just a technicality for Black. The pawns are all on the same side, White's are isolated and advanced (the more advanced, the more difficult they are to defend) and finally Black's king is better placed.

48 Kf2 Kh4 49 Bb6 Kh3 50 Bc5 Kh2 51 Bf8 g6 52 Bc5 Kh3 53 Bb6 Ne7 54 Bc7 Nd5 55 Bd8 f6 56 Ba5 g5 57 Bd2 Kh2 58 Bc1 Kh3 59 Bd2 Nf4 60 Ba5 f5 61 Bc7 Nd3+ 62 Ke3 Nb4 63 Bd6 Nc6 64 Bc7 Kg2

Black's king has penetrated and now the f-pawn will fall.

65 Bd6 f4+ 66 Ke4 Nxd4! 67 Bxf4 gxf4 0-1

After 68 Kxf4 Nxf3 White cannot win the remaining pawn.

Game 71
□ **M.Mahjoob** ■ **D.Laylo**
Dresden Olympiad 2008

---

1 e4 d5 2 exd5 Nf6 3 Bb5+ Bd7 4 Be2

The attraction of 4 Be2 is that White doesn't need to bother memorizing a whole load of lines against various Black set-ups. White tries to make use of the space advantage and also the fact that Black must spend a tempo removing the bishop from d7.

4...Nxd5 5 d4 Bf5 6 Nf3 e6 7 0-0 Be7!

The best move and the most solid – Black doesn't obstruct his pressure along the d-file.

8 a3

8 c4 allows 8...Nb4!? which seems a little artificial but Black can get away with it. After 9 Na3 (if 9 Nc3 Nc2 10 Rb1 Nb4 White must give up the exchange or agree a

draw) 9...Nd7 10 Be3 0-0 11 Qb3 a5! 12 Rfd1 c6 White's a3-knight is out of the game and Black can claim comfortable equality.

8 Re1 0-0 9 a3 Nc6? 10 Bb5! is a nasty move to face, and in J.Degraeve-J.De Wolf, Belgian League 1996, Black felt obliged to play 10...Nb8. I would probably play 9...Bf6 and then 10 c4 Nb6 11 Nc3 Nc6 12 Be3 Qd7, getting ready to put pressure on d4.

8...0-0 9 c4 Nb6 10 Nc3 Nc6 11 Be3 Bf6 (Diagram 13)

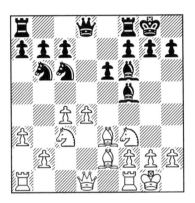
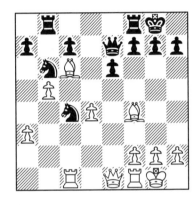

Diagram 13 (W)
Black pressurizes d4

Diagram 14 (B)
Good for White

11...Bg4! is stronger. White has spent a move on the not particularly useful a2-a3, and this allows Black enough time to put pressure on the d4-pawn: 12 b3 Bf6 13 Ne4 Bxf3 14 Nxf6+ Qxf6 15 Bxf3 (it's funny, but the two knights and the pressure on the d4-pawn give Black adequate compensation for the bishop pair) 15...Rfd8 16 Bxc6 bxc6 17 Qg4 (this position was agreed drawn in D.Bronstein-A.Gipslis, Tallinn 1975) 17...a5 18 Rac1 a4 19 b4 (the knight now has some purpose on b6 and Black should concentrate on upping the pressure on d4 with...) 19...Qf5 20 Qxf5 exf5 21 g3 f6 22 Rfd1 Rd7 and is difficult to see how White can make any progress.

12 b4 Bg4 13 Ne4 Bxf3!

The pressure on d4 and c4 is so great that the time is right to determine the position.

14 Nxf6+ Qxf6 15 Bxf3 Nxc4?!

This is dubious, though. 15...Rfd8 was best.

16 Rc1 Nb6

16...Nxe3 17 fxe3 highlights the problem with developing pieces in front of pawns – Black's queenside structure will be ruined.

17 b5 Na5 18 Qe1 Nac4 19 Bxb7 Rab8 20 Bc6 Qe7 21 Bf4 (Diagram 14)

White holds the advantage here: he has the better pieces, more space, and once the d4-pawn has been exchanged he will have the better structure too.

21...Rfd8 22 d5!

Black's position falls apart after this move.

22...e5 23 Qe2 Qxa3 24 Bg5! f6 25 Rxc4! fxg5

After 25...Nxc4 26 Qxc4 the devastating 27 d6+ is threatened.

26 Re4 h6 27 Rxe5 Kh8 28 Re7 Qc3 29 Rd1 Rbc8 30 g3 Rf8 31 d6

Once the second rook enters the fray, Black is lost.

31...cxd6 32 Rxd6 Rf6 33 Rxf6 Qxf6 34 Rxa7 Rf8 35 Re7 Kh7 36 Re6 Qa1+ 37 Kg2 Kh8 38 Qe3 Nc4 39 Qc5 1-0

Black resigned as he is losing material.

Summary

3 c4 is in my opinion not the best continuation for White, as it allows Black to enter the reputable Panov-Botvinnik Attack with 3...c6 4 d4 cxd5. Game 68 shows what may happen if White instead greedily grabs the offered pawn with the 4 dxc6?!. Black also has the option to play 3...e6 – the sharp Icelandic Gambit which offers good practical chances if White is unprepared.

White can play 3 Bb5+ either with the intention of holding on to the d5-pawn with 3...Bd7 4 Bc4 or simply to disrupt the harmony of Black's pieces with 4 Be2. As Game 70 shows, after 4 Bc4 Bg4 5 f3 the best retreat square for the black bishop is c8. 4 Be2, as played in Game 71, takes the position back into something resembling the 2...Nf6 main lines.

Chapter Sixteen

Unusual Lines

- 2...Nf6 3 Nc3
- Second Move Alternatives for White

In this final chapter we take a look at some rarely-played lines, including 2...Nf6 3 Nc3 and attempts by White on his second move to avoid the Scandinavian altogether.

2...Nf6 3 Nc3

1 e4 d5 2 exd5 Nf6 3 Nc3 (Diagram 1)

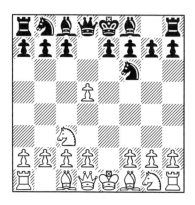

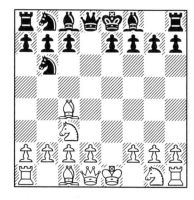

Diagram 1 (B)

An innocuous move

Diagram 2 (W)

The best reply

I have never been impressed with this simple move. I think that it gives Black an easy game simply because White cannot establish a d4/c4 pawn front.

3...Nxd5

 NOTE: This position can also be reached from a line in the Alekhine Defence: 1 e4 Nf6 2 Nc3 d5! 3 exd5 Nxd5.

4 Bc4

I guess this is most challenging move. Alternatively:

a) The unambitious 4 Nxd5 Qxd5 succeeds only in alleviating Black's space worries, as the exchange of knights frees up his position:

a1) After 5 Nf3 Bg4 6 Be2 Nc6! it's noticeable that White no longer has Nc3 to hassle the black queen, and 7 0-0 0-0-0 8 c3 e5! 9 Qa4 e4 10 Bc4 Qh5 left White in trouble in the one-sided game L.Garcia Mengual-D.Campora, Coria del Rio 2006.

a2) If White establishes a pawn centre without challenging the queen then Black should aim to eliminate it immediately: for example, 5 d4 Nc6 6 Be3 e5! 7 dxe5 Qxe5 is fine for Black.

a3) Finally, White can play very dryly with 5 Qf3 when, as Andrew Martin states, playing these positions is a question of attitude. You should not let yourself be disgusted by White's dull play but instead be thankful that you have equalized easily and continue in this frame of mind. G.Calavalle-I.Rausis, Porto San Giorgio 2007, went 5...Qc5 6 Qc3 (White persists, but this time he must accept doubled pawns for his efforts) 6...Qxc3 7 dxc3 e5 8 Be3 Be6 9 Nf3 f6 10 Nd2 Nd7 11 Nb3 Bd6 12 f3 Ke7 13 Rd1 a5 with a better position for Black.

b) Against 4 d4 Black should play aggressively with 4...Nxc3! 5 bxc3 g6!. Black wishes to break the wall of granite with ...c7-c5, opening up the long diagonal and the c- and d-files. For example, 6 Nf3 Bg7 7 Bc4 c5 8 0-0 (or 8 Ne5 Bxe5 9 dxe5 Qxd1+ 10 Kxd1 Nc6 11 Bb5 Bd7 12 Bxc6 Bxc6 13 f3 Rd8+ and Black, with control of the d-file and a better bishop, had a strong position in M.Kulesza-R.Antoniewski, Opole 2006) 8...0-0 9 Re1 Qc7 10 Bf1 Rd8 11 Ba3 b6 12 Qe2 Nc6 13 Rad1 Be6 14 Qe3 cxd4 15 cxd4 Bd5! 16 c3 e6 17 Bb2 Na5 and Black completely dominates the light squares, E.Berg-S.Agdestein, Gausdal 1996.

4...Nb6! (Diagram 2)

4...Nxc3 5 Qf3 e6 6 Qxc3 Qf6 and 4...e6 are solid alternatives.

5 Bb3 Nc6

This move is considered to be the most accurate and the safest. Black starts by controlling the d4-square and introduces the possibility of hunting down the light-squared bishop.

5...c5?! is just too ambitious: 6 Qh5 e6 (6...c4 loses a pawn to 7 Bxc4 Nxc4 8 Qb5+ and I don't think Black has enough compensation after 8...Bd7 9 Qxc4 Bc6 10 f3 Nd7 11 Nge2 e5 12 0-0) 7 d3 N8d7 8 Bg5 Nf6 9 Qe2 Be7 10 Nf3 0-0 11 0-0 h6 12 Bh4 Nbd5 13 Ne4 b6 14 Ne5 Bb7 15 Kh1? (White is planning to attack with f2-f4 but does not take due care; 15 Rad1! is better) 15...Nxe4 16 Bxe7 Nxe7 17 dxe4 Qd4 and Black won a pawn in S.Guliyev-O.Vozovic, Istanbul 2006.

5...e5?! has been known for some time to be dubious: 6 d3 Nc6 7 Nf3 Bg4 8 h3 Bh5? and now White has the wonderful 9 Nxe5!! – it's like something from the 19th century! After 9...Bxd1 10 Bxf7+ Ke7 11 Bg5+ Kd6 12 Ne4+ Kxe5 13 f4+ Kd4 14 Rxd1 Nb4 15 c3+! Ke3 16 0-0! Nxd3 17 Ng3!, as played in E.Rozentalis-Mikenas, Vilnius 1981, mate is unstoppable.

6 Nf3

6 Qf3 is designed to prevent Black from fianchettoing his bishop, but after 6...e6 7 Nge2 Be7 8 d3 0-0 9 a3!? (providing an escape square for the bishop) 9...Kh8 10 0-0 e5 11 Nd5 Nxd5 12 Bxd5 Bg4 Black had no problems at all in L.Galego-A.Silva, Vila Nova de Gaia 2004.

6...Bf5 (Diagram 3)

This is the typical "Scandinavian" move. For those keen on the more aggressive approach of fianchettoing bishops, you will be relieved to know that this is possible too! For example, 6...g6 7 a4!? (forcing Black to concede the b5-square; 7 Ng5 forces Black to shut in the light-squared bishop, but White doesn't seem to gain anything from this manoeuvre, and 7...e6 8 d3 Bg7 9 h4 h6 10 Nf3 e5 11 Be3 Bg4 12 Qd2 Qd7 followed by ...0-0-0 gave Black no problems in N.Rogers-A.Shabalov, Cherry Hill 2007, especially as he has great potential with ...f7-f5) 7...a5 8 d4 Bg7 9 Be3 0-0 10 h3 e6 11 0-0 Ne7 12 Qd2 Nf5 13 Bg5 f6 14 Bf4 (A.Melekhina-A.Shabalov, Cherry Hill 2007) when instead of the extremely bold 14...g5?!, which led to a White advantage, the more solid 14...c6 would have been sufficient.

7 0-0 e6 8 d4 Be7 9 h3 0-0 10 a3 Bf6

Black has handled the position in a typical way, and all that he needs to do now is to free up his game with a ...c7-c5 pawn break.

11 Be3 Na5 12 Ba2 (Diagram 4)

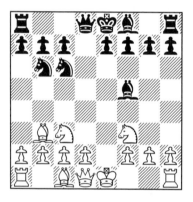

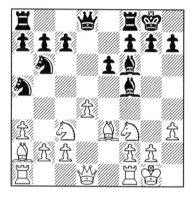

Diagram 3 (W)

The Scandinavian way

Diagram 4 (B)

Black prepares ...c5

We have been following the game J.Horner-D.Smerdon, Port Erin 2007. Here Black could play 12...Nac4 intending 13 Qe2 Nxb2, as after 14 Rab1 N2a4 15 Nxa4 Nxa4 Black threatens 16...Nc3.

In the actual game Black chose an interesting and thematic pawn sacrifice. After 12...c5!? 13 dxc5 Nbc4! 14 Qc1 Bxc3 15 bxc3 Qc7? 16 Bd4 e5?? (unfortunately this natural move is a huge blunder) 17 Nxe5! Nxe5 18 Qf4 White regained his piece with a big advantage and soon won. However, Black's idea was perfectly sound; it was the execution which caused the problem. After 15...Nxe3! 16 Qxe3 Qc7 Black wins either the c2-pawn or the c5-pawn and stands better.

Second Move Alternatives for White

1 e4 d5 2 Nc3 (Diagram 5)

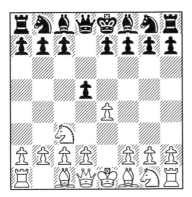

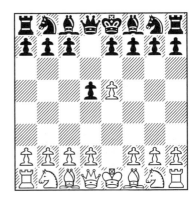

Diagram 5 (B)	**Diagram 6 (B)**
Avoiding the Scandinavian?	Not to be recommended

I remember in 1994, my brother telling me that a certain player by the name of Eric Prié had been defeating everyone in a Paris tournament with the Scandinavian. Eric was doing such a fine job that one opponent resorted to playing 2 Nc3 in an attempt to avoid it! Eric simply played 2...dxe4 3 Nxe4 Qd5 inviting a transposition back to the Scandinavian with 4 Nc3!. White instead chose 4 Qf3, which doesn't achieve anything. In fact it doesn't even threaten 5 Nf6+ as Black has 5...Nxf6!.

2 e5?! **(Diagram 6)** is just a bad move. Black has neither shut in his light-squared bishop with ...e6, nor has he had to waste time supporting the centre with pawn moves, so he should simply play 2...c5! 3 c3 Nc6 4 d4 Bf5 5 Nf3 e6 giving him a great version of the Caro-Kann. Black should place the queen on b6, a knight on f5 and aim to control the c-file. The pawn break ...f7-f6 should be played if White manages to prevent Black from breaking through on the c-file.

2 d4 dxe4 3 Nc3 Nf6 4 f3 takes us to the Blackmar-Diemer Gambit. Those of you familiar with my first book *Play the Caro-Kann* will know that I don't think too much of this gambit. 4...exf3 5 Nxf3 Bf5 6 Bc4 c6 (the most solid formation) and now:

a) 7 0-0 e6 8 Ne5 Bg6! (White has one little trick: 8...Bd6 9 Nxf7! Kxf7 10 Rxf5 wins) 9 g4? (very rash and very desperate) 9...Nbd7! 10 Nxg6 hxg6 11 g5 Qc7 was great for Black in A.Rodriguez-E.Bricard, Toulouse 1998.

b) 7 Ne5 e6 8 g4!? Bg6 9 h4 has been played in a few correspondence games. Black should play 9...Nbd7 10 Nxd7 Qxd7 11 h5 Be4! 12 Rf1 (12 Nxe4 Nxe4 13 Qd3 f5! maintains the strong knight on e4) 12...Bb4 13 h6 Rg8 14 hxg7 Nd5 15 Bd2 Bxc3 16 Bxc3 Nxc3 17 bxc3 Rxg7 and Black is winning.

2...dxe4

2...d4 is possible, while 2...e6 transposes to the French and 2...c6 reaches the Caro-Kann.

3 Nxe4 Qd5

3...Nd7 **(Diagram 7)** is a good choice for those who play 2 exd5 Nf6. The main attraction, when compared to similar positions from the Caro-Kann, is that Black can play ...c7-c5 in one go. For example:

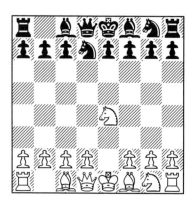

Diagram 7 (W)

An improved Caro-Kann?

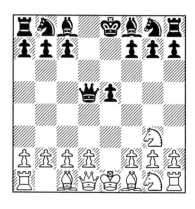

Diagram 8 (W)

Seizing the centre

a) 4 Bc4 Ndf6 (4...Ngf6 gives White the chance to play 5 Bxf7+ Kxf7 6 Ng5+ Kg8 7 Ne6 Qe8 8 Nxc7 Qg6 9 Nxa8 with a complicated position; after 9...Qxg2 10 Qf3 Black is forced to exchange queens as White is threatening 11 Qb3+) 5 Ng5 e6 6 N1f3 Bd6 7 0-0? (this natural move is a mistake as it allows Black to seize the initiative) 7...h6 8 Nh3 g5 9 g4 h5 10 Nhxg5 hxg4 11 Nxf7 Kxf7 12 Ng5+ Kf8 13 f4 b5 and Black was better in K.Kokolias-I.Nikolaidis, Athens 2004.

b) 4 d4 Ngf6 5 Nxf6+ (5 Bd3 Nxe4 6 Bxe4 Nf6 7 Bf3 c6 8 Ne2 Bg4 is equal) 5...Nxf6 6 Nf3 Bg4! (no time has been spent extracting one of White's centre pawns, so it is safe to develop the bishop here) 7 h3 Bh5 8 Be2 (the aggressive 8 g4 is not to be feared: 8...Bg6 9 Bg2 e6 10 Ne5 c6 11 0-0 Nd7 12 Nc4 h5 13 g5 Nb6 14 Ne5 Bf5 and a draw was agreed in T.L.Petrosian-G.Sargissian, Stepanakert 2004) 8...e6 9 0-0 Be7 10 Ne5 Bxe2 11 Qxe2 0-0 12 c3 c5 (this is the advantage – no time has been wasted!) 13 dxc5 Bxc5 14 Bg5 Be7 15 Rfd1 Nd5 16 Bxe7 Qxe7 with an equal position, B.Heberla-A.Beliavsky, Warsaw 2004.

4 Ng3

White's best move is 4 Nc3!

4...e5!? (Diagram 8)

4...Nc6 is also good, and after 5 Nf3 e5 6 b3 Bg4 7 Bc4 Qd7 8 h3 Be6 9 Qe2 Bd6 10 Bb2 Bxc4 11 Qxc4 Nf6 12 0-0-0 0-0 White achieved nothing from the opening in E.Vancini-L.Caselli, Vanzaghello 1998.

After 4...e5, in B.Le Bailly-N.Tripoteau, Fouesnant 2002, White plays too simplistically with 5 Qf3?! Be6! 6 Ne4 Nc6 7 Ne2? 0-0-0 8 a3 h6 9 d3. His passive play was punished severely after 9...f5 10 N4c3 Qd7 11 h3 Nf6 12 Ng3 Bc5 (12...Nd4 also looks very good) 13 Qd1 h5 14 Be3 Nd4 15 Bg5 h4 16 Bxf6 gxf6 17 Nge2 Qc6 18 Nxd4 Rxd4 19 Qf3 Qb6 20 b4 (20 0-0-0 fails to 20...Rf4) 20...Rf4 21 bxc5 Qb2 22 Qxf4 and White resigned. 5 b3 is probably the best course of action, and 5...Nc6 6 Bb2 Nf6 7 Nf3 Bd6 8 Bc4 Qc5 9 0-0 0-0 10 Qe2 Bd7 11 a3 Nd4 reaches an equal position.

Summary

Horner-Smerdon shows how Black should handle the insipid 3 Nc3 after 2...Nf6. Although Black lost the game, his play out of the opening before his blunder on move 15 is instructive.

White cannot trick Black into playing something else with 2 Nc3, as after 2...dxe4 3 Nxe4 Qd5!? the best move is 4 Nc3 transposing to the 2...Qxd5 Scandinavian. For 2...Nf6 followers I would recommend 3...Nd7, when Black obtains a position resembling the Caro-Kann but with the advantage that he can play ...c7-c5 in one go.

2 e5? achieves nothing for White. Black can play 2...c5! and smile in the knowledge that his unsupported pawn strike has been successful. The game continues in a manner similar to the Advance Caro-Kann, except that Black is a tempo up.

Index of Variations

1 e4 d5 2 exd5

2 Nc3 – *307*

2 d4 – *307*

2 e5 – *307*

A: 2...Qxd5

B: 2...Nf6

A) 1 e4 d5 2 exd5 Qxd5 3 Nc3

3 d4 – *218*

3 Nf3 Bg4 4 Be2 Nc6 5 d4 0-0-0

     6 c4 – *218*

     6 Be3 – *221*

A1) 3...Qa5 4 d4

4 Bc4 Nf6 5 d3

     5...c6 – *124*

     5...Bg4 – *128*

4 Nf3 Nf6 5 Be2 c6 – *132*

4 g3 – *135*

4 b4 – *138*

4...Nf6 5 Nf3

5 Bc4

     5...c6 6 Bd2

          6...Bf5 – *102*

5...c6

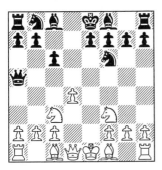

6 Bc4

6...Bf5

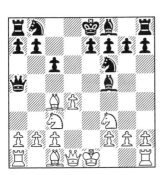

7 Bd2

7 0-0 e6 8 Bf4 – *68*

7 Ne5 e6

    8 0-0 – *89*

    8 g4 Bg6

        9 h4 – *82*; 9 Bd2 – *85*

7...e6

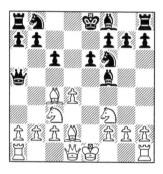

8 Nd5

8 Ne4 – *71*

8 Qe2 Bb4

    9 0-0-0 – *53*

    9 Ne5 Nbd7 10 Nxd7

        10...Kxd7 – *57*

        10...Nxd7 – *59*

    9 a3 – *61*; 9 0-0 – *64*

8...Qd8 9 Nxf6+

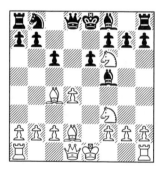

9...gxf6

9...Qxf6 10 Qe2

    10...Nd7 – *23*

    10...Bg4

        11 d5 – *26*

        11 0-0-0 Nd7 12 d5 Bxf3 13 gxf3 cxd5 14 Bxd5

            14...Ba3 – *29*

            14...0-0-0 – *30*

10 c3 – *36*

10 Bb3 – *40*

10 Qe2 – *44*

A2) 3...Qd6

3...Qe5+ – *210*

3...Qd8 4 d4 Nf6 5 Nf3 c6 6 Bc4 Bf5 7 Ne5 e6 8 g4 Bg6 9 h4

    9...Bb4 – *212*

    9...Nbd7 – *215*

4 d4 Nf6

4...c6 5 Nf3 Bg4 – *197*

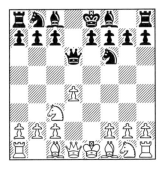

5 Nf3

5 Bc4 – *199*

5 Bd3 – *202*

5 Be3 – *204*

5 Be2 – *205*

5...a6

5...c6 6 Ne5 Nbd7

    7 Bf4 – *189*

    7 Nc4 – *193*

    7 f4 – *196*

6 g3

6 Ne5 Nc6

    7 Bf4 – *167*

    7 Nxc6 – *169*

6 Bc4 – *173*

6 Bg5 – *176*

6 Be3 – *179*

6 Bd3 – *182*

6...Bg4

6...b5 – *147*

7 h3

7 Bg2

B) 1 e4 d5 2 exd5 Nf6

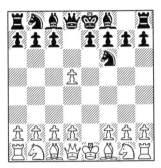

3 Nf3

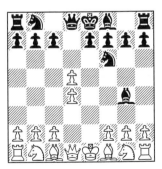

3...Nxd5

4 d4

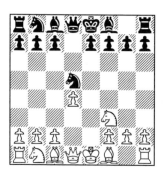

4...g6

Index of Games